"Professionals often zero in on disciplinary differences in
Nesbit Sbanotto, Heather Davediuk Gingrich, and Fred (
and get to the heart of being a better people-helper—the interpersonal helping skills shared across
people-helping disciplines. This is a comprehensive, readable text that is a fully integrated Christian and
psychological model for being an effective helper. Regardless of your discipline or theoretical approach
you'll love it."

Everett L. Worthington Jr., coauthor of *Couple Therapy*

"Every day I look for resources that will help me and others become more effective in helping counsel and
minister to others. Whether you are a beginning student, seasoned clinician, or pastor, *Skills for Effective
Counseling* is a must-add to your library. It is clinically excellent, biblically anchored, and easy to understand
yet filled with immense wisdom and understanding."

Tim Clinton, president, American Association of Christian Counselors

"Wow. What a delightful surprise. This biblically sound, research-based, therapeutically relevant, and
easy-to-read book is a unique, fresh, rich, integrative, and practical resource. Regardless of your therapeutic orientation, you'll find some practical tools to help you to become even more effective. It's a
breath of fresh air for the practicing clinician and will be a resource that you'll turn to often. There are
several chapters alone that are worth the price of the book. If you want to upgrade your therapeutic
toolkit and increase both your confidence and effectiveness, read this book. It's that good."

Gary J. Oliver, executive director, The Center for Healthy Relationships, professor of psychology and practical
theology, John Brown University

"*Skills for Effective Counseling* is well written, comprehensive, and very helpful for training counseling skills,
covering essential microskills with the integration of Christian faith and counseling. This is a much-
needed book for the effective training of Christian professional counselors as well as lay counselors.
Highly recommended!"

Siang-Yang Tan, professor of psychology, Fuller Theological Seminary, author of *Counseling and Psychotherapy*

"Finally! We have been given a competent textbook that tackles the need for training graduate students in
skills for effective counseling that also addresses faith-based integration. Sbanotto, Gingrich, and Gingrich
have given us an excellent tool to understand the relationship of faith-based counseling to secular approaches in a way that will guide us in effective helping processes with those of varied spiritual beliefs."

C. Gary Barnes, licensed psychologist, professor of biblical counseling, Dallas Theological Seminary

"*Skills for Effective Counseling* is a comprehensive yet accessible textbook written from decades of professional practice by the authors. It is for people helpers across a variety of roles—professional counselors,
pastoral care providers, spiritual directors, and life coaches—and features a wealth of training activities,
exercises, and transcript analysis. This is a welcome addition to the counselor education fields."

Gary W. Moon, executive director, Martin Institute and Dallas Willard Center, Westmont College, author of
Apprenticeship with Jesus, editor of *Eternal Living*

"*Skills for Effective Counseling* strives to equip a new generation with listening skills and a constructive
framework to counsel with love in service of Jesus Christ. Forty years ago, Gary R. Collins demystified
counseling and connected basic helping principles with Christian discipleship in *How to Be a People Helper*.
In *Skills for Effective Counseling*, Sbanotto, Gingrich, and Gingrich honor the heart of that pioneering quest.
This is a foundational text that is accessible, intentional, integrative, systematic, and reflective. It is accessible in that it is multiculturally aware, jargon free, and adaptable to ministry. The intentional design to

promote quality-helping encounters is evident in its sequential approach, dialogue samples, and plentiful learning activities. The faith-integrative component is found in comparative tables and discussion. Contemporary counseling links to Christian soul care. Each chapter systematically bridges pivotal empirical findings with elevated conversation. The reader is shown how to increase communication habits that deepen interpersonal relationships and motivate growth. There are countless opportunities for self-reflection with scales to obtain insightful feedback. This book unfolds a helping process that is realistic, hopeful, and, most importantly, biblically faithful. Finally, a faith-sensitive, microskills text for the next generation of people helpers."

Stephen P. Greggo, professor of counseling, Trinity Evangelical Divinity School

"This book combines clarity and reader-friendliness with an academically solid, up-to-date approach to counseling skills. Unusual in drawing on the three perspectives of its authors (a counselor, a marriage and family therapist, and a psychologist), it will be a great text for students and a wonderful resource for practitioners, whatever their people-helping role—including pastors and other church-based workers. The Christian integrative perspective is woven throughout, as well as having its own chapter. A chapter on the systems perspective—rare in such counseling skills books—is an important, welcome addition."

Bradford M. Smith, associate professor of psychology, Belhaven University

SKILLS FOR EFFECTIVE COUNSELING

A FAITH-BASED INTEGRATION

ELISABETH A. NESBIT SBANOTTO

HEATHER DAVEDIUK GINGRICH

FRED C. GINGRICH

IVP Academic
An imprint of InterVarsity Press
Downers Grove, Illinois

InterVarsity Press
P.O. Box 1400, Downers Grove, IL 60515-1426
ivpress.com
email@ivpress.com

InterVarsity Press® is the book-publishing division of InterVarsity Christian Fellowship/USA®, a movement of students and faculty active on campus at hundreds of universities, colleges and schools of nursing in the United States of America, and a member movement of the International Fellowship of Evangelical Students. For information about local and regional activities, visit intervarsity.org.

All Scripture quotations, unless otherwise indicated, are taken from THE HOLY BIBLE, NEW INTERNATIONAL VERSION®, NIV® Copyright © 1973, 1978, 1984, 2011 by Biblica, Inc.™ Used by permission. All rights reserved worldwide.

While any stories in this book are true, some names and identifying information may have been changed to protect the privacy of individuals.

Cover design: Cindy Kiple
Interior design: Daniel van Loon
Images: © poligonchik/iStockphoto

ISBN 978-0-8308-2860-9 (print)
ISBN 978-0-8308-9347-8 (digital)

Printed in the United States of America ♾

Library of Congress Cataloging-in-Publication Data

Names: Nesbit Sbanotto, Elisabeth A., 1981- author.
Title: Skills for effective counseling : a faith-based integration /
  Elisabeth A. Nesbit Sbanotto, Heather Davediuk Gingrich, Fred C. Gingrich.
Description: Downers Grove : InterVarsity Press, 2016. | Series: Christian
  Association for Psychological Studies (CAPS) | Includes bibliographical
  references and index.
Identifiers: LCCN 2016011841 (print) | LCCN 2016017714 (ebook) | ISBN
  9780830828609 (pbk. : alk. paper) | ISBN 9780830893478 (eBook)
Subjects: LCSH: Counseling--Religious aspects--Christianity. |
  Communication--Religious aspects--Christianity. | Pastoral counseling.
Classification: LCC BR115.C69 N47 2016 (print) | LCC BR115.C69 (ebook) | DDC
  253.5--dc23
LC record available at https://lccn.loc.gov/2016011841

| **P** | 29 | 28 | 27 | 26 | 25 | 24 | 23 | 22 | 21 | 20 | 19 | 18 | 17 | 16 | 15 | 14 | 13 | 12 | 11 | 10 | 9 | 8 | 7 | 6 | 5 | 4 | 3 | 2 |
| **Y** | 43 | 42 | 41 | 40 | 39 | 38 | 37 | 36 | 35 | 34 | 33 | 32 | 31 | 30 | 29 | 28 | 27 | 26 | 25 | 24 | 23 | 22 | 21 | 20 | 19 | 18 |

DEDICATIONS

Elisabeth: *To Judy Stephen*—a mentor, counselor and educator overflowing with grace, skill and spirit. You taught me as much in your being as you did in your doing. I am gratefully indebted to you for the impression you have left on the way I counsel, teach and engage my whole being in life.

To my husband, Stephen—you married me in the middle of this project and supported me through it all. You exemplify what it means to *be* a counselor, letting the role and giftings permeate into every aspect of who you are. I am forever grateful for who you are and all that you embody as a counselor, a friend and my partner in life.

Heather: Dr. Fran White taught in the counseling program at Wheaton College Graduate School for several decades. Her demonstration of the skill of empathic reflection in a class role-play, with me playing the counselee, was so powerful that it forever impacted my view of the importance of the skills that are the focus of this book. Without this profound experience, the way I practice counseling, and the priority I give to foundational skills in my teaching, would be very different. I certainly would not have engaged on this book project without her example.

Fred: To my parents, Virgil and Della Gingrich. Dad was a pastor, missionary and theological educator. Mom was the consummate pastor's wife, who even played the piano. Over the decades of their active ministry both spent many hours a week "counseling" hurting people. Neither ever took a counseling or pastoral care course, but they were naturally and supernaturally gifted listeners and compassionate caregivers to hundreds of parishioners. They never told me to become a counselor but didn't tell me not to, so what did they expect would happen!

CONTENTS

LIST OF FIGURES
AND TABLES

INTRODUCTION

AS THE AUTHORS OF THIS TEXT, we are well aware that what we are attempting in this book is a lofty and complex task. We want to help people learn how to be better people helpers. The book is a culmination of our combined decades of working with counselees and students. We hope that you are driven by the same desire that compels us to write the book: a deep spiritual concern to respond to a hurting world in ways that reflect the love of God, the sacrifice of Jesus and the compassion of the Spirit. Learning new skills is not easy; we hope that our efforts to explain and to nurture these skills bear fruit in your own life and relationships, and in your chosen ministry context.

WHAT'S YOUR PEOPLE-HELPING ROLE?

We expect that many who read this book will identify themselves as counselors (or on their way to becoming counselors of some variety), while others of you are in related helping roles that are not specifically identified as counseling roles. Regardless of your calling, whether you are a pastor, spiritual director, life coach, mentor, pastoral care provider, mental health counselor in training or in some other people-helping role, we assume that you care about the psychological-emotional-spiritual well-being of people or you would not be reading this book. We want to assure you from the outset that most everything you read in this book will be applicable to any people-helping relationship, whichever specific role you are in with a particular person. However, vocabulary that is inclusive of all the potential people-helping roles is very cumbersome. Therefore we have chosen to use the term *counseling* in a broad, generic sense to encompass all of the above roles. Similarly, we will use *counselor* when referring to anyone in the helper role, and *counselee* when referring to the individual who is in need of help. If you are not specifically in a counseling role, as you read we invite you inwardly replace the words *counselor* and *counseling* with terms that better fit with your role. We realize that this is easier said than done, but we want to affirm the multiple callings and giftedness in people-helping relationships across the spectrum of ministry to others.

Throughout the book we have included stories from our own experiences. While our own names (Elisabeth, Heather and Fred) and the stories and examples we use are often real, the names of counselees and identifying details of the stories have been changed to protect privacy and confidentiality.

THE STRUCTURE OF THIS BOOK

As a skills text, this book is structured to build one skill on another. In this way the book is to be read and worked through sequentially and not approached topically. We encourage you to read the chapters in order and not jump around, since subsequent chapters will make more sense having read the previous chapters.

We will walk you through a rather systematized yet adaptable structure. There are many ways to help people and many variations in the process of how this can be done. In presenting you with our model of people helping we do not mean to imply that there is only one way or a right way. What we have to offer is our combined experience from unique educational and teaching contexts, a range of ministry and people-helping relationships, and diverse cultural experiences.

Aiming for specific targets. Using skills well involves intentionality. We want you to not only know *how* to use a given skill but also *when* to use it and *why* to use it. For this reason we have divided the book into four sections, each of which focuses on a particular task, or target, within the overall process of counseling. Although all of the skills can be used at almost any point in the counseling process, specific skills are particularly helpful in accomplishing a given target.

The analogy of archery can be a helpful way to illustrate this. As an archer you are aiming for the target and hoping to hit the bull's eye. If you do not even know what the target is, your arrow will at best be useless, if not downright dangerous. A beginning archer will attempt to hit the target but may totally miss. With increased practice at building archery skills, the archer's arrow will soon land somewhere on the target and eventually successfully hit the bull's eye.

We see the counseling process as having four targets: (1) establishing relationship and exploring, (2) deepening, (3) growing and (4) consolidating and ending. As mentioned above, all of the skills covered in this book will be used from time to time in accomplishing each of these targets, but some skills will be directly aimed for with greater frequency at specific points in the counseling process because they are more relevant to the task, or target, at hand.

For example, the skill of confronting will not likely be very useful when the target being aimed at is establishing the counseling relationship. As counselors we have to earn the right to confront, or counselees will not accept our feedback. Confronting may at times be useful when the target is consolidating change, but it is going to be most helpful when the target is deepening awareness of the core of a counselee's issue. Therefore the skill of confronting is covered under target 2 in the book, even though its use spills over into other target areas.

Target 1, "Establishing Relationship and Exploring," will be most important at the beginning of the counseling relationship, while target 4, "Consolidating and Ending," will obviously be the main focus toward the end of the helping process. Sometimes counselees get a certain amount of relief from simply talking to a counselor who seems to understand what they are saying and values them as a person. In this case counselees sometimes end counseling without even entering the hard work that targets 2 and 3 require. These target areas are really the crux of the counseling process because they get to the root of the problem (i.e., target 2, "Deepening") and support the counselee to grow in ways that can be painful and difficult (i.e., target 3, "Growing").

Figure 0.1 below illustrates the relationship between the targets and the core reflecting skills across the counseling process.

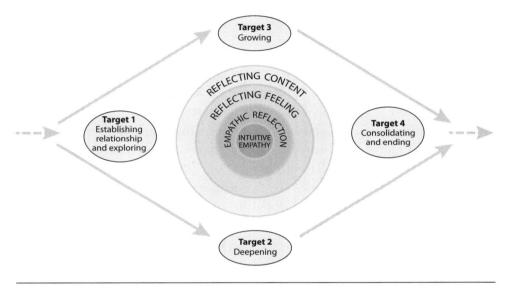

Figure 0.1. The targets and the bull's eye

Common elements in the chapters. In most chapters, in addition to describing the skill focus of the chapter, you will find a number of elements that broaden and deepen your understanding and application of the skill. Our intention is to provide multiple avenues for learning the microskills, coming to the topic from various perspectives.

Questions. Learning new information and new skills requires using multiple sensory modalities (e.g., seeing, thinking, writing and conversing). In most of the chapters there are questions that are intended for you to think about, write down responses to, discuss with others or read more about. We encourage you to slow down your reading and take the time to engage the questions and exercises we suggest. Every time you repeat an idea or a skill, it strengthens the neural pathways required for longer-term memory and skill proficiency. Sometimes there is space in the book to write a response (if you can bear to write in a hard-copy book). Using a learning skills journal (handwritten or creating a file on your computer) would be another way to provide yourself space to write answers down. Electronic versions of this text may have a note-taking feature you can activate to record your answers and reflections.

At the end of most of the chapters there are specific reflection questions related to issues discussed in the chapter. We also encourage you to take the time to engage with them. Other activities will be discussed below.

In many chapters the following elements appear, providing applications of the chapter topic to other contexts and dimensions of the counseling field. The common elements are:

Empirical support. For each skill topic there will be a section that addresses current or landmark studies relevant to the chapter's topic. It is important to us that instructors and students alike recognize the research foundations that undergird the counseling process, demonstrating the complex ways in which God has made people to function and change.

Biblical/theological considerations. Not only is it important to become adept at using the skills, but also we believe that it is essential to recognize and understand the ways in which counseling aligns with scriptural and theological concepts that are foundational to Christian faith. While we have attempted to weave biblical and theological principles throughout the chapters, in each one you will find a special focus on specific ways in which that chapter's topic directly relates to Christian doctrine, biblical teachings or Christian spiritual formation.

Diagnostic implications. Despite the fact that not all of you will find diagnosis relevant to your particular people-helping ministry, we have decided to incorporate "Diagnostic Implications" sidebars in every chapter of the book. Diagnosis is associated with psychological assessment, patterns of psychological symptoms, and categories of mental illness, which point to the benefits of using specific counseling theories and interventions. While foundational counseling skills, such as those focused on in this book, are not generally discussed in light of a given diagnosis, *how* the skills are used with particular individuals can be potentially influenced by the symptoms that they manifest when they fit within a specific diagnostic category. We trust that many of you will find these discussions helpful and may even encourage you to deepen your understanding of diagnosis with further study (e.g., see Seligman & Reichenberg, 2014, for an in-depth, treatment-focused overview of diagnosis; and McRay, Yarhouse & Butman, 2016, for a Christian reflection on psychopathology and diagnosis).

Multicultural application. We recognize that the skills that we are teaching in this book require adaptation for use with counselees from various cultural groups. For this reason most chapters will include a section on multicultural considerations. While not exhaustive, these sections serve to point out ways in which the skill being taught could look or be experienced differently depending on the culture of the counselor or counselee.

Our definition of *multicultural* includes diversity in terms of race and ethnicity, and national heritage and context, as well as encompassing varying religions, immigrant and refugee populations, sexual minorities, age groups, gender, socioeconomic groups and disabilities.

We are quite aware that much of the counseling literature in North America has emerged from a primarily Caucasian, middle-class context. Hence, traditionally, professional counseling has taken place in an office setting, with minimal contact between counselor and counselee outside the counseling hour. This view is being challenged, particularly in the current multicultural counseling and international counseling literature.

Derald Wing Sue and David Sue (2016), prolific writers in the area of multicultural counseling, write that multicultural counseling competence requires that counselors step outside these traditional roles and serve as advocates for their counselees, particularly where social justice issues are involved. This recent emphasis has been added due to increased recognition of the social barriers faced by many counselees from minority groups. For example, a recent immigrant may be in need of social assistance but not have the means to access the help for which he or she is eligible. In this situation Sue and Sue point out that a competent multicultural counselor would not only empathize with the counselee's plight but also take concrete action (e.g., relaying the relevant information to the counselee, helping to fill out the required paperwork, talking to someone in the system on the counselee's behalf).

The form that such advocacy takes will be somewhat dependent on your particular counseling context. For example, if most of your counselees are of lower socioeconomic status or are disadvantaged due to ethnicity, disability or some other factor, you will likely be spending a greater percentage of your time advocating on behalf of your counselees.

Internationally, counseling is gaining recognition in many countries, yet the challenge is to determine the extent to which the Western counseling theories, approaches, skills and interventions are applicable. A helpful, multifaceted reflection on many of these issues can be found in a special journal issue edited by F. Gingrich and Smith (2014).

Relationship application. In this section, we draw applications of the skill being taught to "real life" relationships with counselees, family or friends. As instructors of these skills, we have often been told by students in counseling, chaplaincy, counseling ministries and spiritual direction programs how learning these skills has affected their relationships outside ministry. For instance, parents have noticed that they started talking to their children differently. Spouses and other family members, as well as ministry and professional colleagues, have also benefited from someone in their lives learning these skills.

Ministry application. We are aware that not every reader or student who uses this book is planning to engage in professional counseling. Some of you may find yourselves called to a different people-helping ministry that uses counseling skills in broader ministry-oriented settings. These sections throughout the book look at how a particular skill applies within churches, parachurch organizations or other ministry-based contexts that bring their own unique dynamics and needs to the "counseling" relationship.

While the book is intended to cover a broad range of ministry options in which the skills are foundational, it leans toward preparing students for specific counseling contexts. One way in which this emphasis will be noticed is in the references to the American Counseling Association, the American Psychological Association and other professional counseling organizations. For those in other ministries, there is not a similar central professional home. However, following is an incomplete list of some related organizations. Note that several of these organizations also have codes of ethics that may be more relevant to alternate ministry contexts. Regardless of the ministry context, we believe that the skills presented in this book are helpful in any helping relationship. Application to specific professional contexts will require further training and familiarity with organizations and resources.

- American Association of Christian Counseling—www.aacc.net

- American Association of Pastoral Counselors—www.aapc.org

- Association for Clinical Pastoral Education—www.acpe.edu

- Association of Professional Chaplains—www.professionalchaplains.org

- Christian Association for Psychological Studies—www.caps.net

- Christian Coaches Network—www.christiancoaches.com

- International Christian Coaching Association—www.iccaonline.net

- Renovaré—www.renovare.org

- Spiritual Directors International—www.sdiworld.org

Clinical tips. While generally applicable to all counseling settings, this box will provide helpful hints that are focused on the needs of those working within a more clinical or professional counseling context. Clinical tips will often focus on crucial things to remember and creative ways to apply the information found within the chapter.

Check your understanding. Following a programmed learning approach, these sections within most chapters allow the reader to interact with the chapter's content in a way that engages the reader in various levels of learning, including recognition, application and creation (Anderson & Krathwohl, 2001). This allows readers to build their confidence and competence as they go. Suggested answers are found in appendix A at the end of the book.

Try it out. These sections within a chapter ask readers to apply what they are learning and create interventions based on what they have learned thus far within the text. At times suggested answers can be found in appendix A at the end of the book. At other times readers are encouraged to work with partners or small groups to further develop their understanding of the topic.

Activities. Within several of the chapters are activities that can be conducted as a whole class, in small groups or sometimes alone. They are designed to help readers apply the topic of a particular chapter. Additional activities can be found in appendix B at the end of the book.

Small group exercises. Beginning with the skill of attending (chapter four) and going through the skill of using the here and now (chapter twelve), small group exercises are provided that involve students video-recording themselves practicing the skills in small groups. Clear instructions and templates are provided that allow students to self-evaluate their use of skills, provide better or alternative responses upon review and receive feedback from their instructor with respect to the accuracy of their self-evaluations as well as to the proficiency level of their demonstrated skills. These exercises are meant to facilitate the student's growing ability to not only utilize counseling skills but also self-supervise and self-assess. These exercises are found in appendix C at the end of the book.

THE USE OF TECHNOLOGY IN TRAINING

A brief word about the use of technology is warranted at this point. There are several places where technology can be a considerable asset in the learning of counseling skills:

1. *Observing models* who demonstrate everything from a competent to an inadequate use of the skills. Recordings can be purchased from training companies, and online examples are also available.

2. *Video-recording* your practice sessions (such as with an iPad or tablet). Easy retrieval and functions, such as fast forward and bookmarking a specific location on the recording, are crucial. Some counseling programs provide video recording of sessions, and we strongly recommend this. However, such technology can be expensive. Cheaper alternatives are readily available. In counselor training the use of one-way mirrors to observe your group members' sessions can be very helpful though intimidating. Ideally, clinical supervision should have access to and review actual session recordings.

3. *Audio recording*, while not as useful as video, which allows for observing the nonverbal behavior of both the counselee and the counselor, still can be quite helpful. Using audio recordings to write out *transcripts* of portions of sessions is very valuable, particularly since it engages more than just the visual or auditory senses. Typing a transcript engages the tactile and motor senses, which are helpful in analyzing counselor responses. Even in informal training contexts (e.g., church ministry contexts), recording of practice role-plays and transcript analysis is easily achieved.

4. Commercially available *computer-assisted training programs* (e.g., Casey, 1999) have been available for quite some time and continue to be upgraded. These programs use text and video counseling simulations with a sophisticated prompt-response format that shapes the trainee's responses to become more effective.

5. Of course, class and seminar instruction can be *computer assisted* and *web based*. Interactive computer simulation, and even computer-assisted supervision, career guidance, self-regulation training, and basic cognitive-behavioral therapy can be delivered by computer programs (Hayes, 2008). Counseling training clinics make considerable use of technology (Lee & Jordan, 2008).

6. Last, many products are available to aid with the *administrative* aspects of the counseling process (e.g., note taking, scheduling) and *financial management* in the case of professional counseling.

The downsides of the use of technology must be considered but are often worth the cost:

◆ the financial cost of programs and hardware;

◆ the time required for training and to gain proficiency;

◆ the loss of nonverbal and subtle aspects of communication; and

◆ the maintaining of confidentiality. (Even with the recording of practice sessions, role-playing counselees can reveal personal information. Playing a recording for anyone else without the permission of all who appear in the recording is unethical.)

This is the problem with technology: increased ease and access means increased potential for unethical uses of technology.

A BRIEF WORD REGARDING COUNSELOR
AND COUNSELING PROGRAM ACCREDITATION

There are a number of associations that certify and/or accredit individual counselors, counseling training programs or training programs for related people-helping roles (coaching). For one example, see the American Association of Christian Counselors (www.aacc.net) for a broad range of individual training and certification programs.

For those of you attending an institution accredited by the Council for Accreditation of Counseling & Related Educational Programs (CACREP, www.cacrep.org), the discussion and suggestions within the book are in keeping with CACREP standards and the American Counseling Association Code of Ethics. For a more detailed discussion of CACREP and the specific CACREP standards related to this book, see the Instructor Resource.

Welcome to the beginning of your journey to become a more competent counselor! It is our joy and privilege to walk with you through the counseling skills training process.

THE MICROSKILLS APPROACH

*Let perseverance finish its work so that you may be
mature and complete, not lacking anything.*

JAMES 1:4

CHAPTER FOCUS

SKILL: the skill of learning new skills and identifying targeted skill areas as they relate to the phases of the counseling process

---

PURPOSE: to discuss the goals of counseling, the roles of counselor and counselee, the language of microskills, the process of acquiring new skills, the targeted skill areas of the various phases of the counseling process

---

FORMULA: I learn new skills best by _____. The phases of the counseling process are characterized by the following target areas: _____.

HAVE YOU READ THE INTRODUCTION?

If you have not read the introduction preceding this chapter we suggest you do so before diving into this chapter. It will explain why we have chosen to use particular vocabulary in this book, the specific audiences we are considering and how the book is organized. This chapter will make more sense if you have read the introduction.

A COUNSELING STORY

We will begin this chapter with an extended case description. One of the ways people learn new skills is by reading stories about how others have succeeded, or not, in developing important lessons along their journey. So I (Fred) would like to introduce you to Tommy. As you read this, notice the almost-counterintuitive counseling responses. Counseling is a particular form of communication in which a different kind of conversation occurs.

From the initial phone call, red flags were popping up all over the place. Tommy had previously seen several counselors, and while he now lived in a different town and could not go back to see any of them, I could not help but wonder what I could offer him that the others hadn't. Not only that, but Tommy was a teacher at the same school that my son attended. There would be times that our paths would cross at the school, which could be awkward, a situation I would rather avoid if I could. At least Tommy was not my son's teacher; that would have been a role conflict that would be considered unethical for a professional counselor. I still did not like the situation, but our community was small, so there was no one I could refer Tommy to. I decided to meet with Tommy.

Tommy was amiable, actually a big teddy-bear type. At the beginning of our first session jokes and sports trivia rolled off his tongue, not something that I gravitated to, and this was a bit of a concern as we entered into what is typically a more serious level of conversation. This lack of serious focus was another red flag. Was Tommy going to be able to engage the counseling process?

In an attempt to steer him in a fruitful direction, I gently prodded Tommy to share his story. The theme was a common enough rendition of adolescent boys becoming men, with sports and sex dominating his passions. His previous counseling addressed his search for genuine relationship with women and with men. He had married young, but he and his wife were not particularly close. Their family life was dominated by their three kids. He got together with guys from work to watch sports when he could. He and his family were connected to a church, but they were not involved. The pattern of superficiality in his relationships was clear all the way from his family of origin to his current life circumstances.

His previous counselors, some professional, some pastoral, had been good experiences for Tommy, but all had been short-lived—two to ten sessions and irregular, and they simply had repeated the pattern of superficiality. The counselors had tried a variety of things with Tommy. A college discipler had walked with Tommy through a book on sexual purity and the dangers of pornography. One counselor had used a cognitive-behavioral approach, delving into Tommy's assumptions about his life and challenging his irrational beliefs. A pastor had begun a structured series of Bible studies on intimacy with God. Another counselor had worked on Tommy's distanced relationships with his family of origin. Another pastoral counselor had confronted him with his deficits in being a Christian husband and father and his deficiencies in leading his family.

All of these approaches made sense to me and had proven somewhat helpful to Tommy. But they had ultimately not produced any long-lasting, core change. Outside the session, I prayed for God's direction for Tommy's and my times together.

I was not convinced that pursuing an approach similar to any that prior helpers had used was going to be helpful. I sensed that Tommy would compliantly jump through any hoops that I would set out for him. I figured that he wanted to please others and that he was invested in appearing as though he were working hard. So I expected he would diligently do homework assignments. While on the surface this made him a people helper's dream, I knew that real change would involve something different.

So I resisted the urge to suggest to Tommy that he think, feel or do anything. I became much less directive than was my normal tendency. I was trained in the skills that form the core of this book, and I believed they were helpful. I had instructors and supervisors who had affirmed these as good foundational skills, but they suggested that if you wanted to see deep change in your counselees, you needed to offer more. I believed them. But Tommy had been given the *more* in various forms, and he was struggling with the same issues and themes that had dominated his adolescence and young adulthood. Feeling as though I was being merely a good listener but not much of a counselor, I entered each conversation with Tommy with a commitment to not do what the others had done; instead I was committed to simply being with Tommy, following his lead with regard to topic and pace, offering no homework, not directing his reflections or actions.

Still, my low-level anxiety and my questioning of my competence persisted. I consulted with another counselor about Tommy's "case." I regularly checked in with Tommy regarding how he was responding to and feeling about the counseling. I prayed about it. But each session I felt the urging to not direct, suggest or prescribe anything. I used the skills of this book over and over.

We ended counseling one and a half years later (about forty-five sessions). Tommy had decided to take another teaching position in another state, interestingly in the city where his mother and sister lived, because he had decided he wanted to live closer to extended family. His wife was fully supportive of the move, and Tommy was excited about this new chapter in his own life and marriage.

I met Tommy five years later through a random set of circumstances. We immediately moved beyond the superficial to his spontaneous expression of gratitude for our sessions together. He knew exactly how to express his current situation: "I'm different now. My wife and I connect much more deeply. She sometimes even watches sports with me. I have a relationship with each of my kids. My mom died last year, but we were a family as we grieved. I'm so grateful that I have this chance to thank you for not pushing or pressuring me. I don't know how you knew what I needed, but you got it right. Every other counselor had told me in one way or another that I needed to change. I knew I needed to change, but somehow the homework assignments I completed to make me feel like I was doing something weren't of lasting benefit. I can't really describe what you did to help, but I'm so grateful."

The Goals of Counseling *Are* to:

✓ collaboratively set short- and long-term goals
✓ facilitate the next step of growth
✓ focus on the counselee's needs
✓ foster counselee strengths

The Goals Are *Not* to:

✓ give advice
✓ fix things
✓ convince
✓ help counselees feel better or happier

Most of the time, we do not have the benefit of this kind of long-term feedback. Particularly in this case it was wonderful to receive the affirmation that my instincts or spiritual attunement had been correct. I am grateful to Tommy for the reminder that the skills we are describing in this book are not just foundational or preliminary; they are central to the change process. The research on common factors in counseling theory affirms that however you conceptualize the change process, these skills are at the center. Not everyone has the patience to learn them well. Not all counselees have the persistence to spend forty-five sessions with a counselor, and some counselors seldom see counselees for such an extended period of time, even if they wanted to. But our belief is that the skills of this book will serve you and your counselees well.

We prefer an approach to counseling that is strengths based, rather than focused on psychopathology. A psychopathology approach is based in the medical model of diagnosing disease and focuses on the deficits or problems presented within the counselee. While counselee needs and problems bring them to counseling, it is their God-given strengths, abilities and capacity to heal that will move them forward. This means that throughout counseling we seek to identify and build on the tools, resources, skills and abilities that the counselee already brings to the process rather than primarily focus on what is lacking. While deficits or areas that could use further development are not ignored, they are not the foundation on which counseling builds. This was the situation with Tommy. Previous counselors had focused primarily on Tommy's deficits, which had only made him more resistant to change. Switching the focus to listening carefully to Tommy's perspective on what was happening and acknowledging the attempts he was making to change ultimately allowed his defenses to come down. In time, this more strengths-based approach allowed Tommy to make great strides in the areas in which he had long been stuck.

WHAT COUNSELING IS *NOT*

With the many different uses of the word *counseling* in the English language, it is understandable that there may be some confusion about what counseling is and is not. For example, people might assume that the goal of counseling is simply for the counselor to "give advice" and for the counselee to act on that advice. However, while there may be a time and place for the counselor to offer an opinion or make a suggestion, counseling is built on the idea that, most of the time, the counselee has the potential to make good decisions but is too overwhelmed or confused, having insufficient self-awareness or lacking the support he needs in order to be able to identify or act on what, at some level, he already knows. The irony is that even though the counselee may ask for advice, the counselor adding his or her advice to the mix may actually be unhelpful. Either the counselor does not know the counselee well enough, the counselee resents the counselor's wisdom, or the counselor gives bad advice.

> *The extreme greatness of Christianity lies in the fact that it does not seek a supernatural remedy for suffering but a supernatural use for it.*
> **French philosopher Simone Weil, 1909–1943**

Furthermore, it cannot be our goal in counseling to "fix" the counselee, "make" her do or feel something, or "convince" her of something. This goal puts the counselee in too passive a role and puts too much responsibility and power in the hands of the counselor, violating the premise that counseling is collaborative and counselee focused. It furthermore undermines the belief that the counselee's sense of autonomy and personal responsibility needs to be honored. Tommy's previous counselors had not recognized that in doing what they thought would be helpful to Tommy (e.g., giving him homework to do and making suggestions as to what might be helpful) they were actually disempowering Tommy in his healing process.

> *A gossip betrays a confidence, but a trustworthy person keeps a secret.... So avoid anyone who talks too much.*
> **Proverbs 11:13; 20:19**

Finally, it is not the goal of counseling to make the counselee *feel* better. This can be particularly difficult for counselors who have been drawn to a helping role because they want to alleviate suffering. The irony is that counselees sometimes have to experience even a greater amount of pain than they were aware of initially in order to heal. The goal is to facilitate the counselee in *being* better, which in turn may eventually lead to them feeling better.

THE COUNSELOR'S ROLE

Although multifaceted, the counselor takes on very distinct and specific roles within the counseling relationship. The counselor serves as a confidant, a mirror, a coach and an encourager. As a *confidant*, the counselor is a person with whom the counselee can share personal and intimate things without fear that such information will later be disclosed by the counselor to anyone else. This confidentiality is a foundational element to the counseling relationship, as it provides a space for emotional safety for the counselee (we will explore the limits of confidentiality in the next chapter when we discuss counseling ethics).

> *As water reflects the face,*
> *so one's life reflects the heart.*
> **Proverbs 27:19**

As a *mirror*, the counselor uses both verbal and nonverbal communication to reflect back to the counselee what the counselor sees, hears and experiences within the counseling relationship. As people, we are limited in our self-understanding and rely on the direct and indirect feedback of others to gain self-awareness, insights and understanding of social cues. The counselor as a mirror seeks to reflect back to the counselee, without distorting the message or adding evaluative judgments, in order that the counselee can more clearly see himself and the situation.

> *The wise in heart are called discerning,*
> *and gracious words promote instruction.*
> **Proverbs 16:21**

As a *coach*, the counselor brings his or her experiences and training to the therapeutic relationship in order to gently guide the counselee through the process of cultivating her skills, abilities and aptitudes. In this, the counselor serves as the expert in the counseling process while honoring the counselee's role as expert of her own life. The coach helps to clarify vision, collaboratively design a plan, offer growth opportunities, and provide both challenges and affirmations along the way.

As an *encourager*, the counselor seeks to continuously remain in a position of respect, understanding and hope toward the counselee. While it cannot be expected that every counselor will like or enjoy every counselee, it is necessary that counselors prayerfully and intentionally strive to see, honor and affirm the image of God in every counselee. Whether spoken or unspoken, the counselor as an encourager seeks to affirm and champion the steps of growth and the progress made by the counselee, no matter how small.

> *Anxiety weighs down the heart,*
> *but a kind word cheers it up.*
> **Proverbs 12:25**

Unlike most friendships, counseling relationships are not reciprocal; the participants do not take equal turns sharing struggles, joys and insights. Instead, in counseling, the counselor has the distinct role of coming alongside the counselee in order to facilitate the counselee's growth process. Counseling is all about what the *counselee* needs, not about relational reciprocity. Our goal as counselors is to ultimately work ourselves out of a job by collaborating with counselees to resolve their problems in a way that utilizes their strengths and talents.

The focus of the counselor is always on fostering, facilitating and promoting the growth and the good of the counselee, not on the counselor's needs for growth, affirmation or fulfillment. In working with Tommy, it would have been much easier for Fred to have been more directive; at least by giving homework he could have had more objective evidence of getting somewhere with Tommy, that is, if he actually completed it. Continuing to remind himself that the ultimate goal was what would be beneficial for Tommy allowed Fred to put aside more immediate needs for success and fulfillment. (In chapter two we will discuss further the person of the counselor, that is, what personal qualities and characteristics are necessary for a good counselor.)

THE COUNSELEE'S ROLE

The role of the counselee is much less complex than that of the counselor. Essentially the counselee needs to (1) recognize that something in his life is not the way he wants it to be; (2) seek the support, input or help of another person; and (3) be willing to, at least to some degree, honestly engage in a process of self-exploration and change. The degree to which a counselee can embrace these three elements will vary from one individual to another and may even change throughout the counseling process. Remember it took Tommy several counselors over many years to be able to eventually truly engage in the process. Since many counselees have never before been in a counseling relationship, and others may not have had a good experience in previous counseling, we have found it beneficial not to assume that counselees understand the counseling process as we do. Therefore, we intentionally explain to counselees the respective roles of counselee and counselor at the beginning of the counseling relationship. This way everyone involved is clear as to what the respective roles are and can adjust their expectations accordingly at the beginning of the journey together.

THE CONCEPT OF MICROSKILLS

Long-term goals are often impossible to reach unless they are broken down into achievable short-term goals. So while it is important to collaboratively identify where the counselee eventually wants to end up, much of counseling involves helping the counselee to move to the next step in the counselee's growth process. We all tend to make life changes in small steps. Just as the counselee's long-term goals need to be dismantled into smaller pieces, so too the skills of counseling need to be divided into what have been called *microskills*. Microskills are teachable, learnable segments of new behavior that combine together into the overall skills of counseling.

You have probably noticed that so far we have used the words *skills* or *microskills* repeatedly and interchangeably. Technically, *microskills* refer to the process of taking a large and complicated skill, what has been called a *macroskill* (e.g., skiing or bike riding) and dividing it into smaller, bite-size pieces. If the smaller pieces are mastered, the chances of mastering the larger, more complex skill are greatly improved. Balancing, pedaling, braking, steering and negotiating bumps in the road are all microskills necessary in learning to ride a bike. Likewise, perceiving (chapter four) and attending (chapter five) are microskills that, when combined with each other and

Types of Counselees and Counselors

The solution-focused/brief therapy literature identifies a helpful typology of counselee/ counselor relationships (avoiding labeling people but emphasizing the relationship dynamic in each case).

1. Visitor/Host: This counselee wants to window shop: checking counseling out, minimally investing and leaving other options (such as miracles) open for achieving change. Such counselees are often mandated or pressured to go for counseling or have some ulterior motive (e.g., pleasing someone else). The role of the counselor is to be hospitable and ease the counselee into the process while being clear about what counseling is and is not. The downside of this set of roles is that counseling is potentially much more than being a gracious host.

2. Complainant/Sympathizer: This counselee is interested primarily in discussing someone else in her life who is interpreted as causing the counselee's distress. This counselee wants the other person to change and wants help to get the other person to change. As counselors, in response to what are often sad and even traumatic relationship stories, we feel genuine sympathy, but sympathy does not facilitate change, as this book will emphasize. Counseling requires something more, something deeper.

3. Customer/Consultant: This counselee truly wants to address an issue in his life, desires to change, wants to modify circumstances and is willing to engage in the process—to "buy into" the process. The counselor becomes a consultant of the process, not determining the outcome for the counselee. The power of the counseling relationship is in this dynamic and these roles.

As counselors, we want to invest ourselves in customers and not waste our time and energy on the others, but our skills will go a long way to helping visitors and complainants become customers. Do not give up on visitors and complainants too soon; their fear and anxiety of what counseling will require of them may be what is getting in the way. A counselor's skills can quickly uncover this "resistance" to the process.

For further information see Ziegler, P. B. (2010). "Visitor," "complainant," "customer" revisited. In T. S. Nelson (Ed.), *Doing something different: Solution-focused brief therapy practices* (39-44). New York: Routledge.

added to additional microskills, can help you to counsel effectually. Effective counseling consists of learned and practiced skill; simply desiring to help, having some knowledge of the counseling process, hoping for the best or praying for someone are not enough. There are specific things we can learn in order to be helpful.

THE SKILL OF LEARNING NEW SKILLS

We all know that it is not enough to simply *want* to be good at doing something new; we have to figure out *how* to learn to be proficient at a task. In short, learning new skills is a skill in itself. Some people master it; others struggle repeatedly.

A metaphor: Learning a language. The journey of learning counseling skills is, in many ways, like learning a new language. Initially, you might have some limited vocabulary and a sense of the new language, but despite your confidence and natural language-learning abilities, fluency is a long way off. You may have used

Empirical Support

Hearn (1976) is a foundational research study on programmed learning of counseling skills showing that systematic training of counselors is effective. In 1990, Baker, Daniels and Greeley's meta-analysis compared Carkhuff's human resource training/development model, Ivey's microcounseling model and Kagan's interpersonal process recall model. In the 1980s and '90s these models were the most popular and widely used programs for training students in counseling skills courses. The meta-analysis showed that while all three were effective, there appeared to be a relationship between the length of training and the effect size:

Table 1.1. Comparison of microskills training models

Model	Effect Sizes	Hours of Training
Carkhuff (late 1960s)	1.07 (large)	37
Ivey (early 1970s)	.63 (medium)	19
Kagan (mid 1980s)	.20 (small)	9.5

Source: Baker et al., 1990

More recently, Little, Packman, Smaby and Maddux (2005) combined the Carkhuff and Ivey models into a training program called the Skilled Counselor Training Model, and many additional innovations and variations are found in the literature.

As the research has developed, studies have begun to look at what components (microskills) of the programs produce the largest effect sizes. Kuntze, van der Molen and Born (2009), with a sample of 583 students, studied seven basic skills (minimal encouragements, asking questions, paraphrasing, reflection of feeling, concreteness, summarizing and situation clarification) and five advanced skills (advanced accurate empathy, confrontation, positive relabeling, examples of one's own and directness) and found that each of the separate skills had large effect sizes, except for one advanced skill (examples of one's own), which had a moderate effect size. Another conclusion was that students taking a second (advanced) skill course increased their basic skill levels further as well as began to master the advanced skills; the amount of practice affects the development of skills. There are, unfortunately, no shortcuts.

some of the new language in other contexts as you explain the change, growth and healing process that people undergo. But the depth of fluency needed to engage with a counselee's deep concerns comes with its own structure, style of speech and vocabulary, requiring you to take the natural skills that you bring to this process and build on them.

If you have ever learned a second (or third) language, you understand that the process is both rewarding and frustrating. You know how to say all that you think, feel, see and so on in your native language, and it takes time to build up the same level of vocabulary, self-expression and fluency in the new language. In counselor training, as with language leaning, it may be necessary to *un*learn some of your former "language" of helping in order to *re*learn the new language through systematic engagement with the microskills.

Another metaphor: Learning to drive. The microskills will be taught one at a time and will be sequenced so that they build on one another. They provide the basic structure and framework for the counseling process. When I (Elisabeth) was in driver's education, I was taught that keeping my hands on the steering wheel at the "10-and-2" position, as in the hands on a (nondigital) clock, was the proper way to drive. The idea of 10-and-2 being applied to counseling was first introduced to me by a friend and colleague, Dr. Elizabeth Keller-Dupree, as a helpful way to explain the process of learning the core counseling microskills. Whether you were taught "10-and-2," "9-and-3" or simply to keep both hands on the wheel, there was likely a position you were taught to go back to as your "proper" driving form. If the counseling process is a road on which you journey with a counselee, microskills serve as the 10-and-2 position on the steering wheel as you navigate the counseling process.

However, many of us do not drive with our hands perfectly at 10-and-2 on the steering wheel all the time. In fact, we frequently drive with one hand, or at times may even drive with our knees! But the 10-and-2 position is where we come back to when the road is rough, the terrain is unknown or the environmental conditions are dicey. The same is true in the counseling process. It is important that you learn to "drive" at 10-and-2, proving that you understand and can effectively use the foundational microskills of counseling, so that you can come back to them when you are unsure how to navigate the counseling conversation. Eventually, when you have mastered the 10-and-2 of the microskills, you will slowly take more freedom to incorporate "one-handed" approaches to counseling, and maybe even drive with your knees, positions that are not recommended in driving or counseling but are occasionally necessary!

RATIONALE FOR OUR METHOD OF LEARNING SKILLS

Our rationale for the methods used in this book is drawn from various sources within the education and counseling fields, combining what we see as the best of the methodologies. The well-known taxonomies of cognitive, affective and psychomotor domains in education (Bloom, Engelhart, Furst, Hill & Krathwohl, 1956) suggest that learning new information and skills involves all three domains and is not limited to simply the acquisition of cognitive knowledge (see Anderson & Krathwohl, 2001, for an updated version of Bloom's Taxonomy). Mental skills (the cognitive domain) are essential, but likewise change in feelings or emotional dynamics (the affective domain), and developing manual or physical skills (the psychomotor domain), are each relevant to the effective practice of counseling. Hence learning counseling skills involves the learner cognitively, emotionally and behaviorally.

Learning New Skills Requires:

✓ motivation: a compelling purpose   ✓ receiving feedback

✓ risking   ✓ resisting discouragement

✓ practice and more practice   ✓ persistence

Other influences on our model include Linehan's (1993) approach to helping counselees develop new personal and interpersonal skills. In addition, we will be integrating elements of a programmed learning approach (Evans, Hearn, Uhlemann & Ivey, 2011; Hearn, 1976) in which the learning process is scaffolded, one skill building on a previous skill. Finally, we will also add some of the practical steps of microskills acquisition as identified by Chang, Scott and Decker (2013).

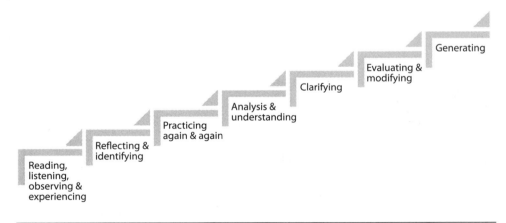

Figure 1.1. Sequenced and scaffolded learning

While we do not often break down the process in much detail, learning a new skill could be summarized in a sequence of steps such as the one in figure 1.1. Humans, as we grow and develop, have the ability to collapse these steps into an almost unconscious sequence. Only when we are really motivated do we make it more intentional in order to master more complex and significant skills.

HOW WE PLAN TO TEACH THE MICROSKILLS

We have chosen to break the process down into five major steps that will form an outline for each of the microskill chapters. While this is a sequenced (one following the other) and scaffolded (building on the previous step) approach, real skill acquisition may be more recursive than this suggests. The need to go back to prior steps and repeat and practice earlier steps that you thought you had already mastered is not an uncommon experience and should not be cause for discouragement. The five steps we will use as an outline are:

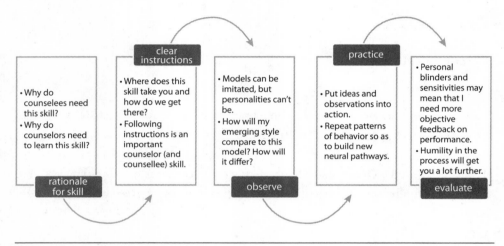

Figure 1.2. Our model of skill acquisition

Step 1: Provide a rationale for the skill. Any time a new skill is pursued the learner must understand why this skill is relevant or important (Linehan, 1993). Therefore, when each new skill is introduced, we will look at *why* it is important. In terms of overall microskill development, research findings show that counselees report higher levels of satisfaction with the counseling process when microskills are used, regardless of whether the counselee is an adult or a child (De Stefano, Mann-Feder & Gazzola, 2010; Kuntze, van der Molen & Born, 2009; van Velsor, 2004).

Step 2: Provide clear instruction. The second step in skill development is to *provide clear instruction* (Linehan, 1993, p. 34). There is little that is more frustrating than being given a task without a clear sense of how it is to be done. In light of this, as each microskill is introduced we will clearly communicate *how* it is to be delivered and used within the counseling process. In many cases, a specific formula will be provided that serves as a template for exactly what to say.

Step 3: Observe an effective model. The third step in skill development is that of *observing an effective model* (Chang, Scott & Decker, 2013, p. xxvii; Linehan, 1993, p. 34). You will be provided with dialogue examples in which an exchange between a counselor and a counselee models the appropriate use of the skill being taught. Beyond the scope of this book are many counseling training videos available that can be watched as good, and not-so-good, demonstrations of the skills.

Step 4: Practice the new skill. The fourth step in skill development flows naturally out of the third and is that of *practicing the new skill* (Chang, Scott & Decker, 2013, p. xxvii; Linehan, 1993, p. 33). It is not enough to simply read about and observe a new skill; making it your own requires multiple forms of practice. In some instances practice will mean reading an exchange between counselee and counselor and filling in the missing blanks within the counselor's response. In other instances, practice will mean generating your own response from scratch, keeping in mind the formulas and guidelines presented along the way. Finally, other instances of practice will ask you to engage with a partner or a small group by taking on the role of counselor and responding to the narrative your role-playing counselee shares.

Step 5: Evaluate. The fifth step in skill development is that of *evaluation* (Chang, Scott & Decker, 2013, p. xxvii; Linehan, 1993, p. 36). Repeated efforts to learn a new skill must be accompanied by feedback so that necessary adjustments can be made to the process. Practicing skills incorrectly would be a waste of time.

Evaluation has two foci: evaluation of self and evaluation from others. *Evaluation of self* is the process by which you reflect on your own work, comparing it to the guidelines, standards or answer keys that are available to you in this process. For written practice activities, this takes the form of comparing your responses to the key at the end of the chapter. For in-class and homework practice activities, this takes the form of reviewing your audio/video recording and comparing your responses to the standards and guidelines you have been given for the skill(s) being practiced.

Evaluation from others is often the most anxiety-provoking part of this process, for in it we invite others to comment on our demonstrated skills. For those who for whatever reason have some sensitivity regarding receiving feedback, this can easily become discouraging and demoralizing. In a later chapter we will address the dynamics of giving and receiving feedback in more depth.

Whether you are evaluating a classmate or you are the one being evaluated, it is important to remember that skill acquisition is a *developmental* process. This means that someone who is just learning a skill should not and cannot be evaluated by the same standard one would use to evaluate someone who has been using a skill for the last ten years. Because of this, we encourage evaluation to be on a Likert scale that looks something like this:

Table 1.2. Proficiency levels for ratings of microskills

Rating	Description
1	***Does not*** use targeted skill appropriately—use of skill is ineffective or demonstrates a lack of understanding as to skill's purpose
2	***Sometimes*** uses targeted skill appropriately
3	***Often*** uses targeted skill appropriately—use of skill is minimally effective or demonstrates basic understanding of skill's purpose
4	***Regularly*** uses targeted skill appropriately
5	***Consistently*** and appropriately uses targeted skill—use of skill is highly effective or demonstrates advanced understanding and proficiency

As you begin this journey of microskill development, your practice attempts early on in the process should *not* yield a score of five unless you are some kind of microskill genius! Your first few practices will likely be around a two or a three, and it may not be until a few months (or years) into counseling experience that you find yourself consistently at a four or five, particularly for the more advanced microskills. As you evaluate one another, be kind, but do not be dishonest in your kindness. Telling individuals that they did a great job when they actually have things to work on does not help them to learn the new skill. Likewise, it is not helpful to nitpick when their overall delivery was appropriate and effective.

THE PROFESSIONAL AND SPIRITUAL DISCIPLINE OF FORMING HABITS

The words *discipline* and *habit* do not evoke positive responses in our contemporary culture. Yet when we think about any professional person, we know that it took them practice to get where they are. We know this is true spiritually as well. Unfortunately, we do not simply grow into new healthy patterns of living and relating; it takes practice. Interestingly, the resistance you might feel in reading the words *discipline* and *habit* are the same reactions your counselees will have when you discuss with them the need to alter life patterns. Developing habits is often considered in the negative, for example, "I have the bad habit of saying 'umm.'" We would like to reclaim a positive meaning for *habit* in the sense of encouraging counselors to develop the good habits of counseling. However, we know from our efforts at failing miserably at New Year's resolutions that breaking old habits and acquiring new ones is harder than we think. This is where our spiritual resources (e.g., meditation, prayer, silence, conversation) can be a useful part of the process of developing *habitus*, the refinement of good patterns of relating to others for their own good, not necessarily ours.

Historical Reflection

Going back to Plato and Aristotle, humanity has been curious about the virtues (prosocial attitudes and behaviors) and how we can help promote virtuous thinking and behaving in others. One of the virtues that church fathers and later theologians (e.g., Augustine and Aquinas) have discussed is the importance of *habitus* (Latin).

Habitus is not simply developing good habits of moral behavior (repetition of automatic behaviors). *Habitus* refers to how repeated actions become internalized as perfected dispositions to act for good. Repeated actions can also become bad habits.

Habitus refers to nonidentical repetition (doing a similar thing over and over); it is a repetition of behavior that "forms beliefs, shapes and modulates emotion, and correctly aligns our appetites and apprehensions" (Hampson, 2012, p. 8). While they become second nature to us, they also evolve and become refined with practice.

Faith itself is a gift from God that we receive, but it is also a *habitus*; we must practice our faith. In the same way that the other virtues must be practiced, counseling skills must be practiced to form in us a way of relating that is not only a nonidentical habitual pattern of responding but a deeply held set of beliefs and potential ways of engaging in helpful behaviors depending on the nuances and contexts of the particular situation. They, too, require continuous refinement.

THE COUNSELING PROCESS

Learning how to ride a bike was one of the metaphors we used for learning counseling skills. The microskills of balance, steering and pedaling are all necessary for the macroskill of bike-riding. But there is not a whole lot of value in learning how to ride a bike if you do not have a destination! Actually arriving at your endpoint involves all of the riding skills as well as knowing how to get there and what to do if there are detours or flat tires along the way.

Similarly, counseling involves a journey that you as the counselor and the counselee take together with a specific destination in mind. Developing good microskills is essential to the success of the trip, but part of the art of counseling involves knowing what microskills to use when. This is where an understanding of the process of counseling is crucial.

While each of the unique helping contexts we are addressing has its own distinctive aspects and styles, the processes of these various helping relationships have a lot in common. All counseling-type relationships consist of two (or more) people who have mutually agreed to go on a journey of growth together, a journey in which one person (the counselor) has the primary goal of facilitating the other person's (the counselee's) growth in a particular area.

The counseling process is not linear or sequential; it is circular and repetitive, more like a spiral, in that at times it feels as if things are being repeated, are not going

Figure 1.3. Spiral with upward trajectory

anywhere or are frustratingly slow. However, the spiral has an overall upward trajectory. We believe that in the repetition, the ups and downs of the process, growth is occurring. Created in the image of God (Gen 1:27), we are complex beings with multiple layers or facets. Therefore, cycling through the layers of our identities at different times, in slightly different ways, aids in the healing process.

THE PHASES OF THE COUNSELING PROCESS: WHAT IS TARGETED WHEN

My (Fred's) master's thesis consisted, in part, of a massive literature review of stages or phases of the counseling process. It is amazing to see the variety of ways in which people can conceptualize it. In 1984 I found over one hundred authors who described the process, and now many more have added their wisdom to describe the process by which people change and grow.

The theoretical underpinnings of phase language. While many of these authors would describe their phases as universal for all counseling processes, the reality is that theoretical orientation often influences how such phases are described. For example, Wright's (1984) five-step model includes: (1) relationship building, (2) exploration of problems, (3) deciding on a course of action, (4) stimulating action and (5) terminating the counseling relationship. The language sounds very behavioral or oriented toward problem-solving approaches. In contrast, the five counseling phases outlined by Young (1992) include: (1) initial contact, (2) commitment, (3) intimacy, (4) untying and (5) termination. The relational terms imply a very different theory of counseling.

The phase challenge. As we considered how we would like to identify phases of the counseling process here, our dilemma was how could we describe them in a way that was not specifically geared to a particular theoretical approach and yet could be of benefit for helping students understand which skills should be used at certain points in the process. The solution we came up with was to discuss the phases in the very simple terms of *early, middle* and *late* phases. The amount of time spent in each phase will vary immensely, depending on the overall duration of counseling with a particular counselee. So, for example, if a particular counselee is in counseling on a weekly basis for a total of eight weeks, the first week or two would constitute the early phase, sessions three through six would constitute the middle phase, and sessions seven and eight would constitute the late phase. In contrast, if counseling were long term, the early phase might be the first year of counseling, the middle phase the next three years, and the final year the late phase.

Targets. We briefly described the concept of targets in the introduction to this book. While using the language of phases helps to give a sense of process over time, the idea of targets relates more to specific tasks or areas of focus that can be most helpful within a given phase of counseling but that can still be useful in other phases. Target 1, "Establishing Relationship and Exploring," is the main target area of the early phase of counseling. Target 2, "Deepening," and target 3, "Growing," are most helpful in the middle phase of counseling, and target 4, "Consolidating and Ending," will be the major focus during the late phase.

PHASES OF GROWTH AND CHANGE IN
BIBLICAL AND SPIRITUAL DEVELOPMENT

It is important to remember the role of the Holy Spirit in the change process. We all have had issues in our lives that have taken time to change. It can be easy to look at counselees and become impatient or discouraged by the lack of progress they appear to be making. It is in these moments that we need to reflect on the process of change in our own lives, noting the time and grace allocated to us by friends, family and the Holy Spirit along the way.

John 16:7-13 reminds us that it is the Holy Spirit's job to convict people of the changes that need to be made in their lives. This same passage also reminds us that sometimes God withholds things from us because they are too much to bear in the moment. God is gracious and intentional in what he reveals to each of us at a given point in time so that we do not become overwhelmed and discouraged. Instead of bombarding us with everything that needs to change, God shows us, piece by piece, where growth is possible. It is the counselor's job to be prayerful and discerning, noting where a counselee is in the change process and keeping in mind that it is ultimately the Holy Spirit's job to convict and motivate toward change.

The emphasis on phases is not merely a twentieth- or twenty-first-century preoccupation. Scripture identifies a phase-like development in growth and change (cf. Prov 9:6; Eph 4:12-16; Phil 3:14). We can see stages of Christlikeness in 1 Corinthians 3:1-3 and Hebrews 5:12-14. As Larkin (1967) puts it, "Divisions of growth are thus a framework for spiritual direction according to the needs and possibilities of different people" (p. 43). Larkin recognizes the need for a framework yet also the need to affirm the uniqueness of each person in terms of how the framework is applied. So, both within Scripture and in psychology, the concept of development is crucial to understanding people, including ourselves.

In order to help conceptualize the various ways stages are understood, in table 1.3 is a summary of the classical stages or phases of spiritual direction (column one). These are aligned with the phases and targets as we are conceptualizing them in the counseling process (column two). As an example of one other phase model in counseling, the phases of treatment of survivors of complex trauma are given in the third column. The language of each is quite different and reflects the focus of the particular helping relationship. Though the language used in classical spiritual direction is perhaps foreign to many of us, it highlights several important dimensions of the counseling process.

Phase one (*purgation*) reminds one of the idea of purging. Purging is not a pleasant experience, but the term is descriptive of the need for people at the beginning of a counseling process to express, either reluctantly or in a gush of words, their pent-up, unprocessed life experience. This purging experience is what some psychoanalysts call catharsis, the venting of built-up emotion in therapy, often related to the counselee's personal stories. Cathartic release, or abreaction, a key element of psychodynamic and person-centered therapy, is considered healing in and of itself (Kearney, 2007; Von Glahn, 2012).

The second phase of spiritual growth, *illumination*, highlights the increased understanding of oneself and one's circumstances and begins the inner change process of reflecting Christlike virtues despite the struggles and frustrations that are an inevitable part of life. Use of the word *virtue* highlights the fact that ultimately the counseling process is about identifying strengths and positive aspects of self, not only pathology and problems.

The third phase, *union*, while using the idealistic language of perfection, suggests a point of completion, not unlike that rather odd term that often is used in the counseling literature, *termination* of the relationship. The important piece of this phase of spiritual direction is the idea of moving beyond oneself to connection with God and others in healthier ways that are characterized by charity (love).

Table 1.3. Comparison of phases of the change process from spirituality, counseling and trauma therapy perspectives

Christian Spirituality[a]	Counseling Process	Complex-Trauma Therapy[b]
Purgation (release of sin and its effects)	Early phase: Target 1: Establishing relationship and exploring	Safety and stabilization
Illumination (growth in virtue and inner renovation)	Middle phase: Target 2: Deepening Target 3: Growing	Trauma processing (integrating the components of traumatic experiences)
Union (with God and others—perfect charity)	Late phase: Target 4: Consolidating and Ending	Consolidation and resolution

Note: The three columns in this chart are not identical, but there are similarities. Each can learn from the other, yet each describes a particular type of helping relationship.
[a]Cf. Coe, 2000; Larkin, 1967; Mulholland, 1993, chapter 8.
[b]Cf. Gingrich, 2013.

The third column in table 1.3 identifies the phases of the counseling process with survivors of complex trauma (e.g., sexual abuse, chronic domestic abuse, ritual abuse). There is a wide range of incidents that can be subjectively experienced as traumatic, whether or not an external observer would necessarily view them as such. However, unresolved trauma will inevitably interfere with life and complicate the healing process. In the first phase a counselee needs to be helped to feel safe in the counseling relationship and to gain some sense of understanding and control of symptoms, particularly ones that are dangerous (e.g., self-harm). In the second phase the focus is on the long, tough work of processing the traumatic events. In the third phase the counselee experiences the resolution of the trauma and often emerges with a new sense of identity and wholeness.

The middle column identifies the three phases of the healing process that we will use in this book, along with the targets of focus. Whether in a twenty-minute conversation or throughout a twenty-week counseling relationship, the three phases are important and typically present. As we briefly overview each phase with its related tasks, it is important to note that the phases are meant to build on one another and must be approached in order. With that being said, it is always possible, and sometimes necessary, to circle back and revisit previous phases in order to effectively journey with the counselees through their stories.

THE HOURGLASS METAPHOR

The counseling process functions much like an hourglass. The top of the hourglass might represent how counselees are initially all over the place—the topics are far-reaching, and the discussion does not go particularly deep. Some of this is intentional on the part of the counselor in order to gather data on all facets of the counselee's life. Gradually specific issues come more into focus, and therapeutic work becomes more narrowly concentrated (the middle of the hourglass). The sand flows quickly, and intensity and depth are increased. Finally the content/topics once again become broader as counselees learn how to generalize what they have learned and apply that to their lives and relationships (the bottom of the hourglass). This hourglass analogy can be helpful in describing the process of counseling both within each individual session and in the overall counseling relationship. The hourglass suggests that timing and control of the process are crucial—too fast or too slow can hamper the process.

Figure 1.4. Hourglass

The top section of the hourglass, initially full of sand. This represents the information, the many details of the story and of the counselee's life. There is often a lot of confusion, and while some counseling goals may be identified, others may be unclear. Target 1 (Establishing Relationship and Exploring) skills will be most effective here.

In more clinical settings, one of the tasks is to gather and organize the information provided by the counselee into a diagnosis. Again, borrowed from medical contexts, the concept of diagnosing a problem is deeply embedded in much counseling literature. An introductory overview of the diagnosis process is provided in the "Diagnostic Implications" sidebar.

Diagnostic Implications

Diagnosis is the categorization of mental disorders. In most ministry contexts diagnosing people is not helpful and is not done. In professional counseling contexts it is required. The world of diagnosing is the world of psychiatry, specially trained medical doctors, who typically meet with patients, listen for descriptions of symptoms and prescribe medication. This is an essential component of mental health services, and as a result psychiatrists are the experts in diagnosis.

This is seen most clearly in the *Diagnostic and Statistics Manual of Mental Disorders* (DSM; APA, 2013) published by the American Psychiatric Association (Note: this is not the American Psychological Association, which also uses the acronym APA.) Because of its technical language, research base and medical aspects, the DSM is a highly specialized document but one that has become very accessible with the help of the Internet. Therefore the general public has become much better informed, which can be both a positive trend, in that people can take greater interest and responsibility for their own mental health, and a negative factor, in that misunderstanding the technical aspects of diagnosis is likely, and there is a tendency to use the language to label others.

The DSM is described as being *a-theoretical* in that it does not assume a particular theory of causation or treatment. However, there are a few alternative, theory-driven approaches to diagnostic categories and treatment (e.g., McWilliams, 2011; PDM Task Force, 2006; L'Abate, 1998).

Professional counselors must become familiar with the DSM and use it frequently, depending on their practice setting. It is advisable for people helpers in other settings to avoid using the DSM. The rationale for not using the DSM is:

✓ the danger of labeling people—sometimes when we label people they end up acting according to their label (think about the profound influence labeling children can have)
✓ the assumption that the DSM includes all mental disorders—it is not the only way of conceptualizing psychopathology
✓ the adherence to the medical model of understanding and treating people—this can be a limiting approach to understanding people holistically
✓ the lack of recognition of the relational component of people's problems—a diagnosis is typically made of an individual
✓ the difficulty in diagnosing crossculturally—symptoms mean different things in different cultures
✓ the rejection of a spiritual/religious worldview

The rationale for using the DSM is:
✓ the ability to study groups of people with similar symptoms and to determine the effectiveness of various treatment approaches
✓ the advantage of being able to focus our helping efforts for specific clients in ways that are evidence based rather than just treating counselees based on our hunches or preferences
✓ the recognition that specific categories of symptoms are more physiologically caused than situationally or dispositionally caused
✓ the ability to distinguish, at least to some degree, biological, emotional, relational or spiritual issues

The DSM is a valuable resource; it has been, and will continue to be, a helpful resource for counselors of all varieties. However, it is a specialization that not all counselors have the luxury to learn well, so caution is warranted. Of most importance in this regard is the recognition that diagnosing is not equivalent to counseling: being a good diagnostician is not the same as being a good counselor. They use different sets of skills.

The narrowing of the hourglass. The counselor is seeking to facilitate the counselee's self-exploration and sense of self-awareness within his or her given situation. There is a narrowing, or clarifying, of the problem or the situation as the counselor and counselee work their way down to the neck of the hourglass. Target 2 (Deepening) skills are essential at getting past what is often a superficial sense of what kind of change is needed early on in the process, into the underlying or deeper issues. This generally marks the beginning of the middle phase of counseling.

Biblical/Theological Connections

At the heart of this book will be what we will call a theology of emotion. As we learn effective counseling skills, we must wrestle with how we view persons, how emotions play a central role in people's problems, how the counseling process must pay close attention to the emotional experience of counselees and how emotions factor into the process of personal and spiritual growth and change (see M. Elliott, 2006, 2014; Peterman, 2013; Scazzero, 2006, for sources on this topic).

A theology of emotion is anchored in the teaching of Scripture on the nature of God; the image of God in which persons are created; the interaction of emotions, cognition, behavior and volition; and the life of Christ. Subsequent chapters will unpack these ideas, which taken together present a preliminary outline of a theology of emotion. We believe such a theological foundation is essential for effective counseling.

We do not take a positive perspective toward emotion for granted, since in our Christian tradition emotions have often been thought of as the part of the person that most likely will lead us into sin. In the history of psychology, emotions have often been considered the cause of dysfunction and immaturity. Take a few moments to assess to what degree you believe/accept these statements as true. Where did these beliefs come from? Do they fit with a biblical understanding of human emotions?

✓ There is a right way to feel in every situation.
✓ Letting others know that I am feeling bad is a weakness.
✓ Negative feelings are destructive.
✓ Being emotional means being out of control.
✓ If I give in to my emotions, I will lose control of myself.
✓ Emotions just happen for no reason.
✓ All painful emotions are the result of a limited or faulty view of God.
✓ If others don't approve of my feelings, it means I shouldn't feel the way I do.
✓ Other people are the best judge of how I should be feeling.
✓ Painful emotions are not really important in life and so should be dismissed.

✓ I must never let my emotions get the better of me. If I do, I will be sinning.

✓ Only prayer can take away emotions that out of control.

✓ Within the mature, spiritual Christian, reason and emotion are in a war, and reason should win.

✓ Behavior is justified because you feel a certain way.

✓ Being emotionally restricted is just the way men are.

✓ Overemotional reactions are just part of being a woman.

✓ Being calm, neither up nor down, is a goal and sign of good mental health.

✓ Being calm, neither up nor down, is a goal and sign of being a spiritual person.

At the narrowest point of the hourglass. The counselor and counselee really zero in on specific aspects of the key counseling goals. There is an intensity and depth to this part of the middle phase of counseling when target 2 skills are being used effectively.

Launching into the base. Everything up until this point in the counseling relationship has led to this point, which could not have been reached without making its way through the funnel. In this part of the middle phase of counseling, target 2 skills continue to be used, and target 3 (Growing) becomes an increased focus as the hard work of growing and changing is at its peak.

Approaching the bottom of the base. As the process fans out and approaches the bottom of the hourglass, the late phase of counseling and target 4 (Consolidating and Ending) come into play. The changes that occurred during the difficult work of the middle phase of counseling now need to be consolidated so that they become permanent. Preparing counselees for leaving the counseling relationship is the final aspect of target 4.

Each phase of counseling builds on the progress made in the previous phase, as long as the related tasks have been accomplished well, with each one serving to bring counselees closer to meeting their goals. See figure 1.5 for a summary of the microskills that are associated with each phase of the counseling process.

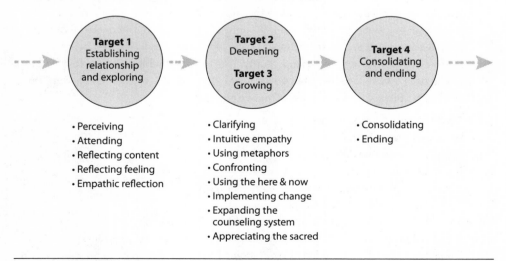

Target 1
Establishing relationship and exploring

Target 2
Deepening

Target 3
Growing

Target 4
Consolidating and ending

- Perceiving
- Attending
- Reflecting content
- Reflecting feeling
- Empathic reflection

- Clarifying
- Intuitive empathy
- Using metaphors
- Confronting
- Using the here & now
- Implementing change
- Expanding the counseling system
- Appreciating the sacred

- Consolidating
- Ending

Figure 1.5. The phases, microskills and chapters

CONCLUSION

We are excited to have you join us on this journey of counseling skill development! Taken piece by piece, the microskills approach helps students build skills one at a time, solidifying a strong foundation in the process of becoming an effective counselor. Like learning a second language or going on a bike trip, the journey is one of excitement and discovery.

In order to learn the microskills necessary for counseling, it is your responsibility to come into this process with at least some degree of purpose (*why* you want to acquire counseling acumen) and intentionality (a proactive and positive attitude toward the process). As your guides on this journey, it is our job, along with your trainers, course instructors or supervisors, to give you some structure and opportunities to practice, but you in turn must provide the time and effort that practice requires. Your instructors' and peers' responsibility is to provide you with feedback as you practice. In response, you will need to graciously accept constructive criticism, recognizing that receiving both positive and negative feedback is essential to successful mastery of a particular microskill. Finally, application is found first within your homework and in-class small group activities, and then within the ministry or clinical contexts in which you may work.

All of this can feel a little overwhelming, but we encourage you to find purpose and motivation that will sustain you through the process. For Christian counselors, at least some of our motivation is not only to learn a professional or personally beneficial skill; it is also to follow Jesus' teaching and example. His concern and love for all people compels us to be as effective in helping others as is humanly possible. But despite a powerful purpose the risks can be overwhelming for some. It is important to consider the costs of discipleship (Bonhoeffer, 1937/1995) in this regard. Perseverance, or as the King James Version calls it, *longsuffering* (Gal 5:22) is a fruit of the Spirit. The Holy Spirit becomes our strength when we can no longer continue in our own strength.

Welcome to the community of counselors, both in secular and the ministry-based environments, who have gone before you. As you learn the skills that can help you effectively care for the souls of others, may you be encouraged, transformed and renewed in your understanding of how God uses each of us to care for one another.

REFLECTION QUESTIONS

1. Think of a skill you have learned in the past (e.g., academic, computer, athletic, music) and reflect on the process. How hard was it? How motivated were you? Did you become discouraged along the way? What were the essential elements in achieving success? What kept you going when it felt like you might never get the hang of it?

2. Based on that experience, how would you complete this sentence: "I learn new skills best by . . ."? Could this be helpful in learning of the new skills of counseling?

3. In learning a new skill, what is the hardest part for you? What gets in the way? How are you going to compensate for this as you learn the skills of counseling?

4. What has brought you to the point of wanting to learn counseling skills?

5. On a scale of one (low) to ten (high), what is your level of motivation for learning counseling skills? What could you do to choose to raise that number by one or two points?

6. How does your faith, your relationship with God, and his body, the church (Christian community), factor into this learning process?

7. How will you handle discouragement when you are feeling stuck or frustrated with the slow development of your counseling skills?

THE PERSON OF
THE COUNSELOR

*We have different gifts, according to the grace given to each of us. If your
gift is prophesying, then prophesy in accordance with your faith; if it
is serving, then serve; if it is teaching, then teach; if it is to encourage,
then give encouragement; if it is giving, then give generously; if it is
to lead, do it diligently; if it is to show mercy, do it cheerfully.*

ROMANS 12:6-8

CHAPTER FOCUS

SKILL: self-as-instrument

PURPOSE: to examine the person of the counselor as a valuable tool within the
counseling process

FORMULA: Some of my strengths are _____.
Some of my weaknesses are _____.
I am _____ and bring _____ to the helping relationship.

THINK OF THREE PEOPLE you know who, in your estimation, are good people
helpers, and write your response to the following:

» For each individual, write a list of the positive attributes you see in them as a
helper.

» As you look at the list for each person, what attributes do they have in common?

» How do they differ from one another?

Now consider three individuals among your acquaintances whom you would definitely *not* put in the category of good people helpers.

» For each individual, write a list of the attributes they carry that put them on your "not a good helper" list.

» As you look at the list for each person, what attributes do they have in common?

» How do they differ from one another?

Counseling is truly a both/and experience. It involves both art and science, knowledge and skill, comfort and challenge, grace and truth. To emphasize one part of each dichotomy over the other is to negate, or at the least to minimize, what the helping process can be. In this chapter we will explore what it means for you to be the most valuable and influential instrument in the counseling room and how to develop each side of the both/and equation.

During this part of the journey, we will ask you to spend time reflecting on who you are, who God has made you to be, and the strengths and weaknesses you embody. Keep in mind that who you are is a work in progress and that, just like counseling, growth is more about engaging the process and less about arriving at some predetermined destination.

SELF-AS-INSTRUMENT: EMBRACING THE ART

Microskills and academic learning are in many ways what comprise the "science" of counseling, as these elements are more concrete, provable and testable. The art of counseling, on the other hand, is found in the person of the counselor and the development of her character, discernment, empathy and attitudes—the development of oneself as a therapeutic instrument. The counseling literature is very clear that the most influential variable in counseling is the person of the counselor and the relationship that is cultivated with the client (Norcross, 2011). It is not a formula or a series of steps to be followed but instead relies on self-reflection, self-awareness and an ability to take constructive feedback from others.

One way to think of this interplay between microskills and self-as-instrument is to use the analogy of the human body. For the purposes of this analogy we will break the body down into two parts: the skeletal system and the internal organs. In counseling, the

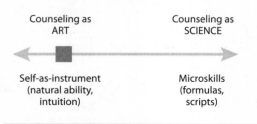

Figure 2.1. Art versus science: Self-as-instrument

microskills and academic learning are analogous to the skeletal system, as they provide the structure and framework of helping, while the development of the art of the self-as-instrument is represented by your internal organs, which sustain life. Without the skeletal system, key organs would be left unprotected and overexposed; without the internal system, there would be no life or energy given to the body. Counseling works in much the same way in that both structure and heart are necessary in order for the process to be truly alive and for the helping relationship to thrive.

Biblical/Theological Connections

How do you understand yourself as a "person"? What do you mean when you think or talk about your "self"? How do you think of yourself as created in the image of God? To what degree are your thoughts, emotions, behaviors and so on part of who you are as a person? How you view yourself as a person will significantly affect how you view your counselees.

The "self" is a central construct in psychology; much has been written about the nature and development of the self. For counselors, helping counselees to form a healthy self is an important task in the counseling process. To do this, it is our belief that the counselor's sense of self is, in many situations, the main instrument by which counseling achieves change. It takes a self to help form a self.

This leads to the question, what is the self? For the Christian, the self, or the core of the person, was created by God in his image (Gen 1:26-27). Theologians, philosophers and biblical scholars have written volumes on the *imago Dei*. At the risk of oversimplifying it, the image of God has something to do with aspects of our personhood, rationality, emotion, imagination and so on. It also involves aspects of our ability to affect the world around us, to have an overall life purpose, as well as our ability to enter deeply into relationships. For centuries, the most common definition of the image of God was humans' ability to think, gather information and use logic, hence the phrase *homo sapiens* (knowing beings). However, is this a one-sided view of God and of persons?

In classically orthodox theology, God is described as impassible; he is not subject to suffering, pain, or the ebb and flow of involuntary passions, like humans are. In the words of the Westminster Confession of Faith, God is "without body, parts, or passions, immutable" (2:1). Another way of saying it is that God cannot be hurt but empathizes and experiences permanent joy. What then do we make of the numerous biblical passages ascribing to God many variable emotions: grieved—filled with pain (Gen 6:6); anger (Num 11:1); angry and shows favor (Ps 30:5); delights, loves, rejoices (Zeph 3:17); loves (Jn 3:16)? Scripture records many other emotions, both positive and negative, that God expresses. Some have argued that these are simply anthropomorphisms, defining God in human terms. What do you think?

While we will be working to cultivate both the science and art aspects of counseling throughout the book, the focus of this chapter will be the art side of counseling—the intuitive and subjective elements that make counseling a uniquely personalized experience.

ONE PROFESSION, MANY PARTS

First Corinthians 12:4-6 tells us, "There are different kinds of gifts, but the same Spirit distributes them. There are different kinds of service, but the same Lord. There are different kinds of working, but in all of them and in everyone it is the same God at work." As much as Paul was speaking to the church in general, this concept also applies to the work that counselors do. Although each of you are here because of some broad common interest in caring for people, you also each possess a different set of gifts, skills, abilities, passions and interests that inform *how* and *why* you care for people. Consider, for yourself,

> » What is it about helping others that appeals to you?

> » A good friend calls you to tell you about something really difficult that happened to him or her that day. How would you likely go about caring for them?

The differences in how people answer these questions can contribute to the type of counseling profession they may go into or the type of counselees they prefer to work with. Similar to medical doctors, who share the same core training but then specialize in, for example, surgery, oncology or pediatrics based on their interests, abilities and temperaments, counselors cannot all be the same. For example, the skills and giftings that are needed to work with someone whom society would consider an "offender" of some sort (i.e., an abusive husband, a sex offender, someone convicted of criminal violence) are different from the skills and giftings needed to work with those in more vulnerable positions (i.e., children, abuse victims, trauma survivors). Just as the church needs people with different giftings to effectively reach the world around them, so the world needs various kinds of counselors to care for various wounds.

The comforter versus the challenger. The counselor who is more of a comforter tends to see how support, affirmation, empathy and comfort could create a sense of safety for the counselee that could then enable the counselee to move forward in a healthier direction. The challenger, in contrast, tends to see how well-meaning con-frontation or challenges to logic, behavior or decisions could facilitate the counselee's ability to understand his situation differently and thus move toward healthier change. There is a time and a place for both types of approaches, but most of the time your counselees will need you to be able to do both.

During my master's program, I (Elisabeth) had a counseling professor who once said to me, "Counseling is knowing how to hold someone and hit them at the same time." He proceeded to say, "And I have no doubt you can do the hitting, we're just going to have to work on the holding while you're here." Of course he was not talking of "hitting" as physical or emotional violence. But the analogy really helped me to see both the strength I brought to the counseling process and where I needed to grow.

It is important for you to determine whether you are naturally more of a comforter or more of a challenger. Do you tend to hear a person's story and see where she might need to be comforted, affirmed or validated? Or do you tend to hear where someone might need to be confronted, challenged or redirected for the purpose of growth and change? Rarely is a counselor only a comforter or a challenger, but most have a tendency to prefer one modality over the other. It is also important to keep in mind that, when healthy, both the comforter and the challenger take on their preferred approach out of the same heart and motivation: to help the counselee grow. Counselors who have honed their craft are able to identify which approach they personally prefer or "default" to but also have the ability to adjust their approach in order to implement what the counselee needs in a given moment.

Comforter	**Challenger**
✓ comforts	✓ challenges
✓ affirms	✓ confronts
✓ validates	✓ redirects

What about you? When you see someone in need of help, how do you conceptualize what help looks like? Does help look like a hug or the emotional equivalent? Does it look like words of affirmation and encouragement and a positive reframe, emphasizing what is already good and right in the counselee? Or does it look more like a gentle challenge to do, think or feel differently, bringing attention to what might need to change or be corrected in the counselee? Once you determine which of the two sides of the dichotomy fits with your more natural inclination, you can begin to work on developing the other aspect.

The priest and the prophet. Throughout this book you will be introduced to psychological concepts and their scriptural counterparts, and vice versa. While psychological language uses the concept of the comforter and the challenger, Scripture also provides a framework for understanding the person of the counselor in the helping process. Ultimately, counseling functions much like any discipleship process: the counselor meets the counselee where he is and seeks to partner with him in moving one step closer toward health and wholeness (for a Christian, this is the sanctification process and growing in Christlikeness). In the Old Testament there were two primary roles, or professions, that had the direct responsibility of helping the Israelites be in right relationship with God and to grow in their relationship with him: priests and prophets. Both roles served to help Israel be in communication with God and to grow in relationship with him, but the direction of the transaction looked slightly different for each. The job of the priest was to intercede *to God* on behalf of the people. He was, in essence, a peacemaker, and the one who facilitated reconciliation and atonement by pleading for God's mercy. In contrast, the prophet's job was to communicate to the people *from God*. The prophet was the truth speaker, both of affirmation and of correction, and served to facilitate change by communicating to the people God's perspective. Similar to the comforter and the challenger, the "priestly" counselor and the "prophetic" counselor both share the same heart and passion—to see people grow in wholeness and righteousness; it is simply that their gifting and approach take on different forms.

The Priest

✓ comforting   ✓ thinking with
✓ confessional   ✓ talking with
✓ interviewing   ✓ affirming truth
✓ listening   ✓ comforting the disturbed

(Carter & Narramore, 1979, p. 114)

What about you? When you consider these two descriptions, do you find yourself more often in the priestly role seeking to comfort and bring reconciliation? Or do you find yourself more in the prophetic role of the truth speaker, seeking to promote growth through challenging people to change? Consider sharing this analogy, along with the comforter-versus-challenger analogy, with close friends or family in your life and ask them what role(s) they have seen you most drawn to over time.

» I am more of a _____ and I bring _____ to the helping relationship.

The Prophet

✓ convicting   ✓ thinking for
✓ confronting   ✓ talking to
✓ preaching   ✓ proclaiming truth
✓ lecturing   ✓ disturbing the comfortable

(Carter & Narramore, 1979, p. 114)

HOW WELL DO YOU KNOW YOURSELF?

Each one of you has a unique and valuable story that has shaped you into who you are. The pieces of your story, and how you choose to understand them, work together to mold your self as an instrument in the counseling process. A critical part of being an effective counselor is self-awareness, which is your ability to know and understand yourself, for good and for bad. Self-awareness includes not just knowing what you like or dislike (although that is part of it) but, even more, awareness of your own emotions, thoughts, motives, values and intentions as you go about life. Self-awareness is generally cultivated through two avenues: (1) self-reflection and (2) input from others.

Self-Awareness Involves Self-Reflection and Knowledge of:

✓ your strengths and weaknesses
✓ how your past affects you
✓ your motivation
✓ your values
✓ receiving input about how others perceive you

Self-reflection. Self-reflection requires you to slow down and observe yourself in a given situation by asking some of the following questions:

◆ Who am I presenting myself to be at this moment? (i.e., the expert? the clown? the nurturer? etc.)

◆ Why did I just say or do that?

  • What am I hoping to accomplish in what I just said or did? Where am I hoping this conversation or interaction will go?

  • How did I feel right before, during and after that interaction? What was I thinking right before, during and after that interaction?

  • What in my past is contributing to how I am responding in the present moment?

◆ When I said or did that, how was it received by others?

  • What meaning might others put toward what I just said or did? How might I have come across to the others in this situation in my tone, body language, word choice and timing?

Knowing your strengths and weaknesses. No one is perfect; neither is anyone all flawed. Healthy self-awareness means that you have the ability to identify both the strengths and weaknesses that you carry with you. It does not mean being prideful or dismissive about your strengths, nor does it mean being self-deprecating or dismissive about your weaknesses. Instead it is about being able to see both sides as part of what contributes to the art of your counseling practice. Keep in mind that strengths in one context may be weaknesses in another, and vice versa. For example, one of your strengths might be perseverance, but you may also have a tendency toward its flip side, stubbornness.

Try it Out

Take a moment and write down five to ten things (traits, abilities, giftings, skills or interests) about yourself that you see as strengths or assets that you bring to a counseling relationship.

Now, choose one of the things you listed above and consider how that strength could potentially become a weakness in a counseling relationship. Explain:

Finally, identify one trait that you consider to be a weakness in yourself:

How might this become a potential strength within a counseling relationship?

Understanding your past. No counselor enters the counseling room completely free of the past or uninfluenced by what has happened in her life prior to that moment. Part of healthy self-awareness is growing in your understanding of how your past has contributed to your present. Please note that we are not saying that your past determines your present or that you are forever defined by your past; rather, we believe that understanding the effects of your past can help to enlighten you as to why you are the way you are. As you consider your past and its influence on your present, some of your recollections will be positive, as they are memories of joy, success, accomplishment, love, encouragement and acceptance. But some of your recollections will be painful, being composed of memories of sadness, hurt, disappointment, rejection, mediocrity or trauma. In both instances, balance, humility and an acknowledgement of the good as well as the not-so-good that exist are important. Getting involved in your own personal counseling is often a good way to facilitate this domain of self-awareness and to consider questions such as:

◆ How has my family of origin or cultural background influenced my sense of self?

◆ How has my family of origin or cultural background influenced my understanding of health, dysfunction, forgiveness, grace, justice and fairness, resolving conflict, success and failure?

◆ How did my relationship with my parents affect the way I now relate to authority and to God?

◆ How did my relationship with peers growing up affect the way I approach friendships today?

◆ What childhood events (illness, rejection, awards and recognitions, parental divorce, moving, abuse, etc.) could be seen as influential in the shaping of my self-concept?

As you begin to explore more of your past, you will likely find that particular events have resulted in the formation of a lens through which you see the world, including the stories of your counselees. The lens is like a framework you have developed in an attempt to make sense of both yourself and others. The goal of self-reflection in this domain is that, as you grow in your self-awareness, your past no longer serves as the lens through which you see the world but instead becomes a tool in your toolbox—a resource you can use when it is appropriate but also a tool that you recognize is not fitting for every situation you encounter. The only way for the issues (good and bad) of our past to move from a lens to a tool is through self-reflection and growing self-awareness, and oftentimes through personal counseling.

Take, for example, a situation in which a female counselor, Glenda, was sexually abused by her youth pastor as a young teenager. Glenda's lens of the world became one in which she distrusted all males, in particular those in church leadership. If Glenda is unaware that this is happening, her negative biases may inadvertently negatively affect her counseling work with a counselee who is struggling in the same area (e.g., agreeing with her counselee that it is unwise to trust any male). However, if Glenda becomes aware that she has trust issues with men, realizes that she has believed the lie that all men are abusers, and works to determine which men are trustworthy and which are not, she is in a much better position to help her counselee wrestle with how to stay safe without cutting herself off from all relationships with men.

Awareness of motivational factors. Being aware of not just *what* you do but *why* you do certain things will enable you to have greater mastery over yourself in a counseling relationship, letting you function primarily out of your strengths and giftings rather than "leaking" your wounds and weaknesses out onto your counselee. Your motivation for helping others will dramatically shape how you define success, as well as how you choose interventions in the counseling process.

Most students, when they are asked why they want to be a counselor, will say something along the lines of "because I want to help people." While this is a great reason to become a counselor, understanding *why* you want to help people and to what end you want to help people are even more important questions. Reflecting on your motivation asks you to dig into the depths of your heart and psyche, to identify what your end goal is and how you will define "success" or "effectiveness" when working with others.

Possible motivations for wanting to help people include the following:

◆ It feels good to be needed.

◆ I appreciate those who were there for me when I needed it, and I now want to give back to others.

- Other people have told me I have a gift for people helping.

- Perhaps, if I help others, I'll be healed in the process.

- I've been told I'm a good listener.

- I see a lot of hurting people in the world and want to do my part to help.

- I'm not sure I'm cut out to be a counselor, but I'm willing to give it a shot.

- I believe that being there for others is a biblical mandate.

- I believe I have gifts of wisdom and discernment, and I want to use them to help people make the right choices in life.

Knowledge of your values. While it is virtually impossible to conduct value-free counseling, part of self-awareness is developing the ability to distinguish between your values, beliefs, motivations, feelings and so on and those of your counselee. Okun and Kantrowitz (2015) state it concisely when they say, "If you are aware of your own values you are less likely to impose them indirectly onto others" (p. 31). You can therefore better facilitate a counselee's growth process from a position of respect and differentiation. Practicing self-reflection on a regular basis serves to sharpen your skills as a counselor while also protecting your counselee from unintended manipulation or value imposition.

It is important to remember that values are not just spiritual or religious principles that guide us. Many Christian students think of "hot topics" such as sexuality, morality and politics when they hear the word *values,* and while these are included, our values are much more nuanced and subtle in most cases. Our values ultimately guide our choices. For example, if you decide to have friends over for dinner instead of going out, is it because you place a higher value (level of importance) on hospitality, or because you place a higher value on frugality? Both hospitality and frugality can be seen as biblical values, but both can also be executed out of prideful and sinful motivations. Be cautious of labeling something a biblical value when it is actually a personal preference. Other topics related to values include:

- *Money and status:* Do you intentionally or unintentionally assume that someone of one socioeconomic status is smarter, wiser, more godly or healthier than someone else? Do you assume that people in one socioeconomic status are in more or less need of counseling services? What assumptions do you make about people who have outstanding debt, wear only designer clothing, drive high-end cars or do not have steady employment?

- *Gender roles:* What expectations do you have for men that you do not have for women in work, ministry, and household or family responsibilities? What expectations do you have for women that you do not have for men?

- *Family composition:* What assumptions do you make about people based on their marital status? Do you think more or less of someone who has never been married, has been married for several decades, has been divorced, is cohabiting, is a single parent, has children or does not want children?

◆ *Parenting style:* How do you react to parents who are authoritarian in their parenting styles versus very permissive? How do you respond to parental behavior that you perceive as somewhat abusive (e.g., yelling at child for a minor infraction)? How do you feel about parents who appear overly passive or permissive?

◆ *Sexuality:* Do you perceive one type of sexual sin or dysfunction (premarital sex, pornography, infidelity, homosexual behavior, etc.) as more problematic than another? Is that hierarchy based solely on your level of comfort or discomfort with the topic, or is it grounded in something else?

◆ *Religion and spirituality:* What assumptions do you make about how healthy a person can be if his or her faith system is different from yours? What assumptions do you make about someone who professes your same faith system but then proceeds to live in a way that you find incongruent with that system?

◆ *Health and wellness:* How do you define a physically healthy person? What role do nutrition and exercise play in your understanding of health? How do you feel toward someone who is significantly more or less disciplined in these areas than you are?

◆ *Giftedness:* Do you respond differently to someone who is obviously gifted in some way (e.g., athletics, music, drama, dance, writing, intelligence) as compared to someone who has no obvious talents, or someone who has disabilities?

Clinical Tip

In its most general sense, countertransference refers to a counselor's emotional reactions to a particular counselee. This can include responses to how the counselee looks or what the counselee says or does. Your past experiences can trigger countertransference reactions, as can your values being directly or indirectly challenged. Not all countertransference is negative. Positive countertransference can be elicited when we really like a counselee or are even physically attracted to a counselee. Understanding, managing and appropriately using our countertransference reactions are essential to helping rather than harming our counselees.

All of these topics, and more, reflect our values—the assumptions, expectations, beliefs and preferences that shape the way we perceive the world. As you reflect on these questions and others like them, the "right answer" is not found in being the most "politically correct" or in figuring out what you think your professor, pastor or community want you to say. Instead, the "right answer" starts with your own authenticity and honesty, and then moves into a place of greater self-reflection and willingness to allow the Holy Spirit to use others to speak into areas that may need to be changed.

Receiving input from others. Input from others is the next step in cultivating self-awareness. It requires a level of vulnerability and teachability that can be risky, but it is essential to the development of self-as-instrument. As you continue on in your journey of becoming a counselor, be intentional in seeking out people whom you trust and who can point out to you the traits, giftings and blind spots that they see in you. Your professors and supervisors will naturally serve in this role as they provide feedback on assignments and in your counseling practice. Additionally, a classmate you connect with or an outside mentor may also be someone to whom you can turn for this valuable input. We encourage you to intentionally invite specific individuals into this role in your life and to directly ask them to share their insights with you.

This may come in the form of a conversation where you say something like, "Kyle, I really respect who you are, and I think you could have good insight into who I am. If you're willing, I would like to invite you to share with me over the next few months what you see as my strengths and the areas I might need to work on. I'll do my best to not be defensive in those exchanges but to dialogue with you about what you share with me." While this process has the potential to be very personally enriching, it also facilitates the development of empathy for counselees who will one day sit in front of you, directly or indirectly asking you for your feedback on their lives.

In addition to developing interpersonal relationships that provide honest input and feedback into your life, getting involved in your own personal counseling is also a critical piece to the development of yourself as an instrument. We are regularly astonished at the number of students who want to be counselors but are unwilling or at least highly resistant to being the counselee themselves. Conversely, we meet many students who want to be counselors because of the impact that counseling has had in their own life; they have personally reaped the benefits and now want to pass them on to others! Putting yourself in the role of the counselee, with all it entails (cost, vulnerability, time, emotion, humility and effort), will serve to cultivate your own self-awareness as well as your empathy for those who will one day trust you to walk with them in that role.

Try It Out

1. Who is someone in your life you might ask to provide input into your self-awareness process? What makes them a safe and desired choice?

2. What do you hope will come from others having input into your self-awareness development process?

3. What hesitations do you have about inviting others into your self-awareness development process?

Questions to Ask Others:

1. What are some strengths you see in me?

2. What are some areas that you see I could grow in?

3. Can you tell me about a time where you were impressed with the way I handled something or responded to someone?

4. Can you identify a time or a situation in which you could tell I was uncomfortable because I was being stretched or challenged? How might you suggest I approach a similar situation in the future?

Diagnostic Implications

One major debate in the counseling field revolves around the pros and cons of looking for pathology (mental illness) in people versus looking at people through the lens of developmental challenges. In the history of psychiatry and clinical psychology, there was considerable emphasis given to identifying symptoms and diagnosing mental disorders. The counseling, marriage and family therapy, and social work fields have tended toward a nonpathologizing approach that instead focuses on normal individual and family development and the many transitions that we all encounter in our lives. In this sense, much mental illness can be seen as development gone awry.

In the context of this chapter, the implications of this are significant. Should we see people, including ourselves, as struggling with a mental disorder or as trying to navigate a developmental transition as best as we can? How you counsel will be somewhat dependent on your view of this issue and how you understand your own challenges. If you see a particular counselee you are meeting with, for instance a young man who is a senior in college, as having anxiety symptoms indicative of an anxiety disorder, perhaps referral to a professional mental health provider is warranted. This could possibly include referral to a psychiatrist for medication assessment. However, if you see this counselee as struggling with a major life transition, with understandable anxiety about succeeding at college, getting a job when he graduates, mounting student-loan debt, a romantic relationship on the rocks and increasing use of alcohol to cope, the developmental lens may be very helpful, and counseling may be warranted.

Of course, our perspective is that both approaches are needed. Sometimes the anxiety is so intense that medication is needed to reduce the symptoms so that the student can cope. And counseling is needed to work through the cognitive, emotional, relational and spiritual implications of this transition.

In terms of the counselor's use of self in the counseling process, it is our own reflection on our personal life transitions, our relationships with family and friends, our emotional coping, and our thinking through issues in our lives that become the foundation of understanding others. It is our own experiences that become the foundation of understanding how people cope, grow and heal. It is not that others will experience things exactly as we did, or that what worked for me will work for you, or that I self-disclose my entire life journey because somehow that will be relevant to you. It is understanding my own process of change that can be helpful to others in their process of change.

SELF-CARE: TENDING TO THE INSTRUMENT

Much of the time, energy and attention of many counselors are spent in caring for others in one way or another. Too often counselors have internalized the belief that their worth and value come from this care that they provide the people around them, which can result in neglecting the care that they need to give themselves. They forget that caring for others is something that must come out of the overflow of who you are. If your own well is not full, you will not have the appropriate resources to overflow onto others. Therefore, self-care is a foundational and critical component of longevity and success as a counselor, and it is our recommendation that you begin practicing it even while in this course.

What is self-care? Self-care involves intentional practices in which you engage to restore, refresh, relax and regroup. Self-care activities can be as unique as you are but generally fall into five domains: physical, mental, emotional, relational and spiritual. These domains often overlap, but they are all important in caring for the whole person.

Physical self-care. Physical self-care includes anything you do to take care of your body. Counselors may have a tendency to focus so much on the emotional domain that they are in danger of neglecting their own physicality. There is value in caring for the physical structure that houses and sustains all that goes on inside. Consider how your ability to think or feel is altered when you are sick or in pain. We often take for granted what the healthy functioning of our bodies facilitates in our lives. As you consider caring for yourself as an instrument, reflect on what you need to do to engage in physical self-care as well as what hinders you from implementing effective strategies:

◆ How does my food intake affect my mental and emotional functioning?

- Do I make sufficient time each day to eat and to drink enough water?

- Do I notice that I feel better or worse after eating certain types of foods?

- Do I use food as an escape or a way to self-soothe, rather than addressing my core emotions and needs?

◆ What type of exercise or physical activity do I engage in to care for my body?

- Do I feel better after aerobic activity (walking, running, etc.) that gets my heart rate up and lets me expel energy?

- Do I feel better after more reflective and stretching-based activity (yoga, Pilates, etc.) that helps me slow down and connect with my body?

- Do I avoid physical exercise and activity, and if so, why?

◆ Do I prioritize sleep and allow my schedule to accommodate the amount of rest my body needs—not just what it can survive on?

◆ What activities can I regularly engage in that contribute to relaxing and restoring my body?

Mental self-care. Caring for your inner world is of utmost importance as a counselor, and that begins with your mind. Philippians 4:8 speaks to this principle when it says, "Finally, brothers and sisters, whatever is true, whatever is noble, whatever is right, whatever is pure, whatever is lovely, whatever is admirable—if anything is excellent or praiseworthy—think about such things." Mental self-care requires you to be intentional about what you put into your mind—what you read, what you watch, what you think about. Furthermore, mental self-care is also about what you give yourself permission not to think about. There will always be more people to consider, more problems to solve, more self-reflection to do, but sometimes mental self-care means allowing yourself to "turn off" and set aside those concerns for a time. This is not escaping and numbing but rather the intentional setting aside of worry, doubt and in-depth reflection and replacing them with laughter, delight, peacefulness and thanksgiving.

◆ What types of television shows and movies do I choose to watch? How might they contribute or detract from my mental self-care?

◆ What types of books do I choose to read? Is my "fun reading" mentally and emotionally beneficial? How so? Do I allow for "fun reading," or does everything have to be professionally and academically relevant? Why?

◆ What role does music play in my thought life?

◆ How comfortable am I with silence in my home, my car, in nature and so on? In the silence, what do I find itself thinking about?

Emotional self-care. Tending to your own heart and feelings allows you to more appropriately give out of the overflow; you cannot give to your counselees that which you do not have. Emotional self-care starts with being authentic, or honest, with yourself about your own emotions. Many counselors have learned to subjugate their own feelings in the name of caring for the feelings of others. Part of self-care then becomes learning to re-engage your own emotions, giving them voice and value. Emotions are a strong part of the inner world of counselors. Their self-care needs to focus on learning how to use their emotions as an asset and not as something that overwhelms or overpowers their life. Regardless of whether you are generally overconnected or underconnected to your emotions, emotional self-care is likely to involve doing your own therapeutic work as the counselee. Emotional self-care also involves cultivating relationships in your life that nurture your heart and care for you—we will talk more about this under relational self-care.

◆ Do you tend to be over-connected or under-connected to your emotions?

◆ What are ways that you can attend to your emotions?

Relational self-care. It always amazes us when we talk with students who only have "friends" in their life for whom they are the caretakers, and yet time and again we meet students who lack truly reciprocal friendships. Part of relational self-care is cultivating relationships in which you are equally attended to, sought out, cared for and nurtured as you do these things for the other person. For many of you this will feel horribly imbalanced, as if you are only "taking" from a particular friendship, but in reality it is simply more balanced than you have experienced before. Reciprocal relationships are often identified by those in which both participants would say that they "get the good end of the deal" in the relationship. These relationships take time and intentionality to both find and cultivate, but it is okay to be picky! Your vocation as a helper will give you the outlet you desire to care for others without needing anything back; your friendships should not have the same structure.

◆ What makes me uncomfortable about not being the "helper" in a relationship?

◆ Who in my life is a reciprocal friend?

◆ Which relationships in my life are not reciprocal? Is there something I can ask for, do or change that might facilitate them in becoming more balanced? Are there some relationships I need to let go of in order to pursue relational self-care?

Spiritual self-care. Care of the soul is deeply important in the life of the counselor. At its root, counseling is about being a conduit for the Holy Spirit to work in someone else's life, and a good conduit needs to not be mucked up or disintegrating due to a lack of its own care. Simultaneously, the conduit needs to always keep in mind that the power, the resource and the change is not of its doing but of something greater and bigger. Spiritual self-care allows the counselor to remain in a place of humility and grace, a place that is awestruck by the honor and privilege it is to walk alongside another person, while simultaneously feeling the weight of that holy responsibility. As a Christian, spiritual self-care includes various elements that can mostly be summarized by (1) involvement in a church community and (2) engagement in spiritual disciplines.

Empirical Support

Tan and Castillo (2014) take a comprehensive look at the literature on self-care as it pertains to counselors, pastors and chaplains. Common themes found throughout the various studies Tan and Castillo reviewed included:

• getting adequate rest

• spending time with friends and family

• spending time alone

• finding and fostering supportive relationships

• receiving ongoing training, supervision and consultation

• setting clear and consistent boundaries, personally and professionally

• pursuing spiritual growth

• pursuing personal growth

• exercising

• engaging in enjoyable hobbies

• asking for and accepting support from others

• developing a routine or ritual when leaving the office to help emotionally and mentally leave work at work

• maintaining and fostering a sense of humor

Involvement in a church community is something that all believers are called to (Heb 10:25) but is often neglected or downplayed because it can be messy and inconvenient. In church involvement we gain teaching and input from others and we have the opportunity to grow relationally and to find reciprocal friendships. Just like in choosing healthy relationships, it is important to be diligent in choosing a healthy (but not perfect) church community. Church often serves four primary purposes: teaching, worship, community and service. In an ideal world every church would do each of these tasks equally well, but the reality is that each church will do one of these tasks better than the others. Our suggestion to you is to consider, in this season of training and development, which task is of greatest priority to you in your pursuit of spiritual self-care right now. Then rank the other tasks and pursue a church community based on that ranking. Just as you will not be able to be all things to all counselees, no church can be all things to every congregant. But if you are aware of your spiritual needs and priorities, it will be easier to identify and connect with the church community that is fitting for you.

Spiritual disciplines are simply any activity that is intentionally pursued for the purpose of deepening your relationship with Christ. The key word here is *intentionally*—whether it is a discipline of thankfulness and celebration, of slowing down or of Scripture memory, the point is that you are purposefully engaging in activities that facilitate your spiritual growth. Disciplines may be things you do on a daily basis, a weekly basis or even a quarterly or annual basis, but they have a position of priority in your life. At the end of this chapter is a list of recommended reading on the topic of spiritual growth and self-care.

Sabbath. Sabbath could technically be included under physical self-care, emotional self-care or spiritual self-care. Because of its significance, though, we thought it fitting to give sabbath its own section. Sabbath is the spiritual discipline of intentional rest, and is something that Western culture is particularly poor in practicing. Even though it is one of the Ten Commandments, sabbath is often disregarded as something to be fit in only after everything else is done and taken care of. Instead, sabbath is meant to be a gift to people, not a burden (Mk 2:27); it is God's way of reminding us that not only is it okay to rest but it is a necessity. In its strictest sense, sabbath is a twenty-four-hour period in which work is intentionally set aside, reminding us that provision comes from God and not from our own strivings. In its essence sabbath is about ceasing the striving, abstaining from the busyness that consumes our culture and taking intentional time to reflect on our dependence on God. We encourage you to prayerfully reflect on the role that sabbath needs to take in your life.

- What does sabbath currently look like in my life?
- What do I fear will happen if I truly take sabbath each week?
- What do I hope will happen if I truly take sabbath each week?

Regardless of the domain of self-care, the need to attend to and care for the instrument of you is critically important to your success and survival as a counselor. It is not selfish, wasteful or weak to take the time or expend the resources to attend to your own needs. Counselors can only give as much as they have, and without self-care their well of resources will dry up. Consider self-care as a way to indirectly but powerfully care for your counselees while simultaneously obeying and honoring the one who has enabled you to serve in that role to begin with.

RELATIONSHIP APPLICATION

The development of yourself as a therapeutic instrument affects not just your work with clients but also the way you approach other relationships in your life. Just think about it—growing in your self-awareness, as well as in your ability to give and receive feedback, is likely to affect your expectations and desires in personal relationships as well. Consider the ways each of the topics discussed in this chapter is part of your personal relationships:

◆ What type of friends do you choose? Are they more comforters or challengers? Do you share similar values? Where are you different?

◆ What strengths do you bring to relationships? What weaknesses do you have that seem to be a theme in your relationships?

◆ How aware are you of the motivations you bring to interactions with friends? What role are you most often trying to live out with them?

◆ How receptive to constructive feedback are you from friends, family, coworkers and bosses?

As you continue on this road toward becoming a counselor (regardless of the professional title you will one day carry), it is likely that you will be changed. You will, hopefully, be changed as you grow in self-awareness, as you learn to let others speak more honestly into your life, as you learn to identify and cultivate friendships of depth and purpose, and as you grow in your understanding of who it is God has made you to be (and not be) in various circumstances. Be prepared for friendships to grow, change and even dissolve as you begin to sharpen and refine yourself as an instrument.

MULTICULTURAL APPLICATION

Every culture places a different amount of value on authenticity and on what North American culture would consider "constructive feedback." In light of this, people from different cultures will be more or less comfortable both giving *and* receiving input from others. For example, when I (Elisabeth) was working in Ukraine, there was conflict among the staff, focused primarily on the director's style of leadership.

Having been brought in as a consultant to help in part with team dynamics, I went to someone I trusted who understood both Ukrainian and American culture and asked what level of confrontation and honest feedback was generally acceptable. He looked me straight in the eye and without blinking said, "Oh, in Ukraine, it is better to lie to someone than to hurt their feelings." In his comment I was quickly reminded of my preference to both give and receive direct and honest feedback, while also being struck with how ineffective such feedback would be to someone who saw it as offensive, rude or domineering.

Contrast this with Dutch culture, in which "constructive feedback" can come from just about anyone in your life, with or without invitation. The baseline cultural assumption in the Netherlands is that it is actually disrespectful not to point out what you see in another person (Buckland, 2006), both good and bad, but the feedback is taken far less personally than it would be even by many Americans.

As you work to develop yourself as an instrument of therapeutic change, reflect on the role that your own culture has had on the value you place on self-awareness, input from others, comforting and challenging, as well as whether emphasis has been placed on the art or the science of counseling. Where you have come from culturally provides you with unique insight and resources in the counseling process, so long as you do your work to grow in understanding who you are and what has contributed to shaping you into that person.

CONCLUSION

The art of counseling requires an intentional counselor who is willing to be self-reflective and open to feedback. Your journey of self-reflection is ongoing—it is less about arriving and more about the process of becoming. It asks you to bring courage, humility, openness and teachability to this training process and into your life as a whole. Thankfully, this is not a journey made in isolation but one preferably done in relationship with others who are able to encourage and affirm you while also speaking hard truths in gracious ways when necessary. As you continue to move through this book and learn new microskills, pay attention to the skills you enjoy and which ones are less natural for you. Be encouraged by the times when your natural abilities are affirmed. When you come across skills that are less natural for you, fight the temptation to see yourself as "lesser" than a classmate who excels in that area, remembering that your unique strengths and weaknesses enable you to work with counselees your classmate may be less suited for—just as their giftings will enable them to work with counselees you may be less interested in. We are one body with many parts, and we need the comforters and challengers, the priests and the prophets all the same.

REFLECTION QUESTIONS (ADAPTED
FROM COREY & COREY, 2011)

1. Under the section "Awareness of Motivational Factors," we provided a variety of motivations for helping. Which of the motivations do you most identify with? What else contributes to your desire to help others?

2. What do you consider a marker of a "successful" helping conversation or relationship?

3. What is the difference between exposing someone to your values or opinion and imposing your values or opinion on someone?

4. What life experiences have you had that could help you better relate to others?

5. What unresolved issues or open concerns exist in your personal life that could affect your ability to work with different kinds of counselees?

6. Who you are today is largely affected by the choices you have made along the way and how you make sense of those choices. What are some specific choices in your life that are particularly significant for who you are today, and how have you chosen to make sense of those choices thus far?

7. Are you aware of the ways you avoid conflict or other anxiety-provoking situations?

8. Do you always feel as though you need to be in control of situations?

9. Do you become irritated when others do not see things the way you do or when others do not respond the way you think they should?

10. Do you often feel as though you must be omnipotent, that you must do something to make others feel better?

11. Are you so problem oriented that you're always looking for the negative, for a problem, and never responding to the positive, to the good?

12. Are you able to be as open with others as you want them to be with you?

13. What additional resources might you pursue to further develop your personal growth and self-reflection?

14. Some strengths I see in myself are: _____

15. Some of the growth areas I see in myself are: _____

RECOMMENDED READINGS ON SPIRITUAL SELF-CARE

◆ *Streams of living water: Celebrating the great traditions of the faith* (Foster, 1998) provides an overview of six timeless traditions in approaching spiritual formation that allow the reader to connect with biblical, historical and modern examples of very different ways in which people pursue and express their relationship with Christ.

◆ *The search for significance: Seeing your true worth through God's eyes* (McGee, 2003) comes with a workbook in the back to help readers process through four different lies that often form the foundation of one's identity, along with God's response, or answer, to those lies.

◆ *Invitation to a journey: A road map for spiritual formation* (Mulholland, 2016) is a wonderful introductory text to the concept of spiritual formation. The author provides insight into how different personality types (based on Jungian typology) approach and reflect God.

◆ *The life you've always wanted: Spiritual disciplines for ordinary people* (Ortberg, 2015) is a wonderful book for learning practical ways of incorporating spiritual disciplines into your day-to-day life. Personal, funny and practical, this book takes the stigma and dryness out of "disciplines" and shows how these activities can become the natural overflow of our love for God.

Other recommendations:

Baker, H. (1998). *Soul keeping: Ancient paths of spiritual direction.* Colorado Springs, CO: NavPress.

Barton, R. H. (2009). *Sacred rhythms: Arranging our lives for spiritual transformation.* Downers Grove, IL: InterVarsity Press.

Benner, D. G. (2002). *Sacred companions: The gift of spiritual friendship & direction.* Downers Grove, IL: InterVarsity Press.

———. (2015). *Surrender to love: Discovering the heart of Christian spirituality.* Downers Grove, IL: InterVarsity Press.

———. (2015). *The gift of being yourself: The sacred call to self-discovery.* Downers Grove, IL: InterVarsity Press.

———. (2015). *Desiring God's will: Aligning our hearts with the heart of God.* Downers Grove, IL: InterVarsity Press.

———. (2010). *Opening to God: Lectio divina and life as prayer.* Downers Grove, IL: InterVarsity Press.

Calhoun, A. A. (2015). *Spiritual disciplines handbook: Practices that transform us.* Downers Grove, IL: InterVarsity Press.

Demarest, B. (1999). *Satisfy your soul: Restoring the heart of Christian spirituality.* Colorado Springs, CO: NavPress.

———. (2009). *Seasons of the soul: Stages of spiritual development.* Downers Grove, IL: InterVarsity Press.

Foster, R. (1988). *Celebration of discipline* (revised and expanded). San Francisco, CA: Harper.

Manning, B. (2002). *Abba's child: The cry of the heart for intimate belonging.* Colorado Springs, CO: NavPress.

———. (2004). *The wisdom of tenderness: What happens when God's fierce mercy transforms our lives.* New York, NY: HarperOne.

———. (2005). *The ragamuffin gospel: Good news for the bedraggled, beat-up, and burnt out.* Colorado Springs, CO: Multnomah.

———. (2009). *Ruthless trust: The ragamuffin's path to God.* New York, NY: HarperCollins.

———. (2009). *The furious longing of God.* Colorado Springs, CO: David C. Cook.

Moon, G. W. (1997). *Homesick for Eden: A soul's journey to joy.* Ann Arbor, MI: Vine.

Moon, G. W., & Benner, D. G. (Eds.). (2004). *Spiritual direction & the care of souls: A guide to Christian approaches and practice.* Downers Grove, IL: InterVarsity Press.

Smith, J. B. (2009). *The good and beautiful God: Falling in love with the God Jesus knows.* Downers Grove, IL: InterVarsity Press.

Tan, S-Y., & Gregg, D. (1997). *Disciplines of the Holy Spirit: How to connect to the Spirit's power and presence.* Grand Rapids, MI: Zondervan.

TARGET 1

ESTABLISHING RELATIONSHIP AND EXPLORING

*T*ARGET 1 IS ALL ABOUT BUILDING FOUNDATIONS and creating a solid base on which the counseling relationship can develop. Target 1 involves using the related microskills to build the relationship with the counselee. This is the main task of the early phase of counseling. Consider your own life experiences and the people with whom you have chosen to confide over the years. Whether consciously or unconsciously, we rarely sit down with a stranger and reveal our deepest and darkest secrets before testing the waters to see whether we feel safe, heard and understood. Just because you may hold a formal position as "counselor" does not mean that you are, or should be, automatically endowed with trust by the counselee. No matter the context or the prior relationship, all counselors must *earn the honor* of hearing the depths of another's story for each individual counselee and *earn the privilege* of speaking into another's story. A counselor earns this honor and privilege by listening well, being respectful of the counselee's story and not rushing the counseling process by jumping to advice giving or confronting.

The foundational microskills that are aimed for in target 1 are typically called the facilitative conditions in the counseling literature. These conditions were first discussed by Carl Rogers (1957/1992). His initial description included six necessary and sufficient conditions for personality change to occur in the counseling relationship (see sidebar "The Facilitative Conditions"). Three of these relate to specific microskills. These skills all work to establish the counseling relationship and begin exploration with the counselee. Each of these three skills-based conditions can be found within the brief descriptions below, but all will be directly or indirectly expanded on in separate chapters to follow.

The Facilitative Conditions (Rogers 1957/1992)

1. Counselor-counselee contact: a relationship between the two must exist, and each person must perceive the other as important.
2. Counselee incongruence: a disconnect exists between the counselee's experience and her ideal self.
3. Counselor's congruence, or genuineness: the counselor is congruent within the relationship. The counselor is deeply involved himself, is not "acting" as if he cares, and can draw on his own experiences (self-disclosure) to facilitate the relationship.
4. Counselor unconditional positive regard (UPR): the counselor accepts the counselee without judgment, disapproval or approval. This facilitates increased self-regard in the counselee, as she can begin to become aware of experiences in which her view of self-worth was distorted by others.
5. Counselor empathic understanding: the counselor experiences an understanding of the counselee's internal frame of reference. Accurate empathy on the part of the counselor helps the counselee believe the counselor's unconditional regard for her.
6. Counselee perception of empathic understanding: the counselee perceives, to at least a minimal degree, the counselor's UPR and empathic understanding.

NONVERBAL SKILLS

Use of the first two skills that are given special attention when aiming for target 1 do not require you as the counselor to say a word. Instead they rely on your powers of observation of both the counselee and yourself as the counselor.

Perceiving (chapter three). How we take in the messages sent by the counselee, whether verbal or nonverbal, is what we mean by perceiving. We begin with perceiving because you cannot, as a counselor, know what you are responding to if you have not first perceived it! Perceiving is a skill because we do not always accurately notice the other and sometimes do not even "see" the person in front of us. This skill involves learning to make observations and being aware of not only what the counselee is *saying* but what he may be *showing* you or telling you by means of his facial expressions and body language, or in the delivery of his words. The skill of perceiving is about listening, watching and feeling what the counselee shares with you.

Attending (chapter four). Just as we use perceiving to take in the verbal and nonverbal messages of the counselee, in attending we learn to pay attention to the nonverbal messages we may either consciously or inadvertently be conveying to the counselee. In other words, we attempt to see ourselves through the counselee's eyes in regard to our own nonverbal messages. These nonverbal messages are communicated through specific attending behaviors that, among other things, include our facial expressions, body language, tone of voice and use of space. While attending is primarily behavioral, that is, focused on specific behaviors exhibited by the counselor, there is also a self-reflective element to attending, because behaviors ultimately reflect the internal world of the counselor. Therefore, self-awareness of our own values, beliefs and attitudes about the counselee and the counselee's situation is essential in order that we may genuinely and respectfully interact with the counselee both verbally and nonverbally.

REFLECTING SKILLS

The purpose of the target 1 reflecting skills is to allow you, as the counselor, to gather all the information that is needed in order to understand the counselee's situation from the counselee's perspective. These skills elicit from the counselee information enabling them to "put their cards on the table." This helps with the exploration aspect of target 1.

The process of exploring, the second focus of target 1, is built on three key reflecting skills: Reflecting content, reflecting feeling and empathic reflection. These are called reflecting skills because the words of the counselor function like a mirror, reflecting back to the counselee what was said without adding to, subtracting from or interpreting the counselee's message.

With reflecting skills we are still in the early phase of counseling, at the top of the hourglass, the widest and most general part of a counselee's story. Each reflecting skill will help move us further down into that hourglass. Reflecting content is the most impersonal and surface-level reflection, as it is focused solely on the facts of the counselee's story. Reflecting feeling moves a step further into the hourglass, engaging the surface emotions of the counselee's story. Empathic reflection then connects the counselee's feelings with the content of her story, going a step further into the hourglass. If target 1 skills have been used well, the counselor and the counselee should have a pretty good sense of what the focus of the counseling conversation, and relationship, is going to be. In terms of the counseling process, at this point the early phase of counseling will be drawing to a close, and the counselee and counselor will be moving into the middle phase.

Each reflecting skill is unique and important in its own way and serves a critical purpose in the counseling process. You are likely to find that you have a natural preference or aptitude toward one of these reflecting skills and may therefore struggle with another. That is completely normal and can often help inform you of the theoretical orientation and approach to change strategies that you are most likely to employ when working with counselees. Nevertheless, every counselor must work on developing increased facility and aptitude with each reflecting skill in order to truly serve and benefit his counselees.

Reflecting content (chapter five). Reflecting content is the first of three reflecting skills that you will be specifically aiming for in target 1. In reflecting content, the counselor is listening for the facts of the counselee's story and summarizing them back to the counselee. In this way, the counselor assures the counselee that the facts, or content, of her story are understood.

Reflecting feeling (chapter six). The microskill of reflecting feeling involves going deeper into the counselee's story and hearing the emotional messages that the counselee is directly or indirectly communicating.

Empathic reflection (chapter seven). This final skill related to target 1 goes even deeper into the counselee's story as the counselor summarizes for the counselee how the content and feelings in his story appear to be connected. In each of these three reflecting skills the counselor is not making assumptions or interpretations but is functioning in the role of a mirror. Using the microskills language, the counselor reflects back to the counselee what she has directly and indirectly heard about the counselee's story.

THE USE OF TARGET 1 SKILLS THROUGHOUT THE COUNSELING PROCESS

In figure T1.1 the relationship between the targets, microskills and the counseling process is illustrated. Target 1 skills not only are helpful early on in the counseling relationship but are foundational skills that you will continually return to throughout the counseling process. In fact, the skills related to target 1 are so critical that when working with some counselees, entire counseling relationships could take place and be successful without ever moving on to the middle phase of counseling or targeting other areas. This was Rogers's (1957/1992) point: the core facilitative conditions are necessary and sufficient for personality change to occur.

For counseling relationships that do move into other phases, mastery of target 1 skills is critical in order to have earned the honor and privilege of going deeper with the counselee and appropriately using the skills related to targets 2, 3 and 4. If target 1 is not mastered before going on to other target areas, it is possible that harm may actually be done to the counselee and the counseling relationship.

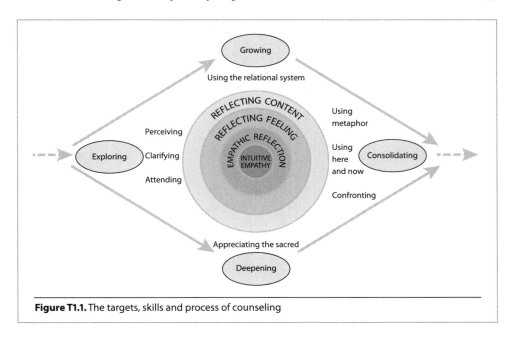

Figure T1.1. The targets, skills and process of counseling

WHAT DO YOU NOTICE?

As water reflects the face, so one's life reflects the heart.

PROVERBS 27:19

SKILL: perceiving

PURPOSE: to develop the counselor's ability to take in the nonverbal communication of the counselee

FORMULA: I notice _____ about this counselee.

*I*N THE MIDDLE OF A TENSION-FILLED conversation with her father, a teenaged daughter asks, "Dad, why are you so angry?!" In response he yells back, with teeth clenched, face red and brow knotted, "I am *not* angry!!!" Which message do you think the daughter will believe, her father's words, which belie feelings of anger, or his tone of voice and facial expressions, which communicate the exact opposite?

Think about a conversation in which you noticed a discrepancy between what someone said verbally and what he or she communicated nonverbally. What was the result?

» Write down your response.

Can you remember a situation where someone you were talking to pointed out a discrepancy between the words you spoke and what your tone of voice and body language conveyed? Were you able to admit to your true feelings?

» Write down your response.

Now that you have spent some time in chapter two reflecting on who God has made you to be and are beginning to get a sense as to the type of "instrument" you might be in the counseling process, it is time to begin focusing more on the specific microskills needed in this journey. *Perceiving* is the first microskill needed within the counseling process. Perceiving is the skill of accurately understanding the overt and covert messages sent by the counselee without judging, distorting or overinterpreting those messages. While perceiving involves picking up both nonverbal and verbal communication, we will focus on nonverbal communication in this chapter because future chapters zero in on accurately perceiving what specific words mean.

A hallmark study, conducted by Mehrabian (1971), found that words account for only 7% of the messages people receive from others, while voice accounts for 38%, and facial expressions contributes a whopping 55%. In light of these findings, it is import for counselors to hone their ability to accurately perceive the nonverbal messages of their counselees.

This chapter will explore the communication process and the four core elements involved that contribute to not just what is said but how it is received and perceived.

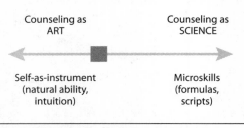

Figure 3.1. Art versus science: Perceiving

Awareness of how this process works will contribute to the counselor's ability to perceive not just the spoken messages of the counselee but the unspoken messages as well, and to avoid inaccurate perceptions. Next we will look at various avenues by which nonverbal communication is shared and how to identify the underlying request or need being expressed in the counselee's message. This ability to take in the unspoken or nonverbal messages being sent by the counselee provides a foundational skill on which every other microskill will build.

AVOIDING INACCURATE PERCEPTIONS

The skill of perceiving depends on the counselor's ability to take in the nonverbal messages of the counselee in a way that does not add to or distort the counselee's intention. One way to help avoid inaccurate perceptions is to be aware of how the communication process works, who the players are and the pieces that are involved. In a helping relationship, the "players" are generally the counselor and the counselee(s); the "pieces" include anything that can contribute to or hinder the communication process. In this awareness the counselor is then able to better account for what she is taking in from the counselee and the counseling relationship at any given time. In the communication literature, one communication model is described as being composed of four distinct elements: the sender, the receiver, the message and the noise, where "noise" is anything that distorts the message of the sender (Anderson & Ross,

1998). Too often people assume that communication is unidirectional, going only from sender to receiver, and that the message gets delivered to the receiver exactly as the sender intended it:

Figure 3.2. Unidirectional message

The reality, however, is that communication is not unidirectional but is instead bidirectional. In bidirectional communication both the sender and the receiver are simultaneously filling both roles. For example, the counselee may be speaking, but the counselor is also communicating through eye contact, facial expressions and body language back to the counselee, who in turn is altering his message or the delivery of the message based on what he has just received from the counselor. At the same time, the counselor is also adjusting her message to the counselee based on the message received and sending feedback. Both participants are sending and receiving at the same time:

Figure 3.3. Bidirectional message and feedback

The concept of "noise" must also be attended to by the counselor, which is where the practices of self-reflection and self-awareness become important. Noise is anything that either the sender or the receiver experiences or brings to the communication process that can alter or hinder the delivery or reception of the message. It can even include environmental factors. Without ongoing self-reflection and well-developed self-awareness, counselors can inadvertently mistake noise as part of the counselee's intended message, can dismiss part of the counselee's message as unimportant, or can interpret noise based on their own biases and experiences rather than understanding the noise through the perspective of the counselee. Any time you have had a conversation with someone where one of you said, "Wait, that's not how I meant it," noise was involved, altering the sending and/or the receiving of the message. It is the counselor's job to be aware of these potential barriers to the communication process and to adapt whenever possible.

Take the following example: I (Elisabeth), was working with Lindsey, an adolescent counselee who had come out of severe abuse and on top of that had some social delays. Most people found Lindsey difficult to work with, as she could be defiant and rather odd in her behaviors. After our first couple of meetings I realized that there was something about Lindsey that bugged me deep inside. As I reflected on all the quirks in Lindsey's presentation—her rolling her eyes, her inconsistent eye contact, her disheveled way of dressing and her overdramatic physical movements—it suddenly hit

Is Noise Always Just Noisy?

A baby screaming in an airplane is no more than irritating noise to the majority of passengers, who will do their best to block it out. But to the infant's mother, the crying is a strong signal that something is wrong and needs attention. The noise is not merely noisy but is a sign of distress. Once the problem is identified and solved (e.g., the baby is fed, or the diaper is changed), the noise goes away.

Similarly, the "noise" our counselees bring to the communication process may be an indicator of underlying problems. The counselor's theory of counseling will in part determine which noise to simply ignore or which aspects require significant exploration. For example, a cognitive-behavioral therapist will tend to focus on mental noise, working toward changing the thought patterns that interfere with healthy functioning, including good communication. Theories that focus more on emotions or subjective experience will tend to focus on emotional noise. In psychodynamic circles, emotional responses that counselees have to the counselor are labeled transference. From some psychodynamic perspectives, working through the transference is actually considered the core of the therapeutic process, certainly much more than simply background noise.

me: Lindsey reminded me of someone else I knew named Karen! I had been interpreting Lindsey's behaviors as I would have interpreted similar behaviors from Karen. In reality, Karen and Lindsey both had some social delays and some odd behaviors, but the reasons for them were vastly different in each girl. The noise in my head meant that I was jumping to conclusions and imposing my thoughts and feelings about Karen onto Lindsey. When coming from Karen, the behaviors that I perceived were often signs of laziness, defiance and an unwillingness to take responsibility for herself. Conversely, in Lindsey those same behaviors were indicators of her trauma, and they spoke to her level of woundedness, fear and loneliness in life. Once I was able to recognize what was going on inside myself, I was more accurately able to interpret the noise that impeded my ability to accurately perceive Lindsey's presentation and could then better meet her in her needs as a counselee.

Noise can be mental, including thoughts about other people and events, or worry and expectations regarding the upcoming counseling conversation. Noise can also be emotional. For the counselor, emotional noise would include feelings about the counselee (for good or bad), feelings about the counseling process, feelings about people or events outside the counseling room, or feelings you have about yourself. Mental and emotional noise on the counselor's part have similarities to the psychodynamic concept of countertransference that we referred to in chapter two. Elisabeth's initial response to her counselee, Lindsey, was an example of countertransference. Of course counselees will also have emotional reactions to you that may interfere with clear communication. Noise can also be physical, including both environment and your own physical condition. Environmental noise includes things such as room temperature, seating, lighting and literal noises, while your physical condition includes things such as being hungry, tired, sick or in physical discomfort or pain.

Sender (counselee) — *message/feedback* — Receiver (counselor)

Figure 3.4. Clouding of the bidirectional message and feedback

We have found it helpful for students to take thirty seconds to five minutes prior to entering a counseling situation to "check in" with themselves, making note of the things that may add noise to the conversation so that they can eliminate all of the noise that they possibly can in an attempt to create an environment where the counselee can be heard and understood with as much clarity and purity as possible.

Take a moment to pause. In the space below, write down the noise that you notice in your mind, emotions and physical space right now. How might this noise affect your ability to accurately receive someone else's messages?

Mental noise:

_____

Emotional noise:

_____

Physical noise:

_____

Possible impact on communication:

_____

ELEMENTS OF NONVERBAL COMMUNICATION

Being aware of the communication model we just described, and how the sender, receiver, message and noise all work together, provides the structure for what we are going to look at next. Nonverbal communication consists of the collection of factors, aside from actual spoken words, that contribute to both the message and the noise in any exchange. It includes how the voice is used (rate of speech, pitch, volume and inflection), body language and use of personal space, physical characteristics and personal presentation (clothing, hygiene, style). The interaction between father and daughter described in the opening lines of this chapter is an example of a discrepancy between nonverbal aspects of communication and the words being spoken.

Nonverbal communication is critical to the counseling process because it gives insight into the unconscious of the counselee. It also serves to either challenge or validate the verbal messages that the counselee may send. In nonverbal communication layers of meaning are often seen and expressed, deception is channeled, and feelings are primarily expressed. As Mehrabian (1971) found, 93% of a message is communicated nonverbally, and therefore much attention should be given to what it may have to say.

Voice related. Just because something is nonverbal does not mean it is inaudible; perceiving includes *how* something is said by the counselee, not just *what* is said. Perceiving counselee pitch, tone, rate of speech and use of inflection all become informative pieces of data that are helpful in gaining a deeper and more thorough understanding of counselees and their situations.

Vocal *pitch* is best understood as how high or low someone's voice is. While everyone's voice tends to function within a given range, the pitch within that range can vary depending on mood and intention. Additionally, vocal pitch has been shown to influence the receiver's perception of the sender's dominance, leadership abilities and attractiveness (Klofstad, Anderson & Peters, 2012). Similar to pitch is vocal tone. *Tone* has to do with the sender's attitude. For example, someone may speak in a formal tone or a playful tone. Tone also can often communicate the underlying emotion the sender has with respect to the topic at hand, the person to whom they are speaking or the person about whom they are speaking.

Rate of speech has to do with how quickly someone speaks—is she a fast talker or a slow talker? Individuals' rates of speech can be influenced by their personality, culture and emotional state. For example, people who are really excited will often quicken their rate of speech, while those who are sad or depressed may slow their speech. Anxiety can result in either quickened or slowed speech, depending on the person. Ultimately, perceiving rate of speech in a counselee is about noticing how your counselee usually speaks and noting when their rate of speech increases or decreases.

Inflection has to do with where in the sentence, and where in each specific word, a counselee places vocal emphasis and whether his or her tone rises or falls. For example, to change a statement into a question, the speaker changes their inflection. Consider "You ate a sandwich for lunch" versus "You ate a sandwich for lunch?" When spoken out loud, the vocal quality that marks one phrase as a statement and the other as a question is inflection. Inflection can also be heard when emphasis is placed on one or more words in a given sentence. For example, "You went to the *movies* with him?" communicates a different emphasis than "You went to the movies with *him*?" In either case, when the speaker places emphasis on the italicized word, thereby raising their inflection, the meaning of the sentence is altered.

Body related. The skill of perceiving also includes the ability to observe and accurately interpret the way a counselee uses or presents his body. This can include his use of physical space as well as autonomic responses.

Diagnostic Implications

While there is concern in the broader culture and in the mental health professions about the possibility that attention deficit/hyperactivity disorder (ADHD) is overdiagnosed, it is clear that it has been and continues to be a very helpful way of understanding a complex set of symptoms, often first observed in childhood. Identifying a child as having ADHD can help teachers and families recognize that this child has difficulty with aspects of relationships, termed social intelligence by some authors (Goleman, 2006), that are assumed normal for many other children.

One of those assumed functions that others are able to do without even thinking about it is to pick up on, recognize as significant, and utilize social cues in conversations and social situations. People simply differ in their ability to do this. For some individuals, limitations in these areas cross a threshold, making them diagnosable as ADHD or a related disorder. There is also an opposite tendency that could be called the highly sensitive person, an individual who is so attuned to social cues that he or she is unable to filter out the significant from the less important social cues. Both are a challenge in counseling relationships, but we will focus here on low perceptiveness of both counselors and counselees.

Counselors. There are counselors who, for whatever reason, are not naturally adept at perceiving the verbal and nonverbal nuance in counseling conversations. Thankfully, to some degree, this is a skill that can be learned and improved on by doing exercises like those attached to this chapter. However, for some counselors it will never be as easy as it is for others. If this describes you, it does not mean you should not be a counselor. A simple, intentional strategy may help immensely: encourage counselees to think about the counseling relationships as a different kind of relationship—one in which we do not make assumptions and we identify what might be obvious in other relationships. Specificity, clarifying meaning or repeating important things may simply need to be a greater emphasis for a counselor for whom tuning into verbal and nonverbal cues is more easily overlooked. This can result in really clear communication and is actually good advice for a lot of married couples and families, who often make far too many automatic assumptions about what the other means.

Counselees. Difficulty in accurately perceiving others is a relatively common occurrence for counselees. At least part of the problem for many counselees is the inability to read social cues or the tendency to misread social cues. Such counselees may not even be aware that they are not picking up on social cues very well. In one way, being oblivious to this interpersonal dynamic may be a gift in that they do not get bogged down in what others can get lost in—the endless, subtle nuances of complicated relationships. However, more often than we may like, the counseling process is focused on helping counselees to accurately see and hear what others in their lives are attempting to communicate, minimize automatic assumptions about what they observe, and develop ways of talking about this in their relationships. The counseling relationship becomes the laboratory in which the skills of social intelligence can be learned.

How counselees use *physical space* is of particular importance. For example, do they talk with their hands, expanding their sense of self into the greater physical space around them, or do they seem to try to take up as little space as possible in the room or the chair? What assumptions or interpretations do you make about how they use their space: Do you see large gestures as a sign of confidence or arrogance? Do you see using less space as timidity, insecurity or humility? Does the counselee create a physical barrier between herself and the counselor with the use of holding a pillow, crossing her arms or moving furniture between herself and the counselor as a way of communicating the desire for emotional distance or protection? As with any type of perception, being aware of your personal biases, preferences and past experiences is necessary in developing an accurate understanding of the intention and meaning in the counselee's behavior.

Other body-related components to perceiving are the counselee's *autonomic responses.* Autonomic responses are physical responses that are not always consciously controlled by the counselee, such as pupil dilation, perspiration and heart rate. Autonomic responses are influenced by cognitive, physical and emotional triggers and connect with the body's fight-or-flight response system (Chudler, 2014; University College London Institute of Cognitive Neuroscience, 2011). For example, does the counselee's face or chest begin to flush when he talks about something embarrassing or emotional? Do the counselee's eyes dilate, as if afraid, when he talks about a traumatic event? Does the counselee appear agitated and "twitchy" as he shares about a guilt-inducing event? In poker, players call these responses "tells"—the behaviors, moments or physical responses that the counselee is generally unaware of and that reflect an underlying core emotion.

Personal presentation. We each make assumptions based on the personal presentation of others. While we have been cautioned against stereotypes and "judging a book by its cover," we all still do it—and often for reasons rooted in past experience. For example, what gut assumptions do you make about the intelligence, decorum and culture of a woman with big hair, perfectly applied makeup and a southern drawl? What about a man with a missing front tooth, a "beer belly" and tattered jeans? The important part of perceiving in this arena is to recognize our biases and assumptions and then proceed cautiously, letting the individual counselee support or challenge our presuppositions. It can be challenging to acknowledge and articulate one's biases to a supervisor or peer as they may sound "politically incorrect," judgmental or disrespectful, but it is important to remember that it is that which is left unreflected upon and unacknowledged that ultimately gets imposed onto the counselee. Biases and assumptions about a counselee's physical presentation may also be positive, leading the counselor to assume valued or positive traits and abilities in the counselee without evidence or experiential support. Whether our biases are negative or positive, remember that the skill of perceiving is to *accurately* understand the messages of the counselee, without adding or subtracting from them.

While it is rarely, if ever, appropriate to share such biases with a counselee, it is necessary to acknowledge and work through biases with a supervisor or professor. Every person, and therefore every counselor, carries assumptions, stereotypes, and likes and dislikes regarding the nonverbal presentation of others. It is the effective counselor who can acknowledge his biases and learn to work both with and through them.

Areas of consideration regarding physical presentation:

♦ *Body height*: What assumptions, impressions or judgments do you have regarding short men? Tall women? Tall men? Short women?

♦ *Body weight*: What assumptions, impressions or judgments do you have regarding men/women who are overweight or obese? What about lanky men? Skinny women? Those with possible plastic surgery?

Consider the Following Scenarios

If you were completely honest with yourself, what perceptions do you have of the following counselees? What assumptions do you make regarding their intelligence, investment in the counseling process, social skills, personality traits, likability, sexuality, workplace accomplishments and so on?

Jamie is a forty-five-year-old female who is five-foot-six and approximately 255 pounds (significantly overweight by North American standards). Always appearing clean, she does not wear makeup and regularly dresses in masculine-style jeans and a tucked-in button-down flannel shirt. Her hair, although long, is straight and stringy, and always pulled back in a low ponytail. She smiles readily but is very short and direct in her style of speech, offering little variation in tone or inflection.

From this description, do you like Jamie? Do you feel comfortable around her? What assumptions do you make about her? What would draw you to her, and what would leave you hesitant or apprehensive about her? How does your impression change if Jamie is Caucasian? Black? Latina? Or Asian? What if Jamie were male?

Andy is a twenty-eight-year-old male who is five-foot-eleven, with a very toned, tanned and attractive physique. His hair is always perfectly coiffed, and his clothes are both stylish and well put-together. He wears just enough cologne to be noticed but does not overpower the room. Andy's posture is perfect, and he seems to take up more space in the room than his body would naturally need. His face is more serious, although he smiles easily, and he speaks quickly.

From this description, do you like Andy? Do you feel comfortable around him? What assumptions do you make about him? What would draw you to him, and what would leave you hesitant or apprehensive about him? How does your impression change if Andy is Caucasian? Black? Latino? Asian? What if Andy introduced himself as Andrew and not Andy? What if Andy were female?

◆ *Clothing*: What assumptions, impressions or judgments do you have regarding counselees who dress very fashionably? Who dress according to the norms of a deviant subculture? Who are mismatched? Whose clothes are unkempt or unclean?

◆ *Hygiene*: What assumptions, impressions or judgments do you have regarding a counselee whose hygiene is not up to cultural standards? Whose hair is always greasy? Who smells like body odor? Whose cologne or perfume is too strong for your liking? Whose body hair is unkempt (a man whose beard is "out of control," or a woman who wears tank tops with unshaven armpits or skirts with unshaven legs)?

REQUEST TYPES

Up until now we have we have focused on perceiving the nonverbal aspects of communication. In this section we shift our focus somewhat to paying attention to what counselees are actually requesting of us, whether or not they are conscious of what lies underneath their apparent request.

The concept of *request types* (Gazda et al., 2005) has to do with reading the overarching theme of a conversation. Within any conversation the counselee is implicitly or explicitly making one of four types of requests to the counselor. It is up to the counselor to appropriately discern what the counselee is really asking for and then provide the appropriate counselor response. The four counselee request types and the appropriate corresponding counselor responses are the following (Gazda et al, 2005, p. 51):

1. request for action → appropriate action

2. request for information → appropriate information

3. request for understanding and involvement → facilitative response

4. request for inappropriate interaction → polite decline to participate

Request for action. A request for action involves the counselee wanting the counselor to actively do something. The request may be explicit, such as "Can you please hand me a pen?" or it can be implicit, such as "I don't have an appointment scheduled with you next week." In the implicit request, the counselee is implying that she would like to make an appointment with the counselor but may be uncertain how to go about such a request or may fear that the request would be denied. Unlike an explicit request for action, which is easy to identify, an implicit request may sound more like someone is letting you in on his internal thought process. Regardless of how the request for action is made, it is necessary for the counselor to carefully discern whether fulfilling the request would be in the best interest of the counselee and the therapeutic relationship.

Request for information. A request for information does not ask the counselor to *do* anything for the counselee other than to share his knowledge about a particular topic. Similar in many ways to a request for action, requests for information may be implicitly or explicitly made: "I don't know how to get to the airport from here" versus "Can you give me directions to the airport from here?" As you continue to develop your skills as a counselor, you will increasingly be able to hear and discern not just the surface request being made but the underlying need as well.

Request for understanding and involvement. The majority of counseling conversations are likely to fall within the domain of requests for understanding and involvement. The majority of this textbook is meant to provide you as counselors with the tools to respond to these requests in ways that are honoring and facilitative for the counselee. This type of request may not sound much like a request but may instead sound like someone "venting" or sharing their thoughts out loud. Requests for understanding and involvement are the ones most commonly made in interpersonal relationship, as each individual invites the other to gain insight into the thoughts, feelings and experiences of the other. The challenge for many counselors is that they, in their desire to "help people," end up turning a request for understanding and involvement into a request for action or a request for information, which will inevitably result in the counselee feeling frustrated and misunderstood.

A stereotyped example is seen in a scenario in which a wife comes home and starts complaining to her husband about how much she dislikes her boss and how rude or micromanaging her boss is. In return, her husband, misinterpreting his wife's request for understanding and involvement, begins offering suggestions as to how his wife could talk to her boss (a request for action) or otherwise improve the workplace situation. In doing so the husband heard both a request for action (responding with "Have you tried . . .") and a request for information (responding with "Did you know that legally . . ."). In the context of counseling, unless you are sure that the request being made by the counselee is for action or information, assume it is a request for understanding and involvement.

Request for inappropriate involvement. The final request type is one that is far less enjoyable or pleasant for the counselor. A request for inappropriate involvement is any request that asks the counselor to do or say something that violates the norms, ethics, laws or social standards of a particular helping context. This can also include, but is not limited to, gossip or rumors, excessive or "chronic complaining," "solicitation of a dependency relationship" or "encouragement of activities that are counter to the benefit of other persons or the organization" (Gazda et al., 2005, p. 52).

For example, a counselee might say something like, "So, I heard that Sarah is also a counselee of yours, and she and I work in the same office together. I don't know if you know this about her, but she is a basket case!" It is a request for inappropriate involvement because it is both gossip and implicitly asking you to break confidentiality about who is or is not your counselee. It can be tempting to engage this type of request with a rebuttal or refutation of some sort, wanting to defend the person (known or unknown) who is being talked about. Conversely, it can also be tempting to want to pretend to ignore what the counselee said, hoping that silence will allow the conversation to move on to other topics. Unfortunately, silence can also serve to undermine the relationship between you and the counselee, and may passively encourage him to continue such conversations rather than avoid them. Instead, requests for inappropriate interaction need to be addressed directly but politely. In the above scenario, you as the counselor may respond with something such as, "This time that we have together is to talk about you, and what's going on in your life. It is not ethically appropriate for me to talk about whether someone is or is not a counselee of mine, and it doesn't sound like talking about Sarah will be beneficial to the goals you've identified for our time together." It is important to remember that most counselees know if their request is inappropriate in some way, and when you redirect the conversation they are likely to feel embarrassed. It is not your job to protect counselees from their feelings, but it is your job to communicate respect, clarity of boundaries and affirmation of them as a person whenever possible.

Regardless of the type of request being made by the counselee, it is the counselor's responsibility to perceive what is being asked by the counselee and to respond appropriately given the setting, relationship and context of the conversation. Throughout this book you will be developing the skills to meet this objective, but for the time being it is sufficient that you can simply identify the request type with accuracy.

PERCEPTION, INTUITION AND THE SELF-AS-INSTRUMENT

The skill of perception is often difficult to explain, let alone concretely teach, due to the high degree of "art" that it requires. Perception includes all of the concepts and principles we have explored thus far but also involves intuition. While good intuition may tend to be viewed as something individuals either naturally have or do not have, intuition can actually be developed based on learning that has taken place in previous situations (Witteman, Spaanjaars & Aarts, 2012). For example, your past interactions with children will likely inform you that a child running toward you with her arms spread wide open and a smile on her face means that she wants to be hugged or picked up by you. It does not take a highly intuitive individual to perceive what that child is communicating nonverbally. It will take greater intuitive ability, however, for an individual to perceive that a shyer child is expressing the same desire for affection simply by being able to identify the look of longing in the child's face. In this way intuition helps you to "decode" what you are taking in and gives you an understanding of what you can expect particular facial expressions, voice tones or other nonverbal messages to mean based off your stored experiences and observations in the past. Remember the good news, that even if you are not naturally highly intuitive, you can cultivate your ability to tune into the intuition you do have in order to make better use of it.

Try It Out

In the exchanges below, identify the request type that the counselee is making. Answers can be found in appendix A at the end of the book. Options include (1) request for action, (2) request for information, (3) request for understanding and involvement and (4) request for inappropriate interaction.

1. Counselee: Before I sit down and dive in to what's happened this week, I really need to use your restroom. Where is it?

Request type: _____

2. Counselee: Oh my goodness, you won't believe it! I found out this week that I got a full-ride scholarship to my dream school! I am so excited!

Request type: _____

3. Counselee: I have a killer migraine today. Could we turn the overhead lights off and only have the table lamps on?

Request type: _____

4. Counselee: I don't even know where to begin, this week has been so awful! My baby-sitter just up and quit last night. I don't know what I'm going to do next week because she was supposed to watch the kids Wednesday through Friday while my husband and I are both away on business trips!

Request type: _____

5. Counselee: Ugh, I just met the other counselor down the hall. I don't know how you work with her. She seems really mean and rather snooty too.

Request type: _____

6. Counselee: My son just got diagnosed with ADHD. I know that's one of your specialties, so can you tell me a little bit about it?

Request type: _____

7. Counselee: My mother just got diagnosed with Alzheimer's, and I'm just so over-whelmed. I don't know anything about how to care for someone with dementia, and there's just so much to take in. I wish there was an *Alzheimer's for Dummies* book I could read.

Request type: _____

As with any art-based ability, perceiving is more susceptible to counselor history, personality, mood or physical state. For these reasons, a counselor's ongoing self-awareness of the impact of these kinds of things on her ability to accurately perceive what is happening with a particular client is an essential element of honing the self-as-instrument.

Intuition, Skill Training and the Holy Spirit

How do you know whether the potential insight you have about what is happening with your counselee is the Holy Spirit speaking to you, your intuition or the result of the counseling training you have received? We believe it can be all of the above! If you ask the Holy Spirit to guide you in your helping role, God can potentially answer your prayer by increasing your intuitive sense. He can also use the knowledge you have gained through training and experience by bringing certain aspects to mind that are relevant to a given situation.

Earlier we mentioned the concept of countertransference, which can be broadly defined as a counselor's "emotional response to a [counselee]" (Corey, 2013, p. 77). Countertransference is an emotional response that feels as if it is based solely on the counselee but can also be influenced by experiences with someone the counselor identifies, often unconsciously, as similar to the counselee in one way or another (e.g., Elisabeth emotionally reacting to Lindsey as though she were Karen). This latter type of countertransference can significantly hinder a counselor's ability to accurately perceive what is happening with a counselee. However, countertransference can also be a very informative and beneficial tool when it is approached with high levels of self-reflection and ultimately self-awareness by the counselor. For example, if you realized in the middle of a session that you were feeling angry, you could ask yourself the following questions: "Why am I feeling angry right now? Is my anger related to what this particular person is saying or doing, or am I reacting to something or someone else? How can my anger help me to accurately perceive my counselee?" In this particular situation, it could be that the counselee is overtly expressing sadness or depression, but that by identifying your feelings of anger, you are able to perceive underlying anger in your counselee.

Perceiving Is *Not*

✓ assuming that a counselee's behavior means the same for her as it does for you
✓ jumping to the conclusion that you know what the counselee means
✓ imposing the counselor's thoughts, feelings or beliefs onto the counselee

In your attempts to use countertransference in this way, there is the added danger that you could be projecting your own emotions onto your counselee, emotions that

Biblical/Theological Connections

It is common in Western cultures to view a person, and ourselves, as having parts: body, soul, spirit, mind and so on. Freud's distinction among the id, ego and superego, along with the conscious and unconscious mind, adds to this tendency to define parts of self. Therefore, in terms of communication, it is common to assume that there is explicit communication (e.g., verbal statements) and metacommunication (communication about the explicit communication—tone, pace, etc., as well as underlying feelings and motivations). All of these assumptions about "parts of self" can be very helpful in counseling but sometimes can lead to a view of the person that elevates one part of the person above other parts, that growth and healing only happen beneath the surface.

In Christian thought we often read Scripture through the lens of parts of self and quickly become confused because Scripture talks about the parts differently in various passages. For instance, take the well-known verse "Love the LORD your God with all your heart and with all your soul and with all your strength" (Deut 6:5). This verse can be used to suggest that persons are composed of parts, identified as heart, soul and strength. However, a careful study of this verse and the other places in Scripture where it is referred to paints a different picture (Beck, 1999). Jesus in Matthew 22:37 names the "parts" heart, soul and mind. In Mark 12:30 the "parts" are named heart, soul, mind and strength. Mark 12:33 refers to heart, understanding and strength. Luke 10:27 refers to heart, soul, strength and mind. Add to this that these verses were written in two languages, Hebrew and Greek, and that claiming equivalence between words in different languages is a challenge.

So what is the point? The emphasis of these verses is not on the parts of the person but that we are to love the Lord with everything we are—with all of our personhood, including our emotions, thoughts and behaviors. One part is not elevated above the others. Created in the image of God, humans are better understood as whole, integrated beings rather than beings who are made up of parts. However, it is helpful, in certain contexts such as counseling, to acknowledge the underlying motivations and meanings, and even internal self-contradictions, in our journey toward personal wholeness.

really are not the counselee's at all! Accurate perceiving does not assume that the counselee's facial expressions, body movements and other nonverbal communication mean for him exactly what they would mean if you did them. Additionally, countertransference does not mean that you are free to project meaning onto a counselee just because that behavior meant something for someone else once upon a time. Perceiving is taking in the counselee's nonverbal behavior and using your own emotions and past experiences *grounded on* your understanding of who the counselee is in order to make meaning of what you have observed. This art requires a skillful balance of learning who your counselee is and what a given behavior or response means for her with knowing who you as a counselor are and the meaning you intuitively ascribe to nonverbal behaviors.

We would encourage you, as a class, to discuss ways in which you have (or could) work to develop your perceiving skills. Some examples we would suggest include the activities listed at the end of this chapter.

MULTICULTURAL APPLICATION

Being attuned to both verbal and nonverbal cues is at the heart of perceiving what counselees are experiencing. The problem, however, with accurately perceiving what is going on with counselees who are from a different cultural background than their counselors is that the same cues may have totally different meanings in a counselee's particular cultural context (Garrett & Portman, 2011). The same is true for gender (Robinson & Howard-Hamilton, 2000). Therefore there is a high likelihood of totally misinterpreting the counselee.

Differences in the meanings of words, even within the same language, can certainly vary among cultural groups. We will address the multicultural implications of word usage in chapter eight. While tuning into variation in how words are understood is essential, differences in nonverbal communication can be even more complex. The use of *personal and interpersonal space* (proxemics) varies greatly. For example, Arabs, Latin Americans, Africans, South Americans, French, black Americans and Indonesians are all generally more comfortable in closer proximity to another person than are European Americans (Nydell, 1996). This has implications for how the office space is set up and how much permission you give counselees to adjust the seating.

Gender can also play a role. I (Heather) remember asking my therapist, a male, whether he was willing to roll his chair closer to mine in order to bridge what felt to me like a huge interpersonal chasm created by the seven feet of distance that was his default physical distance from me. When he moved his chair closer to me I immediately felt more relaxed. Of course, the counselor has to feel that his own interpersonal boundaries are not being violated by acquiescing to such a request.

The use of *bodily movements* (kinesics), including amount of eye contact, types of gestures, facial expression and posture, also vary by culture (Chan & Lee, 2004). In European American culture, for example, avoidance of eye contact could be interpreted as discomfort, resistance or lack of respect, while in other cultures eye contact is considered undesirable and disrespectful (Pedersen & Ivey, 1993). Smiling can indicate shame or embarrassment in some cultures, and laughter can have differing meanings (Sue & Sue, 2016). It was only after many years in the Philippines that I (Heather) came to understand that when a group of men laughed when my young son fell off his bike and hurt himself, they were not actually being rude and insensitive but were, rather, attempting to show sympathy. Even the extent to which facial expression is shown is valued to greater or lesser degrees depending on culture. It took me many months to begin to perceive the subtle variations of facial expression with a counselee who was Chinese. Head movements (Jensen, 1985), shaking hands (Sue & Sue, 2016) and specific gestures (LaBarre, 1985) also vary by culture.

Vocal cues (paralanguage), such as pauses, silences, loudness of voice, inflections, rate of speech and silences are also culturally driven (Sue & Sue, 2013). Care needs to be taken to not misinterpret vocal cues. For example, in European American culture, a soft voice could be perceived as insecurity, shyness or low self-esteem, while in an Asian context a soft voice could potentially have these meanings or merely connote respect and good manners.

When working with diverse counselees, you will need to continually check whether what you are perceiving is accurate. This may mean frequent use of reflecting content and feelings (see chapters five and six) as well as asking for clarification (chapter eight). It certainly means coming to the helping relationship with the stance of a learner and an attitude of humility.

CONCLUSION

The skill of perceiving is a fundamentally art-based technique, built on the counselor's ability to make observations about a counselee's nonverbal communication and then ascribe accurate meaning to those observations. Perceiving includes, but is not limited to, hearing the request type that underlies the counselee's words, picking up the meaning behind the counselee's vocal characteristics (such as tone, inflection and rate of speech) and cluing in to how a counselee communicates through his physical characteristics and use of his body. Perceiving is not projection but instead asks the counselor to learn what specific nonverbal behaviors mean for a specific counselee given his unique personality, background and culture. When working with multicultural counselees, particular care is needed to ensure that what you are perceiving is accurate.

REFLECTION QUESTIONS

1. On a scale of one (low) to five (high), how attuned are your perceiving skills? Provide three examples.

2. If you had to guess, are you likely to be more distracted by your own mental, emotional or physical noise? Why?

3. Of the topics addressed in this chapter, which nonverbal characteristics of others do you tend to be most aware of? Why do you think that is?

YOUR PRESENCE
IN THE ROOM

Who is like the wise?
Who knows the explanation of things?
A person's wisdom brightens their face
and changes its hard appearance.

ECCLESIASTES 8:1

CHAPTER FOCUS

SKILL: attending

PURPOSE: to develop the counselor's self-awareness regarding his or her own nonverbal communication

---

FORMULA: I notice _____ about how I may be coming across.
I notice that I'm doing _____, which may come across as _____.

ONE DAY, WHEN I (ELISABETH) was in middle school, my mother asked me to clean the living room. I was not upset or annoyed, as this was a normal request in our house, so I said, "Okay, Mom." My very kind, patient mother quickly stopped me and said, "Freeze your face, go to the bathroom, look in the mirror and tell me why I think you're mad at me." What I found when I looked in the mirror was a face that did not reflect how I felt inside. Instead, my face looked flat, detached and almost angry, while inside I felt calm, peaceful and generally okay with life. It was here that I became aware that my "default face" was not all that pleasant. I had a responsibility to learn how my nonverbal messages came across to others and to work toward congruence between what I felt on the inside and what my face and body language showed on the outside.

This is the act of attending—learning how to use nonverbal communication to convey the messages you intend to send and learning what your default face and body language say to others. Whereas perception is what you take in from others, attending is what others are likely to perceive, or take in, from you. As with perceiving, attending is both art and science but leans more heavily on the side of art.

There are two elements to attending: what you *show* externally and what you *bring* to the conversation as a person. What you show externally refers to your outward expressions or behaviors that a counselee could observe, as well as what a counselee may pick up about the environment that is created through the physical setup of the counseling room. What you bring is everything that happens on the inside of you that contributes to your ability to genuinely attend. We will begin with a discussion of external ways in which a counselor demonstrates attending to her counselees and will then move into the internal elements that contribute to a counselor's ability to be present and attend.

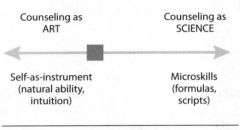

Figure 4.1. Art versus science: Attending

Discovering Your Default

Over the course of the next week, whenever you walk by a reflective window or a mirror, "freeze your face" and observe what others see:

✓ Does your facial expression match your internal emotion?

✓ If someone did not know you, what would they assume you are thinking or feeling based solely on what is shown on your "frozen" face?

THE EXTERNAL ASPECT OF ATTENDING: WHAT YOU SHOW

As was discussed in chapter three, nonverbal communication includes both voice- and body-related elements. Voice-related elements include things such as vocal pitch, rate of speech and inflection. Body-related elements include such things as use of space, physical presentation and involuntary or autonomic responses. Just as you, as the counselor, take in each of these elements from your counselee, your counselee is also observing them in you and making assumptions about who you are based on them. For this reason it is of utmost importance that you are aware of how others might perceive you, even if it is difficult for you to be honest with yourself about aspects of how you come across that you may not want to acknowledge. If you are unsure as to how others perceive you, try asking good friends and even classmates the following question: "Think back to one of the first interactions, if not the first interaction, you and I had. What was your initial impression of me based on my facial expressions, body language and style of dress? What assumptions did you make about my personality, temperament and likeability?" Be prepared for both flattering and unflattering remarks!

Following is a discussion of various aspects of the ways in which counselors can intentionally or inadvertently show aspects of themselves to their counselees.

Voice related. Increasing our awareness as to how others may hear or perceive us allows us the opportunity to become aware of instances where our voice does not accurately communicate our internal state of being. For example, I (Elisabeth) am very aware that I can often come across sounding more serious or definitive than I feel because of my tone, my inflection and my more serious default face. Because I realize this about myself, I will often be very intentional in conversations with counselees to make sure that my tone has an added amount of lightheartedness or playfulness when that is the true intention of my words.

Empirical Support

The work of Sherer and Rogers (1980) as well as that of Sharpley, Jeffrey and McMah (2006), spanning decades of research, demonstrate a timeless truth: the nonverbal messages from the counselor significantly contribute to the effectiveness of therapy. Specifically, when counselors use "high-immediacy nonverbal cues" (p. 699; i.e., close therapist-client distance, eye contact, etc.), counselees perceive significantly higher levels of liking, acceptance, empathy, warmth, genuineness, status and responsivity from their counselor. Furthermore, "clear and unequivocal expression of interest, excitement and enjoyment appear to be positively linked with client experiences of rapport" (Sharpley, Jeffrey & McMah, 2006, p. 354). As such, a counselor who is able to use nonverbal communication in a genuine and masterful way is likely to be "rated as possessing superior therapist interpersonal skills and as being a more effective therapist" (Sherer & Rogers, 1980, p. 699).

Nearly everyone hates the sound of their own voice on a recording, but it is a great way to gain a greater awareness of some of the voice-related nonverbal messages you could send to a counselee. Are you a fast or slow talker? A person who inserts "umm" frequently? Do you laugh or giggle at inappropriate times? Does your inflection go up at the end of every sentence, turning everything into a question? Do you sound overly serious? These elements and others can all be discerned by simply recording yourself in normal conversation and playing it back. (Be sure to get appropriate consent from friends or relatives who might also get recorded during this process, explaining to them that the purpose of the recording is to analyze yourself.)

Now that you have listened to a recording of what you actually sound like, look back on chapter three and review the discussion of vocal pitch, tone of voice, rate of speech and inflection, but this time apply it to yourself. What might counselees perceive about you, based on these elements of nonverbal communication?

Body related. As mentioned earlier, we are not always aware of the myriad ways our body communicates to others by nonverbal means. From our facial expressions, to our use of space, to the physical presentation of ourselves, we must be attentive to the ways in which counselees may perceive us.

Diagnostic Implications

As with so many other personal characteristics, people naturally vary considerably regarding their tendency and ability to pay attention to internal experience and how they convey themselves externally. We admire and seek to emulate those who are attuned to their internal experience and can act and interact from that ability to be completely attuned to how they come across to others. In one sense this describes someone who is wise.

We also know people who are not attuned to their internal experience and how they come across to others. This is clearly seen in people with certain personality disorders—for instance, borderline (BPD) and histrionic personality disorder. BPD is characterized by extreme internal distortion and instability. The moods of individuals with BPD can fluctuate dramatically. Their sense of self is unstable and distorted. They are impulsive and prone to self-harm. The core of this disorder is the chaotic internal experience that cannot be contained and "leaks" out in interpersonal relationships.

For counselors, the ability to simultaneously attend to both their internal experience and to a counselee's description of her life and circumstances requires counselors to have, inside their own minds, an ongoing internal dialogue between their self (values, emotions, thoughts, etc.) and how they are interacting with and being perceived by the counselee. In cognitive therapies this ability is referred to as self-talk, and while counselors need to teach counselees to self-talk, they also need to be able to do this themselves within the session. Learning the intentional, calming skills of meditation and mindfulness can help give increased, nonjudgmental attention to internal experience. Becoming more aware of how one is coming across to others is the additional component of attending. Both components are missing in severe disorders like BPD, and both are required for effective counseling relationships.

Facial expressions. My (Elisabeth's) mom was trying to get me to pay attention to my facial expression when she told me to freeze my face and take a look in the mirror. How we hold or move our face can "speak" very loudly to others. As you are reading this, freeze your face and take an internal scan of how the muscles in your face feel. Is your brow furrowed? Is your jaw tight? Are your lips pursed, frowning or smirked? With your face still frozen, go and look in a mirror. Does your internal scan match the external reflection? If not, what is different? Now, looking in the mirror, arrange your face into the expression that you would most like to have when talking with a counselee, and take an internal scan of what *that* face feels like. If your default face does not match this chosen "helping face," take time each day to repeat the process of looking in a mirror, finding your helping face and noting how it feels. Over time this may help you to "reset" your default face.

While the default face of some counselors is one of pensiveness or stoicism, others default to one that is overly smiley and happy looking. While a warmer, more positive, default face can initially be more inviting to a counselee, this same facial expression can be problematic when a counselee is sharing something painful or communicating something difficult. Responding to a counselee's grief, sorrow, fear or anxiety with a smile is obviously inappropriate, yet it can be an automatic, unintentional response on the part of a counselor. The goal is for the counselor's facial expressions to be congruent with the mood of the story the counselee is communicating.

Mirroring. There are various ways of understanding the concept of mirroring, each nuanced in its own way. For the purposes of this training process, we are defining mirroring as a skill of using nonverbal communication to reflect back the nonverbal messages perceived in the counselee. For example, mirroring occurs when, as a counselee is telling you a story of delight and excitement, he smiles, and you smile back. You are *mirroring* the counselee's nonverbal expressions, showing him on your face what you perceive on his face. The same thing can happen with negative affect. For example, if a counselee begins to tell you about the death of a dear loved one, she may start to cry or to look sorrowful. While you as the counselor may not start to cry or carry the same level of emotion that the counselee does, mirroring would involve you putting your face into a more melancholy or sorrowful position, reflecting back the sadness that you perceive within the counselee. Care must be taken, however, not to mirror facial expressions that are actually incongruent with the counselee's story. For example, sometimes people will smile when they are describing intense pain, perhaps as a way of attempting to minimize the extent of their hurt or out of fear that you will not validate the intensity of their emotion. In such cases you will need to intentionally *not* mirror your counselees' facial expressions, because most of the time they will be unaware that they are smiling and may wonder why you are making light of their pain!

It is important to remember that mirroring is not mimicking a counselee's presentation but is more closely aligned with matching his presentation. It is using your nonverbal communication, whether that be in facial expression, body posture or vocal quality, to reflect back to the counselee that you are accurately perceiving what they are communicating to you.

Presentation of physical self. The presentation of your *physical self* is also part of effective attending. Rightly or wrongly, people make assumptions about another's personality, social class, values and likeability based on how that other person physically looks. In light of this, it is important for counselors to consider how their counselees will perceive their physical presentation, including their personal hygiene as well as their clothing and sense of style. Cleanliness is of utmost importance for a counselor. The last thing anyone wants is to walk into an office and sit within three feet of a counselor who smells of body odor, whose teeth have not been cleaned, whose breath is in desperate need of refreshment or who has clearly not showered in multiple days!

Beyond basic cleanliness, other areas of physical presentation may be influenced by culture. For example, a counselor's choice of clothes and style reflect her ethnicity, socioeconomic status and personality. Whether male or female, how you dress yourself needs to take into consideration what would be suitable for your given clientele. For example, there was time when I (Elisabeth) was teaching at a university but also worked as the counselor in a residential foster care facility. On the days that I went from teaching in the morning to the foster-care facility in the afternoon, I would often bring a change of clothes. For my university students, it was important that I dressed professionally, in business-casual to business style. But for the foster-care facility, those clothes would have created a social barrier between my counselees and me, so I would regularly counsel in jeans and a casual top, as my counselees were all coming out of poverty and neglectful environments where they had little to no financial resources. One rule of thumb is to dress equal to or one professional level up from how your counselees dress. So, for example, while the counselees in the foster-care facility often wore sweatpants or jeans, my choice to wear jeans kept me at a comparable level of style.

While a suit and tie would generally be considered overkill for male counselors, if your counselees are professionals who come to sessions in suits, then you should at least wear a dress shirt and tie if not a suit with the jacket hanging visibly nearby. T-shirts may be okay in informal, residential settings, but a shirt with a collar is going to be suitable more often for men. Jeans may be suitable in some settings, but not in others, and ripped jeans should always be avoided in professional settings. Additionally, shorts would not generally be permissible in an office setting.

While both male and female counselors need to pay attention to what their clothing portrays to their counselees, modesty in clothing is of paramount importance, particularly for women. Regardless of your counseling context, your choice of clothing should never serve to draw attention to you or your body in a way that could be perceived as provocative, sensual or anything other than professional. This means that women should not wear tops that reveal cleavage, spaghetti-strap tops or skirts that show a lot of thigh when they sit. Clothes that are tight-fitting and accentuate or draw attention to curves should also be avoided. An outfit that is as stunning as evening wear but too dressy for the office can similarly draw attention to yourself in ways that are not helpful in a counseling relationship. This does not mean that women cannot dress femininely or in ways that are flattering to their figure, but it does mean to be attentive to how a counselee is likely to perceive you and your style. Similarly, male counselors need to dress modestly. Tight-fitting clothing should be avoided, and shirts should be buttoned in ways that do not show much chest or chest hair.

Space related. How a counselor approaches the use of space is also part of nonverbal communication and proper attending behavior. Use of space refers to how counselors physically use the space around them, how they arrange the environmental space in which the helping conversation takes place and how they use the energetic space around them. Let's start from the farthest sphere and work inward.

Environmental space. How a counselor arranges the *environmental space* in which a helping conversation takes place is of high importance. Depending on the type of counseling you will be doing, you may or may not have control over your physical environment. Ideally, though, you will have some influence over things such as the type of furniture as well as the way the furniture is arranged in the room. The color and décor you select, and even the type and amount of lighting, all become a form of nonverbal communication to counselees.

The type of furniture and décor that is appropriate will vary somewhat depending on who your counselees tend to be. For example, if you are seeing primarily upper-class people who are paying a top fee to see you, a sophisticated look with more expensive furniture would be appropriate. In a not-for-profit counseling agency or a church setting, there would not be the same expectation of luxury, although chairs should still be as comfortable as possible. Similarly, if a room is used primarily with adolescents or children, care should be taken to create a space where they will feel comfortable.

It is also important to make sure that chairs, loveseats or couches are all at the same height. If the counselor's chair is higher than the counselee's, for example, it potentially creates a further power differential, with the counselee feeling inferior. On the other hand, if the counselee is in the higher chair, the counselor could feel disempowered. Similarly, if the counselor is in a chair that is somehow bigger or better than the counselee's, the helping relationship can be subtly affected.

You also want to arrange the furniture so that there are no physical barriers between you and your counselee. The presence of such physical barriers often serves to non-verbally communicate an emotional distance or self-protectiveness on the part of the counselor, just as it does if done by the counselee. For this reason counselors should generally avoid sitting on the other side of a desk from a counselee. Similarly, it is better to have end tables than a coffee table, although a low coffee table would not likely create as strong a barrier as a desk. There may be exceptions to this general rule. For example, in a prison setting where there is potential risk of violence, a physical barrier such as a desk might actually be a good idea.

The type of lighting used also communicates something to counselees. Lamps, for example, tend to communicate a warmer and more familiar environment than do overhead fluorescent lighting. The light is "softer" and thus more likely to contribute to a calmer feel within the counseling room. Some counselees, though, may feel more comfortable with the use of less intimate forms of lighting. Part of the art of counseling is sorting out which setup is better for which counselees.

The use of color within the counseling room is related to this same principle. Studies have shown that different colors and hues evoke different emotions (Boyatzis

& Varghese, 1994; Elliot & Maier, 2007; Kaya & Epps, 2004). Thus utilizing colors that are soft and yet rich can create a feeling of warmth and groundedness in a room (i.e., browns instead of black, a cranberry red instead of a cherry red, a navy or slate blue instead of a bright teal, and muted instead of bold tones).

In regards to décor, it is often tempting for counselors to put items of personal significance around their office. While this is not automatically a bad thing, it is important to remember that you want to decorate your office so that *counselees* are comfortable there. An out-of-the-way picture of loved ones can serve to personalize who you are to counselees, but multiple photos of loved ones directly facing the counselee can serve as a distraction or point of discomfort for counselees who may need a counselor to remain more anonymous in their minds, or who may interpret the photos as a reminder of what they do not have in their own life. Items such as crosses, Bibles or other religious artifacts can also serve as a double-edged sword. For counselees who share the same faith as their counselor, these items can be seen as points of connection. These same objects, however, could be equally as divisive if counselees do not share the same faith as their counselors or if they come from a background in which religion was used in an abusive manner. Hanging diplomas, licenses and certifications in a visible but off-set location is generally accepted practice and can offer reassurance to counselees as to the qualifications of their counselor.

Personal space. How close the counselor and the counselee sit to each other is one aspect of personal space. It is worth noting that cultural factors will influence what is considered comfortable or normative in this domain (see "Multicultural Application" below). Within Western culture, the closer two people are in conversation, the more intimate or personal the conversation is perceived to be. In the United States, when two people are four to twelve feet apart, the conversation is generally perceived to be more of a professional or broadly social interaction, whereas under four feet is a more personal interaction, and less than eighteen inches implies a rather intimate conversation (Anderson & Ross, 1998). Within a counseling relationship, a distance of approximately three feet is preferable, when measured from one person's knees to the other person's knees (Young, 2009).

Gestures. Another area to pay attention to that is related to personal space is the use of gestures. Individuals who talk with their hands and arms nonverbally communicate a larger physical presence than those who speak with their arms at their sides. Gestures can at times be helpful—for example, they can be a way of adding emphasis to a message—but they can also be distracting or overwhelming for particular counselees (e.g., those who come from backgrounds of abuse or other trauma). Therefore it is best to be observant of how a counselee utilizes gestures and then match, or mirror, him or her in your use of gestures.

Touch. A good analogy for the use of touch in counseling is that of a power saw. When cutting down a decent-sized tree, a power saw is much more efficient and takes far less energy than using an axe. However, if you do not know how to properly use a power saw, you can severely injure yourself or someone else. Similarly, judicious use of touch can be immensely helpful in counseling, but it can also be harmful.

A sexual relationship of any kind with a counselee is strictly prohibited by all ethical codes in the mental health professions. But even if the counselor's touch has no sexual intent, it is easy for some counselees to misinterpret the meaning of touch. Sexual abuse survivors, for example, may not be able to differentiate touch that is intended to show compassion and touch that is sexual in nature.

While asking permission before touching a counselee is a good practice, a "yes" response does not necessarily indicate consent. Counselees who do not have a strong sense of self or feel little personal power may not be able to refuse, despite feelings of discomfort. Therefore you will need to carefully observe whether counselees' nonverbal cues confirm or deny their verbal assent.

Some counselors attempt to solve the dilemma by only touching counselees of the same gender as themselves. Such a stance, however, assumes heterosexuality; it does not take into account the possibility that a counselee may be confused about his or her sexual orientation or may identify as a homosexual.

One way to deal with these complexities is to just not touch counselees at all in order to avoid the possible traps. Unfortunately, this option closes the door to some of the benefits to counselees of using touch. For example, touch used appropriately can be healing for counselees who have only experienced touch as abusive or exploitive, helping them to begin to discern between healthy and unhealthy touch.

If you do decide that touch could be therapeutic with a particular counselee, we suggest the following guidelines:

1. Always ask permission to touch, but do not assume that an initial "yes" implies consent. Acknowledge that counselees may not be comfortable with touch and that it is okay for them to refuse.

2. Carefully observe the counselee's nonverbal responses to both your request and the touch itself.

3. If you do touch a counselee, always process with them what the experience was like so that you can determine whether it was helpful or not.

4. For your own protection against accusations of malpractice, it is a good idea to video-record sessions where touch is used.

5. Discuss the issue with your supervisor.

Energetic space. The concept of energetic space is both the most personal and the most abstract. It refers to the energy that you as a person carry into a room. One way to think about this concept is to use the analogy of an engine's RPMs. Some people go through their days revved up consistently high, while others exude a lower, more laid-back energy. Another way to think about energetic space is to consider how "big" or "small" a presence someone has. We have a well-loved colleague who fills a room with her "big" presence. She talks loudly, laughs loudly and exudes boundless energy. We definitely know when she is around (and miss her when she is not there!).

The amount of energetic space you take up may largely be due to personality temperament. There are some people who are simply more high strung or energetic, and the people around them can feel this. It is as if there is a whirlwind spinning around their bodies. Others have personalities that are rather subdued and naturally more understated, and it is as if the space around them is a soft, barely palpable breeze.

Energetic space can also be directly related to how anxious or comfortable individuals are with their own sense of self, or, within the helping context, how confident they are in their counseling role. Whatever the reason for the particular energetic space you take up when in your role as a counselor, it is important that you are aware of the energetic space that you take up in a room and that you are reflective about what contributes to that energy. Do you, for example, take up more or less energetic space when you are anxious? How would you describe the RPM levels that go on inside of you in an average interaction compared to a counseling interaction? The crucial question is, "How is the energy I'm exuding affecting this particular counselee?" If it is having a negative effect, you will need to make adjustments.

Volume of speech and speed of speech both affect the amount of energetic space you take up, making these areas you can specifically work at adapting. Our colleague with the "big presence" we referred to earlier works with extremely emotionally wounded individuals, so she intentionally softens her tone and slows down her speech so as not to overwhelm such counselees. Large gestures also contribute to a sense of largeness of presence and energetic space, so they too can be toned down. Similarly, if your counselee's energetic space has the effect of overriding your therapeutic contribution, you can work at speaking more loudly and more quickly, as well as using more expansive gestures. If you cannot adapt sufficiently, you may need to consider referring the counselee to someone more compatible.

If you are uncertain about what you show to others, start asking those around you about their perceptions of you. Listen for patterns or repeated comments and themes that others provide, and then consider whether the nonverbal messages you are sending are congruent with who you see yourself to be and how you feel, and whether those are the messages you want to be sending to counselees.

S.O.L.E.R.

Part of the science of attending that comes out in what you show to counselees has to do with the specific ways in which you position and move your body within a counseling conversation. This science of attending is abbreviated by the acronym S.O.L.E.R. (Egan, 2014, pp. 77-78), which stands for:

- sit **Squarely**
- maintain an **Open** posture
- at times, **Lean** in
- demonstrate appropriate **Eye** contact
- **Relax**

In chapter one we compared learning microskills to the driving school instructions to keep your hands at the 10-and-2 position on the steering wheel at all times, when in reality many of us drive one-handed. S.O.L.E.R. serves as your 10-and-2 of attending. When the terrain is unfamiliar, when the conditions are dire or when the counselor is tired, this is the posture to acquire. Without practice it will not feel familiar or comfortable, but with practice it will teach your body that "When I'm in this posture I'm focused and paying attention." While someday you may be able to comfortably "drive one-handed," we strongly suggest that for the remainder of this course you remain in S.O.L.E.R. for every counseling conversation, role-play or small group activity in order to train your body to attend in a way that does eventually feel comfortable for you while at the same time creating a comfortable environment for your counselees.

Sitting squarely means that you, as the counselor, position your body to face the counselee as if there are parallel lines running from your shoulders to her shoulders, and from your hips to her hips. You should have an upright posture, with your back straight and your shoulders back. Sitting squarely communicates to the counselee that you are present and that you are focusing your attention on him. This posture also helps prevent you from getting distracted by peripheral activity.

In actuality it may be helpful not to face your counselee quite straight-on but rather to angle the chairs slightly so that the counselee can look into space while thinking, but with just a slight shift of the head can meet your gaze. We would still consider this position "sitting squarely."

Maintaining an *open posture* means that your arms are at your sides, possibly resting on your thighs, and that both feet are set firmly on the ground. No limbs are to be crossed, as this can communicate being closed or guarded. We actually recommend that effectively nothing is crossed, including not folding your hands in your lap (effectively crossing fingers across one another) and not crossing your ankles, at least while you are in the training process. For many people this is a very unnatural position, as it leaves them feeling exposed and vulnerable, which is exactly why it is in the best interest of counselees for counselors to learn to be comfortable in this posture.

There is a time and a place to *lean in* to the conversation. This movement generally takes place as a nonverbal way to close the gap between the counselor and the counselee, often taking place when the counselee's emotion increases or the story the counselee is telling intensifies, or as a way of nonverbally offering reassurance to the counselee that the counselor is present with her at that moment. I (Elisabeth) once had a supervisor who referred to leaning in as a "nonphysical hug." It is important that the counselor does not start from the lean-in position, as there is then no way to step closer in to the counselee's story if it intensifies. Be selective in when you choose to lean back and return to S.O.L.E.R., as an ill-timed lean back can be perceived as disengaging from the counselee and his or her story.

Clinical Tips

Regularly video-recording yourself while you are in the counselor role can be eye-opening. When you review the recording, look for the following:

1. Is your facial expression congruent with what you intended to convey at that moment?

2. Do you notice yourself exhibiting any distracting mannerisms?

3. Are you using S.O.L.E.R.?

4. Does your counselee seem to misinterpret your body language?

Eye contact is likely the most culturally influenced element of S.O.L.E.R. and should therefore be treated accordingly. Within Western culture, maintaining steady but not fixated eye contact is a sign of engagement with and respect for the person with whom you are speaking. Conversely, in Native American culture, steady eye contact can be perceived as disrespectful and threatening (Garwick, 2000). Regardless of cultural norms, what is critical is that when a counselee looks to find you with his eyes, your eyes are there for them to connect with. I (Heather) knew a survivor of sexual abuse who did not make eye contact with her counselor for six months because of the intense shame she felt. However, out of her peripheral vision she could see that her counselor's eyes were on her. This reassured her that when she did make the courageous move to lift her eyes, she would meet the caring gaze of her counselor. Your default, then, should be to maintain eye contact, allowing the counselee to decide whether or not to break eye contact.

Now that we have encouraged you to change your posture and have asked you to sit in a way that is likely not how you hang out with friends over coffee, we are going to remind you to *relax*. It is rather impossible to execute this element of S.O.L.E.R. if the other four elements have not become second nature to you, and that requires practice. While a few of you may already sit in S.O.L.E.R., most of you will need to take the remainder of this course practicing in and outside class before relaxing will be a regular part of this posture, but we promise it does come!

WHEN WORDS ARE NOT *REALLY* WORDS

In most languages there are space-filling phrases that are technically words, but both the speaker and the listener interpret them as nonverbal messages. In English we call these *minimal encouragers*, and in the counseling relationship they are used by the counselor as road signs to the counselee. We consider them an attending skill, as they do not actually contribute verbally to the content of the counseling interaction but instead serve as signposts along the way, demonstrating the counselor's ability to listen and track with (attend to) the counselee. In English, examples of minimal encouragers are:

"Uh huh."

"Mmhmm."

"Yeah/yes."

"Go on."

"Huh."

"Oh."

"Right."

"Okay."

The key to minimal encouragers is that they are to be used *minimally*, so as to not interrupt or distract from what the counselee is saying. As with any other attending skill, it is important for the counselor to take note of how the counselee is perceiving the behavior and to adjust accordingly. For example, when minimal encouragers are perceived to be attempts at interrupting the counselee, male counselees are more likely to perceive the interruption as an attempt to control or direct the conversation, where women are more likely to perceive the interruption as a gesture of support (Wood, 1995). As the name implies, minimal encouragers are designed to provide encouragement to the counselee that she is being heard, but to do so in a way that does not distract or interrupt from the flow of the story (Young, 2009).

THE INTERNAL ASPECTS OF ATTENDING: WHAT YOU BRING

Beneath what you show counselees is what you bring within your own person. These are the things that happen under the surface in your mind and in your heart. They are more art than science, because there is no formula, no script and no fail-proof test to say whether you are or are not doing them correctly. But, true to any art, experts in the field can identify good art and bad art, and while there is no empirical test, good art and good attending are intuitively known by their observers.

You bring your head. While much of attending has to do with how a counselor communicates nonverbally through environment and physicality, a large part of attending also has to do with how a counselor thinks about the counseling process. For example, the *attitudes* that a counselor brings into the counseling relationship can significantly influence her ability to attend to the counselee. In terms of attitudes regarding the perceived role of the counselor, whether you see the counselor's role as one to fix, help, facilitate or guide changes the attitude with which you approach a counselee. Attitudes about how or why people seek counseling also contribute to your ability to attend; do people come for counseling because they are "broken," "wounded," "stuck," "crazy" or "utilizing resources"?

Gazda et al. (2005) introduce the concept of *verbal villains*, which are things that counselors say in an attempt to be helpful but which inevitably only serve to negate or minimize the counselee's emotions. We would like to take Gazda et al.'s concept of verbal villains one step further and consider that what comes out in spoken form ultimately starts as a thought that reflects how the counselor is approaching or attending to the counseling relationship. Ultimately, they reflect the counselor's attitude toward problem solving. As we explore different types of verbal villains, consider the following questions for each one:

1. Whom do you know who utilizes this particular verbal villain in their interpersonal or helping conversations? How do you feel when they respond in such a way?

2. What is likely the positive intent of the counselor who approaches a counselee or a counselee's story from this perspective?

3. In what ways could this verbal villain be ineffective or harmful to a counseling relationship?

4. Provide an example of what this might sound like in a real-life conversation.

The following list (based on Gazda et al., 2005, pp. 62-67) is not exhaustive, so we encourage you to identify or create the verbal villain persona that most aptly reflects who you are. Because verbal villains generally come from a well-intended, even if misguided, place within the counselor, it is our belief that every person has at least one verbal villain that, if left unchecked, can arise in conversation.

◆ *The coach* effectively tries to get the counselee to "walk it off" by staying busy and following the regimen for recovery that the coach gives, emphasizing the importance of keeping active and pushing forward.

◆ *The detective (AKA the journalist)* focuses exclusively on the content of a counselee's story, wanting to know the who, what, when, where and why. Feelings are neglected or even completely ignored in the name of getting all the facts or details of the story.

◆ *The diagnostician* believes that if a problem can be labeled, then it is effectively solved, requiring no further action or explanation.

◆ *The doctor* attempts to diagnose the problem (like the diagnostician) and then prescribe a solution. "Take two aspirin and call me in the morning" offers overly simplistic directives without much personal connection.

- *The florist* seeks to find and affirm the good in the counselee, using compliments, optimism and positivity in order to keep emotional distance from the unpleasantness of the counselee's story.

- *The guru* responds to counselee emotion and stories with clichés or, within Christian contexts, may implement Bible verses and proverbs in the same manner.

- *The hangman* effectively blames the counselee and his past behavior for the situation or problem at hand, identifying what he should or should not have done in order to have altered the course of events.

- *The historian* attempts to relate with and connect to the counselee by using self-disclosure and telling stories about their own life rather than listening to and offering true empathy for the counselee's story.

- *The (un)holy spirit* speaks as if he knows what the future will hold, knows how others in the counselee's life will respond or knows what will or will not, or should or should not, happen in the counselee's life.

- *The magician* tries to make the counselee's problem disappear, negating its significance or even its existence.

- _____ is the title of my personal verbal villain.

- My personal verbal villain can be described as: _____
  _____
  _____

See appendix B for a "Try It Out" activity related to verbal villains.

You bring your heart. In addition to what is going on in your thoughts, much of attending has to do with what is going on in your heart and how you feel in the room with the counselee. This is, at its essence, the art of human presence. *Human presence* is the relational quality of attending and being present in heart and mind, not just in physical body. We would venture that all of us have had a conversation with another person in which we thought, "I know you are physically here with me, but I feel like you are a hundred miles away." That is a case of someone not being present to you.

On the other side, we would hope that each of you has had at least one conversation in your life in which you walked away feeling as if you had the full and undivided attention of the person with whom you were talking. That is human presence. We cannot teach you to have presence; it is fully art. We can encourage you, though, to identify someone in your life who has good presence and watch them so that you can model yourself after him or her. When we think of someone with good human presence, we think not just of the description above but of some tangible qualities as well. People who are present sit comfortably in S.O.L.E.R., as if they could be there all day; they give the impression that there is nothing in their minds or weighing on their hearts other than the well-being of the counselee. All electronic devices are silenced, put away and functionally do not exist within that conversation. Counselors who are fully present have also learned to silence the potentially distracting, chattering noises in their heads, knowing that they will be focused on in good time. This too takes practice and, more specifically, discipline.

Two other characteristics contribute to human presence: Authenticity and warmth. *Authenticity* (discussed more thoroughly in chapter twelve) is the quality of being genuine or congruent. In essence it means that who you are and what you feel on the inside is reflected in who you are on the outside; there is no deception or falsehood in how you present yourself to a counselee. Ultimately, as we grow in self-awareness, we also grow in our ability to be authentic. It is impossible to be truly present when you are attempting to present yourself in a way that is misleading or inauthentic to your true self.

Warmth is the quality of nonverbally communicating caring to the counselee through means such as tone, posture, facial expressions and other nonverbal mediums. Warmth is rarely a characteristic that is felt in isolation; it is often accompanied by respect, empathy and authenticity. As a part of human presence, a warm counselor brings an attentiveness with their eyes, facial expressions, body posture and gestures to the counseling relationship and nonverbally creates an environment between the counselor and the counselee that is inviting, comforting and safe. A genuine smile from the counselor can be an example of communicating warmth to the counselee. An inauthentically warm counselor is quickly perceived by the counselee as untrustworthy, unsafe and disrespectful—just like sitting by a picture of a fire is not the same as sitting by the fire itself. Similar to the physical quality of warmth, the opposite of a warm counselor is one who comes across as "cold" or "icy," "uninviting" or "sharp." We will talk in more detail about the art of being fully present with a counselee in chapter seven, "Connecting Empathically."

» Whom do you know with good human presence?

» How do you experience his or her presence?

» What physical image do you see when you think about warmth that could serve as a metaphor for the emotional quality of warmth?

» What image or metaphor might you use to describe the concept of authenticity to someone not in this class?

Values are the principles you hold about what is important in life. You likely have values about money, what makes a healthy relationship, how time is spent, what it means to be a "good person" and any host of other topics. Your values are informed by your personality, your past experiences, your family of origin, your faith system and the culture in which you grew up. They are included in your "heart" because values often go beyond logical conclusions and encapsulate that which has become significant to you through thoughts, feelings and experiences. It is impossible to conduct "value-free" counseling (Richards & Bergin, 2005), but it is imperative that counselors learn to identify their own values and so have more control over how and when those values are expressed to counselees (ACA, 2014). Specifically, if counselors are aware of their own values around various topics, they are less likely to impose those values onto their counselees and more likely to be able to respect their counselees' right to have their own values, separate from the counselor's.

Biblical/Theological Connections

In the book of Psalms there are many references to our faces reflecting our emotions, including our feelings toward ourselves, others and God. Many times the phrase "hiding our face" is used, and often it is associated with hiding our face in shame (e.g., Ps 44:15). We are encouraged to seek God's face (e.g., Ps 27:8) and to rejoice when his face shines on us (e.g., Ps 104:15). The face, as well as other parts of our body, manners and even clothing, reveal our internal condition, but the problem is that we are frequently unaware of what we are communicating nonverbally.

Socially attuned adults are often pretty skilled at "reading between the lines," at sensing what is the truth behind the words. We pick up the hints conveyed by others about their deeper emotions, and in some segments of society these skills are highly valued, for instance in working with criminals. However, in counseling, these skills are only justified in their use if we first attend to our own nonverbal expression. For Christians, Jesus' mandate is clear: "Why do you look at the speck of sawdust in your brother's eye and pay no attention to the plank in your own eye? How can you say to your brother, 'Let me take the speck out of your eye,' when all the time there is a plank in your own eye? You hypocrite, first take the plank out of your own eye, and then you will see clearly to remove the speck from your brother's eye" (Mt 7:3-5).

In regard to attending, values come into play in the counselor's ability to truly be present with a counselee whose values are either very aligned with the counselor's or different from the counselor's. When a counselee's values differ greatly from the counselor's it can be difficult for the counselor to remain present and attend to the counselee, as his mind is constantly trying to create a framework for why and how a counselee sees the world in a particular way. Unless the counselor has done his own work in understanding the development of his own values, this process can be very distracting and hinder the attending process. In the case that the counselor is comfortable with differing values, this can actually increase the counselor's ability to attend, as he will be more focused on the nuances of what the counselee has to say—both verbally and nonverbally. Conversely, though, when a counselee and a counselor have very similar values, a counselor can become lazy and inattentive because the counselor assumes he knows where the counselee is coming from without truly taking in all the messages that the counselee is sharing. Regardless of whether you as a counselor have aligned or very disparate values from a counselee, the presence of values will influence your attending.

Bringing head and heart together. Ultimately, a counselor's head and heart come together in the joining of her attitude and values as they are expressed in respect to a counselee. From a counseling perspective, this is similar to what Rogers (1961/1992) referred to as "unconditional positive regard," which he defined in the following way:

> When the therapist is experiencing a warm, positive and acceptant attitude toward what *is* in the client, this facilitates change. It involves the therapist's genuine willingness for the client to be whatever feeling is going on in him at that moment—fear, confusion, pain, pride, anger, hatred, love, courage, or awe. It means that the therapist cares for the client, in a non-possessive way. It means that he prizes the client in a total rather than a conditional way. By this I mean that he does not simply accept the client when he is behaving in certain ways, and disapprove of him when he behaves in other ways. It means an outgoing positive feeling without reservations, without evaluations. The term we have come to use for this is unconditional positive regard. Again research studies show that the more this attitude is experienced by the therapist, the more likelihood there is that therapy will be successful. (p. 62)

Young (2009) summarizes this concept by explaining that "positive regard does not mean that helpers must approve of every client behavior. Rather, the helper must respect the personhood of each client and believe that all persons have inherent worth" (p. 20). This aligns very well with the Christian idea of seeing and honoring the *imago Dei*, the image of God, within each person. Whether counselees are Christians or not, they, too, have been made in the image of God and deserve to be treated with the same honor as anyone else (Gen 1:27).

A counselor does not have to like or agree with the decisions a counselee has made or is making, but a large part of respect is the ability to recognize and honor the freedom and choices that God has given to all people (yourself included). A counselor's ability to respect, or recognize the *imago Dei*, within a counselee can significantly influence her ability to attend. If a counselor respects a counselee, she is more likely to be present and focused in her attending abilities, whereas a counselor who does not respect her counselee is likely to be unable to be fully present and attend to the counselee. Not respecting a counselee is likely to also affect the counselor's ability to perceive, and therefore attend to, the counselee accurately.

Some counselees will be easier for you to respect than others. For example, I (Heather) initially have a much easier time showing unconditional positive regard to victims of abuse than I do perpetrators of abuse. Recognizing that many perpetrators have themselves been victimized helps me to look beyond their horrific behavior to where they themselves carry pain and fear. I also tend to react negatively to individuals who come across as narcissistic or entitled. In order to successfully work with such people, I have to remind myself that Christ loves them as much as he loves individuals to whom I am more naturally drawn. If you are not able to authentically care for a counselee at some level, you will not likely be able to be of help.

Who you are as a counselor, particularly your values, attitudes and ability to respect counselees, will affect your ability to accurately attend to your counselees. If you find yourself struggling with any of these areas, consider reviewing chapter two and some of the activities suggested therein, talking with a professor or supervisor or becoming a counselee yourself in order to explore possible roadblocks.

MULTICULTURAL APPLICATION

In the previous chapter we discussed how both verbal and nonverbal behavior can be easily misinterpreted by counselors who are in a helping relationship with a counselee of a different cultural background. The same can be true in reverse: a counselee can easily misinterpret your attending behaviors. You will not be able to change everything about your communication style. A more realistic goal is to at least have the knowledge that you may be misread and that you may need to adjust your behavior to some degree. Certainly you can broach the subject that misinterpretation can be expected and that you desire to clear up any potential misunderstandings (Day-Vines et al., 2007). The counselor is often seen as an authority figure, which in some cultures may hamper the counselee's ability to be direct about such matters. Therefore it may be up to you to initiate such discussions (see chapter twelve, "Using the Here and Now"), giving your counselees lots of permission to be up front while also recognizing that it may be very difficult for them to be honest with you because of their cultural norms. Good multicultural perceiving skills (see chapter three) will help you know whether your attending behavior is appropriate for the context. However, given the complexities of perceiving crossculturally, you may need to regularly seek confirmation that your meaning is clear to your counselee.

Appropriate ways to greet someone vary among cultures. Therefore, if you know ahead of time that you are seeing someone from a culture you are not familiar with, you could do a brief internet search to make it less likely that you will offend your new counselee before you even leave the waiting area. For instance, in some Muslim cultures shaking hands with the left hand would be considered a grave insult (Sue & Sue, 2016).

As mentioned earlier, physical proximity varies among cultures. While living in the Philippines, I (Heather) once had a very distraught client enter my counseling office for the first time, bury her head in my lap and sob! While this was unusual even for that culture, I think it is highly unlikely that even a very upset Caucasian would do the same in Canada or the United States. Although in highly relational cultures such as the Philippines, the counselee will likely prefer sitting in closer proximity to the counselor than would be true in more individually focused cultures, ultimately you as the counselor need to feel comfortable with a given physical proximity so that your discomfort does not end up negatively affecting the therapeutic relationship.

As mentioned earlier, the meaning of eye contact also varies among individuals from different cultures. We suggest the following rule of thumb: you as the counselor should keep your gaze on your counselees, allowing them to make the decision to glance away or make no eye contact at all if they wish. If you get to know another cultural group well enough to recognize that this would not be appropriate, of course you should adjust. You will need to be careful not to misinterpret the meaning of lack of eye contact on the part of a counselee from a different culture from yours.

When conducting play therapy crossculturally, counselors need to consider which toys are appropriate for the context. Play-therapy kits that are manufactured for a Western context will not likely work well in countries where children have never been exposed to such toys or where the toys are not culturally relevant. For example, the typical dollhouse that would be part of a play therapy room in Canada or the United States would be nonsensical for a child living in a house made of bamboo with woven banana leaves for a roof! Makeshift toys such as cut-out dolls, sticks, stones, pebbles or feathers are more likely to be helpful as counseling aids.

CONCLUSION

Utilizing nonverbal communication, attending provides the first messages sent from counselor to counselee. Attending skills include body language, facial expressions and the emotion or intentions that you as the counselor bring to the counseling relationship. As you continue to build on your counseling skills, remember to pay attention to how you use nonverbal communication to express your presence to the counselee.

REFLECTION QUESTIONS

1. Which verbal villain do you find yourself gravitating to the most? Why do you think that is?

2. If you didn't know you, how would you describe your resting face?

3. Which types of counselees do you think you might have the most trouble having a respectful attitude toward (e.g., counselees who are perpetrators of abuse, or are belligerent, angry, self-deprecating, dependent, narcissistic, etc.)?

4. What values or beliefs do you currently hold about others that may hinder your ability to attend well? What are some specific steps that you can take to further explore these values and beliefs and their impact on the counseling relationship?

IDENTIFYING THE PIECES OF THE STORY

*Whoever can be trusted with very little
can also be trusted with much.*

LUKE 16:10

CHAPTER FOCUS

SKILL: reflecting content

PURPOSE: to verbally summarize back to the counselee the content, or facts, of what they said

FORMULA: In other words, _____.
What I'm hearing you say is _____.
To wrap things up, when you came in today you said you wanted to talk about
_____, and then we also explored _____.

» Who in your life tends to remember key details or events in your life (i.e., the person that calls to see how an appointment went, when you only mentioned it in passing)?

» What do you feel when someone remembers details about your life?

"Tell me what happened." Perhaps you have been in situations where all you were looking for, all you initially needed, was for another person to hear your experience and understand the facts of what you had been through. The sense of safety and freedom, and the experience of being cared for that can result from another human seeking to understand the facts of the event as it unfolded, can often be a critical first step to individuals uncovering what they feel about a situation, let alone what to do about it. Conversely, you may have experienced frustration at someone jumping in to offer premature solutions or making false assumptions before taking the time and care necessary to hear and understand your perception of what transpired.

Reflecting content serves to lay the foundation of mutual understanding between counselor and counselee before proceeding into more personal or intimate parts of the counselee's story. It is the foundation on which reflecting feeling and empathic

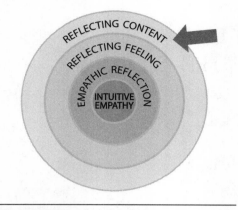

reflection (which will be fully discussed in future chapters) are based. In figure 5.1 we see the progression of reflecting skills, starting with reflecting content. While each reflecting skill brings the counselor and counselee closer to the heart of the counselee's story, it does not mean that landing in one of the outer rings is not necessary or beneficial. For some counselees, it will be important for rapport building to take the circles one at a time.

Figure 5.1. Aiming for reflecting content

WHAT IS CONTENT, AND HOW IS IT REFLECTED?

"Just the facts, ma'am." This phrase, often attributed to the 1950s television show *Dragnet*, succinctly captures the essence of the skill of reflecting content. All that is being asked of the counselor is to hear and reflect back to the counselee the who, what,

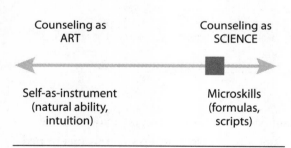

when, where and how of his story. Note that the why of the story is not generally included in this reflecting skill, as it can be considered interpretive unless the counselee directly states the why to the counselor.

Another way of conceptualizing the skill of reflecting content is to think of it as paraphrasing. When

Figure 5.2. Art versus science: Reflecting content

you paraphrase what has been said to you, you are choosing to reflect back the main elements of someone's story. In this skill, you are not required to reflect back everything that the counselee said, nor are you required to say it back exactly as he said it—that would be parroting. You are also not reflecting back the counselee's feelings. Instead, you are striving to hear the most important facts, as understood by the counselee, and say them back in order to confirm your understanding of his situation. Reflecting content can also be thought of as identifying the salient features of the *context* of the counselee's felt experience. Without an idea of the context, it is difficult to understand the emotional reactions or the behavior of the counselee.

Response Sentence Stems

✓ It sounds like . . .

✓ It might be that . . .

✓ It seems as though . . .

✓ If I'm hearing you correctly . . .

✓ It's almost like . . .

The formula for how to reflect content is: "In other words _____ " or "What I'm hearing you say is _____."

Reflecting Content Is

✓ paraphrasing

✓ summarizing the key facts

✓ identifying the context

There can be alternate beginning "stems" for the formula, but they all have the function of leading into a reflection (see "Response Sentence Stems" sidebar). For an example of how the formula can be used, let's say that a counselee comes into your office and says the following:

Counselee: Oh my goodness, it was such a busy weekend! My best friend from college flew in from out of state, and we just spent the whole time going from one activity to another. On Friday I picked her up from the airport, and we went straight to my favorite dinner spot, and after that to this amazing jazz bar downtown. Then Saturday we did brunch at this delicious local place that I love and then went to an art exhibit that we were both dying to see. By the time Saturday evening rolled around we had caught up on so much and had such a great time, but we were really exhausted, so we decided to just order in pizza and watch a movie. Sunday we went to church in the morning, and I got to introduce my college friend to all my local friends—I love when my worlds collide! It was just such a wonderful weekend!

If you, as the counselor, were to reflect content it might sound something like:

Counselor Response Option 1: In other words, your best friend from college was in town this weekend and you two got to spend a lot of time together doing things you really love.

Counselor Response Option 2: What I'm hearing you say is that you got to spend this weekend with your best friend from college doing everything from eating well to exploring the city to just having time talking and being together.

Note that in both counselor response options the reflection only addresses the content of the counselee's story and does not include how the counselee *feels* about the weekend. Also, the responses are not elaborate or overly wordy but instead seek to summarize or paraphrase the key elements of the counselee's story.

Try It Out

Using the following counselee statement, identify the content of the story:

Counselee: Last night was my final dance recital for the year. My dad said he was going to come, but at the last minute he texted my mom to say he wasn't going to make it. It's the third time this month that he's promised to be somewhere but then didn't come. I didn't find out that he wasn't there until after the recital, which was good because I really did do a good job and I'm afraid I would have messed up more if I'd known he'd bailed again.

What's the content? Identify all of the following that you can (see appendix A for possible answers):

Who (who is involved in this story? list them all):

_____

_____

What (what took place?):

_____

_____

When (when did these events occur?):

_____

_____

Where (where did this story take place?):

_____

_____

How (how did these event take place or come to be?)

_____

_____

Now that you have identified all the key facts of the counselee's story, put them together as to reflect content in one concise sentence.

_____

_____

_____

Counselor: _____

_____

THE PURPOSE OF REFLECTING CONTENT

Reflecting content is not a skill that most people use as a regular part of casual conversation. It is instead more of a therapeutic skill used to hold the dialogue together. It is like the toothpick that holds a hamburger or sandwich together: Although the toothpick is not the main focus of the meal, it serves an important function. Similarly, reflecting content holds the therapeutic dialogue together and sets the stage for other types of interventions. The skill of reflecting content serves two main purposes:

1. to help both the counselee and the counselor make sure the basic facts of the counselee's story are jointly understood, and

2. to clarify or make sense of what the counselee has shared without having to ask a direct question (Ivey, Ivey & Zalaquett, 2014).

Empirical Support

The value of reflecting content is seen throughout the literature and within various domains of counseling (Egan, 2014; Ivey, Ivey & Zalaquett, 2014; McCarthy, 2014; Taylor, 1980). Reflecting content is also referred to as summarizing or paraphrasing. Regardless of its label, this skill allows for the facts of the counselee's story and the context of the problem to feel heard, which serves to help the counselor join with the counselee. As Ivey, Ivey and Zalaquett (2014) state, "Accurate paraphrasing can help clients complete their storytelling" (p. 158). McCarthy (2014) demonstrates that the use of microskills, including the use of paraphrasing, was "positively correlated with successful client outcomes" (p. 3).

Being able to accurately and concisely reflect content back to the counselee functions as a way for the counselor to earn the right to engage with the counselee at a deeper and more personal level. It shows that you, as the counselor, have heard the counselee and therefore can be trusted as the story goes deeper. Building on Jesus' language in Luke 16:10, "whoever can be trusted with little [such as boring facts] can also be trusted with much [such as deep and vulnerable feelings, motives and hurts]."

WHAT REFLECTING CONTENT IS *NOT*

Reflecting content, although very simple, can also be very difficult because it is not a common way of communicating in casual conversation. It is important to recognize that reflecting content is *not*:

Biblical/Theological Connections

"Just the facts, please." We hear versions of this phrase all around us. Especially in the legal system, there is a strong desire to clear away the cobwebs of extraneous opinions and emotional reactions and get to the true facts of the story. This is what happens in counseling too. Facts, feelings, opinions and values all get messed up with one another and are hard to sort out. This is no easier for Christians than for those who do not claim faith in God. It is not like God automatically gives us the ability to discern the truth. The New Testament says we are to know the truth, seek the truth, live by the truth, speak the truth, teach the truth, worship in truth, share the truth, rejoice in the truth and obey the truth. The facts matter and need to be sought and clarified. In addition, the promise is made in John 8:32 that the truth will set us free.

But ultimately in the New Testament the truth is described as a person. Jesus states, "I am the way and the truth and the life" (Jn 14:6). Truth comes to life in a relationship with the one who is true. This is why we are told to share the truth in love (Eph 4:15). Biblical truth and theological principles are always revealed and shared through the lens of the person of Jesus. Following in his way, with integrity, justice, mercy and grace (Mt 9:13; 12:18; 26:16; Jn 1:14, 17), takes harshness and possible insensitivity out of the equation. It is the emotional component of who we are, and who Jesus is, that allows the content, the details of our lives, our story, to become real and life giving.

◆ *void of emotion:* Often students seek to add to their reflections of content because of how flat or emotionally detached it can seem. It is because of this that the use of nonverbal communication when reflecting content becomes of critical importance, as it is especially in tone and facial expressions that a counselor can communicate connection and caring, even if all he or she is doing is verbalizing content.

◆ *parroting:* Parroting takes place when the counselor says back to the counselee what she has heard, word for word and tone for tone. There are times when reflecting content will repeat many of the counselee's words, but it is important that the counselor then pay particular attention to his tone of voice and nonverbal messages so as to avoid sounding condescending or mocking.

◆ *curiosity seeking:* Reflecting content needs to focus on the facts that the counselee finds important rather than the details you find intriguing. Your reflections need to be about what facilitates the counselee's process and not simply on what you find interesting or want to know out of your own curiosity.

Diagnostic Implications

There are a number of psychological disorders where counselees' narratives of their life journey and circumstances are problematic. Those suffering a psychotic disorder are out of touch with reality. For those with schizophrenia, for example, the terms *word salad* or *disorganized speech* are used to describe words or phrases that are spoken but not coherent or connected in any meaningful way. Reflecting content is almost impossible in these situations. For others, the narrative is more cohesive, but the content is problematic (e.g., when paranoia or magical thinking is involved). Delusions (thinking disturbances) and hallucinations (perceptual or sensory disturbances) are also common symptoms of psychosis.

While reflecting content traditionally has not been used with psychotic individuals for fear of reinforcing symptoms, some authors have suggested that reflecting can be a way to connect with such counselees, thereby both building the therapeutic alliance and attempting to understand their subjective experience (see the fictional account of a counselee with schizophrenia in *I Never Promised You a Rose Garden* [Green, 1964/2004]).

Anytime Activity

Find the facts (see appendix A for possible answers). In the following vignettes, underline the content of the counselee's story. Then reflect content using one of the formulas provided in this chapter:

"What I'm hearing you say is _____."

"In other words, _____."

Vignette 1:

Counselee: Oh my goodness, you would not believe the weekend I've had! It was just the best! On Friday my best friend surprised me and flew into town for my thirtieth birthday. We went to my favorite restaurant for dinner, and then Saturday we got to go to breakfast before spending the day hiking. Then in the evening my best friend had arranged for a group of friends to all meet at my favorite restaurant for dinner and karaoke. It was just an amazing weekend!

Counselor:

_____

_____

Vignette 2:

Counselee: I just don't know what I'm going to do. I found out yesterday that my company is downsizing. My boss informed me that at least half of our department will be without a job by the end of the year. I don't know what to do.

Counselor:

_____

_____

Vignette 3:

Counselee: Prom is in two weeks, and I'm *so* excited! Jack asked me to be his date, and I couldn't be happier. I bought this beautiful blue dress with sequins; it makes my eyes really shine. Jack and I are going to double-date with my friend Kate and her boyfriend, Zach. It's going to be the best night ever!

Counselor: _____

_____

Vignette 4:

Counselee: Tomorrow's football game is going to be really important. My coach has said that scouts from three major universities are coming to check me out. This game could mean the difference between a college scholarship or working through school.

Counselor: _____

_____

Vignette 5:

Counselee: Next week I'm going to China on a business trip. I've never been to Asia before, and I'm kind of nervous, I'm not quite sure what to expect. Plus, this is a really big deal for our company, and I want to make sure everything goes according to plan.

Counselor: _____

_____

CONCLUDING THE CONVERSATION WITH A REFLECTION OF CONTENT

Reflecting content is a skill used throughout a counseling relationship, but it becomes particularly important at the beginning and at the end of the conversation. We have discussed how at the beginning it is used to affirm that the counselor has heard and understood the facts of the counselee's story. This in turn helps counselees gain a greater understanding of the details for themselves. Reflecting content also has a very important role at the end of a counseling session or conversation, as it serves the function of being a summary of what the counselor and the counselee discussed in their time together. A sample formula for this summary statement might sound like: "To wrap things up, when you came in today you said you wanted to talk about _____, and then we also explored _____."

Taking time at the end of a counseling conversation to summarize what has been discussed helps both the counselor and the counselee leave the conversation with clarity and closure. It also serves as a confirmation to both participants of what was discussed and can cast vision for what may be explored next time. This in part reflects content but also adds an additional element. A sample formula for this type of summary reflection might be something like: "Today we explored _____. And, in light of that, we'll likely pick up there next time and continue discussing _____."

Whether viewed as the bookends of the counseling conversation or as the toothpick that holds everything together, reflecting content is a critical component to effective counseling.

Check Your Understanding

For the following exchanges, identify the "best" reflection of content given what you now know about reflecting content. Rate each response as additive, comparable or subtractive and provide an explanation as to why that response earned that rating. Author ratings and explanations can be found in appendix A. Note that a response can be simultaneously additive and subtractive.

✓ An additive response includes excessive content or adds to the counselee's story in some way.
✓ A comparable response appropriately summarizes the important content of the counselee's story without adding or leaving out key facts.
✓ A subtractive response neglects to reflect key factual content within the counselee's story.

1. Counselee: I am just swirling with so many different emotions. My brother got arrested for drug possession last night. It's the third time he's been arrested, and I just don't know that he'll ever turn his life around.

Counselor:

a. Your brother got arrested last night for the third time.

Rating: _____

Explanation: _____

_____

b. You're worried about your brother getting arrested.

Rating: _____

Explanation: _____

_____

c. Your brother has a serious problem with his drug use.

Rating: _____

Explanation: _____

_____

d. Yesterday was a hard day.

Rating: _____

Explanation: _____

_____

2. Counselee: You won't believe everything that happened since I saw you last! My best friend decided to move from out-of-state to just down the road from me, plus I got a promotion at work, and I won a vacation from the radio station! It's like every area of life is perfect right now.

Counselor:

a. What I'm hearing you say is that a lot's happened since I saw you last.

Rating: _____

Explanation: _____

_____

b. In other words, in a very short period of time something wonderful has happened in multiple areas of your life!

Rating: _____

Explanation: _____

_____

c. A lot of good things happened since I saw you last, but you still don't have a boyfriend.

Rating: _____

Explanation: _____

_____

d. Your life is perfect.

Rating: _____

Explanation: _____

_____

MULTICULTURAL APPLICATION

Reflecting content is a skill that can be useful in most crosscultural situations. Unlike reflecting feeling, which could be potentially problematic with counselees from some cultural backgrounds (see chapter six), reflecting content can be a relatively safe way of connecting with counselees and helping them to feel understood. Another advantage of reflecting content is that if you have not actually grasped your counselee's meaning, a situation that is more likely to come up with a counselee who is from a different culture than you, there is opportunity for the counselee to give you feedback and for you to get clarification as to what is the intended message.

The main danger we see in using this skill crossculturally is that in some cultures it is disrespectful to correct an authority figure. A counselee from such a culture may hesitate to give you the feedback that you are off track, and you might continue on oblivious to your error. If this pattern repeated itself, the helping relationship would obviously suffer.

RELATIONSHIP APPLICATION

In most "real life" relationships reflecting content is primarily used at the beginning of a friendship or the beginning of a complex story. Facts and details are easier to share than personal emotions and facts. As you get to know someone and become familiar with the key people and the ongoing situations in his or her life, reflecting content becomes less and less important as much of the content of the conversation is already mutually understood. However, there are times when the details of a story are complex or the facts need extra attention, and in these situations coming back to content and reflecting content can be of significant value.

In our culture, there is a lot of joking about gender differences, much of which is either very weakly supported by research or so exaggerated that it is of little value. One such supposed gender difference is that women prefer to hear all of the details of a story ("tell me all the details"), whereas men just want to get the end of the story ("tell me what happened!"). Whether or not this is true in terms of the particular counselee you are working with, it does raise the issue of differences in how much people want to spend time telling, listening and exploring the content of a story. In general, we need enough content in counseling to know how the situation or person affected the counselee. It is not the details that matter so much as it is how people, particularly the counselee, were affected.

MINISTRY APPLICATION

Reflecting content can be invaluable in all kinds of ministry settings. Perhaps its greatest value is in confirming that you have heard the other person's intended meaning. In congregational meetings or committee meetings, for example, tensions can rapidly escalate when people misunderstand each other. The group facilitator is in an excellent position to reflect content for clarification; however, others in the group can also use this skill when necessary.

Similarly, it is essential that pastors, mentors and spiritual directors ensure that they are accurately hearing what the individual to whom they are ministering is communicating, whatever the context (e.g., making wedding plans or funeral arrangements, determining what a directee's desires are for his or her relationship to God, discussing an interpersonal conflict and so on).

CONCLUSION

Reflecting content is incredibly important to the progression of the counseling relationship. It provides structure and context, which in turn helps deeper and more vulnerable conversation to emerge. When utilized with attending skills, reflecting content does not have to be void of emotion or personal connection, but it still must focus verbally only on the perceived facts of the counselee's story. Take the time to incorporate this skill, building a foundation on which you may earn the opportunity to go deeper with your counselee.

REFLECTION QUESTIONS

1. As you read this chapter, what do you anticipate being the most challenging part about reflecting content in a counseling setting?

2. What aspects of reflecting content do you see as beneficial to the counseling relationship?

VALIDATING EMOTION

There is a time for everything . . .
a time to weep and a time to laugh,
a time to mourn and a time to dance.

ECCLESIASTES 3:1, 4

CHAPTER FOCUS

SKILL: reflecting feeling

PURPOSE: to reflect back the explicit emotion of the counselee

---

FORMULA: You feel _____.

Do you remember hearing the old love song with the first line "Feelings, nothing more than feelings" (Morris Albert, *Feelings*, RCA Records, 1974)? Popular music tends to focus on emotions. There are many songs that express the excitement and passion of romantic relationships or, conversely, the pain of unrequited love or the agony of betrayal or rejection by a loved one. Similarly, the words of contemporary Christian music are full of emotion. There are songs that focus on our love for God, our gratitude for his love and care, our joy in his presence, our desperation for relationship with him and our sense of helplessness without him. The book of Psalms is full of examples of raw emotion of every variety. It is clear that we are emotional beings and that our feelings are important aspects of who we are. Before we go farther, take thirty seconds to write down all the feeling words that come to your mind below. They can be positive, negative or neutral, but they should be words and not phrases:

_____

_____

_____

See the end of this chapter for an extensive list of feeling words.

In the last chapter we discussed reflecting content as being the skill that lays the foundation of mutual understanding between the counselor and counselee regarding the facts of the counselee's story. Reflecting feeling is the other foundational

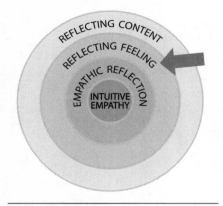

skill that allows the counselee to begin to feel heard, understood and known by the counselor (Egan, 2014). The difference between these two skills is that reflecting content only references facts, while reflecting feeling only references the affective experience of the counselee. While distinctions are sometimes made among terms, we will be using the words *affect, emotion* and *feelings* somewhat interchangeably. Therefore, when we reflect someone's affect or emotion, we are reflecting his feelings.

Figure 6.1. Aiming for reflecting feeling

WHAT ARE FEELINGS, AND HOW ARE THEY REFLECTED?

The feelings in a counselee's story are the elements related to the counselee's internal experience. While emotions may be externally expressed in vocal tone, pitch, volume or language selection, feelings are first an internal experience. As the counselor, it is your job to not just listen for the content of a counselee's story (the facts) but also grasp how what has happened has affected the counselee emotionally. This expression

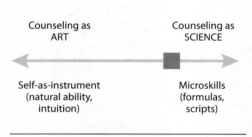

of emotion can be either explicit (i.e., in *what* the counselee says) or implicit (i.e., in *how* a counselee says it). Without addressing these internal aspects, the counselee is unlikely to feel heard.

Most of us are in helping roles with people because we want to alleviate suffering in some way or another. However, attempting to take away someone's pain

Figure 6.2. Art versus science: Reflecting feeling

before they have fully experienced it or worked through it can actually hinder the healing process. In fact, often the pain becomes more intense in the process of healing. An analogy with respect to physical pain could be having a deep wound cleaned out by a physician before stitching it up. If the doctor ignores the dirt, the wound will become infected and fester, creating even more serious problems. Similarly, you as the counselor need to be able to help counselees acknowledge and sit with even the most negative of emotions. Ignoring them or passing over them quickly potentially will hinder healing.

Counselees can communicate their emotions both explicitly and implicitly. Explicit expression of emotion is when a counselee directly states how she was or is feeling. For example, a counselee might say, "When my boss told me I didn't get the promotion, I was so angry I could spit!" In this scenario the client's expressed or explicit emotion is anger.

Diagnostic Implications

Care needs to be taken when reflecting the feelings of counselees with personality disorders (PD). There is a polar tendency in those with PDs to either exaggerate emotion or avoid emotion. Whereas many counselees have difficulty identifying and expressing their emotions, those who fit diagnostic criteria for histrionic personality disorder or borderline personality disorder tend to be overly dramatic in their expressions of emotion. A relatively minor hassle in day-to-day living is often blown out of proportion for such counselees. Reflecting feeling by the counselor tends to encourage further expression of feelings on the part of the counselee, sending the counseling process into an emotional morass.

Similarly, as a counselor you need to exercise caution in how much you reflect back the self-inflated, overly "me-focused" emotions of individuals, for instance with those who fit criteria for narcissistic personality disorder. For the person with antisocial personality disorder, reflecting emotions can become a way the counselee can manipulate the counseling process by essentially pretending to care when in fact he lacks any sense of shame or remorse and can even enjoy causing harm to others (e.g., through murder, theft, emotional manipulation or destruction of property).

In an opposite way, reflecting feeling may get a counselor very little traction when dealing with a schizoid or schizotypal counselee. Without getting into the nuances of these disorders, these are people who typically express very little emotion (see "Diagnostic Reflections" in chapter seven on alexithymia).

Another category of concern is those with serious depression and anxiety symptoms. Reflecting feeling can serve to deepen and intensify negative and anxious feelings and may lead to an increased likelihood of self-harm behaviors.

On the other hand, implicit emotions are never directly stated but are implied based on other verbal and nonverbal factors (Dael, Mortillaro & Scherer, 2012). For example, a counselee might say, "My boss just told me I didn't get the promotion. How could he make such a decision? I had been counting on that raise, and now I don't know how I'm going to make ends meet for the rest of the year." Let's say that the counselee made this statement with a raised voice, a clenched fist and a scowl on his face. Taking into consideration the counselee's nonverbal messages and the words in his actual statement, you could also conclude that the primary emotion is anger. Whether or not you reflect the underlying anger will depend on factors that will be discussed in chapter nine, where we zero in on reflecting implicit underlying feelings. Our focus in the current chapter is on reflecting the explicit feelings, but because it is important to understand the distinction between the two, we wanted to at least introduce the concept of implicit feelings here.

An Encouraging Perspective

In our experience students who naturally tend to hear content may struggle to hear implicit emotions, and students who naturally tend to hear implicit emotions often struggle to identify content. Be encouraged that both skills can be learned, and be gracious to yourself as you discover which elements of the counseling process come more or less naturally to you. In all likelihood, if you struggle one week you'll find some footing the next week.

Feelings, whether implicitly or explicitly expressed, fall into two categories: positive emotions and negative emotions. Positive emotions are the feelings that most of us like to have: happy, excited, content, peaceful, hopeful and so on. Negative emotions, on the other hand, are the emotions that most of us do not enjoy experiencing: sad, angry, disappointed, upset and hurt, to name a few. Keep in mind that a negative emotion is not a "bad" emotion but rather tends to be an unpleasant emotion. As a counselor it is not your job to help a counselee only experience positive emotions (Hankle, 2010). God has given us a range of emotions, similar to the range of emotions that he himself feels (e.g., Ps 7:11; 11:5; Jer 31:3; Zeph 3:17). To limit the spectrum of emotions that God has made available to us as his creation is to hinder the fullness of his image being expressed in us.

The formula for how to reflect feeling is: You feel _____.

Using this simple formula involves inserting a single affective word to describe the primary emotion that you hear or perceive in the counselee's story. The key to this formula is its simplicity: only one affective word per reflection. This simplicity is actually one of the most challenging elements of reflecting feeling. Too often students want to attach a meaning or an explanation to the emotion when reflecting feeling is simply being the verbal mirror that reflects back to the counselee the emotion that was implicitly or explicitly heard by the counselor. The only modification that can be made to the above formula is if the counselor were to add a modifier that amplifies the emotion, such as *really*, *very* or *extremely*. Minimizers such as *sort of*, *kind of* or *a little* are not allowed, as they minimize or diminish the power of the emotion being reflected.

Another common error that counselors-in-training make is that they are often tempted to put a bunch of affective words in the reflection. This may be the result of insecurity, limited affective vocabulary or a desire to address every feeling in one reflection rather than taking the time to address one emotive element at a time. Note that the formula above has no "and" in it; you only get one emotion per reflection, so

Biblical/Theological Connections

Our theology is often not very reflective of who Jesus really was. We read about his teaching, the stories of his ministry, the meaning of his death and resurrection, but overlook the degree to which he was fully and completely a human being. Were the reports of his emotional expression simply faked, so that he could appear to experience what we experience? Hebrews 4:15 reads: "For we do not have a high priest who is unable to empathize with our weaknesses, but we have one who has been tempted in every way, just as we are—yet he did not sin." So if he is like us in all respects except sin, then, we believe he experienced both a similar variety and a similar intensity of emotion as any of us.

✓ "a man of suffering, and familiar with pain" (Is 53:3)
✓ grief at the tomb of Lazarus (Jn 11:35)
✓ joy in welcoming children (Mk 10:16)
✓ anger at Peter, at the Pharisees, and in the temple (e.g., Mt 23:13)
✓ disappointment at the denial of Peter (Lk 22:61)
✓ love and tenderness, using the analogy of a hen gathering her chicks under her wings (Lk 13:34)
✓ sadness, shown by weeping (Lk 19:41)
✓ deeply distressed (Mk 3:5)
✓ enraged: "You unbelieving and perverse generation" (Lk 9:41)
✓ compassion: "his heart went out to her" (Lk 7:13)
✓ amazement (Lk 7:9)
✓ anguish (Lk 22)
✓ fear in the garden (Mt 26:37-44)

Two quotations to consider:

"Jesus felt compassion; he was angry, indignant, and consumed with zeal; he was troubled, greatly distressed, very sorrowful, depressed, deeply moved, and grieved; he sighed; he wept and sobbed; he groaned; he was in agony; he was surprised and amazed; he rejoiced very greatly and was full of joy; he greatly desired, and he loved" (Hansen, 1997, p. 43).

John Calvin, commenting on Matthew 26:37, states: "Certainly those who imagine that the Son of God was exempt from human passions do not truly and sincerely acknowledge him to be a man" (King, 1850).

it is best to start developing some affective vocabulary that can describe complex emotions! There will be times that a counselee's story has multiple feelings involved. In this situation, start with the most dominant, most important or clearest emotion first, and then use subsequent reflections of feeling to capture other pertinent emotions.

Let's go back to the sample scenario in the last chapter, but this time let us read for affect and not content.

Counselee: Oh my goodness, it was such a busy weekend! My best friend from college flew in from out of state, and we just spent the whole time going from one activity to another. On Friday I picked her up from the airport, and we went straight to my favorite dinner spot, and after that to this amazing jazz bar downtown. Then Saturday we did brunch at this delicious local place that I love and then went to an art exhibit that we were both dying to see. By the time Saturday evening rolled around we had caught up on so much and had such a great time, but we were really exhausted, so we decided to just order in pizza and watch a movie. Sunday we went to church in the morning, and I got to introduce my college friend to all my local friends—I love when my worlds collide! It was just such a wonderful weekend!

Try It Out

Using the following counselee statement, identify the explicit and implicit emotions in the counselee's statement (see appendix A for possible answers).

Scenario 1:

Counselee: I'm so disappointed. Last night was my final dance recital for the year. My dad said he was going to come, but at the last minute he texted my mom to say he wasn't going to make it. It's the third time this month that he's promised to be somewhere but then didn't come. I didn't find out that he wasn't there until after the recital, which was good because I really did do a good job and I'm afraid I would have messed up more if I'd known he'd bailed again.

What is the feeling? Identify all emotions explicitly and implicitly communicated by the counselee, noting whether they are positive (+) or negative (-), and provide a reflection of feeling of the explicit emotions:

Explicit emotions: _____

Implicit emotions: _____

Reflection of feeling: _____

Scenario 2:

Counselee: Oh my goodness, I am so excited I can't even stand it! I just found out that I got accepted to my top choice for college *and* I got a scholarship too! I feel like I'm in a dream. I never thought this would actually become a reality. There is so much to do between now and August, my head is spinning with excitement!

What is the feeling? Identify all emotions explicitly and implicitly communicated by the counselee, noting whether they are positive (+) or negative (-), and provide a reflection of feeling:

Explicit emotions: _____

Implicit emotions: _____

Reflection of feeling: _____

If you, as the counselor, were to reflect feeling, it might sound something like, "You feel really happy!" or perhaps, "You feel excited!" depending on which emotion fits better with the counselee's facial expression and vocal tone. The only other explicit emotion expressed by the counselee in this scenario is feeling exhausted. Depending on the counselee's nonverbal messages and context, implicit emotions expressed by the counselee could include wiped out (as long as the positive emotions have also been reflected), energized, revitalized and delighted. Remember that with reflecting feeling, you are not explaining why or how the counselee has a particular emotion, you are simply reflecting the emotion that is expressed by the counselee.

THE PURPOSE OF REFLECTING FEELING

While reflecting content sets the foundation of a therapeutic conversation by communicating to the counselee that the facts of his or her story are understood, reflecting feeling solidifies that foundation. For many people, the sense of feeling understood comes in the form of having their emotions heard (Egan, 2014). In the therapeutic relationship, reflecting feeling is the first skill that a counselor can use to demonstrate that the subjective experience of the counselee is understood, not just the objective (fact-based) elements of what he or she is conveying. Similar to reflecting content, reflecting feeling serves two primary purposes:

1. to help both the counselee and the counselor make sure the affective experiences of the counselee's story are jointly understood, and

2. to clarify or make sense of how the counselee perceived and affectively experienced his story, without having to explain or defend why the counselee felt a certain emotion.

Being able to accurately and concisely reflect back a counselee's feeling serves to take the conversation slightly deeper than reflecting content, building trust and a sense of more personal connection between the counselor and the counselee.

It is important to remember that when a counselor reflects feeling, she is reflecting the feelings of the *counselee* and not the feelings of the situation. For example, it is appropriate to say "You feel discouraged," but saying "That's discouraging" is not. The first reflection places the emotion within the possession of the counselee—the counselee feels discouraged. The second reflection changes the affective word to an adjective and uses it to describe a situation or circumstance. Doing this distances the counselee from the emotion, rather than facilitating the counselee's understanding and ownership of his own feelings.

WHAT REFLECTING FEELING IS *NOT*

Explaining what reflecting feeling is *not* can shed further light on what reflecting feeling *is*. Therefore, reflecting feeling is *not*:

- *agreeing:* Often students are hesitant to reflect feeling when they are not sure whether they agree with the counselee's emotional response to a situation. For example, reflecting back "You feel disrespected" when you, as the counselor, do not see why the counselee felt disrespected in a given scenario, often leaves students feeling as if they are agreeing with or condoning the counselee's emotion. In reality, you are neither agreeing nor disagreeing with the validity of the counselee's emotion by reflecting feeling. You are simply being the verbal mirror, saying back to the counselee what you have heard her say, implicitly or explicitly. While there is a chance that some counselees may interpret your reflection as agreement, most will simply feel heard and understood.

- *proving:* Reflecting feeling does not include any explanation, justification or rationale for the counselee's emotion, so do not add one! Reflecting feeling does not ask the counselor to provide any type of proof for why a counselee feels a certain way. Keep it simple and just reflect the feeling, nothing more.

- *imposing:* Just as it is not the counselor's responsibility to agree with or approve of the counselee's emotion, neither is it the counselor's responsibility to tell the counselee what he *should* feel in a given situation. This often comes in the form of a beginning counselor trying to reflect feeling in order to impose an emotion rather than simply reflect an emotion. For example, let us say the counselee describes a scenario in which he received poor customer service. The counselee factually describes the situation and summarizes his emotional reaction

Empirical Support

When working with children, play therapy often is used instead of talk therapy (Allen, Folger & Pehrsson, 2007). It is in play that children often re-create the situations and emotions in their real-life worlds, attempting to work out the tensions, confusions and hurts. Instead of verbally expressing their anger or sadness, they will likely express their emotional experiences in the themes or story lines of their play (Ray, 2004). In these situations the toys that the child chooses to play with become representatives of themselves or the people in their lives. In light of this, reflecting feeling with children often looks like reflecting the feelings that a particular toy is expressing in the child's play. For example, the child throws a toy dog across the room while saying, "He's mean. I don't like him!" to which the counselor responds, "You are really angry with the mean dog." The use of reflecting feeling in this situation, and in play therapy in general, serves to increase the child's awareness of emotions as well as increase the child's own affective vocabulary (van Velsor, 2004). Although it should be done carefully, as children can sometimes feel threatened by reflecting feeling, "reflecting feeling helps children become aware of emotions, thereby, leading to the appropriate acceptance and expression of such emotions" (Ray, 2004, pp. 32-33).

by stating that he felt disappointed by the conversation with customer service and he wishes a different result could have been obtained. In listening to the story, the counselor notes that she would have felt disrespected, shut down or condescended to, had she been in the counselee's position. If the counselor were to reflect any of these emotions to the counselee, instead of disappointment, the counselor would be imposing her feelings rather than reflecting the counselee's emotions.

RATING REFLECTIONS OF FEELING

Not all reflections of feeling are made equal. Keeping everything in formula ("You feel _____") is one important element, but then there is the issue of choosing an accurate affective word for your reflection. Choosing a feeling word that is in the ballpark of your counselee's emotion is the first step, but from there it is important to assess whether the feeling word you choose is *additive, comparable* or *subtractive*. An additive reflection often includes implicit or underlying feelings. It can also add additional commentary, such as an explanation for the counselee's emotion. A comparable reflection accurately identifies an affective synonym for the counselee's communicated emotion. Finally, a subtractive reflection minimizes or completely ignores the counselee's emotion.

For example, if a counselee says, "It was a good day. I'm really pleased with what I accomplished at work!" then the following are examples of each type of reflection of feeling:

◆ *Additive reflection of feeling:* "You feel ecstatic!" In this situation, the feeling word is *ecstatic,* and it is additive because it reflects a significantly stronger emotion than the counselee has explicitly expressed.

◆ *Comparable reflection of feeling:* "You feel satisfied." The feeling word in this reflection is *satisfied,* and it neither adds to nor minimizes the counselee's expressed emotion. It accurately mirrors the level of emotion that the counselee has expressed and, in this case, uses some of the counselee's own language.

◆ *Subtractive reflection of feeling:* "You feel kind of content." The feeling word in this reflection is *content,* and it is subtractive because it minimizes the counselee's emotion in two ways, either of which would be subtractive on their own: (1) When "kind of" is placed before a feeling word, it diminishes the strength of that feeling and can communicate to the counselee that the emotion reflected is not acceptable in its fullness. (2) In this situation the word *content* does not fully represent the counselee's emotion and minimizes the level of the happiness or satisfaction the counselee has expressed.

Clinical Tips

1. If you get a defensive reaction when you reflect feelings, back off and try reflecting content for a while before going back to reflecting feeling

2. Use caution when reflecting the feelings of those who are severely depressed if it looks as though your reflections are deepening despair or suicidal feelings.

3. If you really are not sure what the counselee is feeling, it is better to clarify rather than risk an inaccurate reflection.

4. Use a comparable level of reflecting earlier on in the counseling process, saving additive levels for after the counseling relationship has been firmly established.

5. Use sparingly with counselees who have personality disorders or psychotic disorders.

The goal in all comparable reflections of feeling is to accurately reflect the counselee's explicit emotion. If an error is to be made, it is better to make an additive reflection than a subtractive one. The reason for this is that most counselees will still feel heard and understood by reflecting a feeling that overshoots their emotion and will then correct the counselor with the more proper feeling word of lower intensity. On the other side, a subtractive reflection of feeling can communicate to counselees that they are not truly heard or understood, or that the intensity of their emotions is not allowed by the counselor.

MULTICULTURAL APPLICATION

As we alluded to in the previous chapter, reflecting feeling can be potentially problematic when working crossculturally. Some cultures, for example Chinese and other Asian cultures, value not letting emotions show (Rothbaum, Morelli, Pott & Liu-Constant, 2000). This can also be true of American men (Wong & Rochlen, 2005). Therefore, if you use "feeling" language when a counselee has not explicitly used such language, it could be experienced as very threatening because you may have inadvertently torn off her "mask."

This does not mean that you should never reflect feelings with multicultural counselees! What we would suggest, however, is that you begin with reflecting content and gradually interject reflecting feeling while carefully assessing your counselee's verbal and nonverbal reactions. If you pick up any discomfort, you should go back to reflecting content. You could also try reflecting feeling in a more indirect way, that is, instead of saying "You're feeling anxious," you might say, "Some people might feel anxious under those circumstances." In emotionally restrictive cultures individuals may not be very tuned in to their own feelings. Increasing emotional self-awareness can therefore be an important part of the healing journey. For these reasons your counselee can potentially benefit greatly from you reflecting back his feelings. The key is to time the use of this skill so that the risk of creating resistance is minimized and the chances of it being constructive are maximized.

Check Your Understanding

For the following exchanges, identify the "best" *reflecting feeling* response given what you now know about reflecting feeling. Provide a rating (additive, comparable or subtractive) and an explanation for your selection and rating. Author selections and explanations can be found in appendix A.

1. Counselee: I am just so pissed, I can't believe my brother pawned my drum set!

Counselor:

Whoa. I can't believe he did that. What did he pawn it for?

Explanation: _____

_____

You feel kind of upset.

Explanation: _____

_____

You feel irate.

Explanation: _____

_____

Your brother pawned your drum set.

Explanation: _____

_____

2. Counselee: I can't believe it! I got accepted to Harvard for law school!

Counselor:

You feel ecstatic!

Explanation: _____

_____

You're excited because you got into Harvard.

Explanation: _____

_____

What kind of law do you want to practice?

Explanation: _____

_____

You feel shocked.

Explanation: _____

_____

3. Counselee: I just don't get it. I studied and studied and studied. How did I fail that mid-term?

Counselor:

You feel betrayed.

Explanation: _____

_____

You feel really discouraged.

Explanation: _____

_____

Man, that's really disappointing.

Explanation: _____

_____

You feel confident.

Explanation: _____

_____

MINISTRY APPLICATION

Reflecting feeling is an often-overlooked and yet very important skill within a ministry context. As all three of us have worked and volunteered in various ministry settings, we have seen times where well-meaning ministers skip over emotions in order to jump to the "more important" spiritual matters. While we would agree that the spiritual aspects of a situation are important, we would also insist that emotional matters need to be addressed. For many people, building a foundation of trust requires that they feel safe and heard as they share the content and emotion of their stories before they are able or willing to allow anyone access into the spiritual elements of their story. This is particularly difficult to do when it is quite apparent that the counselee's behavior is sinful. For example, in a case where a Christian is rationalizing involvement in an extramarital affair, the spiritual distortion is obvious and will need to be confronted at some point (see chapters seven and eleven). However, if the counselee does not first feel heard, your premature attempts to point out sinful behavior will fall on deaf ears, and you will likely lose any future opportunity to have any further influence.

It is not only in situations of blatant sinful behavior that feelings need to be first addressed. In Psalm 22 David both explicitly and implicitly communicates a lot of difficult emotions in his cry to God. Before David can rest in his worship and praise of the Lord, he first needs to honestly express his mostly negative emotions. We are no different today. Oftentimes people need the freedom and the safety to honestly express their doubt, anger, hurt, confusion, fear and seemingly unmet hopes before they are able to rest or find peace in spiritual truths that surpass earthly circumstances. Just as David was allowed to express emotion first and spiritual truth second, you may need to offer your counselees the same patience, grace and space to follow David's process.

CONCLUSION

Reflecting feeling is simple in its formula and delivery but provides the counselee with a sense of feeling heard and understood at a level that goes beyond facts. It is not a skill of interpretation but of reflection, being the verbal mirror to that which has been communicated by the counselee. Drawing on the counselor's ability to hear both explicit and implicit emotion, this skill continues the process of earning the right to speak into the counselee's story, building the foundation of mutual understanding between the counselee and counselor. Utilizing the affective vocabulary list at the end of this chapter, continue to expand your vocabulary of feelings.

REFLECTION QUESTIONS

1. Do you find hearing emotions easier or harder than hearing content?

2. When listening for emotion, do you hear the implicit or the explicit emotion the loudest (i.e., what the counselee *says* or what you perceive them to *mean*)?

3. What about reflecting feeling do you anticipate to be the most challenging? The most enjoyable?

More
intense

adore, captivated, cherished, confident, daring, delighted, devoted to, ecstatic, elated, enamored, energetic, enthusiastic, euphoric, exhilarated, fantastic, fascinated, glowing, great, idolize, infatuated, joyful, loving, marvelous, optimistic, overjoyed, passionate, powerful, riding high, sensational, sensuous, terrific, thrilled, wonderful

admire, affection, amused, appreciated, attached to, cared for, caring, cheerful, close, committed to, connected to, content, excited, fine, fond of, friendly, glad, good, grateful, happy, hopeful, important, in high spirits, intimate, lighthearted, like, nurturing, peaceful, pensive, playful, pleasant, pleased, positive toward, prized, proud, relaxed, respectful, responsible for, satisfied, secure, serene, stimulated, successful, surprised, tender, thankful, thoughtful, trusting, turned on, up, valuable, warm toward, worthwhile

Less
intense

adrift, afraid, agitated, alone, aloof, ambivalent, annoyed, anxious, apart from others, apathetic, apprehensive, at fault, at loose ends, at the mercy of, bad, belittled, blah, blamed, blew it, blue, bored, bothered, bugged, concerned, confused, crummy, depressed, disappointed, disconcerted, discouraged, discredited, disorganized, distant, distrustful, disturbed, doubtful, down, emasculated, embarrassed, embroiled, empty, excluded, failure, fearful, finished, flustered, foggy, frustrated, full of questions, gloomy, goofed, helpless, hesitant, ill at ease, impatient, in a bind, in error, inadequate, incapable, incompetent, incomplete, ineffective, inefficient, inept, inferior, insecure, insignificant, irritated, isolated, jittery, jumpy, lacking, laughed at, left out, let down, lonely, lonesome, lost, lost face, low, mad, mean, melancholy, minimized, mistreated, mixed-up, nervous, offended, on edge, overlooked, painful, paralyzed, perplexed, perturbed, pessimistic, pissed off, put down, put out, puzzled, regretful, rejected, remorseful, remote, resentful, ridiculed, sad, sarcastic, scared, self-conscious, selfish, shaky, shot down, shy, skeptical, slandered, small, sorrowful, sorry, stupid, taken for granted, tearful, threatened, ticked off, timid, tired, troubled, turned off, unappreciated, uncertain, uncomfortable, undecided, uneasy, unhappy, unimportant, unsure, upset, uptight, used, useless, vulnerable, washed up, weak, weepy, worried

abandoned, abused, aggravated, alienated, all alone, angry, anguished, antagonistic, ashamed, awful, baffled, barren, belligerent, bewildered, bitter, bleak, burned out, cast off, confounded, contempt, crippled, critical, criticized, crushed, cut off, debased, defamed, defeated, deficient, degraded, dejected, demeaned, demoralized, depreciated, desolate, despair, desperate, destroyed, devalued, devastated, discarded, disgraced, disgusted, dismal, dismayed, distressed, dread, enraged, estranged, exasperated, exploited, exposed, fighting mad, forsaken, frightened, furious, good for nothing, grief-stricken, grieved, guilty, hate, hateful, hopeless, horrible, horrible, horrified, hostile, humiliated, hurt, immobilized, impotent, in a dilemma, in a quandary, in despair, indignant, inferior, infuriated, intimidated, isolated, miserable, mocked, mortified, nauseated, neglected, outraged, overwhelmed, panicky, petrified, powerless, rotten, ruined, scorned, seething, slammed, spiteful, terrible, terrified, terror-stricken, tortured, trapped, unforgivable, vengeful, vicious, vindictive, violent, whipped, worthless, wounded

More
intense

Notes

- English has a very rich emotional vocabulary; each word carries unique meanings and nuances.
- There are a lot more negative words than positive words.
- This list is far from exhaustive. Additional words/phrases are the many metaphors and colloquial expressions that can express emotion (e.g., "I'm on top of the world").
- There is considerable overlap of categories, and there are even some words that can have either positive or negative connotations depending on tone of voice or context (e.g., "I'm feeling fine").
- There are a number of ways we intensify meaning by adding qualifiers, for example, "a little," "kind of," "sort of," "very," "really," "severely," "extremely," etc.

Figure 6.3. Affective vocabulary chart

CONNECTING EMPATHICALLY

So in everything, do to others what you would have them
do to you, for this sums up the Law and the Prophets.

MATTHEW 7:12

SKILL: empathic reflection

PURPOSE: to build relationships with counselees so that they feel heard holistically and better understand their own situation

FORMULA: "You feel_____ (feeling word) because_____ (content)."

*T*HINK BACK TO A SPECIFIC SITUATION in your life when you were in deep emotional pain and someone attempted to be helpful but instead made things worse. What did this individual do or not do that added to your distress? What did you need from this person instead?

» Write down your responses.

Now reflect on a time where the result was the opposite; you were in agony and the person with you was helpful in some way. What in particular helped you to feel well cared for?

» Write down the thoughts that come to mind.

Chances are that in the first scenario you did not feel heard or understood. The individual may not have taken the time and energy required to really listen. Or perhaps this person offered quick solutions by giving advice, quoting a Bible verse or simply switching the conversation to their own issues or something else.

By contrast, in the second scenario, you likely felt emotionally connected to the person at that moment, sensing that they understood what you were going through or at least that they were making a concerted effort to understand and be with you in your pain. This kind of emotional presence, or "being with" another person, is empathy.

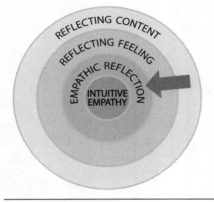

As Matthew 7:12 (the so-called golden rule) reminds us, we not only like to be treated well by others, but also we are commanded to treat others the way we would like to be treated. So if we like it when others empathize with us, God calls us to treat others empathically. This chapter focuses on how to get better at doing this.

Figure 7.1. Aiming for empathic reflection

WHAT IS EMPATHY?

When I (Heather) was an MA student in counseling, I had an experience that profoundly affected me as a counselor. The professor in my skills course asked for a volunteer to role-play a counselee for a class demonstration on empathic reflection. A friend's difficult situation had been on my mind, so I decided that I could role-play her situation and agreed to be the counselee. What astounded me is the depth of emotion I began to experience, despite my nervousness at being in front of the class, as the professor skillfully used empathic reflection. I actually began to cry. And this wasn't even my own personal problem! As I went back to my seat, I told my classmates that I was role-playing someone else, and they couldn't believe it either. From that time onward, I was fully convinced of the power of empathy. This has not only benefited my counselees but has greatly affected the priority I give to empathy training in my teaching.

Carl Rogers (1957/1992), one of the grandparents of contemporary counseling, defined empathy as the ability "to sense the client's private world as if it were your own, but without ever losing the 'as if' quality" (p. 829). Rogers goes on to explain that this concept means that you, as the counselor, can "sense the client's anger, fear, or confusion as if it were your own, yet without your own anger, fear or confusion getting bound up in it" (p. 829). Empathy enables counselors to step into

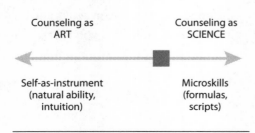

Figure 7.2. Art versus science: Empathic reflection

their counselees' space without bias or imposition while still connecting to their counselees' thoughts, feelings and experiences in an authentic way.

The first part of Rogers's definition, that is, the ability to identify with someone's experience, is similar to the expression "walking in another's shoes." This does not mean that you should try to imagine how *you* would feel in a similar situation (which is the tendency of most people), but rather that you attempt to understand how *your counselee* would feel in that situation, given their genetic makeup, personality, family background and other life experiences.

Listening: The Hardest or the Simplest Thing to Do

Benner (2015) compares therapeutic listening to what some spiritual directors describe as "listening with one ear to the directee [counselee] and one ear to the Spirit" (p. 187). Similarly, we need to think carefully "about how a therapist actually does this in the midst of all the other things to which we need to attend—our own thoughts, our associations to our thoughts as well as to the unconscious elements of our interaction, the words and nonverbal communications of the counselee, and the movement of the Spirit of God within our spirit."

Therapeutic listening is not, therefore, a simple matter. "I judge it to be the hardest and yet at the same time most important part of the therapist's contribution to psychotherapeutic process" (p. 187).

Brené Brown (2012) describes empathy as "the real antidote to shame" (p. 74) and as a "strange and powerful thing." "There is no script. There is no right or wrong way to do it. It's simply listening, holding space, withholding judgment, emotionally connecting, and communicating that incredible healing message of 'You're not alone'" (p. 81).

On one hand, hard; on the other, simple. Which is it? What does appear to be common across all skilled people helpers is that listening is of crucial importance.

This is an essential distinction and bears repeating. Imagining how you would feel in a particular situation may come close to how your counselee feels, but it also might lead you in the wrong direction. While self-disclosure is an important counseling skill (see chapter twelve), it is often overused and misused. The goal of empathy is to understand how the person you are with feels in the situation, not how you would feel. It is not about you.

An example is the emotion of shame. I (Heather) know what it is like to feel shame, because I have experienced situations in which I have felt humiliated or embarrassed, or have behaved in ways that I would rather no one else ever finds out about. Now consider an Asian counselee who describes feeling intense shame because he placed second instead of first in his class at school. I have never felt shame in this situation. Rather, I might feel overjoyed at doing so well, or perhaps some mild disappointment that I just missed the top honor. As a counselor who was raised in the West, what I must do is relate to his experience by imagining how *he* feels in that situation, given his culture, family background and personality, rather than projecting how I might feel onto him.

While sensing and describing what counselees are going through is of utmost importance in counseling, overidentification can potentially be destructive. If you get lost in your counselees' overwhelming feelings, you lose objectivity. It risks becoming about you, not them. When your feelings begin to interfere with your ability to intervene in ways that could help them move forward in their journey, you are at risk for burnout or compassion fatigue. You cannot feel what your counselees feel, but you can use your own experience with personal emotions to better understand what they feel as unique individuals in unique circumstances.

CHRISTIAN FOUNDATIONS OF EMPATHY

There are countless examples of how Jesus models for us this concept of empathy in his interactions with others. For instance, the Samaritan woman at the well was amazed that Jesus understood both her illicit sexual behavior as well as her yearnings for greater meaning in her life (Jn 4:4-26). Jesus also clearly understood the rich young ruler's dilemma of being torn between serving him and having to give up his wealth (Mk 10:17-22). Another example is Jesus' perceptive understanding of the motivation behind the apparently senseless act of the woman who anointed his feet with costly perfumes and wiped them with her hair (Lk 7:37-39).

Biblical/Theological Connections

In theological language, empathy is best illustrated by the incarnation (Benner, 1983). Though created in God's image, we are unlike God in so many ways. God chose to bridge the distance between his total otherness and our humanity by putting himself into human form, flesh and blood, so that he would comprehend the cognitive and emotional dimensions of human experience (Phil 2:6-8). Because of the gift of his son to us, we can know and experience God's love, care and blessing. The rich theological language and literature exploring the incarnation model for us the central therapeutic value of empathy—we love because he first loved us (1 Jn 4:19).

Benner suggests that this desire and ability to purge others of their badness by taking the evil into themselves is a possible interpretation of the *imago Dei*, in each person.

The incarnation as a model for counseling suggests that therapists are able to absorb sickness and suffering and therefore transform the counselee's inner world.

Not only does Jesus demonstrate empathy in how he relates to people, but in his unique position of being both God and human he can empathize both with God the Father and with us. In this sense he could be seen as the ultimate empathizer. Isaiah prophesied about Jesus, stating,

He was despised and rejected by mankind,
a man of suffering, and *familiar* with pain. . . .
Surely he *took up our pain*
and *bore our suffering,*
yet we considered him punished by God,
stricken by him, and afflicted.
But he was *pierced for our transgressions,*
he was *crushed for our iniquities;*
the punishment that brought us peace was on him,
and by his wounds we are healed. (Is 53:3-5)

Describing Jesus, Paul says,

Who, being in very nature God,
did not consider equality with God something to be used to his own advantage;
rather, he made himself nothing
by taking the very nature of a servant,
being made in human likeness. (Phil 2:6-7)

Paul eloquently describes Christ's ability to walk in the shoes of people without losing his sense of self as fully God and fully man. In a similar way, the writer of Hebrews expresses Jesus' unique ability to empathize and feel with people by stating, "For we do not have a high priest who is unable to empathize with our weaknesses, but we have one who has been *tempted in every way, just as we are*—yet he did not sin" (Heb 4:15).

Empirical Support

The prosocial benefits of empathy are multiple and supported by extensive research. For instance, empathy:

- reduces prejudice and racism
- increases altruism (helpful even if it goes against one's self-interest)
- is good for marriage; it deepens intimacy, increases relationship satisfaction and helps resolve conflicts
- decreases bullying and aggressiveness
- promotes heroic acts
- counters inequality, and inequality can reduce empathy (e.g., people show less empathy when they attain higher socioeconomic status)
- is good for business
- is good for health care

Adapted from The Greater Good Science Center at the University of California, Berkeley, "What Is Empathy?" http://greatergood .berkeley.edu/topic/empathy/definition.

Throughout Scripture we see the concept of empathy being explained, instructed and modeled. Integral to the Christian experience and growth process is the need to both give and receive empathy from each other and from God himself. Paul, in Romans 12:15, expresses succinctly what it means to reflect empathically when he says, "Rejoice with those who rejoice; mourn with those who mourn." Again, this imperative is not that we must fully live out the same experiences as one another, but instead it calls us to connect with and share in the experiences of another. It is the feeling *with* that is so vitally important to human relationship and connection.

Additionally, Proverbs 18:13 speaks to the importance of listening well before responding, stating, "To answer before listening—that is folly and shame." In other words, it is disrespectful and even absurd for a counselor to talk before taking the time to find out what the counselee is really trying to say. True empathy is not about proving that you are a good listener; instead, it is the act of communing with the counselee, and that can only be done after the counselor has listened well and truly heard the counselee's story.

COGNITIVE AND AFFECTIVE EMPATHY

There are two components of empathy: the cognitive and the affective. With the cognitive aspect, you as the counselor can cognitively, or intellectually, understand the counselee's emotion and the cause (content) of that emotion. As its name implies, cognitive empathy stays in your head and is a mental acknowledgment of the counselee's situation. Conversely, affective empathy involves an emotional response or connection to the counselee's affect.

In *cognitive empathy* you are primarily using your mental capacities to figure out what a counselee is experiencing. This could involve, for example, going through a mental checklist of feeling words to see which one might best fit, crafting a succinct yet descriptive summary of content and then reflecting back the feelings and content you have decided would be the most helpful. During this process the counselor can feel somewhat disconnected emotionally from the counselee. This is particularly noticeable when you are learning the skill and it seems artificial. However, the ability to come up with the best feeling word for the situation, paired with an accurate and focused content reflection, is an enormously helpful skill. It is the cognitive component of empathy that is the primary skill focus of this chapter. This skill will involve using your intellectual perception skills and reflection skills to demonstrate your understanding of what the counselee has said. Empathy that is only felt or understood internally by the counselor and not expressed in some way is not empathy in the eyes of the counselee.

In contrast to cognitive empathy, in *affective empathy* the counselor's emotions are engaged and you as the counselor feel *with* the counselee. Affective empathy is a unique skill in that it is the first that we have discussed so far that asks the counselor to actually *become* someone different, not simply *do* something different. Another way of saying this is that this skill is not just about a counselor's external behavior toward a counselee but requires the counselor to shift internally. As mentioned earlier, a good counselor should be able to step into someone else's experience and "rejoice with those who rejoice; mourn with those who mourn" (Rom 12:15). This goes beyond just learning the right thing to say (i.e., cognitive empathy) by cultivating within the counselor the ability to *be* connected with the feelings and experiences of another human being. The challenge is to do this *without losing your sense of self* so that you can maintain enough objectivity and presence of mind to allow you to also use cognitive empathy.

Losing Your Sense of Self Happens When You Listen to a Counselee's Story and:

✓ feel as if you lived through it yourself

✓ feel a need to rescue, fix or erase the counselee's problem because it is too difficult for you to hear

✓ cannot identify how your feelings, thoughts and perspectives differ from those of the counselee's

It is easier to learn cognitive empathy than it is to learn affective empathy. This is because affective empathy is to some degree intuitive. As long as there is even a tiny seed of such intuition, affective empathy can be developed and can grow over time with attention and experience. So we encourage you to begin with cognitive empathy while nurturing your ability to connect emotionally with your counselees so that you can give them the gift of your authentic presence without losing your sense of self.

Of course, for empathy to be done correctly and fully, it must be both part of the counselor's being *and* part of his doing. A good counselor has the ability to both cognitively and affectively empathize, but each counselor's use of and comfort with both aspects of empathy will differ based on her own personality and approach to counseling. For example, if you are naturally more of an affectively empathic person, developing your empathy skills will be more about putting words to your affective experience of another person and learning to keep your emotional response in the realm of empathy without overstepping into sympathy (which we will talk more about shortly). If you are more of a cognitively empathic person, your process will likely involve working on being more present in the moment with a counselee and experiencing the story she has to tell. And, for some of you, both components of empathy will be a challenge, so start with developing cognitive empathy and grow from there.

LEARNING THE SKILL OF EMPATHIC REFLECTION

We now look at how to combine the skills of *reflecting content* and *reflecting feeling* into a compound skill that results in an ability to connect with counselees through empathic reflection. This is the linchpin skill of effective counseling: the ability to link together the what and why of the counselee's feelings is paramount.

In keeping with the skills we have learned thus far, basic-level empathy is expressed as an interchangeable response or a reflection. As a reflection, there is no additive interpretation at this time; you are simply being the verbal mirror for what the counselee has provided in the conversation (intuitive or additive empathy will be introduced in chapter nine). The purpose of expressing empathy is to enable counselees to feel heard holistically in that both the facts and the feelings of their story are accurately reflected back to them. Connecting through empathy is seen as the primary connecting skill in the counseling process. It connects counselor to counselee while simultaneously connecting the counselee's own thoughts and feelings.

The levels of empathy. This new skill of empathy requires the counselor to truly begin integrating all previously learned skills, from attending to perceiving to reflection. To begin with, the counselor must attend to both the verbal and the nonverbal messages of counselees as well as their context. As you listen to counselees, you are striving to set aside your own biases and judgments in order to hear their perspective and to listen for the core messages of what they are communicating. A helpful empathic response will increase rapport. It will also enable counselees to remain focused on their issues while simultaneously developing and clarifying important parts of their story.

Empathy Scale

Level 1: This response is hurtful to the therapeutic relationship, as it directly or indirectly tells the counselee that the counselor is not listening, does not respect the counselee or does not understand the counselee. The counselor's reflection could be any of the following:

✓ ignores or dismisses the counselee's emotion (e.g., changes the subject)
✓ contradicts the counselee's emotion
✓ condescends (as if from a superior to an inferior)
✓ is argumentative
✓ states or infers that the counselee is deficient for feeling the way that he does (e.g., stupid, ignorant, foolish or childish)
✓ gives advice
✓ shifts the focus onto what the counselor finds interesting or important, rather than what the counselee has expressed
✓ completely misinterprets the counselee's emotion (e.g., stating that the counselee feels happy about something when she is actually feeling scared)
✓ a different skill is used, but so inappropriately that empathy is virtually absent

Level 2: This empathic response in some way misses the mark of what the counselee has communicated but is not as harmful as level one. Specifically, this response could be any of the following:

✓ notably detracts from or minimizes the counselee's emotion, but still reflects a feeling within the same broad category of emotion

✓ is stated as a question, not a statement

✓ is accurate regarding something the counselee said previously in the conversation but is "behind" the counselee's current point in his story

✓ a response in which the goal is not empathic reflection but an appropriately used different skill

Level 2.5: In this category of empathic reflection the response is missing something. The counselor's reflection could be the following:

✓ is accurate as it pertains to the feeling reflected but lacks adequate content reflection. While intended to be an empathic reflection it in essence is only reflecting feeling; it qualitatively communicates empathy to the counselee due to its accuracy or delivery but lacks attention to context

✓ slightly misses the mark of what the counselee has communicated

Level 3: At this level an empathic response accurately reflects the counselee's feelings and content without adding to or subtracting from what she has communicated. The counselor's reflection could be any of the following:

✓ is fully reciprocal or interchangeable with the counselee's explicit statement

✓ is an accurate depiction of the counselee's situation and/or state of being

✓ does not go deeper than the counselee's expressed feelings

✓ does not minimize or negate the counselee's expressed feelings

Levels 4 and 5: At these levels the empathic response goes beyond what the counselee has stated and is beyond the scope of this chapter. We will cover this more in chapter nine, so for the time being limit your reflections to a level three and stay with the feelings and content that the counselee has communicated.

As a more integrated skill, empathy can be communicated on various levels. In this chapter we will explore levels one through three, while chapter nine will explore levels four and five. The goal with empathy is not necessarily to always use the highest level available, but instead to use the level that is most suitable for a particular counselee in his or her current situation. Within this chapter, you are striving for a level-three empathic response.

While empathic reflection is an essential skill that should be frequently used throughout the counseling process, the other skills in this book are also important. There will, therefore, be times when conveying empathy is not your primary goal, because you are more focused on skills such as clarifying or confronting. However, it is vital that you are aware of how empathy levels are affected even when showing empathy is not your primary purpose at that moment. For this reason we believe that any counselor response can and should be rated on the empathy scale.

In most counseling situations, a level three response is your "home base" for the counseling process, as it provides a safe and effective way for counselees to feel heard and for counselors to confirm their understanding of their counselees' stories. From this point forward, regardless of the skills you add to your "technique toolbox," a level-three empathic reflection is the best skill to use when you do not know what to do.

How empathy is verbally expressed. In any empathic statement there are two parts: the feeling and the content. Drawing on the skills you learned in chapters five and six, you are now looking to link those two concepts. Instead of simply reflecting the facts or content (chapter five) or reflecting the emotion (chapter six), we are now attempting to draw some connections and communicate an understanding that a certain feeling has arisen in light of or because of a specific fact or piece of content.

The formula for a level three empathic reflection is: You feel _____ (feeling word) because _____ (content).

Diagnostic Implications

In the history of psychopathology, alexithymia is the psychiatric concept used to describe people who are devoid of empathic skills. Specifically, they:

✓ have difficulty identifying feelings in themselves and others
✓ struggle to distinguish between their own feelings and bodily sensations such as emotional arousal
✓ have difficulty describing their feelings to other people
✓ have limited ability to imagine things and therefore have few fantasies
✓ are responsive to external stimuli and cognitively process the external world with little reference to their internal world

While not a DSM diagnosis, it plays a significant role in autism spectrum disorders, some personality disorders, conduct disorder and substance abuse, and, of course, it wreaks havoc in marital and family relationships. The capacity for empathy is a significant correlate of mental and relational health.

Empathy is often used simply to track with (or follow) the counselee. In this case, empathy serves to say, "I hear that you feel a particular way because of this particular situation." No more, no less. An example of this, in its simplest form, might look like the following dialogue with a twenty-five-year-old male counselee:

Counselee: I'm really disappointed with myself. It's Friday evening, and I'm behind in my responsibilities for work. That means I had to bring files home with me tonight and will spend most of Saturday finishing up all the things I'd wanted to do in the office during the week.

Counselor: You feel disappointed because you are bringing work home this weekend.

In this scenario "disappointed" is the feeling, and "bringing work home" is the content. The counselee clearly stated his own emotion and then proceeded to provide content. You, as the counselor, simply condensed his statement and reflected it back more concisely. In so doing you were able to show that you heard both the feeling and the content of the counselee's message, thus expressing empathic understanding. In putting together the above response, think back to chapters four and five in regard to reflecting content and reflecting feeling. Notice that an empathic reflection is simply a compound sentence where you are joining the two previously learned reflection skills:

Reflecting content: "You had to bring work home this weekend."

Reflecting feeling: "You feel disappointed."

At other times, empathy is used to help the counselee see connections between feelings and content that he may not have previously put together, at least not out loud. Again, even in this instance, we are not adding to the counselee's story; we are simply reflecting what he has already communicated, but in a succinct way. It is preferred that you do not simply parrot back the same affective word that the counselee has used, as parroting can communicate to the counselee that you only heard his words, not that you understood his situation. Instead, challenge yourself to find an accurate and fitting synonym whenever possible. An example of this might look like the following dialogue:

Counselee: It's Friday evening, and I'm behind in my responsibilities for work. I don't know what I'm going to do. I was supposed to go to a friend's birthday party tomorrow, but now I'm going to have to work all day instead. This is so not how I wanted to spend my weekend! I just wish I could enjoy my weekend like I'd planned.

Counselor: You feel disappointed because this weekend isn't turning out how you had planned.

In this scenario, the feeling is "disappointed," and the content is the "weekend isn't turning out how you had planned." Unlike the previous situation, the counselee did not provide you with a direct statement about how he was feeling but talked around the idea of being disappointed and implied this emotion instead. In this case, it is then the role of the counselor to provide a feeling word that helps capture what the counselee is feeling, *without adding to or subtracting* from the counselee's emotion.

» What other feeling words might the counselor have used instead of *disappointed* to capture the counselee's emotion? (Consult the vocabulary of feelings at the end of chapter six.)

While an empathic reflection is any statement that includes both feeling and content, the simplest expression of this skill is stated as: "You feel _____ (feeling word) because _____ (content)."

As with reflecting feeling, you may only include *one feeling word at a time* in your reflection. As you will recall from chapter six, limiting yourself to reflecting only *one* feeling word allows the counselee to respond to something that is clear and concise. Saying "You feel annoyed and overwhelmed and disappointed because you have to work this weekend" leaves the counselee with too many feelings to think about and respond to. What if you are accurate in reflecting "annoyed" and "disappointed" but not accurate with "overwhelmed"? Giving too many feeling words in one empathic reflection can indirectly communicate that you do not actually understand how the counselee feels. Instead, pick the most pressing or most representative feeling word to reflect first. You can always reflect additional emotions later. Better yet, you can use situations like this to develop your vocabulary of feelings, adding words to your repertoire such as *exasperated*, *perturbed* or *despairing*, depending on the intensity of emotion you sense a counselee is expressing.

Also, remember that a reflection is always a statement, not a question, so watch your intonation. When you turn a reflective statement into a question, you inadvertently communicate to counselees that they are difficult to understand and that you are not actually able to hear their emotion and experience, which is the exact opposite of what empathic reflection is supposed to accomplish. Do not let "You feel disappointed because this weekend isn't turning out how you had planned" turn in to "You feel disappointed because this weekend isn't turning out how you had planned?" If you are uncertain as to whether you understand the counselee's perspective, continue with your best attempts at basic reflections of content or reflections of feeling, but be willing to take the risk of making a mistake. Your goal initially is not to find the most perfect feeling word every time but rather to at least choose words that are within an appropriate range of emotion, which will demonstrate to your counselees that you understand their stories.

If your empathic reflection is close to being accurate, counselees will feel heard and will continue on with their story. If you miss the mark completely, counselees will likely correct you, explicitly or in more subtle ways, but will still hear that you are trying to understand them. Then, after they correct you or try again to express themselves, they will continue their narrative. Your role is to continue to listen well, having incorporated their most recent response so that your next reflection may be more in range with their emotional experience. It is important to note that counselees will often repeat their story or key elements of their story when they do not feel heard. Therefore, if you find yourself with a counselee who seems to be talking in circles or rehashing the same story time and again, it may be helpful to examine your empathy statements to determine whether your choice of feeling words may need to go deeper, be more specific or be more nuanced.

Formulas can be useful aids to learning a new skill. However, as you become more comfortable with the basic formula for empathic reflection, you will be able to experiment with modifying it. As it stands now, the formula is very direct in order to keep the skill as clean and uncomplicated as possible. As you grow in your use of empathic reflection, keep in mind that many counselees may respond better to a more indirect approach. For example, prefacing the formula with stems such as "I think I hear you saying . . . ," "It's almost like . . . ," "It sounds like maybe . . ." and "I'm wondering whether . . ." gives counselees greater permission to disagree if counselors are not quite on the mark. Be careful not to jump to these stems first, as they risk communicating to a counselee that you do not understand her or that she has not been clear in her communication with you.

Response Sentence Stems

✓ I wonder whether . . .

✓ It sounds like maybe . . .

✓ Perhaps you feel . . .

✓ It might be that . . .

✓ It seems as though . . .

✓ I think I hear you saying . . .

✓ If I'm hearing you correctly . . .

✓ It's almost like . . .

✓ Could it be possible that . . .

✓ I could imagine you feel . . .

EMPATHY IS STILL EMPATHY, EVEN OUT OF FORMULA

Empathy is a unique skill in that it can be put into formula, and it can be expressed in tone, facial expressions and body language, and even within other skills. In light of this, nearly any skill can be experienced by the counselee as facilitating empathy or diminishing empathy within the counseling relationship. The essence of empathy is that it expresses understanding of the counselee's situation, both affectively and experientially. For some counselees the most empathic thing a counselor could do is to reflect feeling: "You feel devastated." In a situation like this, the reason for the devastation may already have been reflected or mutually understood, or the content may be of little significance to the counselee because the emotional aspect of the situation is of such high significance to the counselee.

Questions are an important clarifying skill, but by their very nature questions lack empathy. If you totally understood the subjective experience of a counselee, you would not need to ask for clarification! That is why the highest rating on the empathy scale that a question could typically attain is a level two. An exception would be a question that is prefaced by an empathic reflection, or where an empathic reflection is embedded within a question. For example, "When you were crouched in the corner of the room after hearing the outside door open, feeling absolutely terrified, what was going through your mind?" In this case the counselor is asking about the counselee's thoughts, but content and feelings have both been accurately reflected, making the empathy rating for this statement a level three.

Similarly, other skills, when appropriately used, would likely be rated at a level two unless an empathic reflection is embedded in them. For example, an authentic response of "I'm so happy for you!" would likely be rated at a level two on the empathy scale and a level four on the authenticity scale (see chapter twelve). However, a counselor response of "I'm so happy to hear that you are really excited about your promotion! You've worked hard for that!" would be rated at a level three on the empathy scale.

As a rule of thumb, when an activity in this book asks you for an empathic statement or reflection, we are looking for you to respond in formula. But, moving forward, every response can be evaluated on the empathy scale, regardless of the actual skill used. This serves to demonstrate that every response out of a counselor's mouth has the potential to build or diminish the counselee's sense of being empathically understood.

Check Your Understanding

For the following exchanges, identify the "best" *empathic* response given what you now know about empathic reflection. Rate each response on the empathy scale and provide an explanation as to why that response earned that rating. Author ratings and explanations can be found in appendix A. *Note: It is possible for there to be more than one response at each rating level.*

1. Counselee: Every day at school Jayden takes my lunch. I don't want to be a tattletale, but I get really hungry.

Counselor:

Dude, that's totally a bummer.

Rating: _____

Explanation: _____

_____

You feel confused about what to do when Jayden takes your lunch.

Rating: _____

Explanation: _____

_____

What a jerk! I bet that makes you super mad.

Rating: _____

Explanation: _____

_____

I remember when I was in third grade and this kid, Tyler, always took my lunch. Finally, one day, I just punched him, and he never took my lunch again!

Rating: _____

Explanation: _____

_____

2. Counselee: Pastor Tim, I really want to go on the high school camping trip this weekend, but because I broke curfew last week my parents said I can't go. It's just not fair!

Counselor:

It sounds like you're angry that something you did last week is affecting what you want to do this week.

Rating:

Explanation:

Well, I guess you did it to yourself, huh? If you hadn't broken curfew you'd get to come. Maybe next time you'll think ahead a little more.

Rating:

Explanation:

I'm really sorry, Kaitlyn, I know you wanted to come camping with everyone. Maybe next time.

Rating:

Explanation:

Maybe you should talk to your parents again and see if they can move your punishment to another weekend.

Rating:

Explanation:

3. Counselee: I just don't know what to do. It's my senior year of college, and all my friends know exactly what they want to do with their lives, and many of them already have jobs lined up, but I feel just as confused as I did before I began college. I wish I knew what God wanted for my future.

Counselor:

It can be really difficult to navigate major life transitions when you're confused about where you're going and what God wants for you.

Rating:

Explanation:

I wonder who you've talked to about this dilemma and what kind of suggestions they've had for you.

Rating: _____

Explanation: _____

_____

Well, Jacob, I think I know you pretty well, and I've always wondered whether God was calling you into missions work. You love people, you enjoy learning about new cultures and you pick up languages easily. I don't know, but maybe it's something you should consider.

Rating: _____

Explanation: _____

_____

As you look at your life after college approaching, you feel really uncertain as to what's next.

Rating: _____

Explanation: _____

_____

4. Counselee: My husband and I just can't seem to get on the same page! I can't keep having this same fight over and over again. It's maddening!

Counselor:

You feel exasperated by the ongoing conflict between you and your husband.

Rating: _____

Explanation: _____

_____

You're aggravated because you and your husband can't seem to find resolution on this topic.

Rating: _____

Explanation: _____

_____

Man, that's really annoying. I hate it when my spouse and I can't come to an agreement. I don't know how you've put up with it for so long.

Rating: _____

Explanation: _____

_____

At least your husband is talking to you. That's an improvement from last month. I know it would be nice if you could come to an agreement, but look on the bright side.

Rating: _____

Explanation: _____

_____

5. Counselee: I'm really sad. My daughter, her husband and their three children are moving away at the end of next month. Our family has always lived so close together, and now they're moving halfway across the country. I know it's the right decision, and it's in their best interest as far as personal and professional growth, but I'm just so sad to see them go.

Counselor: I completely understand your sadness. It's hard to see family move far away.

Rating: _____

Explanation: _____

_____

Why are they moving so far away? Did one of them get a really great job, or couldn't they find something here in the area?

Rating: _____

Explanation: _____

_____

It feels bittersweet to see your children make good choices for themselves when those same good choices take them away from you.

Rating: _____

Explanation: _____

_____

I know it's sad, but think of how much fun you'll have getting to visit them in their new home and all the great memories you guys will make exploring their new city!

Rating: _____

Explanation: _____

_____

WHAT EMPATHY IS *NOT*

As much as it is important to recognize what empathy *is*, it is also pertinent that we explore what empathy is *not*.

◆ Empathy is *not* sympathy. Sympathy happens when the "as if" aspect of Rogers's definition is lost and you can no longer distinguish between which emotions are yours and which emotions are the counselee's. In sympathy, you are feeling *for* the counselee rather than feeling *with* the counselee.

◆ Empathy is *not* agreeing with the emotions or the reactions of the counselee. Instead, empathy is simply expressing that you hear that the counselee feels a particular way in light of a particular situation or circumstance. Remember that empathy is a reflection, and just like a mirror, it is meant to simply reflect back what is there—without judgment or interpretation.

◆ Empathy that is unexpressed is *not* empathy. If you internally think to yourself, "I totally understand what this person is feeling," but never share that understanding with the counselee, you have not been empathic. Likewise, it is not empathy to simply say "I understand," as it raises the question of *what* you understand. Some counselors have the rare gift of exuding such empathy by their very presence that counselees can sense their empathy through their nonverbal communication. However, in order for empathy to be received, it most often must be concretely shared and done so verbally in a reflective statement that links emotion with content.

◆ Empathy is *not* a question. Empathy is a reflective *statement*, so watch your inflection. It is far too easy, because of counselor insecurity or self-doubt, to turn "You feel happy because you got engaged" into "You feel happy because you got engaged?" (note the question mark!). One reflects understanding, while the other indirectly questions why or whether the counselee actually feels happy.

◆ Empathy is *not* emphatic. Empathy is not trying to be pushy or to prove, emphasize or convince a counselee of anything. If you are *emphatic* you are unlikely to be *empathic*!

RELATIONSHIP APPLICATION

Empathy is a primary prosocial skill. It is a skill that we are not formally taught growing up but that is at the center of all healthy relationships. Therefore it should be of no surprise that it is not only an essential counseling skill but a core concept in many highly regarded relationship, marital, parenting and family psychoeducational programs and therapies. The Relationship Enhancement program (www.nire.org), Emotionally Focused Couples and Family Therapy (www.iceeft.com) and Love and Logic parenting programs (www.loveandlogic.com) are three examples.

Many who intentionally learn empathy skills to assist them in responding to counselees find that it has a powerful impact on their personal relationships. It can alter and defuse conflict scenarios and increase closeness. The relationship application of empathy often goes beyond the basics of expressing empathy to helping both parties in a conversation to express a concern, listen nonreactively and respond empathically. This pattern of communication is a challenge to implement amid the busyness of daily family life, let alone in the midst of a relationship conflict, but the benefits are enormous. In addition, the application of empathy to growing healthy relationships extends way beyond the counseling or ministry context. This is an interpersonal skill necessary across all domains; family, education, business and dare we say, politics and international relations.

MULTICULTURAL APPLICATION

Empathy, more than any other skill, has the potential to build bridges within multicultural settings. Regardless of gender, religion or any other cultural distinctive, humans have emotions, and those emotions are affected by their surroundings and their situations. As empathy asks the counselor to connect with the shared humanness between themselves and their counselees, it has the potential to cut through cultural boundaries, biases or differences and center in on the universal aspects of our emotional experiences. It is important to remember that empathy does not mean that you have felt exactly the same way, have lived through a similar circumstance or even that you agree with the feelings of your counselees, but rather that you hear from them how a particular situation affected their emotions. In light of this, cultural boundaries have the ability to be minimized if you can hear how counselees are emotionally affected by their situations. Using empathic reflections, you have the ability to show respect to counselees who are culturally different from you simply by demonstrating that you have been able to hear them without judgment or accusation.

Nevertheless, some cautions are in order. In cultures that value hiding outward expressions of emotion, the use of too many feeling words may feel threatening. In such cases, affective empathy in the form of empathic presence may be most appropriate initially, while reflecting content rather than feelings. Multicultural counseling experts Derald Wing Sue and David Sue (2016) suggest that less direct forms of empathic reflection may be more appropriate when working with certain cultural groups. As mentioned previously, the skill formula used in this chapter, "You feel _____ (feeling word) because_____ (content)," is very direct. Sue and Sue suggest that counselors pay particular attention to the verbal and nonverbal cues of counselees after reflecting content and feeling in order to test out how it is being received. If discomfort is apparent, a more indirect reflection might be more appropriate (see "The Formula for Empathic Reflection" above).

Sue and Sue (2016) also point out that cognitive empathy can be demonstrated to counselees of diverse cultures if counselors show that they understand their counselees' worldviews. Recognizing that family, for example, may have important influence on decision making, or that counselees have faced discriminatory experiences such as racism or sexism, may help counselees feel understood. Conversely, counselors who lack awareness of their own cultural biases, or who do not realize that others may hold cultural values that are different from their own, are unlikely to be able to adequately empathize with a counselee from a culture different from their own. Such counselors would benefit from receiving specific training in multicultural competence.

MINISTRY APPLICATION

There is a tension in pastoral care and related activities between being prophetic, pastoral and priestly (see Carlson, 1976). These overlapping roles, seen in Jesus' ministry, reflect aspects of ministry relationships. The prophetic-confronting, pastoral-teaching and priestly-confessional roles each require solid and extensive use of the foundational skill of empathy. None should be used without careful application of empathy skills. Listening and understanding the people being ministered to are not enough. We must be able to express our understanding in ways that connect to the ministry recipient. This is true of spiritual directors, preachers, Bible study leaders, chaplains and other ministry providers. Even if the primary ministry focus is the human-divine relationship rather than the human-human therapeutic relationship, the person in the ministry role will be of limited assistance if he or she does not also pay attention to the human ministry relationship. For example, directees who do not feel that their spiritual directors understand the struggles they are having as they attempt to walk more closely to God, or directees who sense that their spiritual directors are not hearing what their spiritual yearnings are, will not likely continue seeking soul care from those individuals.

Clinical Tips

1. Empathy is sometimes criticized for being too passive and not action oriented enough. However, well-timed and expressed empathy does not detract from change and action but sets up the possibility, the conditions and the motivation for change and action to follow. For example, empathy can be used in problem solving or brief, solution-focused approaches (Cade & O'Hanlon, 1993; Turnell & Lipchik, 1999).

2. Empathy can be expressed nonverbally as well as verbally, though nonverbal communication can easily be misunderstood. Men, however, may find it easier to express empathy nonverbally as a precursor to learning the verbal skill.

3. The way to gauge the accuracy and effectiveness of an empathic statement is to notice the counselee's response. Just because you thought your empathy was right on target does not mean it was.

4. When in doubt about what to say next, empathize.

The many "love another" passages in Scripture describe what the church should look like. The problem is that most people do not automatically empathize, which easily results in the church becoming characterized by something other than loving relationships. Empathy is not a fruit of the Spirit given just to certain spiritual giants in the church; it is a skill that thankfully can be learned so that churches can become Christ's body in the world.

> » How could your church better demonstrate empathy, teach empathy and practice empathy?

CAUTIONS IN THE USE OF EMPATHY

As with any relationship, the answer to most questions about what is best to say next is "It depends." Ultimately it is not a formula but a highly trained and nuanced intuitive sense that points the way forward. Following are a number of cautions, each of which could take a lot of time to explain in full. However, we hope that these cautions will raise your awareness of the complexity of the counseling relationship.

◆ Empathy is not the best response in the midst of a crisis; a crisis calls for a more directive approach from the counselor that promotes the counselee's physical safety first. The therapeutic power of being understood comes later, as we attempt to make sense of the crisis and integrate that experience into our lives.

◆ Highly emotional counselees may benefit more from cognitive empathy (understanding the situation and details) rather than affective empathy. Empathic reflection can result in further emotional decompensation for highly emotional people.

◆ Real-time empathy (i.e., empathizing with the counselee about the counseling relationship, here and now, in the room) is harder to accept—it introduces a lot of vulnerability into the relationship and is potentially threatening and intrusive. But this is often when the greatest change happens. Counselees make use of the dynamics of the real therapeutic relationship with you to alter their relationships outside counseling. This is discussed more in chapter twelve.

◆ For various reasons, students and counselees sometimes balk at learning a skill like empathy, but life is full of skill learning, and so is the vocation of counseling. When teaching empathy skills to laypeople or couples and families, empathize with the resistance to learning the skill, but remind them of the empirical support and the personal benefits of good empathy in relationships.

◆ Empathy "costs" the counselor—giving out more empathy than you are receiving through your own personal relationships can quickly result in compassion fatigue.

◆ Empathy skills can be misused by manipulative and exploitive people. True empathy is never used for the counselor's gain but is for the counselee's benefit.

A SAMPLE COUNSELING DIALOGUE WITH MARY

Skills used: reflecting content, reflecting feeling and empathic reflection

Background on the conversation: The counselor and counselee have met together once previously. The counselor started the session by following up on a situation the counselee had mentioned during the last session. We pick up the dialogue from there:

| **Counselor:** | *So, Mary, last time we were talking you mentioned that you were going to a birthday party for your nephew this past weekend. You said last time that you were nervous about how the party would go because of some tensions between you and your brother.* |

SKILL	reflecting content or summary statement
Although it includes feeling words, it is not about reflecting feeling or empathy and is instead simply summarizing the content of the previous conversation.	

| **Mary:** | *Yes, you're right. My nephew's first birthday party was this past Saturday. I was so nervous about going to the party. As I mentioned last week, my brother and I have had a rather tense relationship since he got married a few years ago. We haven't spent much time together in recent years, and even before his marriage our relationship was tense, so I just didn't know what to expect.* |

| **Counselor:** | *You were really quite anxious about this weekend's party because of the past tensions in your relationship with your brother.* |

SKILL	empathy, level 3
feeling = nervous or anxious content = because of the past tensions in your relationship	

| **Mary:** | *I was super anxious! So much so that I didn't really want to go. But, at the same time, I love my nephew, and I really want to be involved in his life, so there was no way I was going to miss his birthday.* |

| **Counselor:** | *Because you really care about your nephew, you went to his birthday.* |

SKILL	empathy, level 3
feeling = care content = went to his birthday	

| **Mary:** | *I do. I love that little boy so much. It was nice to be at his birthday party and get to celebrate the little guy. At the same time, it was hard to be really present with my nephew while my brother was hovering. I'm always so afraid that my brother is going to disapprove of what I say or do.* |

Counselor: *You feel really apprehensive around your brother.*

SKILL	empathy, level 3
feeling = apprehensive content = around your brother Although this is not in perfect formula, the connection is still made between what is felt by Mary and the content that evokes that emotion.	

Mary: *I am super apprehensive around my brother. I don't want to say or do something he'll disapprove of. I always feel like he's judging me and that because I didn't make the same choices in life that he did that I'm not good enough. See, he was super driven and responsible—going to college, getting married, now having a baby. I graduated high school five years ago, have changed jobs a handful of times, had a couple of failed relationships, and I still don't know what I want to do with my life. I don't think I've been irresponsible, but he still sees me as his slacker little sister.*

Counselor: *You feel judged by your brother because you two have taken different paths in life.*

SKILL	empathy, level 3
feeling: judged content: have taken different paths in life	

Mary: *It's just, honestly, I wish my life had turned out differently too. I would have loved to be married and be established in my career by now, but I just haven't felt God leading me that clearly into either of those situations. I wish my brother understood that.*

Counselor: *You feel misunderstood.*

SKILL	reflecting feeling

Mary: *I do feel misunderstood. And now, with my nephew around, I want so badly to be involved in his life. But each time we're all together I can just feel how much my brother disapproves of me and the path I've been on. I wish I could explain to him what this journey has been like from my perspective. I will say that our interactions have slowly gotten better over the last year, and I'm hopeful that because of my nephew we'll get more opportunities to interact and come to a better understanding of one another.*

Counselor: *You feel hopeful that your nephew could serve as a bridge between you and your brother.*

SKILL	empathy, level 3
feeling = hopeful content: your nephew could serve as a bridge between you and your brother	

Try It Out

Below are brief dialogues between a counselor and counselee. In section A, fill in the appropriate feeling word and content (level three), completing the formula. In section B, create your own level-three empathic reflection.

Section A:

1. Female counselee: I cannot believe it, I was so shocked this weekend when David proposed! It was the best birthday present ever!

Feeling: _____

Content: _____

Counselor: You feel _____

because _____

2. Counselee: I just don't know what I'm going to do. My babysitter canceled for tonight, and I have this work dinner that I absolutely cannot miss. If I'm not there I could literally lose my job, and now I only have an hour to find a new babysitter.

Feeling: _____

Content: _____

Counselor: You feel _____

because _____

3. Counselee: I just found out I didn't get into the college I wanted. I am really, really disappointed, and now I have no idea what I'm supposed to do come next fall.

Feeling: _____

Content: _____

Counselor: You feel _____

because _____

4. Counselee: I was convinced I lost my wallet this morning on the bus, but this amazing person found my wallet with my business card inside and brought the wallet to my office before lunch. I don't know what I would have done if he hadn't been so kind.

Feeling: _____

Content: _____

Counselor: You feel _____

because _____

5. Counselee: I work so hard, and my boss never seems to notice. I stay later than everyone else, I volunteer more than anyone else, and all I want is a simple recognition that I'm an asset to our team. Is that too much to ask?

Feeling: _____

Content: _____

Counselor: You feel _____

because _____

Section B:

6. Counselee: Oh my goodness, last night was horrific! I was walking up on stage to sing my solo and completely tripped over *nothing*! My sheet music went everywhere as I landed on my hands and knees. It was awful!

Feeling: _____

Content: _____

Counselor: _____

7. Child counselee: It's just not fair, every other kid in school gets a new backpack every year, but not me. My mom says mine is still in good shape and I don't need a new one. I know it looks fine, but I want a new one like everyone else!

Feeling: _____

Content: _____

Counselor: _____

8. Adolescent counselee: I just moved here at the beginning of the semester, and I miss my old friends. It's really hard being the new person and not knowing anyone. I wish I had better friends here, or just some people I could hang out with on the weekends.

Feeling: _____

Content: _____

Counselor: _____

9. Student counselee: I just got my grade back from my statistics midterm and found out I made an A! I studied so hard for that exam, I can't believe it actually paid off!

Feeling: _____

Content: _____

Counselor: _____

10. Counselee: I feel unbelievably sad after this morning. I had to take my dog to the vet and have him put down.

Feeling: _____

Content: _____

Counselor: _____

CONCLUSION

Potentially the most important skill a counselor can learn, empathy serves as a foundational bridge between counselor and counselee. Through the use of empathic reflection, counselees are able to feel heard and understood by their counselors. Hopefully they are then better able to understand themselves as well. Beginning with cognitive empathy and fostering affective empathy, counselors use this skill to demonstrate their ability and willingness to feel *with* their counselees, without counselors losing their own sense of self. Moving forward, this skill underlies every other part of the counseling relationship. When you do not know what to do, empathize.

REFLECTION QUESTIONS

1. What additional empathy examples can you think of that are found in Scripture?

2. Reflect on the incarnation as an example of empathy.

3. What do you anticipate will be your major obstacle in learning empathy?

4. How could your church benefit from expressing more empathy? How could your church teach and practice more empathic forms of conversation?

DEEPENING

AND GROWING

TARGET 1 SKILLS ARE INTENDED TO HELP DEVELOP a foundation on which to build the counseling relationship and begin exploring the issues for which a counselee seeks help. The reflecting skills of target 1 offer a counselee the opportunity to feel safe and be heard, which can be all that someone needs, particularly if he came in only with a request for understanding and involvement. So it is possible that work with some counselees never goes beyond the target 1 skills. But what do you do if reflecting is not enough, if there is more to discover and changes that need to be made?

The skills of targets 2, "Deepening," and 3, "Growing," provide the next steps. Target 1 skills set the stage and allow the counselor to earn the privilege to tread into the deeper, more subjective and more vulnerable territory that can be unearthed in the middle phase of counseling. Therefore, move slowly, cautiously and intentionally into using target 2 skills, and remember that your target 1 skills are always available to you. Do not leave them behind!

Target 2 and target 3 skills are primarily used in the middle phase of counseling. However, some target 2 skills, particularly clarifying skills, can be used in the early phase as well. Target 3 then builds on all the skills from targets 1 and 2. The difference between targets 2 and 3, and the primary reason for separating these skills into the two targets, is the difference in *how* the skills are used.

For example, the intuitive empathy and clarifying skills of target 2 are used to deepen affective experience and cognitive awareness of the counselee. Target 3 then takes that awareness a step farther by encouraging counselees to take intentional steps to ensure that this awareness makes a lasting difference for them in how they think, feel and act.

As a counselor, you will go back and forth between targets 2 and 3 throughout the middle phase of counseling in that as target 2 skills successfully deepen a counselee's experience in a particular area, you will shift your aim to target 3 in order to help that increased awareness take root and grow so that change is implemented in some form. That is why deepening (target 2) and growing (target 3) are shown as parallel processes in figure T2.1, rather than as target 2 goals preceding target 3 goals. There is a reciprocal movement between them throughout the middle phase.

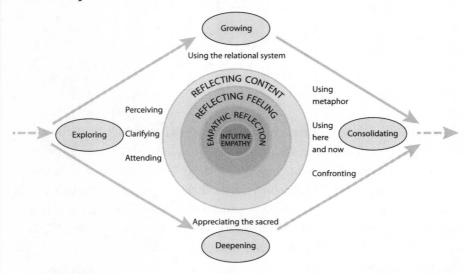

Figure T2.1. The targets, skills and the process of counseling

TARGET 2: DEEPENING

Target 2 builds on the solid foundation of target 1 skills and moves with the counselee into deeper levels of understanding and awareness of both the current situation and future possibilities. While working on this target area, the counselor gains understanding and awareness of the counselee, and the counselee develops self-understanding and self-awareness. Remember that the counseling process is about the *counselee's* growth, not about the counselor's ability to prove that he or she has good helping abilities or satisfying his or her own curiosity. Therefore the target 2 microskills are focused on what will further the counselee's abilities to make sense of herself and the situation. Note that the skills addressed through aiming for target 2 get progressively more insightful, risky and powerful, with *clarifying* being the least invasive skill and *immediacy* being the most intrusive skill. The greater the potential a skill has to provide depth, forward movement and insight, the greater the potential that skill also has to hurt, harm or overwhelm the counselee and the counseling relationship if used incorrectly. Target 2 skills should be approached with respect, caution and intentionality by the counselor. They should be used only when they are in the best interest of the counselee and after a sufficient foundation has been established through successful completion of target 1.

Clarifying (chapter eight). This skill uses both open-ended questions and prompts to encourage the counselee to elaborate on, specify or in some other way clarify what he has already said. The purpose of this skill is to provide the counselee with the opportunity to examine, and thereby better understand, the hows and whys of his or her situation. It will be important to note that the clarifying skill is meant to facilitate the *counselee's* understanding of his situation and is not a tool to appease the counselor's curiosity about details.

Intuitive empathy (chapter nine). The second skill related to target 2 builds on the foundational skill of empathic reflection that was used to accomplish target 1. Intuitive empathy is a more advanced skill, as its use depends on the ability of the counselor to make inferences about the counselee's feelings and to connect to deeper emotions than what the counselee may initially present. In this, intuitive empathy goes beyond a reflective skill, as it is no longer simply about being the counselee's mirror but instead asks the counselor to read between the lines and affectively connect to the counselee's experiences.

Expanding therapeutic options (chapter ten). The third skill within target 2 is the use of metaphor. This chapter engages advanced skills that rely more heavily on "art" and intuition than any other skills learned thus far. The use of metaphor, symbols and imagery in the counseling relationship involves engaging the counselee's imagination in order to better understand and express abstract experiences in more concrete ways. For many counselees, being able to describe their experiences in pictures unlocks layers of understanding and growth.

Confronting (chapter eleven). The fourth target 2 microskill involves pointing out apparent discrepancies between aspects of a counselee's verbal or nonverbal communication with respect to perception, affect or behavior. The purpose of the skill of confronting is not to "catch" the counselee in a contradiction but to offer the counselee the opportunity to examine or explain apparent contradictions in order to move toward greater congruency in life.

Using the here and now (chapter twelve). The final microskill that is aimed for in target 2 is that of using the here and now, the immediate in-the-room experience of each other. Using the here and now allows the counselor to point out what she is picking up in the moment. This observation can be about the counselee's nonverbal presentation or use of physical space, or the observation can be a reflection of what is relationally going on between the counselor and the counselee in the moment. It also involves the use of self-disclosure, in which the counselor shares something about herself that directly relates to what the counselee is sharing or experiencing in the moment. This skill is the most difficult target 2 skill to use appropriately, since it involves both reflection and intuitive perception, thus increasing both the power and the risk of the skill. Therefore reflecting the here and now has the potential to evoke strong feelings of vulnerability and emotional exposure for the counselee, and thus it must be handled with caution, respect and empathy.

While the exploration aspect of target 1 will result in an initial set of counseling goals, it is not until the target 2 skills result in a deepening awareness of what is really going on under the surface that the underlying issues come to light. By the time target 2 tasks have been accomplished, both counselor and counselee will be able to fill in the blank in the following sentence: "So the core issue(s) needing work are _____." These goals can be as concrete or as abstract as the counselee needs them to be, though it will be important to help the counselee make the goals as concrete as possible so that progress in counseling can be assessed.

TARGET 3: GROWING

Developing strategies for implementing change is the primary skill of target 3. Target 2 and target 3 skills go hand in hand in that, as there is deepening awareness of what the core, underlying issues are as a result of utilizing target 2 skills, the need for implementing change in a particular area becomes clearer, necessitating the use of target 3 skills. Therefore throughout the middle phase of counseling, focus will go back and forth between target 2 and target 3.

Too often counselors want to jump to solutions, actions and advice giving, thinking that these are the things the counselee *really* wants or needs. But in reality the counseling process is more about enabling counselees to better understand themselves and their situations so that *they* can discover or create solutions for *themselves*. Therefore target 3 skills are to be used in a collaborative fashion and at a pace that fits the counselee's needs.

Implementing change (chapter thirteen). Implementing change in counseling often involves both internal and external change. In 1988 Larry Crabb, well-known Christian counselor and spiritual director, wrote a popular book with the title *Inside out: Real change is possible if you are willing to start from the inside out.* The point of the book is well intended; so often in the church, and in society at large, we focus on external behaviors and try to change those. Crabb's point is that real change happens internally. However, it is our contention that well-rounded change happens in both directions, inside out and outside in. The verse at the beginning of this chapter from James 2 makes a similar point. We will look in more detail at this internal/external dynamic in chapter thirteen.

Related to this view of change is the foundational principle we see in Scripture of change requiring both the stopping of old and starting and new internal and external experiences (see Eph 4:22-25 as an example of this put on/put off dynamic). The counselee may want to extinguish something undesirable internally or externally. The process might be about adding or implementing something positive, and/or taking steps to reduce and eliminate other things, or working to prevent relapsing into something previously experienced as negative.

Change may be implemented in one or more of four domains of growth: (1) cognitive, focused on changing how the counselee thinks about her situation; (2) affective, focused on changing how the counselee feels about her situation; (3) behavioral, focused on changing what a counselee does in her situation; and (4) spiritual, focused on the counselee's relationship to God and/or issues of ultimate meaning. Different theoretical orientations to counseling are related more closely to one or more of these domains of growth. Regardless of the theoretical orientation you as a counselor choose to implement, when aiming for target 3 the counselor helps the counselee to look at where the counselee has been, compares it to where the counselee would like to be and helps the counselee implement appropriate change strategies to meet specific goals.

When aiming for both targets 2 and 3, the focus may expand from the specifics that initiated counseling to other areas of life. The counselor may encourage the counselee to generalize what has changed and apply it to other contexts. We will focus on two of these areas, which encompass much of life: expanding the therapeutic system and recognizing the sacred.

Expanding the therapeutic system (chapter fourteen). In this chapter we discuss how the principles that apply to using microskills with individual counselees can be adapted for expanded use with a larger system of two or more counselees. Some of the topics include maintaining balance within the counseling relationship, creating enactments, identifying relational patterns and focusing on process (relational patterns) rather than content (the specifics of a particular situation).

Attuning to the Holy Spirit and spiritual themes (chapter fifteen). While spiritual themes may emerge at any point in the counseling process, and we have addressed spirituality at numerous points in the book, this chapter will focus specifically on what it means to recognize the sacred and integrate spirituality into the counseling relationship. Whether or not a counselee holds the same faith beliefs as his counselor, it is important for the counselor to develop awareness and dependency on the Holy Spirit within a counseling session and throughout the counseling relationship. Otherwise we can fall into the trap of believing that the responsibility for the counselee's growth rests solely in the hands of the counselor (or the counselee).

HITTING THE WALL: THE IMPASSE

One indication that the middle phase of counseling is about to be entered is when a counselee shows resistance to going further. This can be experienced in a variety of ways by both counselor and counselee: for example, the sense of "hitting the wall," "spinning your wheels" or "treading water," or the counselee coming late to sessions, projecting blame onto you or others, not completing homework assignments, overspiritualizing and so on. At other times resistance may show itself through difficulties in the counseling relationship, for example, with the counselee getting angry at the counselor. On the counselor's part, the "impasse" may be experienced as sessions dragging, being bored, starting to feel frustrated or increasingly disliking the counselee.

Beginning counselors, in their frustration of being at an impasse and seemingly not getting anywhere, may assume that this means that the counseling process is at an end. In contrast, what is often happening is that counselees are fearful or reluctant to do the deeper work that is the focus of target 2 or to do what it takes to implement the changes necessary for lasting growth, which is the focus of target 3. It can take skillful empathic reflection, intuitive empathy and confronting to help counselees do the difficult work that targets 2 and 3 require.

ZEROING IN

Search me, God, and know my heart;
test me and know my anxious thoughts.

PSALM 139:23

CHAPTER FOCUS

SKILL: clarifying

PURPOSE: to help facilitate the counselee's deepening understanding of his or her story

FORMULA: Tell me more about _____.
What is it about_____ (content) that feels_____ (feeling word)?

I (ELISABETH) HAVE A DEAR FRIEND, JILL. We regularly have conversations that sound like this:

Jill: Oh my goodness, you would not believe what we did this weekend. It was so fun! Brian and Bob and Rachel and Laura were all there. But then, you won't believe it, he said that he was planning to move to Tibet at the end of the summer. I mean, I think that's a great fit for him, but she really wasn't happy about it.

Elisabeth: Umm, Jill, who's the "he" that's going to Tibet? And who's the "she" that's upset about it?

It can be a bit tricky following a story when you do not know who "he" or "she" is! Jill can often get so wrapped up in the story she is telling that such details get missed. While we will be discussing far more nuanced needs for clarification, this provides a humorous example of a situation where parts of a story need further elaboration.

Up until this point in the counseling relationship, the counselor's role has been to be the verbal mirror for the counselee, reflecting back what she hears from the counselee. In most counseling conversations there comes a point where greater clarity is needed in order for the counselee to move forward and be able to identify

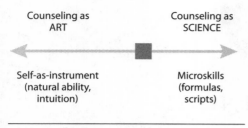

Figure 8.1. Art versus science: Clarifying

the specific nature of the problem or topic of conversation. While good reflecting skills can indirectly provide clarification to the counselee, the skills that are part of target 2 serve this goal directly, beginning with the skill of clarifying.

WHAT IS CLARIFYING?

The skills of target 1 serve the purpose of establishing relationship by setting a foundation for the therapeutic conversation and for allowing the counselee to feel heard and understood. Now, as a skill that is part of target 2, "Deepening," the broad category of clarifying helps in the new goal of elaborating on and gaining a deeper understanding of the characteristics and contributions of major elements within the story. Specifically, clarifying builds on the foundation set up through use of target 1 skills and begins to delve deeper into the meaning and possible significance found within the various elements of the counselee's story. Rather than being one specific skill, clarifying is actually a category of skills that help the counselee, and secondarily the counselor, to narrow the focus of the counseling conversation onto the areas of greatest significance, importance or confusion in order to bring greater understanding and clarity. The category of clarifying includes the specific skills of prompts, open questions and signposts. While all of these skills serve to help clarify the details, focus or nature of the counselee's story, each skill serves a slightly different purpose.

A counselee will often use a word or phrase that is vague in its nature, such as *frustrating, disappointing, unpleasant, enjoyable* or *hurtful*. It can be tempting for counselors to assume they know what counselees mean by particular words or phrases when in reality that word or phrase may have a very different nuance to each counselee. Clarifying skills are useful in focusing in on such words or phrases in order for the counselee to be able to better elaborate on and explain what that word or phrase means to him in that particular situation. It is important to remember that clarifying skills are to be used *first* for the benefit of the counselee's understanding and only *secondarily* for the counselor to be able to better understand the counselee. Additionally, while clarifiers can be used to gain insight into the details or content of the counselee's story, it is best to use clarifiers to focus in on the counselee's affect and to gain a better understanding of his or her emotions (Hill & O'Brien, 1999; Tamase & Katu, 1990).

Prompts. A prompt is a *statement* that invites the counselee to talk further about a particular element in his story that you, as the counselor, think might bring clarity to the story. A prompt inquires about one element at a time, giving the counselee the opportunity to expand on that single component before moving on to another.

The formula for this skill is: "Tell me more about _____."

An alternative formula is: "I was wondering _____."

It is very important that any prompt remains a statement and that the counselor's inflection does not go up at the end of the sentence, turning it into a question. By keeping a prompt as a statement, many counselees feel less threatened or on the spot to defend or prove what they are being asked to clarify and instead feel heard and invited to expand on something that may need further elaboration. For an example of how this might sound in an exchange, let us say a counselee comes into your office and says:

> **Counselee**: I am so nervous for this wedding. My best friend is getting married, and the wedding is on Saturday. I'm super excited for her, but, man, I am just so nervous!
>
> **Counselor**: Tell me more about feeling nervous.
>
> Or
>
> **Counselor**: I was wondering what feels so nerve-racking for you about this wedding.

The reasoning for the counselor's use of a prompt in this situation is of the lack of clarity or certainty about what in this scenario is evoking feelings of nervousness for the counselee. The counselor might suspect that they understand, assuming that the nervousness is related to the logistics of the wedding itself, but it could actually be a wide variety of concerns, from logistics to the appropriateness of the marriage to having to give a toast to anticipated conflict between family members. The list could go on and on. Note that the counselor's response was focused on emotion and kept simple. While a prompt may focus on content, it is best to focus on an emotion when possible. By inviting the counselee to say more about feeling nervous, the counselee's response is likely to simultaneously elaborate on the emotion as well as provide greater detail regarding the content of the story as he expands on the initial statement. The use of a prompt additionally allows greater freedom to the counselee to take the conversation where he needs it to go.

Empirical Support

Although open questions can be a valuable part of the counseling process, the research on the effectiveness of questions is mixed (Benn, Jones & Rosenfield, 2008). Rautalinko (2013) found that well-timed reflections "improved ratings of the counsellors and the observed working alliance, but open-ended questions did not" (p. 24). Similarly, Brodsky and Lichtenstein (1999) also found that too many questions can get in the way of developing a collaborative relationship with a counselee. Therefore, use questions sparingly and rely instead on reflecting skills to build and maintain a therapeutic relationship with your counselee.

Questions. Finally, after seven chapters, you get to ask questions! Our guess is that many of you are excited about this development, while others of you are equally as nervous about how to reintroduce them into your toolbox now that you have worked so hard on your reflecting skills. Just like many other skills, questions have their appropriate time, place and formula. They serve a unique purpose among the clarifying skills: inviting the counselee to explore his or her perceived connection between the feelings and content of the story being told.

Although we have not included questions among the target 1 skills, some questions will be necessary as part of the problem exploration aspect of target 1. However, use of too many questions can potentially interfere with the relationship-building aspect of target 1. Therefore we have included questions as part of target 2, when they can be used for deepening awareness.

Closed Questions

✓ can be answered in a single word, such as *yes* or *no*
✓ do not require the counselee's elaboration

At the end of this chapter is the "Question Cube," which further elaborates on types of questions and their use. For our purposes in this chapter we will present two types of questions: closed questions and open questions. *Closed questions* are any question that can be answered by a "yes," a "no" or with a specific piece of information that does not require elaboration. Examples of closed questions include:

◆ Did you go to the movies last night?

◆ Is school going well?

◆ What is your favorite color?

◆ Do you like pizza or hamburgers better?

◆ Did you . . . ?

◆ Do you . . . ?

◆ Have you . . . ?

◆ Will you . . . ?

◆ Won't you . . . ?

◆ Could you . . . ?

◆ When do/did . . . ?

While the counselee may choose to elaborate on a closed question, the grammatical structure of the question does not require the counselee to respond with anything other than yes or no, or to provide a very specified or limited response. There are times in the counseling process where closed questions may be useful, but they are generally limited to the initial intake or to times in which the counselor needs a detail clarified in order to continue "tracking" or making sense of the counselee's story. As a general rule, you should avoid all closed questions in a counseling conversation (Brodsky & Lichtenstein, 1999; Tamase & Katu, 1990).

The other type of question is an *open question*. The opposite of a closed question, an open question does not prematurely force the counselee into a predetermined or limited-choice selection of responses. Instead, open questions allow the counselee to expand, explore and elaborate as much as they would like. Examples of open questions include:

- What was your favorite thing about this weekend?

- How would you describe your weekend in the mountains?

- In what ways did you enjoy your economics class?

- When you realized you were going to be late, what did you do?

- What made you decide to call your parents?

Open Questions
✓ invite elaboration
✓ do not limit the counselee's response options

Some possible stems for open questions include:

- How . . . ?

- What . . . ?

- In what ways . . . ?

An open question does not lead the counselee toward a preconceived response or set of responses but instead allows the counselee to address what she sees as important, significant or relevant to the question. In a counseling setting, an open question will often ask the counselee to further elaborate on the connection she sees between the content and the feelings in her story.

One possible formula for an open question is: "What is it about _____ (content) that feels _____ (feeling)?"

While not every open question will fit this formula, it is a good place to start, as it serves to follow up on the empathic statement made to a counselee and can actually be perceived as quite empathic in and of itself as it demonstrates an understanding that a particular emotion is connected with particular content. The same rule applies to open questions as applies to empathic reflection in that a counselor is to include only one emotion at a time in his response.

Why you cannot ask "why." You will notice that a very popular stem is missing from the list of open questions, despite being grammatically open. This is the stem of "Why . . . ?" Although a why question is technically an open question, it is not considered appropriate within the counseling conversation. Read the following why questions to see whether you can determine what might be the reasoning behind this rule:

- Why did you do that?
- Why did you think going to the party would be a good idea?
- Why didn't you call your mom if you knew you were going to be late?

As you read each of these questions, what emotions can you imagine getting stirred up in the counselee who would be on the receiving end? A why question can put people on the defensive, feeling as if they have to prove or defend their actions, feelings or previous statements (Brodsky & Lichtenstein, 1999). In a counseling relationship, the counselor should strive to create an environment where the counselee feels safe and understood. Asking a why question can undermine this goal in an instant. It is important to practice turning a why question into either a what question or a how question, or a prompt instead. For example:

Counselor why question: Why did you do that?

> **Counselor open question**: What were you feeling (or thinking) in the situation that led you to make that decision?

> **Counselor prompt**: Tell me more about your decision to do that.

Counselor why question: Why did you think going to the party would be a good idea?

> **Counselor open question**: What was it about going to the party that was appealing to you?

> **Counselor prompt**: Tell me more about why going to the party was appealing to you. (Note that in this prompt the *why* is embedded. Although it is still a part of the counselor's response, by embedding it in the prompt much of the sting is taken away. If you have a particularly sensitive counselee, this may still cause a bit too much defensiveness, so be attentive to how the counselee responds when you use this prompt.)

Counselor why question: Why didn't you call your mom if you knew you were going to be late?

> **Counselor open question**: What led you to decide to not call your mom when you realized you weren't going to make it home before curfew?

> **Counselor prompt**: Tell me more about not calling your mom.

While it takes practice and intentionality, every why question has an alternative grammatical form that can minimize defensiveness and encourage greater elaboration and clarity from the counselee.

Diagnostic Implications

Professional counseling involves a number of discrete activities in which clarifying skills are required. For example, intake interviewing, diagnostic interviewing, mental status exams, and suicide and addictions assessments are all examples of applications of clarifying skills (see Sommers-Flanagan & Sommers-Flanagan, 2014, for detailed descriptions of each of these forms of interviewing).

The temptation for many counselors is to try to find a set of questions that will suffice for the majority of counselee situations encountered. Conducting more structured forms of interviewing, in which the same set of questions is followed in the interview, has helpful applications, for instance, at intake, in research or when trying to fine-tune a diagnosis or do a risk assessment. However, the majority of counseling is less structured in its use of questions and alternative ways of clarifying a counselee's experience.

Psychological testing, and the related use of questionnaires in many forms of counseling, can be exceptionally helpful to the counseling process. Even in pastoral counseling and spiritual direction contexts, questionnaires can be useful in providing additional information and clarifying the severity and extent of a counselee's experience. Particularly the use of brief assessments can provide quick, helpful baseline information of counselee functioning (e.g., depression or anxiety) and/or feedback regarding counseling progress (Greggo, 2016). Also, spiritual assessments can be helpful in clarifying or pointing to additional aspects of a counselee's experience.

Cautions with questions. Although questions can be very resourceful and facilitative to the counseling process, there are some cautions that need to be taken when using questions.

Be Very Careful with Questions That Are:

✓ closed   ✓ forced-choice
✓ begin with "Why?"   ✓ leading
✓ multiple

1. *Limit your questions.* When I (Elisabeth) was in my master's-level skills class, our instructor told us that we were allowed only three questions per fifty-minute session. While most of the time that number is a bit extreme, he made his point: use questions judiciously. It is a good rule of thumb that any question needs to be

followed by an empathic statement or a reflection of some kind. This will help you, as the counselor, slow down and truly listen to the counselee's response. It also will help the counselee not to feel as if they are in the middle of an interrogation!

2. *Multiple questions lead to confusion.* When you ask several questions in a row without waiting for an answer, your counselee is left with the dilemma of which question to answer. Generally the counselee will answer the last question you pose. When I (Heather) make this error, I am generally thinking aloud; I have not taken the time to formulate the question I really want to ask before opening my mouth! It is better to give yourself the time you need than to potentially create more confusion for your counselee.

3. *Forced-choice questions limit responses.* Some questions can be asked in the form of a multiple-choice test. This is actually a particular category of closed questions. For example, "Did you quit your job because you found one you liked better or because of difficulties at your former job?" The counselee's reason for finding different employment might actually be "none of the above"! Your counselee may have been laid off or fired. Or perhaps your counselee's spouse found a job in a different city and your counselee then needed to look for work in the new location. Maybe the youngest child began kindergarten and your counselee is ready to go from part-time to full-time employment. The point is, there can be countless reasons for choices that people make. An open question is always a more appropriate intervention. There is a valuable exception to forced-choice questions. Similar to the parenting strategy of limiting options for a child (e.g., would you like cheese or a banana?), a counselor may need to limit the choices in order to move the process along. For example, would you like to spend the remainder of our time today discussing possibilities for handling your frustrations with your spouse, or your concerns about work (implying that we are not going to go back to the unfocused string of complaints about everyone in your life)?

4. *Leading questions take you in the wrong direction.* While some leading questions are closed questions and already no-nos in this process, some leading questions can be delivered in an open format. Open questions that are leading communicate the counselor's opinion, perspective or value regarding the counselee's story. For example, a counselee may have shared extensively about a tenuous relationship with her parents, who live out of state. The holidays are coming up, and the counselee is discussing possible travel plans for Christmas. The counselor holds a strong value that family should be together for Christmas and believes that it would be good if the counselee were home with her parents for Christmas. The counselee has made it clear that she wants to do Christmas with her friends this year. As the counselee is discussing possible travel options, the counselor

asks, "When in all those plans are you going to see your parents?" A leading question can be far more subtle, but regardless of content a leading question will prompt or encourage a desired response from the counselee rather than following the counselee's lead.

Signposts. Signposts are the least used clarifying skill and one that not every counselor will find helpful. On the other hand, a signpost can also serve as an incredibly empathic clarifier, honing in on the single emotion that matters most to the counselee. Unlike prompts and open questions, which are likely to be used in varying degrees by all counselors, signposts seem to "fit" for some counselors and not for others. A signpost is a simple one- to two-word phrase that is reflected back to the counselee to note comprehension by the counselor and to encourage the counselee to continue. Make sure that it is a statement and not a question. For example, using the same exchange:

> **Counselee**: I am so nervous for this wedding. My best friend is getting married, and the wedding is on Saturday. I'm super excited for her, but, man, I am just so nervous!
>
> **Counselor**: Nervous!

In this exchange the counselor identifies a single word or simple phrase that captures the focus of the counselee's comment. The word is stated back, with appropriate inflection, to capture the counselee's meaning. Just like road signs when driving, a verbal signpost says, "This is where you are." And, just like a road sign, the counselee hears that statement by the counselor and can either keep going if the counselee agrees that it is in fact the "road" he is on, or the counselee can correct the counselor if it is not the correct "road." Be careful when using this skill to keep it as a statement and not let your inflection turn it into a question. A signpost that is communicated as a question can communicate challenge, judgment or misunderstanding to the counselee, leaving the counselee feeling unheard or defensive.

Check Your Understanding

Using the following counselee statements, write a possible prompt, open question and signpost (if applicable) that could be used as a counselor's response. See appendix A for possible answers.

Counselee 1: Today was the best day ever! From beginning to end it was just amazing. I truly couldn't have asked for it to go better.

Counselor 1 *prompt*: _____

Counselor 1 *open question*: _____

Counselor 1 *signpost*: _____

Counselee 2: I don't know what I'm going to do. I am just so devastated by the fact that I didn't get the promotion at work that I was up for. I mean, I just don't understand how that happened.

Counselor 2 *prompt*: _____

Counselor 2 *open question*: _____

Counselor 2 *signpost*: _____

Counselee 3: I know I need to have this conversation with my mom, but it's just tricky.

Counselor 3 *prompt*: _____

Counselor 3 *open question*: _____

Counselor 3 *signpost*: _____

WHAT CLARIFYING IS *NOT*

As we have discussed thus far, clarifying skills facilitate the counselee in exploring, expanding and elaborating on a particular component of his or her story. Clarifying is to be used for the benefit of the counselee in the pursuit of gaining greater understanding of the area or topic that needs attention or resolution. Just as it is important to remember what clarifying skills *are*, it is important to know what they are *not*.

Becoming a detective. Previously, in chapter four, we discussed the verbal villains that every counselor encounters in the counseling process, those well-intended ways of thinking and speaking that ultimately ignore or invalidate a counselee's emotions. With the introduction of clarifying skills, counselors who struggle with being a "detective" need to be extra careful in their use of questions. Remember that questions are to be used for the counselee's betterment and increased understanding, not to appease the counselor's curiosity.

A detective or journalist verbal villain is concerned with content-based questions and filling in details that may or may not be relevant from the perspective of the counselee. As a general rule, given enough time, a counselee will share the details that matter to him and that are pertinent to the story. I (Elisabeth) often fight the detective verbal villain in my head. I love details and facts! One of the ways that I keep my inner detective in check is by asking myself a simple, albeit morbid question: "Is the question I want to ask a 'How did your mother die?' type of question?" Let me explain. Let us say a counselee comes into your office, brokenhearted and grief-stricken by the death of her mother. She proceeds to tell you all about how the family is struggling now that Mom is gone and how devastating her death has been to the counselee. Now, you as the counselor are likely thinking, "I wonder how Mom died." On one level this could be an important question to have answered, as the anticipated impact on a person or family could be different if Mom died suddenly or had been ill for years. But, to the counselee, this is already a known detail—they do not need it clarified, and in all likelihood the counselee will provide this information as you give her the opportunity to elaborate on the story. Furthermore, by asking such a question, you are likely to distract the counselee from what she needs to talk about, and you could possibly communicate a sense of disrespect or impatience for her process.

Chasing rabbit trails. Similar to becoming a detective, clarifying skills are not for the use of chasing rabbit trails. When a counselor is chasing a rabbit trail, they are pursuing a line of details within a counselee's story that are secondary to the primary needs or interests of the counselee. While the rabbit trail may be of some therapeutic interest and possibly even some relevance, the timing is inappropriate. For example, a counselee may have come in to talk about his grief related to the recent death of his mother. Rather than focusing on the counselee's current emotional experiences and concerns, the counselor uses clarifying skills to explore the counselee's previous experiences with grief or the counselee's current relationships with other family members. While both of these topics may eventually prove relevant and pertinent to the counselee's process, pursuing them too soon can short-circuit the counselee's ability to explore and detract from the emotion or concern that the counselee sees as most relevant.

Clinical Tips

1. When in doubt, empathize.
2. Closed questions can hinder the therapeutic relationship and leave a counselee feeling defensive.
3. Open questions can allow counselees to expand on their story, but they should be used sparingly.
4. Ask questions that further counselees' understanding of themselves or their story. Avoid questions that simply serve to appease your own curiosity.

Action oriented. Rather than drawing attention to possible future behavior or actions, clarifiers are to focus on the counselee's continued exploration and growing understanding of her emotions in a given context. In the next section of the book we will discuss target 3 (Growing) skills, which are intended to help counselees move toward substantial growth and implementing change in their life. Clarifiers for target 2 are to be used for the purpose of gaining deeper understanding. Questions such as "How would it feel if you tried . . . ?" or "What would happen if . . . ?" are target 3 questions. As discussed previously, target 2 and target 3 skills are both particularly relevant in the middle phase of counseling. What is important is that you know which target you are aiming for as you use clarifying skills.

Inserting your opinion. Using clarifiers well requires a counselor to do some instantaneous and in-the-moment self-reflection as to his or her motives and intentions. If counselors are not careful, they will find themselves using clarifiers as a way of inserting their own opinions or perspective, rather than using clarifiers to help the counselee explore his or her own emotions. Take the following example:

> **High school senior**: I'm really stoked to be going to LA for college next year. I can't wait to get out of this boring farm town and see all that the world has to offer!

> **Youth pastor**: Tell me what's so bad about going to school here in town.

While this is technically a prompt, the implication is clear that the youth pastor thinks the student should stay closer to home. The response lacks empathy or acknowledgement of where the student is coming from. A better alternative would sound something like: "What is it about going to LA that has you so excited?" This open question serves as an empathic question, reflecting the student's feelings and content while inviting the student to elaborate further.

Biblical/Theological Connections

Getting to the heart of the matter, zeroing in, as we have called it in this chapter, reminds me (Fred) of the biblical story of King Solomon in 1 Kings 3. It is the story of two mothers, one whose baby died in the night. Come morning, both mothers claim that the living baby is hers. It is a sad, desperate story. One mother knows that the living baby actually is hers and is frantic at the thought of losing him. The other mother is grieving but cannot accept the horrific reality that not only is her baby dead but she inadvertently caused his death by rolling over on him in her sleep. Whose baby is alive and well? Solomon, with a brilliant, macabre suggestion, says that they will cut the baby in half in order to resolve the dispute, allowing the mothers to get half a baby each. Of course, the real mother exclaims "No!" and tells Solomon that the other mother can have the baby in order to save his life. Solomon, in his emotionally informed wisdom, knows that this is the real mother and gives the baby to her.

This is a fascinating, strange story of legal decision making that utilizes emotional attunement in the cause of justice. Getting at the root of an issue, being discerning and judicious with questions and other clarifying skills, requires sensitivity to the emotional and relational dynamics of the situation, and it is both a gift from God and a skill that can be developed.

Shortcuts to feelings. The cliché question asked by counselors is, "How do you feel about that?" This question should rarely, if ever, come out of a good counselor's mouth for a couple of reasons: (1) You sound like a cliché, and counselees are unlikely to take you seriously. Whenever possible, avoid sounding like a TV therapist! (2) In most situations, if you have to ask this question, you have not used target 1 skills well enough. The majority of the time, if a counselor uses effective reflecting skills the counselee will communicate his or her feelings either through spoken or nonverbal communication. It is a rare occasion in which a counselee has remained so content focused in sharing his story that an emotion is not evident. This question, therefore, is not needed to encourage the counselee to begin discussing his emotion. The other difficulty with asking individuals how they feel is that, ironically, in order to answer the question they have to switch to cognitive "head" mode, which takes them out of the affective "heart" mode that you are asking about!

RELATIONSHIP APPLICATION

One of the difficulties that couples often face is that each member assumes that they know what their partner means without taking the time to clarify. Teaching couples to slow down their communication process so that they take the time to make sure they really understand each other can be very helpful. Good communication takes time, and in our busy lives we constantly seek short forms (e.g., texting abbreviations), risking miscommunication.

In the field of marital and family counseling, significant attention has been given to the difference between content questions and clarifications, and process questions and comments. This is a key skill in effective work with groups of people. Simplistically, when looking at a river, the content is the water (Is the water clear? Is it cold? Is it shallow? Where does it flow from and to?), and the process is how is it flowing (Is it flowing fast with rapids, or is it slow and lazy? Are there bends in the river? Does it merge with another river?).

Examples of content questions are:

◆ How old are you?

◆ Where did you go after that?

◆ What was the fight about?

◆ What was the last thing you did with your son?

Examples of process questions are:

◆ What made you decide to tell me that?

◆ What do you think she heard when you said that to her?

◆ What is the difference between what you are saying and how you are saying it?

◆ What is the purpose of this argument?

◆ If you hadn't spent two hours arguing yesterday, what else would you have done?

As counselors, we need enough content—and clarified content—to get the counselee's story and to move forward in counseling. But the goals of counseling have a lot more to do with process.

MULTICULTURAL APPLICATION

Clarifying is an essential skill to use in multicultural helping situations. It is impossible to know everything about every culture or even everything about a single culture. After six months of immersion in Filipino culture, I (Heather) believed that I had come to learn a lot about relational dynamics within that context. Eight years later I realized just how much I did not understand and maybe never would.

One of the challenges in counseling across cultures is that even when using a common language, the same words can convey different meanings in various cultures. For example, when Filipinos say yes, they could actually mean "yes," "no," "maybe" or "I don't know!" Only upon clarifying would someone outside the culture, or perhaps even another Filipino, be able to know what was actually being communicated. In the United Sates, saying that a presentation "bombed" implies that it was a failure, whereas in Britain, the same word indicates that it was a great success (Hil & William, 1998, as cited in Murphy & Dillon, p. 105). Obviously, these differences set the stage for potential disaster within the helping relationship.

Clarifying can also be helpful in determining the meaning of nonverbal cues such as those discussed in chapter three. Particularly in multicultural settings, it is much better to clarify what you are seeing in terms of gestures, facial expression, tone of voice and so on than to jump to a wrong conclusion. Your ability to clarify cultural aspects that are confusing to you by asking questions or requesting that the counselee expand on what she is saying can make the difference between establishing a good helping relationship or failing to do so. In fact, not doing so may mean that you do not get anywhere in the counseling process, increasing the risk of the counselee prematurely ending it.

While it may be difficult to admit that you do not know whether you are hearing someone correctly, an attitude of humility will go a long way toward helping put counselees at ease. They will not likely expect you to know much about their culture and will usually welcome the opportunity to teach you more about it. Your admission of ignorance through seeking clarification will also serve to reduce the power differential between counselor and counselee by acknowledging that the counselee is the expert when it comes to his own culture.

MINISTRY APPLICATION

Clarifying can be immensely helpful when working with people in churches or other ministry contexts. It is tempting to make assumptions about individuals because of their group affiliations when they may or may not feel the same way or hold the same views as others in their group. Clarifying their reasons for seeking you out in the first place is essential, as well as continuing to clarify matters as you go. If your assumptions about what they are asking for are incorrect, your relationship will be hindered, and they will likely not continue meeting with you.

I (Heather) remember talking with a seminary professor who had questions about his faith. He could not be honest about his doubts in his place of ministry and so had sought out a counselor outside his particular ministry context to confide in. Unfortunately, it did not occur to that counselor that a seminary professor could possibly have such struggles. The counselor assumed that the problem was with the work environment rather than with deeper faith issues within the professor. By not clarifying what the professor meant by "struggling," the counselor totally missed what the professor was attempting to reveal, and the professor never did feel safe enough within the counseling relationship to fully explore and work through his doubts.

A SAMPLE COUNSELING DIALOGUE WITH MARCO

Skills used: reflecting content, empathic reflection and clarifying

Background on the conversation: Marco is a seventeen-year-old junior in the high school at which you are the school counselor. Marco comes to talk with you about his plans after graduation next year but is a little confused about the direction in which he would like to go.

Counselor: *Hi, Marco, it looks like we got your career aptitude results back. Now, remember that this assessment just provides a starting point for our conversation. It summarizes the categories of jobs you said you might be interested in. I'd like to go over them with you and see whether you agree or disagree with these recommendations.*

Marco: *Sounds good. I'm kind of excited to see what the results say.*

Counselor: *Wonderful. Okay, so according to this, it says that you have interests in what Holland calls the social and realistic domains. Basically it means that you like to work with people and you like to work with your hands. I'm wondering whether that initial assessment seems accurate to you.*

SKILL	prompt
This clarifying skill is used to "check in" with the counselee before proceeding further.	

Marco: *I think both of those things make sense. I really love working with my hands. My uncle has been teaching me carpentry for the last couple years, and I just love getting to create something out of a seemingly plain block of wood.*

Counselor: *You really enjoy the creative elements of carpentry.*

SKILL	empathic reflection
Although this does not perfectly fit the empathy formula, it links the counselee's emotion (enjoyment) with content (carpentry).	

Marco: *I really, really do! What I don't totally understand is the social category you mentioned. Don't get me wrong, I don't dislike people, but I'm not very extroverted, and I'd much prefer working alone to working with others on a project.*

Counselor: *The social category does not seem as fitting to who you see yourself to be.*

SKILL	reflecting content

Marco: *Not at all. I have friends and all, but the thought of doing a job where I had to be around people, talking and interacting all day, sounds exhausting.*

Counselor: *Ongoing interaction with other people sounds really tiring to you. Sometimes the social category includes teaching or helping others and does not necessarily mean a very extroverted or interactive job. I'm wondering whether there are any situations that would allow you to teach or help others that would feel less exhausting and more invigorating to you.*

SKILL	empathic reflection, prompt

Marco: *Oh! I didn't think about teaching, I absolutely love getting to teach other people carpentry!*

Counselor: *What is it about teaching carpentry that you enjoy so much?*

SKILL	open question
The use of an open question here allows the counselee to elaborate in a way that is less encumbered and could potentially lead to greater insight for the counselee.	

Marco: *All of it! I love all of it! Last summer I actually started teaching carpentry to my little brother and to a couple of friends from school. It wasn't anything formal, but it was a super fun experience. I got to make something with my hands in the process, but I also got to see other people go from clumsy and unskilled to becoming a creator in their own right. I even like how teaching carpentry makes me have to think about what I do and why I do it, and then break that down into specific steps to teach someone else.*

Counselor: *Even though you initially weren't sure whether a social description was fitting for you, the thought of teaching carpentry to others is very exciting to you.*

SKILL	empathic reflection, summary statement

There is a tendency to fall into ruts with how we ask questions. We find a way that is comfortable and then stick to it. For instance, the humorous caricature of the counselor asking "How did that make you feel?" can become irritating for the counselee who struggles with identifying and expressing how he feels. Reflect on the many ways there are to ask questions in creative ways. The cube below indicates options in format, subject and orientation. However, there are even more options to consider. A common way of varying your questions is to ask them with a past, present or future focus.

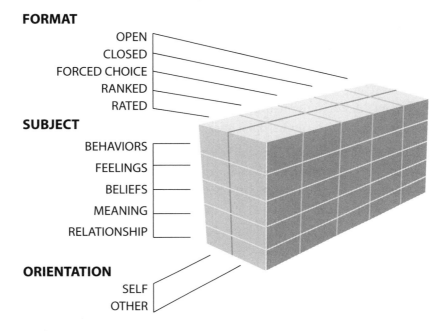

Question format:
- Open: How was it for you when she moved away?
- Closed: Did you grieve?
- Forced choice: Did you keep in touch, or did you cut off the relationship?
- Ranked: Was this harder or easier than when your brother moved away?
- Rated: On a scale of one to five, with five being the hardest, how hard was this experience for you?

Question subject:
- Behaviors: What did you do after she drove off?
- Feelings: How did that feel?
- Beliefs: How do your beliefs about relationships relate to this experience?
- Meaning: What did her leaving mean for you?
- Relationship: What impact has her leaving had on your other relationships?

Question orientation
- Self: Overall, how has this affected you?
- Other: How did it affect others who knew her?

Ways to use the question cube:
- Change up the ways you ask questions. Avoid getting caught in a rut by always asking the same type of question.
- Even if you want to focus on feelings, for instance, changing the format or orientation can elicit a different response from the counselee.
- Practice asking different combinations of questions, e.g., an *open* question about *meaning* focused on *others*.

Figure 8.2. The question cube. *Source*: Brown, 1997, p. 29.

CONCLUSION

The use of clarifying skills when you are aiming for target 2, "Deepening," ushers in the opportunity for further elaboration, exploration and discovery within a counselee's story. Prompts, open questions and signposts serve the purpose of facilitating the *counselee's* further understanding of the deeper elements of her story. Remember to earn the right to use clarifiers by utilizing empathy as much as possible and making sure that the relationship-building skills of target 1 have not been rushed through.

REFLECTION QUESTIONS

1. When you think about someone engaging you in conversation, are you likely to be more responsive to prompts, open questions or reflections? Why?

2. Consider someone in your life with whom you deeply enjoy having conversation. Think back to a significant dialogue with this person. What skills did they use to elicit more from you? In hindsight, what effect did their choice of clarifying skills have on you and your sense of comfort in the conversation?

CONNECTING DEEPLY

The purposes of a person's heart are deep waters,
but one who has insight draws them out.

PROVERBS 20:5

SKILL: intuitive empathy

PURPOSE: to help counselees connect not just conscious feelings with content, but underlying feelings, motives, values, fears and beliefs to their current reactions and experiences

FORMULA: You feel_____ (feeling word) because_____ (value/belief/motivation).

*T*HINK ABOUT A TIME when you felt angry.

» Describe the context and circumstances, including why you felt angry.

Anger is usually considered a secondary emotion; that is, there is usually a deeper, primary feeling behind the anger, such as hurt or fear.

» What might that deeper feeling be for the situation you just described?

As emphasized in chapter seven, empathic reflection is the core skill necessary for developing and maintaining a solid helping relationship. To feel heard by another human being is powerful, but to feel heard at the deepest levels of our beings can be truly life-changing. This is where intuitive empathy comes in. Using this skill appropriately is not easy, though, as the following story attests.

I (Heather) was *so* excited! Several years after I graduated with my MA, I was in a counseling session with a counselee I had been meeting with for several months when suddenly I had a "light bulb" moment. I knew with absolute certainty what my counselee's core issue was! This would change the course of my counselee's life. Trying to temper my enthusiasm, I made my intervention: "Sue, it sounds as though you have been feeling rejected by your father your whole life, and now it's really hard to trust that any man will be there for you." Inwardly I was congratulating myself. Sue was going to think I'm the best counselor ever! But then my bubble burst . . . "No," Sue replied, shaking her head, "I don't think that's true at all. . . . It's just that Joe and Ed are such jerks. . . . My dad's great!" I had to bite my tongue to keep from insisting that I was right. Obviously either I was wrong or Sue was not ready to face the truth. I figured that time would tell which it was.

Indeed time did tell. Two years later (yup, you heard me correctly . . . not two sessions, not two months, but two *years* later) Sue excitedly bounced into the session, hardly able to contain herself. "I realized this week what's been going on with me all this time! Dad was just never there for me. I mean, he was there physically, but emotionally he was totally unavailable. That's why I'm always giving guys such a hard time! I just assume that they will shut me out, just like Dad always has!" After doing some empathic reflections, I tentatively asked whether she remembered me making the same connection a couple of years ago. "No, we've never talked about this before!" she exclaimed.

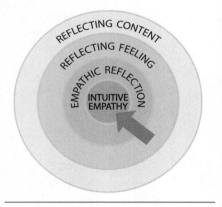

Figure 9.1. Aiming for intuitive empathy

What did I learn from this experience? It was certainly encouraging to have the confirmation that I had been correct in what I had picked up two years previous. But the biggest lesson was about timing. Just because I was intuitive enough to see what was under the surface of Sue's awareness did not mean that she was ready to hear it. Therefore, what had the potential to be a level five on the empathy scale in actuality became a level one.

WHAT IS INTUITIVE EMPATHY?

The skill of intuitive empathy takes us deeper into the clarifying process that is the focus of target 2. Intuitive empathy, also called additive empathy or deep meaning, builds on the skill of empathy that was covered in chapter seven but goes beyond merely reflecting and into a more artful form of intervention requiring good perceiving skills, including well-honed intuition (Okun & Kantrowitz, 2015). The purpose of this skill is to help counselees connect not just conscious feelings with content but to also become aware of the feelings, motives, values and beliefs that underlie their conscious reactions and experiences.

This is the first skill we have looked at that truly begins to blend artful intuition with skilled practice. The formula for this skill is pretty much the same as for reflecting basic empathy, but the implementation is somewhat different. A counselor's ability to accurately use the formula is based on something internal within the counselor: an intuitive awareness and perception of the deeper meaning behind a counselee's overt communication (Turock, 1978). As with other advanced skills, intuitive empathy is a skill that one must earn the right to use, as it brings greater potential for depth and insight but also greater potential to hurt or harm the helping relationship if delivered inappropriately in timing or wording.

The formula for intuitive empathy looks like this: "You feel _____ (feeling word) because _____ (value/belief/motivation)."

Intuitive empathy builds on the basic empathy scale, finding its home in levels four and five. Review the first three levels (see chapter seven), then focus on the expanded explanation of levels four and five. Note that one major separation between basic empathy and intuitive empathy is the additive nature of intuitive empathy (Chang, Scott & Decker, 2013). Basic empathy is simply reflecting the feelings and the content as presented in the story by the counselee. Intuitive empathy *adds* to this presentation, stepping into the counselee's deeper and yet unspoken feelings.

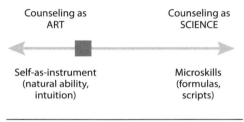

Figure 9.2. Art versus science: Intuitive empathy

Intuitive Empathy Scale

Level 1: This response is hurtful to the therapeutic relationship, as it directly or indirectly tells the counselee that the counselor is not listening, does not respect the counselee or does not understand the counselee. The counselor's reflection could be any of the following:

✓ ignores or dismisses the counselee's emotion (e.g., changes the subject)

✓ contradicts the counselee's emotion

✓ condescends (as if from a superior to an inferior)

✓ is argumentative

✓ states or infers that the counselee is deficient for feeling the way that he does, e.g., stupid, ignorant, foolish or childish

✓ gives advice

✓ shifts the focus onto what the counselor finds interesting or important, rather than what the counselee has expressed

✓ completely misinterprets the counselee's emotion, e.g., stating that the counselee feels happy about something when she is actually feeling scared

✓ a different skill is used, but so inappropriately that empathy is virtually absent

Level 2: This empathic response in some way misses the mark of what the counselee has communicated but is not as harmful as level one. Specifically, this could be any of the following:

✓ notably detracts from or minimizes the counselee's emotion but still reflects an emotion within the same broad category of emotion

✓ is stated as a question, not a statement

✓ is accurate regarding something the counselee said previously in the conversation but is "behind" the counselee's current point in their story

✓ the goal is not empathic reflection but an appropriately used different skill

Level 2.5: This is a category of empathic reflection in which the response is missing something accurate as it pertains to the feeling reflected, but it lacks adequate content reflection. While intended to be an empathic reflection, it in essence is only reflecting feeling; it qualitatively communicates empathy to the counselee due to its accuracy or delivery but lacks attention to context.

✓ slightly misses the mark of what the counselee has communicated

Level 3: At this level an empathic response accurately reflects the counselee's feelings and content without adding to or subtracting from what he has communicated. The counselor's reflection could be any of the following:

✓ is fully reciprocal or interchangeable with the counselee's explicit statement

✓ is an accurate depiction of the counselee's situation and/or state of being

✓ does not go deeper than the counselee's expressed feelings

✓ does not minimize or negate the counselee's expressed feelings

Level 4: This empathic response begins to go beyond what a counselee has stated and reflects implicit or underlying feelings of the counselee. At this level a counselee is likely to perceive the statement as insightful, feeling as if the counselor's statement "clicked" with who they are and what they are going through. A response at this level may:

✓ identify emotions that are just under the surface of the counselee's awareness

✓ reflect a theme rather than a specific piece of content in the counselee's story

✓ put words to an emotion that the counselee has only be able to talk around rather than talk about directly

✓ use stronger affective language than the counselee because of the messages within the counselee's nonverbal communication

Level 5: In this most advanced level of empathy, the counselor's response significantly adds to the affect and meaning expressed by the counselee but does so in a way that is still accurate and provides a deep sense of understanding for the counselee. At this level the counselor's verbal and nonverbal responses accurately reflect the affect, meaning and intensity of the counselee's deeper feelings. A counselee is likely to perceive a level-five statement as being beyond insightful and almost magical in the level of depth, insight and understanding expressed by the counselor. Often a level-five response garners a counselee response of, "I never would have thought that, but that's exactly what I'm feeling. How did you know that?!" A level-five response may:

✓ bring awareness to deeper emotions of which the counselee was not yet conscious

✓ focus on the core issues (e.g., emotions, identity) and ingrained patterns of the counselee, rather than on the counselee's affective response to a given situation

Intuitive empathy asks the counselor to draw from what we call "shared humanness" in order to understand what might be happening beneath the surface for the counselee. Shared humanness is the idea that, in a given situation, most people will experience similar emotions because it is how God has made us to respond. While we do not all experience the exact same emotion in a given situation, we are likely to experience an emotion similar to what someone else experiences. For example, a situation that evokes fear in one person may evoke apprehension, anxiety or nervousness in another. While the emotions are each different, they all fall within the same broad category. This shared humanness allows a counselor to consider what the counselee might be experiencing, even if the counselee has not stated it directly. The idea is not for counselors to project onto their counselees how they would feel if they were in the counselee's shoes but instead use their own self-awareness as a starting point.

Diagnostic Implications

In the "Diagnostic Implications" sidebar in chapter seven, we discussed alexithymia. This condition, characterized by the inability to identify, distinguish between, describe and imagine one's own and others' feelings, is a symptom of several DSM (APA, 2013) disorders. While the DSM typically describes these disorders as discrete categories, DSM-5 has introduced the idea of several disorders existing on a continuum or spectrum. This dimensional approach is helpful in understanding the schizophrenias, bipolar mood disorder, post-traumatic stress disorder, obsessive-compulsive disorder and panic disorder. The most well-developed diagnostic continuum is the autism spectrum disorder (ASD). This new diagnosis incorporates several previously considered discrete disorders, including Asperger's and autism.

Prior to DSM-5 it was common to hear the phrase "high-functioning Asperger's" to describe a child or an adult, most likely male, who was able to function reasonably well in social situations but perhaps exhibited some inability to "go deep" emotionally. An essential feature of ASD is "persistent impairment in reciprocal social communication and social interaction" (p. 53) or "deficits in developing, maintaining, and understanding relationships" (p. 50). If an ASD individual is having trouble in social relationships, it is quite likely that they will also have difficulty in seeing the deeper aspects of emotional experience in self and others. Without this ability, or with limited ability in this regard, it is likely that counseling will not progress to the level of intuitive empathy. As a result, other, more concrete, behavioral skills must be taught in counseling.

A good analogy for intuitive empathy is reading poetry. When one reads poetry, the surface meaning is not always all there is to the story. There are symbolism, metaphor and subtleties that lead the reader to conclude that there is deeper meaning conveyed than is apparent at first glance. And, just like reading poetry, there may not be one "right" interpretation, but there can be "wrong" ones.

Biblical/Theological Connections

Jesus had the unique ability to read a person's deepest wounds and hidden longings. The story of Jesus meeting the Samaritan woman at the well illustrates this clearly (Jn 4:5-30). Despite vast cultural distance between Jesus and the woman (ethnicity, religious, gender, economic differences), he intuits the personal and spiritual issues the woman is living with and points her to a relationship with God that will quench her spiritual thirst and feed her hunger for purpose and meaning.

Can we expect that kind of deep understanding in all counseling situations? Of course not! Our own biases can prevent us from understanding at such depth. Our counselees must be willing to engage in honest conversation. The social context must provide opportunities to transcend our cultural isolation. Our hearts must be open to hear and respond to the deep longings in people's lives.

Intuitive empathy as a reflecting skill. As a reflecting skill the purpose of intuitive empathy is to verbally say back the feelings and content that have been communicated by the counselee in some way but of which the counselee may be not fully aware. Unlike our basic reflecting skills, intuitive empathy seeks to add some level of interpretation to an otherwise simple reflection. Take, for example, your bathroom mirror. Your bathroom mirror only does basic reflection—it does not interpret your hair as being "good" or "bad" in the morning, nor does it give you any rationale for why your hair looks the way it does. However, you likely have some strong opinions about what you see in the mirror! What you "see" goes beyond what is actually reflected because you likely automatically add internal commentary. Intuitive empathy would be like someone else looking into that mirror and having the ability to not only see what is actually reflected but also pick up on what you "see," that is, be able to reflect back both the image and your internal commentary about that image. As a reflecting skill, intuitive empathy takes the counselee further into his or her emotions, deepening awareness of not just his or her emotions but the motives, values, beliefs and themes that inform those emotions.

Intuitive empathy as a clarifying skill. Intuitive empathy also serves as a clarifying skill. As a clarifying skill, intuitive empathy uses additive reflection (a reflection that goes beyond what was communicated by the counselee) to dig deeper and gain greater understanding into the counselee's emotions and experiences. Going beyond the clarifying skills of chapter eight, intuitive empathy seeks to clarify motives, values, beliefs and themes within a counselee's stories. This serves to take the counselee beyond the surface emotions and content of her story.

Clinical Tips

1. Intuitive empathy goes below the conscious level of awareness of the counselee. For this reason, intuitive empathy will often be perceived as somewhat confrontational.

2. Intuitive empathy should be preceded and followed by basic-level empathic reflections. This way you can make sure that you are picking up the counselee's reaction to your use of intuitive empathy as well as help to keep counselees from becoming too freaked out that you are "reading" them so well!

3. Minimize your use of intuitive empathy early in the counseling process and increase your use of it once the helping relationship is well established.

4. Remember that timing is everything! You may be right on about what is really happening with the counselee, but if he is not ready to receive it, your use of intuitive empathy can impede rather than further the healing process.

A SAMPLE COUNSELING DIALOGUE WITH SARAH

Skills Used: reflecting content, empathic reflection, clarifying, intuitive empathy

Background: You have been working with Sarah on a weekly basis for over a month now. Trust and an appropriate level of therapeutic rapport have been built between the two of you. Where the dialogue picks up, you are twenty minutes into your fifth meeting with Sarah. *Note: we give two potentially appropriate counselor responses for the last counselor response so that you can see the difference between intuitive empathy at a level four and at a level five*

Sarah: *As you know, my husband and I have been trying to get pregnant for the last ten months. It's been exhausting, and the past couple of months have left me feeling rather discouraged. What if we can't ever get pregnant? What if there's something wrong with me? I don't know what we'd do if we couldn't have a child.*

Counselor: *After ten months of trying you feel weary and are beginning to ask some hard questions.*

SKILL	empathy, level 3
feeling = weary content = ten months of trying; beginning to ask some hard questions	
In this response, "weary" implies both the exhaustion and the discouragement felt by Sarah. It is neither additive nor subtractive in nature but serves as an interchangeable response that accurately summarizes what Sarah said.	

Sarah: *I am weary! It's just so daunting. I mean, I had this plan ever since I was little: go to college, get married, work to save money for a few years, have a baby, go down to part time for a couple of years, have another baby. You know?*

This wasn't in the plan. This wasn't how things were supposed to go.

Counselor: *This was not how the plan was supposed to go.*

SKILL	reflecting content, no feelings reflected

Sarah: *No, not at all! I never cared about a career, or making money, or climbing some ladder. I started there because college was expected in my family and because we weren't financially ready to have children. But, now that we're ready, it's not happening, and I don't know what to do. What am I going to do if we can't get pregnant?*

Counselor: *You feel scared because having a baby is so important to you, but you're still not pregnant after ten months of trying.*

SKILL	intuitive empathy, level 4 (counselee does not use any feeling words, but "scared" can be inferred)
feeling = scared value = having a baby	

Sarah: *I'm so scared. I've been so focused on what we need to try next and how exhausted that's made me. But, yeah, I'm really scared.*

Counselor: *Tell me more about what scares you about not getting pregnant.*

SKILL	prompt

Sarah: *Well, I think I'm scared about a lot of things. I'm scared that it means there's something wrong with me. I'm scared that my husband will be disappointed, because he's always wanted kids. I'm scared that we can't afford to adopt and so we'll be childless forever. I'm scared that I'll never get to be a mom. I'm scared that I'll be left feeling alone and left out when all my friends have kids and I don't. I'm scared that everything I envisioned for life and family in the future won't happen—and then who will I be?*

**Counselor:
(option 1)**   *For you, not getting pregnant connects to a lot of other parts of your life. Specifically, you feel overwhelmed by fear because your vision for life has always involved being a mom.*

SKILL	intuitive empathy, level 4
feeling = overwhelmed by fear belief = your life plan always included motherhood	
The idea of being overwhelmed is not stated by Sarah but is implied—if the counselee does not agree with the reflection, the level would go down to a 2 on the rating scale.	

OR

Counselor: **(option 2)**	*It's like every aspect of your life is somehow connected to being a mom. The idea that you might not be able to have children feels devastating to you. It sounds as though what feels most terrifying of all is that you have no sense of identity apart from having children . . . almost as though the entire reason for your existence may be gone.*

SKILL	intuitive empathy, level 5 (provided counselee agrees with counselor's reflection)
	feeling = devastating, terrifying belief = no reason to exist
	The feelings of "devastating" and "terrifying" are implicit within Sarah's statement and by themselves would put the reflection at a level four. Adding the content, or belief, of "no reason to exist" bumps the response up to a five. The counselee has opened the door to the identity struggle she is facing, but the idea of her reason for living being affected is much deeper.

Check Your Understanding

Using the following exchanges, identify the skill used by the counselor, rate it on the empathy scale if applicable, and provide an explanation as to why the response earned that rating. Author's ratings and explanations can be found in appendix A. *Note: It is possible for there to be more than one response at each rating level.*

1. Counselee: I don't know what I'm going to do! I can't believe my dad is making us move right before my senior year of high school. It's so unfair! I have lived in this house my whole life; this is where my friends are, where my church is and where all my memories are. How can they ask me to start over now? My parents should know that I don't like change, I don't make friends easily and that I'm really shy. I wish we didn't have to move. I just want everything to stay the same.

Counselor:

You feel angry because your family is moving.

Skill: _____

Empathy Rating: _____

Explanation: _____

_____

You feel scared.

Skill: _____

Empathy Rating: _____

Explanation: _____

_____

Moving is really hard. I'd be super upset, too, if I were you.

Skill: _____

Empathy Rating: _____

Explanation: _____

_____

You feel scared because stability is really important to you.

Skill: _____

Empathy Rating: _____

Explanation: _____

_____

2. Counselee: I got the job! I got the job! I got the job! I worked so hard for this, and I can't believe it all finally paid off. Ever since I was in high school I wanted to be a doctor. I'd watch movies and TV shows about people who had mysterious illnesses and would see how the doctors worked so hard to find ways to heal people. It was so amazing to me. And, here I am, now with a job at the Center for Disease Control. Being on the frontlines of disease and death but knowing I might be able to offer someone a chance at renewed health, there's no greater calling than that.

Counselor:

Ugh, I get nauseous just thinking about anything medical.

Skill: _____

Empathy Rating: _____

Explanation: _____

_____

You feel overjoyed at the opportunity to work for the CDC!

Skill: _____

Empathy Rating: _____

Explanation: _____

_____

You feel invigorated working as a doctor because being able to care for the health of others is so important to you.

Skill: _____

Empathy Rating: _____

Explanation: _____

_____

What is it about being a doctor that makes you feel alive?

Skill: _____

Empathy Rating: _____

Explanation: _____

_____

3. Counselee: My dear Joe continues to decline. I've been able to care for him at home for the last year, but his Alzheimer's is getting so bad that I don't know how much longer I can keep him at home. After fifty-seven years of marriage, I can't imagine our home without Joe in it. But I also can't imagine how I can give him the level of care he needs right now. I've contacted various nursing homes in the area, and I think I know which one will be best for Joe, but I feel like I'm failing him. I'm his wife, I should be the one taking care of him, that's what I promised fifty-seven years ago. But, maybe, taking care of him means getting him better care than I can offer. Oh! I'm going to miss my Joe.

Counselor:

Joe's Alzheimer's is getting worse, and you don't know what do to.

Skill: _____

Empathy Rating: _____

Explanation: _____

_____

You feel like a failure because you have to put Joe in a nursing home.

Skill: _____

Empathy Rating: _____

Explanation: _____

_____

You feel torn because you want the best care for Joe, and that means putting him in a nursing home.

Skill: _____

Empathy Rating: _____

Explanation: _____

_____

You feel deep grief because Alzheimer's is taking your husband from you.

Skill: _____

Empathy Rating: _____

Explanation: _____

_____

WHAT INTUITIVE EMPATHY IS *NOT*

As an advanced skill, intuitive empathy carries with it the tension of greater risk and greater reward. Similar to clarifying skills, intuitive empathy brings counselees deeper into their emotions, and with that into a deeper level of vulnerability. It is important, in light of being in such sensitive and personal territory, that a counselor remember what intuitive empathy is *not:*

◆ Intuitive empathy is *not* essential, or even appropriate, for every counselee or for every counseling conversation. Where basic, reflective empathy can and should be used in nearly every context, intuitive empathy is reserved for times when the therapeutic relationship is strong enough and the goals of counseling are conducive to getting at deeper issues that are beneath a counselee's conscious awareness. A counselor must earn the privilege of embarking into such personal and vulnerable territory. Part of the art of using intuitive empathy well is knowing when to use it and when to hold back.

◆ Intuitive empathy is *not* the goal of every empathic statement. In most counseling conversations a level three, reflective empathy statement is the goal: to meet the counselee where he or she is. Intuitive empathy can be immensely powerful, which can make it both immensely effective when the timing is right and ineffective or even damaging if used incorrectly. The analogy of the power saw that was used in our discussion on touch (see chapter four) can also be applied to intuitive empathy; a power saw is a great way to cut down a large tree, but if you do not know how to use it correctly, you could injure someone badly. Similarly, the power of intuitive empathy can potentially overwhelm counselees when it is coming at them repeatedly and without a chance to process or take in the insights. Use intuitive empathy sparingly, being sure to continue using your perceiving skills to look for signs that the counselee is either connecting with your level-four and level-five reflections, getting overwhelmed or confused by them or even getting defensive. A good counselor gauges where a counselee is and what a counselee can handle, meeting him where he is and helping him move one step further. It is of greater skill to have insight and to temper that insight to the pace of the counselee than it is to "show off" by using intuitive empathy prematurely.

RELATIONSHIP APPLICATION

The ability to use intuitive empathy generally takes time and intentionality in getting to know the other person and how she thinks, feels and perceives the world. Additionally, it is an advanced skill that cannot be taught as much as it can be developed. What separates casual friendships from close friendships and therapeutic relationships is the presence of intuitive empathy. In close friendships or intimate romantic relationships, intuitive empathy is often experienced when one person seems to "just know" what the other is thinking, feeling or needing before it is spoken and sometimes even before the other person is aware of it for themselves. Just as in a therapeutic relationship, utilizing intuitive empathy in a personal relationship should be done with discernment and patience, and never as a way to manipulate or exert power over the other person.

Empirical Support

In *Counseling across cultures* (Pedersen, Lonner, Draguns, Trimble & Scharrón-del Rio, 2016), the authors discuss at length the valuable concept of cultural empathy. Cultural empathy expands beyond the individualistic Western perspective and extends empathy to a more "inclusive perspective focusing on the individual and significant others in the societal context" (p. 13). As such, "inclusive cultural empathy [is] based on a more relationship-centered perspective" (p. 13). The authors posit that:

Inclusive cultural empathy has two defining features: (1) Culture is broadly defined to include cultural teachers from the client's ethnographic (ethnicity and nationality), demographic (age, gender, lifestyle broadly defined, residence), status (social, educational, economic), and affiliation (formal or informal) backgrounds; and (2) the empathic counseling relationship values the full range of differences and similarities or positive and negative features as contributing to the quality and meaningfulness of that relationship in a dynamic balance. (p. 18)

MULTICULTURAL APPLICATION

Due to cultural differences, using intuitive empathy may be more of a challenge with diverse counselees. This skill involves the ability to be nuanced in the use of language and to read nonverbal cues well. Intuitive empathy is generally one of my (Heather's) strengths, but I have felt like a neophyte in some crosscultural counseling situations because I could observe body language that told me that my counselee was reacting emotionally, but I had no clue as to what was really going on with them! This is where the clarifying skill of the previous chapter should be utilized.

I have found, though, that my ability to use intuitive empathy increased as I was given the opportunity to meet on an ongoing basis with particular counselees. As I got to know them better, I was increasingly able to recognize their unique behavioral and affective patterns and make inferences from them. This requires hard work and persistence but is rewarding in the end.

If the counseling situation is one that requires intuitive empathy, but you do not see progress in your ability to use this skill with a particular counselee, you may need to refer the counselee to someone else. I came close to that point with a Chinese counselee whose facial expressions and tone of voice were so well controlled that I could not pick up the affective nuances. I finally admitted my limitations to her, and we discussed the possibility of her seeing a Chinese counselor. The Chinese community she was a part of was relatively small, so she was hesitant to see someone for counseling that she would invariably cross paths with in other settings. She agreed to verbalize her internal world to a greater extent, which then allowed me to use clarifying skills. As I came to know her better, she became more comfortable letting down her guard, and I was increasingly able to effectively use intuitive empathy in our times together.

MINISTRY APPLICATION

Sitting with people as they lie in a hospital bed, terribly ill or facing death, draws on a unique set of abilities within a counselor, pastor or chaplain. Every skill you have learned up until this point remains critically important, but the ability to provide intuitive empathy can be an incredible gift at that moment.

For example, an older man in hospice is outwardly angry that his son has not come to visit all week. Through the counseling conversation, intuitive empathy may bring to light that his anger is actually covering a deeper feeling of fear of being alone, fear of being forgotten or fear of feeling insignificant to those closest to him. A counselor who only focuses on the content of the son not visiting may miss the deeper heart-longings of the counselee, who is looking for affirmation and validation of his significance as a person.

The topic of death is sometimes avoided by family members or medical personnel, even when it is clear that the individual is dying. This presents the patient with a dilemma. The patient may want and need to talk about their fears, but sensing that their family members are either unable to face reality or that they are trying to protect the patient, she may not feel permission to bring up the topic. You offer a great gift to such an individual by using intuitive empathy to bring out any underlying fears or concerns that you sense are there.

CONCLUSION

The advanced skill of intuitive empathy is one of great power and significance within a counseling relationship. As with other advanced skills, its potential for insight is matched with its potential for harm when used inappropriately. Reflecting back a counselee's deepest hopes, fears, beliefs or motivations takes both skill on the part of the counselor and rapport between counselor and counselee. When the privilege to use this skill has been earned, and it is delivered with precise timing and insight, the potential for counselee growth and insight is immeasurable!

REFLECTION QUESTIONS

1. Now that you have learned basic reflective empathy and intuitive empathy, which do you think comes more easily to you? Why?

2. In what ways might the skill of intuitive empathy benefit you in relationships with friends and family, and in professional or ministry contexts?

3. What is likely to be your biggest challenge in utilizing intuitive empathy appropriately?

EXPANDING THERAPEUTIC OPTIONS

What shall we say the kingdom of God is like, or what parable shall we use to describe it? It is like a mustard seed, which is the smallest of all seeds on earth. Yet when planted, it grows and becomes the largest of all garden plants, with such big branches that the birds can perch in its shade.

MARK 4:30-32

CHAPTER FOCUS

SKILL: using metaphors

PURPOSE: To examine the use of metaphor and imagery with respect to the microskills. How can our imaginations be a resource in counseling to explicate, expand or create and deliver metaphors?

FORMULA: It's like _____.
It feels like _____.
What kind of image comes to mind as you focus on how you feel?

THINK ABOUT HOW YOU ARE FEELING at this point in your studies. You are ten chapters into this book. How are your studies going? While we commonly respond to a question like this with an affective word or phrase, sometimes a metaphor may even better describe and add nuance to your description of your emotional state. For example, the expression "I feel like I'm between a rock and a hard place" has no affective words in it but communicates well how someone feels.

» Draw or use word pictures (no affective words allowed) to complete the following statement: At this point in my training I feel like . . .

Using metaphors as part of your counseling with individuals can be extremely helpful, as illustrated by the following case scenario. I (Heather) had been meeting with Mandy, a middle-aged woman, for several months. Rapport had been developed fairly quickly, and we had established some clear counseling goals. In terms of therapeutic process, we were just about at the neck of the hourglass when I started to feel stuck. It was as though the grains of sand had clumped together and movement had ceased. On the surface everything looked fine. At a deeper level, however, I sensed that Mandy was holding something back, but I did not know what it was. After several sessions of treading water, I decided to take the plunge. I used a metaphor to express what I was intuitively sensing: Mandy was resisting my attempts to engage her at greater depth. It went like this:

Heather: Mandy, for several weeks now I've been feeling frustrated in our sessions. I'm trying to help you get closer to some of your core relational issues, but I feel like I'm not getting anywhere. It's like you're behind some kind of barrier, like there's a Plexiglas wall or something . . .

Mandy: Darn! I was hoping you wouldn't notice! It's not really a Plexiglas wall, though, it's more like I've barricaded myself inside a castle!

Heather: Tell me more about the castle . . .

Mandy: Well, it has really thick walls with a gate that's deadbolted shut, and only tiny barred windows that have a sliding panel. Even when the panel is open, someone from the outside can't see in. It also has a deep moat with water filling it, and a huge drawbridge that can only be controlled from inside.

Heather: That sounds like quite the fortress! What was your reason for building it?

Mandy: It's safer this way. I've been so hurt by so many people I've decided I shouldn't let them or anyone get too close to me. Thus the fortress.

Heather: So if you're inside the fortress, where am I?

Mandy: You're on the other side of the moat, and the drawbridge is up. I can see you by sliding back the window cover in the gate a little, but you can't really see me. We can hear each other's voices, though.

Heather: Well, that explains why I've been feeling distance between us! There has been a huge barrier! How would you feel about letting me gradually get closer to you, so that you had time to adjust and assess whether I'm safe, risking just a little at a time? I know it seems really scary now, but I would love to not have those barriers between us. You would be the one to decide how close you let me get each week.

Mandy: Hmmm. OK, I'm willing to give it a try, as long as you don't try to storm the door and push your way in. I'll work on letting you gradually approach.

Over the ensuing weeks Mandy was true to her word. The next session she let down the drawbridge and allowed me to stand outside the door and talk with her. The week after that she slid back the covering to the window and let me see her face in the shadows as we talked. The following session she opened the castle gate a crack, after which she opened it fully and we talked across the threshold. Finally the exciting day came when she actually invited me into the castle. From there counseling progressed quickly, and my sense was that the sand in the hourglass was flowing freely again.

WHAT IS METAPHOR?

Metaphor has traditionally been viewed as a "linguistic expression using words from a *source* domain to talk and refer to something in a *target* domain" (Gelo & Mergenthaler, 2012, p. 159). *Source* refers to the concrete language that is linked to the more abstract *target* concept (Robert & Kelly, 2010). Mandy's use of the analogy of a castle, for example, utilized a literal, concrete idea to describe the more abstract concept of relational defensiveness.

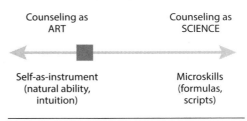

Figure 10.1. Art versus science: Metaphor

Metaphors are used in our everyday language. We suspect that some of you did not even notice the references to water that we used as a metaphor in the first paragraph. For example, "On the surface [of the water] everything

---

Conventional Metaphors

Animals:
- ✓ an elephant in the room
- ✓ an albatross around your neck
- ✓ letting the cat out of the bag
- ✓ mama bear

Various:
- ✓ weathering the storm
- ✓ don't judge a book by its cover
- ✓ melting pot or cultural mosaic
- ✓ snowball effect
- ✓ shooting the messenger
- ✓ ground zero
- ✓ bad apple
- ✓ no-win situation
- ✓ biting the hand that feeds you
- ✓ cabin fever
- ✓ moral compass
- ✓ slippery slope
- ✓ tunnel vision

Body:
- ✓ broken heart
- ✓ lending a hand
- ✓ cold feet

Athletics:
- ✓ faceoff
- ✓ false start
- ✓ jump the gun

What is the value of these examples in counseling dialogues?

---

looked fine"; "At a deeper level"; "After several sessions of treading water, I decided to take the plunge [dive into the water]." These are *conventional metaphors*, while those that are originally created to communicate a specific concept, such as Mandy's castle analogy, or the Plexiglas analogy, are *unconventional metaphors* (Gelo & Mergenthaler, 2012, p. 160).

The purposes of metaphors, or figures of speech, in literature are multiple; essentially they are a form of compressed or abbreviated communication attempting to convey extended meaning by connecting or paralleling current topics with other, common images in the culture. As such, they enrich and deepen understanding, communicating nuance as well as possible further meaning. However, used ineffectively, they can also serve to confuse.

Biblical/Theological Connections

The verse at the beginning of this chapter uses the metaphor of the mustard seed to describe the kingdom of God, a central theme of the New Testament. Metaphor plays an essential part in Scripture's efforts to make known and to make clear faith concepts. Another example in Scripture has been adopted by many evangelical Christians throughout the world when they are known as being "born again." John 3:3 combines the two metaphors by stating that "Jesus replied, 'Very truly I tell you, no one can see the kingdom of God unless they are born again.'" Many faith concepts rely heavily on metaphors to help us more deeply understand aspects of our faith. God as "Father," Jesus as "savior" and the Holy Spirit as "counselor" are all rich metaphors used to extend and deepen our understanding.

Other examples of biblical metaphors express important theological truths: salt and light (sharing spiritual truth), sheep without a shepherd (being spiritually lost), whore or prostitute (unfaithfulness), running the race (perseverance in the faith), armor of God (spiritually protecting ourselves), bride and bridegroom (Jesus' relationship to the church) and body of Christ (the community of believers).

It is important to realize that there are segments of the Christian world, and possibly counselees as well, who are quite suspicious of the idea of using our imaginations and thus using metaphors. At the end of the chapter is a reflection on this issue that provides a biblical foundation for the use of our imaginations.

FUNCTIONS OF METAPHOR

There are many good reasons to use metaphor to communicate. The frequent use Jesus made of parables indicates that he understood the power of story to communicate difficult truths (Blomberg, 2012). Both Old and New Testament writers made frequent use of metaphor (Diel, 1975/1986). The book of John, for instance, uses many metaphors for Jesus (see "Word Pictures" sidebar). Many cultural groups use narratives and proverbs that are metaphorical in nature even more than do Westerners (see "Multicultural Application" later in this chapter).

Metaphor not only is helpful in communication but is also a vehicle for change, which makes its use beneficial within helping relationships. Many suggestions have been made for how specifically metaphor can be beneficial in this context (cf. Barker, 1985; Collins, 2012; Faranda, 2014; Robert & Kelly, 2010; Tay, 2012). While not all-encompassing, Lyddon, Clay and Sparks (2001) have identified five functions of metaphor, which we believe correspond well with the use of the microskills you already have been developing. The five areas are: (1) relationship building, (2) accessing and symbolizing emotions, (3) uncovering and challenging coun-selees' tacit assumptions, (4) working with counselee resistance and (5) introducing new frames of reference (p. 270).

Relationship building. Metaphors can be used to develop therapeutic rapport. We have discussed previously the importance of reflecting content, reflecting feeling and empathic reflection as part of target 1, "Establishing Relationship and Exploring." Finding the best word to accurately reflect the counselee's meaning was emphasized as vital to successfully communicating to the counselee that the counselor under-stands what he or she is experiencing. Metaphor can accomplish the same thing by using conventional metaphors instead of specific words. For example, using the met-aphor "torn apart" reflects the meaning of the counselee's word choice of *conflicted*.

See the sidebar "Conventional Metaphors" for other examples of simple, conven-tional metaphors that can be helpful.

Word Pictures for Jesus from John's Gospel (Greggo, 2007)

These metaphors are used to communicate an aspect of who Jesus is: Word, Light, Lamb of God, Messiah, Living Water, Bread of Life, Gate, Good Shepherd, Resurrection, Way, Truth, True Vine, Advocate.

These metaphors provide more than just a description of who Jesus is. For instance, Jesus calls himself the Bread of Life, an image to suggest a source of nourishment used to nurture and support life. Or he calls himself the Way, a pathway and a guide encouraging discernment and wisdom on the journey.

Similarly, "worn out" could be a helpful comparable paraphrase of *tired* or *fatigued*. See table 10.1 for other examples of simple, conventional metaphors that can be helpful; metaphors that depend on obscure or antiquated references are generally less helpful unless the counselee is a native English speaker. Over time language changes, language differs geographically, and language is highly unique to the individual, so it is necessary to listen closely to your counselee's use of vocabulary and align your own word choice to theirs.

Metaphors can also be used to help orient counselees to the helping process. For instance, a counselor might decide to use the metaphor of a *journey* to describe the helping process. This could include describing the counselee as the one making the journey, with the counselor (or God or the Holy Spirit) walking alongside as a companion. To further the analogy, the counselee is the one making the decisions as to whether to stay on a given road, change the route or even modify the destination. However, the counselor can point out alternative routes along the way, make the counselee aware of various transportation options, indicate dangers en route, watch out for rest areas and/or suggest the possibility of new destinations or via points. The helping relationship may be enhanced in that such a metaphor may help counselees better understand the overall process, thereby possibly becoming more willing to engage it.

Table 10.1. Metaphors and their meaning

Metaphor	Affective Meaning
"torn apart" or "of two minds"	conflicted
"worn out" or "washed up"	tired, fatigued, exhausted
"over the moon," "on top of the world," "on cloud nine"	ecstatic
"bury your head in the sand"	in denial
"at a fork in the road"	needing to make a difficult decision when each choice is equally valid
"running around in circles"	confused, anxious
"at loose ends"	uncertain
"in a bind," "feeling stuck," "between a rock and a hard place"	frustrated, confused, afraid
"running on empty"	desolate, sad, spent (deenergized), depleted
"lost face"	shamed

Accessing and symbolizing emotions. Recently a five-year-old child told me (Heather) that she had a "pain in my heart." We had been visiting Rocky Mountain National Park in Colorado and were at almost twelve thousand feet, where it is more difficult to breathe. I initially misunderstood her, thinking that she was attempting to communicate that the altitude was negatively affecting her physical well-being, when she began to cry, wailing, "I miss my Mommy!" It is not only children who have difficulty recognizing their emotions and/or using affective language; our adult counselees can also struggle, but they may have an easier time using metaphor.

Amy, a sexual abuse survivor, had cut off her feelings for as long as she could remember. When asked what she was feeling she had no idea how to respond. Using metaphors connected to her physical sensations helped her to begin to identify her emotions. For example, she began to connect "a lump in my throat" with sadness, "butterflies in my stomach" with anxiety, and "a furnace in my belly" with anger. Somatic symptoms or physical symptoms serve as even more powerful metaphors for people of some cultural groups (see "Multicultural Application" below). Such metaphors may be initiated by the counselee and reflected back in emotional language by the counselor, serving as an alternate way to reflect feeling or reflect empathy.

Metaphor could also be initiated by the counselor as a way of using the skill of intuitive empathy. For example, the counselee may verbalize that he feels sad, when by looking at facial expressions and listening to the tone of voice the counselor may reflect back, "It looks like you're really torn up inside." Similarly, the skill of immediacy could be utilized through metaphor if the counselor observes tears forming in the counselee's eyes and states that "It looks as though a river is ready to begin flowing."

Empirical Support

One of the cutting-edge areas of research in the mental health field is studying the brain. Studies involving imagery are no exception. Studies have shown that:

- Imagining something produces long-term structural growth in the areas of the brain being stimulated (Siegel, 2007).
- Neural image formation appears to be closely connected to how we develop a sense of self (Damasio, 2012).

- The midbrain area, rather than the cortex, seems to be where self-image begins to form (Faranda, 2014).
- Visual images, emotions and motor functions are connected in the brain (Faranda, 2014).

These findings give further evidence for the usefulness of metaphor and imagery within helping relationships.

Uncovering and challenging counselees' tacit assumptions. Counselees are often not fully aware of their own assumptions about themselves and the world, and they may feel threatened by attempts to increase their awareness. One advantage that metaphors offer over other types of communication is that they are more indirect (Barker, 1985). The nonverbal nature of the imagery that is evoked by use of metaphor is also thought to engage both hemispheres of the brain (Faranda, 2014) as well as tap into basic memory and retrieval systems (Schaub & Schaub, 1990). These all contribute to the ability of metaphor to bypass a counselee's defensive reactions, thus increasing the chances of such a confrontational intervention being well received.

Counselees who have been abused as children may, for example, have erroneous perceptions of God (Gingrich, 2013). Counselors may find that God is viewed as unsafe, particularly if the counselee's abuse was at the hands of his or her father. Therefore, introducing the metaphor of *God as father* can potentially tease out an underlying belief that no one is safe, particularly father figures. The counselee's assumption may fit better with a metaphor of *God as judge*. Changing the metaphor to *Jesus the Good Shepherd* may help the counselee's perception to shift to a more accurate, realistic one.

Working with counselee resistance. The ability for metaphor to decrease defensiveness, as discussed above, works particularly well when dealing with counselee resistance (see chapter eleven for further discussion on resistance). Going back to an earlier example, when Mandy was not willing to engage in the process necessary to continue forward in counseling, Heather introduced the metaphor of sensing as though Mandy was behind Plexiglas. Mandy was then able to develop and deliver her own castle metaphor, which ultimately led to a therapeutic breakthrough. Simply saying "I sense that you're not feeling safe enough with me, Mandy, to really work through the fear you're experiencing" may have felt threatening and perhaps resulted in even greater resistance. In this case the microskill of relational immediacy (see chapter twelve) with metaphor was used to counter Mandy's fear of proceeding to the next step of healing.

The microskill of confronting by pointing out discrepancies can also be done using metaphor. A direct confrontation of a counselee who is showing irresponsible behavior at work could be made by saying, "You've told me that you want to eventually be promoted to manager, yet you came late for your shift twice last week, didn't show up once and are now in danger of losing your job!" Using metaphor, the same confrontation could be made by saying "You've indicated to me that you want to soar like an eagle to success at your job, yet through some of your choices these past couple of weeks you're actually in danger of crashing on the rocks below." Overuse of this way of confronting could backfire (another metaphor!), but with someone who is defensive and with whom metaphor has been previously helpful, it can be quite effective.

> *The imagination, since it is a faculty of the natural mind, must necessarily suffer both from its intrinsic limitations and from an inherent bent toward evil. . . . A purified and Spirit-controlled imagination is, however, quite another thing, and it is this that I have in mind here. I long to see the imagination released from its prison and given to its proper place among the Sons of the new creation. What I am trying to describe here is a sacred gift of seeing, the ability to peer beyond the veil and gaze with astonished wonder upon the beauties and mysteries of things holy and eternal.*
>
> **A. W. Tozer (1959)**

Introducing new frames of reference. Metaphors provide the opportunity for counselees to view themselves or their situations differently. Tom was a child-abuse survivor who used the metaphor of a "piece of glass, shattered into a hundreds of pieces" to describe the pain and helplessness he felt. Tom's counselor took his metaphor and modified it, talking about how stained-glass windows are the result of taking pieces of glass and creating something unique and beautiful from them. This reframe was able to give Tom renewed hope. He realized that nothing could take away the horror of his trauma, but that God could take his brokenness and fashion something new and good from the pieces of his life. Such a metaphor is likely to be helpful only if the counselor is authentic in his or her belief that change for this particular counselee is possible. Metaphors used in this way would be rated as fours or fives on the authenticity scale and as such have a confrontational element to them (see chapters eleven and twelve).

Diagnostic Implications

By its very nature the DSM-V diagnosis of dissociative identity disorder (DID) involves metaphor. While the external reality is that an individual with DID is actually one person with one body, the internal reality of someone with DID is experienced as many people of different ages, abilities and physical characteristics. The internal worlds of people with DID can vary greatly. Some have described themselves as a house with multiple levels and various rooms on each floor, with different identities living in each room. Others' internal structures involve multiple kingdoms or islands, with each having its own organizational structure. The possibilities are only limited by imagination. In order to work effectively with those who have DID, counselors must be able to enter their counselees' subjective worlds, explore them and ultimately help them modify their metaphors so that they better fit reality.

For instance, one dissociated identity of a counselee with DID saw herself as the angel of death. Entering into her metaphor, I (Heather) explored it further, only to discover that she believed that her role was to kill the body. On pointing out that the body I saw did not have the black wings and claws that she believed she had, her metaphor began to shift. Eventually she came to view herself as the terrified child she had been when she was sadistically tortured. After more time and much hard work, she was able to recognize that she was not actually a child but was actually one part of a whole person who had been shattered as a result of childhood trauma. Being able to introduce helpful metaphors, and being able to work with, extend and modify the counselee's metaphors, is an essential skill in working with such counselees.

A child counselee once told me (Heather) the following joke: "How do you eat an elephant?" The answer? "One bite at a time!" Out of all of the possible jokes she could have shared, she chose one that could be viewed as a metaphor for how to approach difficult therapeutic work. Subsequently I have told the joke to a number of counselees who were feeling overwhelmed about the obstacles to recovery still facing them.

GUIDELINES FOR USING METAPHOR

We have discussed some of the functions metaphors have in counseling, along with some specific examples that were used to illustrate these functions. Now we are going to look at some guidelines for how to best use metaphor. A number of authors have suggested protocols for working with metaphor (e.g., Kopp & Craw, 1998; Sims, 2003; Sims & Whynot, 1997). However, we have concluded that the guidelines suggested by Bayne and Thompson (2000), as a result of their research on clinical usages of metaphor, encompass what is most beneficial. Their delineation of specific steps to take in using metaphor within a helping relationship expands on Strong's (1989) original three strategies for responding to counselee's metaphors. They are: (1) recognize that a counselee has moved from literal communication to figurative, that is, that he is using metaphor; (2) decide whether or not to respond to the metaphor immediately or remember for future use; and (3) choose either deliberately or intuitively one of Strong's three strategies: (a) explicate, (b) extend and (c) create and deliver (pp. 48-49).

Clinical Tips

1. If your counselee has a good imagination, there is a good chance that she will work well with metaphor.

2. Metaphor can be very helpful with complex trauma survivors/child-abuse survivors.

3. Ask multicultural counselees about use of metaphor (e.g., proverbs, stories) within their cultures.

4. Symbols in dreams are ultimately metaphors. The guidelines for using metaphor discussed in this chapter can also be applied to dream work (cf. Benner, 1998, chap. 8).

Recognize that a counselee is using metaphor. The first step is to recognize that a counselee is speaking figuratively. While at times a counselee's use of metaphor will be very obvious, at other times you may not recognize the switch in mode of communication. This may be particularly true for conventional metaphors that have become ingrained in our speech. For example "I jumped the gun," "I guess I'd rather bury my head in the sand" and "It may be sink or swim" are all colloquial expressions that use metaphor but may be easily missed because of common usage.

Decide whether or not to respond to the metaphor immediately or remember for future use. As discussed in chapter three, there are many things that you as a counselor will perceive in your counselees. Part of the art of counseling is to determine whether what you are picking up has particular significance, and if you conclude that it does, whether to respond right away or to remember it for use at a future time. This ability develops over time as counselors learn to trust their intuition. Everything counselees say or do ultimately goes through this same evaluative, decision-making process. Determining whether and when to respond to a counselee's use of metaphor is no exception.

Choose one of Strong's three strategies: Explicate, extend, or create and deliver. Once you have decided to respond to a counselee's metaphor, you have three options of how to proceed.

Explicating what is implicit. It is important that counselee and counselor come to a shared understanding of the meaning of the metaphor. Therefore, what has been communicated implicitly must be made explicit. This can be done through reflecting feeling/empathic reflection, using intuitive empathy or clarifying the meaning of the metaphor. For example, if a counselee exclaims, "I'm at the end of my rope!" the counselor could respond, "It sounds as though you're feeling hopeless" (reflecting feeling), "You're feeling so hopeless that you're thinking of ending your life" (intuitive empathy) or, "What does being at the 'end of your rope' mean for you?" (clarifying).

Therapeutically extending or modifying the metaphor. This is where the counselor takes the counselee's metaphor and adds to it or changes it in some way, enabling the counselee to reframe his or her experience. The following example comes out of Bayne and Thompson's (2000) research using actual case material. The counselee uses the metaphor "I'm walking a tightrope," and the counselor extends the metaphor by responding, "You are in/have joined the circus." The counselee says in reply, "Yes, and I'm juggling at the same time" (p. 40). Notice how the extensions to the original metaphor give even greater insight into the counselee's felt experience.

Another real-session example extends the metaphor in a different way. In this one the counselee states, "I'm on a raft out to sea." The counselor responds by asking a number of clarifying questions, such as, "How big is the raft?" "What does it look like?" "Do you feel safe on it?" "What does the sea look like?" "Can you see land?" "Can you swim?" "What would happen if you let go of the raft?" "What do you see around you?" (Bayne & Thompson, 2000, p. 42). Getting these clarifications goes beyond the previous strategy of making explicit what has been implicit, in that the counselee is forced to dig deeply into her own metaphor in the process, learning much.

Creating and delivering therapeutic metaphors. The third option is for the counselor to create his own metaphor in response to a counselee's metaphor in order to open up new possibilities. An example would be one discussed previously, of a counselee viewing himself as "pieces of shattered glass" (expressing hopelessness) and the counselor developing her own metaphor of the counselee becoming a "stained-glass window" (expressing hope and the possibility of beauty). Similarly, a counselee could express that "I'm at the end of the road," and the counselor responds with, "I wonder whether there are any hiking trails nearby that could take you where you want to go?"

Strong does not seem to encourage counselors to create their own metaphors except in response to a metaphor that a counselee has introduced. However, as mentioned previously, we believe that it can also be beneficial at times for counselors to present their own metaphors, such as Heather did with the metaphor of the Plexiglas barrier. In this case it was the counselee who responded with her own metaphor, that of the castle. If a particular metaphor is initiated by the counselor, as with any intervention, the key is not to impose it on the counselee but rather to offer it, then be prepared to work with whatever the response is.

Check Your Understanding

For the following exchanges, identify whether each response is explicating, expanding or creating and delivering a metaphor (see guidelines above). Evaluate the intervention based on where you think it might lead (*Note: there is no right or wrong here; the goal is to get you thinking about the implications of a particular response.*) See appendix A for possible answers.

1. Counselee: I feel like I'm living in a soap opera!

Counselor:
It's like things are spinning out of control!

Type of response: _____

Evaluation: _____

_____

You just never expected that there would be so much drama in your life. It all feels unbelievable to you.

Type of response: _____

Evaluation: _____

_____

What feels like the most important scene?

Type of response: _____

Evaluation: _____

_____

2. Counselee: It's like he's just trampling me underfoot . . .

Counselor:
You're feeling kicked around and ground into the dust.

Type of response: _____

Evaluation: _____

_____

What's it like to feel trampled underfoot?

Type of response: _____

Evaluation: _____

_____

It's like you feel disregarded, and it hurts so much.

Type of response: _____

Evaluation: _____

_____

3. Counselee: I feel like I'm drowning.

Counselor:
The waves are just so huge that you're trying to stay afloat, but you keep getting pulled under.

Type of response: _____

Evaluation: _____

_____

You're feeling totally overwhelmed.

Type of response: _____

Evaluation: _____

_____

It's like everything is crashing down on you.

Type of response: _____

Evaluation: _____

_____

COUNSELING APPROACHES AND TECHNIQUES CAN ALSO BE METAPHORS

Expressive counseling approaches, such as art therapy, dance/movement therapy, music therapy, sensorimotor therapies, play therapy and, in similar ways, equine-assisted therapy, adventure therapy and related modalities essentially are utilizing a person's ability to communicate in metaphors as the counseling modality. The artistic expression, the music, the particular movements, the play are all metaphors for what is being experienced by the counselee. Emotional, cognitive, behavioral and relational dynamics are encoded, often unconsciously, in the therapeutic modality.

A number of the major counseling therapies, such as Gestalt therapy, also make extensive use of metaphor. Working with symbolic expressions in therapy is a related therapeutic process in which the symbol represents an intrapersonal and interpersonal dynamic. Interpreting the meaning of the particular expression for the counselee is the challenge.

It is also interesting to note that a number of counseling theories make use of metaphors to name important concepts in the theory. Psychoanalytic therapy refers to the defense mechanism of displacement, which is a metaphor for how a bowl of water overflows when a stone is placed in it. Likewise, we defend ourselves against pain or anxiety when we focus on the stone rather than the bowl of water. Practitioners of stress inoculation training (SIT), a type of cognitive-behavioral therapy, make use of a medical metaphor. Similar to how vaccinations contain a harmless form of a disease in order to create antibodies against the disease, counselors using SIT create situations in the counseling session that are experienced as stressful. This enables the counselor to train a counselee to develop skills to help her handle stress. The theory is that successfully managing these stressors is then protection against future forms of stress and other varieties of stress in life.

The "Pagdadala" Model—"Burden-Bearing"

Decenteceo (1997), a Filipino psychologist/researcher, found that the metaphor of burden bearing accurately depicted emotional/psychological health or distress for Filipinos. He defined burdens as responsibilities, which could take the form of relationships or tasks. When burdens are perceived as light, there is no problem, but when they are subjectively experienced as heavy, burdens create distress. Similarly, whether or not burdens have been freely accepted and/or whether the individual was adequately prepared to carry the burden also had an impact. While there are many such burdens in a relationally oriented culture with many obligations to family, and one in which there is a lot of poverty, "most Filipinos carry their burdens lightly" (p. 88). Helping relationships, then, involve coming alongside individuals in order to help them carry their burden more lightly or to help them reach their destination. Notice how the metaphor of burden bearing is combined with the metaphor of going on a journey and has numerous biblical connections (e.g., Mt 11:28-30; Gal 6:2).

In emotionally focused couples therapy, one technique is called "catching the bullet." It refers to the metaphorical strategy of the counselor who reaches out and catches the hurtful comment shot from one partner at the other and reinterprets it as a bid for connection (Johnson, 2004b). The frequent use of the technique of reframing by many contemporary therapies is a metaphor for how changing the frame—the context of an event or experience—can alter the meaning of the experience for the counselee, just as a picture frame can change the look of a painting. For instance, reframing depression or sadness as anger turned inward is a common therapeutic understanding.

RELATIONSHIP APPLICATION

Mason (1985), in an almost poetic book about Christian marriage, uses an example of one's spouse being like a giant oak tree growing in the middle of your apartment. Everywhere you walk in the apartment, everything you do is overshadowed by the oak tree. You cannot ignore it; it is even difficult to go around it. It must be factored into everything you do. Watching TV, getting a snack out of the refrigerator, leaving the apartment, all require one to consider the oak tree. While this is an improbable metaphor and jarring in its implications, it illustrates the degree to which the single person, living alone, must adjust when he or she chooses to marry. Perhaps if more people considered their spouse an oak tree, we would have less selfishness in marriage.

Such is the richness of metaphor when reflecting on relationships. Ultimately, the passion and intimacy, as well as the despair and pain, that are present in close relationships are difficult to verbalize. Metaphor becomes the way to describe the mystery.

MULTICULTURAL APPLICATION

I (Fred) remember an episode of *Star Trek* in which the captain is stranded on a planet with only one other humanoid. The natural tendency is mistrust, self-preservation and fear of violence. To avoid this outcome the two attempt to communicate. Despite the universal translator (I can't wait for that invention!) the two are unable to communicate even basic meanings. The problem, it turns out, is that the other humanoid only communicates using idioms, proverbs, stories and historical references rooted in his culture. In our language it would be like communicating about a massive disaster in which many were killed by saying "9/11," or saying "the interstate was gridlocked" to talk about really bad traffic. Even when the other figures out what is happening, communication is almost impossible because the *Star Trek* captain has none of the historical references from the other's culture.

I think of this episode whenever I am feeling really lost with a counselee. We are both speaking the same language on the surface, but how we are using words and conveying meaning is radically different. How much more so are the communication problems between people speaking different languages?

Imagine if God chose to communicate with us only by use of metaphor and story. For example, the snake in the garden could refer to deception in relationships, or Abraham sacrificing Isaac could refer to obeying God at all costs. These may be familiar references to us, but for an unchurched or non-Christian culture, they would be meaningless unless some of this heritage was shared, as is true for Muslims and Jews.

This is the challenge of crosscultural communication using figurative language. Such language can significantly extend and deepen meaning, yet it can also confuse and distract. All cultures communicate extensively through metaphor, or the use of proverbs or stories. Christ used a culturally relevant means of communication when he used parables to reveal deep truths about God. Mwiti and Dueck (2006), in their book *Christian counseling: An African indigenous perspective*, encourage African counselors to make use of local proverbs and stories in their counseling work with other Africans. If you get to know one culture well enough, you may become acquainted with particular metaphors and proverbs and could make use of them in your counseling work with a counselee from that culture.

Even if you are not in a position to know a culture that well, you can listen for proverbs that your counselee introduces and clarify their meaning. If you are not tuned in to the possible benefits of making use of proverbs, the moment may slip by unnoticed. At a minimum, you will have lost a potentially valuable opportunity to be helpful in a culturally meaningful way. The danger, though, is that your counselee interprets your silence as lack of permission to bring up something similar in the future. Similarly, unpacking a counselee's metaphor or getting him to further expand on a story are ways of showing interest as well as gleaning helpful information about the counselee's world.

A FEW ADDITIONAL WORDS ABOUT PROVERBS

Related to the topic of metaphor is the apparently universal use of proverbs—commonly spoken and understood wise sayings rooted in a language and cultural context. Even within a particular language, different subgroups and generations within the culture will develop unique proverbs. In a counseling context proverbs can be useful in communicating common wisdom and in contrasting a counselee's experience with broader conceptions within the culture. They provide a lens against which the current conversation can be compared, contrasted or affirmed.

Colloquial expressions or idioms are a further variation on this theme. Again, we stress the unique cultural context of such forms of language. Notice in the table below the very unique "flavors" of these proverbs, representing three unique cultures geographically, racially and in terms of historical time.

Variable and intriguing use of language can be very helpful in counseling conversations, but the caution must always be acknowledged: the counselor must be familiar with the counselee's culture in order to accurately communicate these relatively complex forms of language.

MINISTRY APPLICATION

There are many possibilities for using metaphor in broader ministry contexts.

Explicit use of biblical metaphors. That metaphor is so commonly used in the Bible means that when it is deemed appropriate to make explicit use of Scripture, there are a plethora of metaphors to choose from that may be helpful. For example, the metaphor of Jesus as our shepherd, taking tender care of us little lambs, can potentially be very comforting. Biblical metaphors can sometimes be used even with non-Christian counselees. For example, counselees who do not acknowledge Christ would not likely be comfortable with the idea that they may be caught in a spiritual battle between God and Satan. However, they may very much feel the effects of being on a battleground, and using the metaphors of choosing "light" over "darkness" with respect to decisions they make might be very helpful.

Table 10.2. Proverbs across cultures

Twentieth-century North American English	Twentieth-century African (Press, 2011)	Old Testament—selected verses from Proverbs 15
• No man is an island. • Keep your friends close and your enemies closer. • There's no place like home. • Never look a gift horse in the mouth. • God helps those who help themselves. • Cleanliness is next to godliness. • Actions speak louder than words. • Practice makes perfect. • Beauty is in the eye of the beholder. • The grass is always greener on the other side of the fence. • Do unto others as you would have them do unto you. • Don't count your chickens before they hatch.	• We dance, therefore we are. • Life has two legs: male and female. • One's generation is like a different country to another's generation. • Life is lived forwards but understood backwards. (Congo) • One can think best when at rest. (North Africa) • What you help a child to love is more important than what you help her to learn. (Senegal) • Treat the earth well; it was not given to you by your parents but was loaned to you by your children. (Kenya) • To dance is to be healed, reconciled and restored.	• ¹A gentle answer turns away wrath, but a harsh word stirs up anger. • ³The eyes of the LORD are everywhere, keeping watch on the wicked and the good. • ⁵A fool spurns a parent's discipline, but whoever heeds correction shows prudence. • ¹³A happy heart makes the face cheerful, but heartache crushes the spirit. • ¹⁴The discerning heart seeks knowledge, but the mouth of a fool feeds on folly. • ¹⁶Better a little with the fear of the Lord than great wealth with turmoil. • ¹⁷Better a small serving of vegetables with love than a fattened calf with hatred. • ²⁰A wise son brings joy to his father, but a foolish man despises his mother. • ²²Plans fail for lack of counsel, but with many advisers they succeed.

Inner healing prayer/Theophostic ministry. Most inner-healing prayer approaches use visual imagery of some kind. Some use guided imagery, for example, suggesting that counselees visualize Jesus there with them in some way. Other approaches invite the counselee to imagine themselves as a child, perhaps of a particular age. Metaphor is invariably a part of such approaches. See Gingrich (2013, pp. 178-80) or Appleby and Ohlschlager (2013, chaps. 2-3) for a discussion of the benefits and dangers of using these approaches.

Spiritual direction. Among the many applications of biblical and other metaphors to spiritual growth are the numerous uses of what the psychological literature calls *archetypes*. An archetype is an ideal, prototype or symbol that represents something core or foundational in human experience. Carl Jung is the psychologist most frequently credited with exploring common shared archetypes that are experienced across cultures and across generations. Based loosely on the Jungian archetypes, myriad authors have extended Jung's archetypes to point us to the common, shared spiritual aspects of our journey with Christ. While the spiritual direction literature frequently crosses over into studying spiritual growth in other religions, not only

Christianity, there are some commonalities in many religions to the archetypes of the warrior, sovereign, seer and lover (cf. Tallman, 2005).

The fascinating element that relates to this chapter is that archetypes are universal metaphors that can be used to describe the spiritual journey in its challenges, dangers and rewards. When spiritual directors or counselors refer to biblical characters as archetypes and exemplars of the ups and downs of the spiritual journey, we are essentially suggesting they are metaphors for our own lives with Christ, and their lives enrich ours through the power of our God-given imaginations.

CONCLUSION

The use of metaphor in counseling is one of the most art-based skills discussed so far in this training process. Drawing on counselor intuition and cultural awareness, the creative options are endless for how metaphors can be applied within the counseling relationship. When delivered well and at the right time, the use of metaphors and parables can expand counselees' understanding of the story they are telling and can give them language for feelings that could otherwise go unspoken.

REFLECTION QUESTIONS

1. What metaphor would you use to describe your life or your outlook on life?

2. Over the next day or two, pay particular attention to your use of language and write down any time you find yourself using a metaphor or referencing a proverb. Is there a theme or pattern to the types of metaphors you use?

3. What metaphors do you notice in other people's speech? Notice what is communicated by specific metaphors. How do you think the use of these metaphors helps or hinders communication?

EXCURSUS: A DEEPER LOOK AT THE BIBLICAL FOUNDATION FOR THE USE OF IMAGINATION IN COUNSELING

The contemporary psychological equivalent to imagination is the concept of visualization. Sports psychologists frequently have athletes employ the technique of visualization to improve performance; imagining yourself winning is an effective strategy for helping you achieve it. Typically, visualization consists of imagining, with as many senses as possible, actually doing a specific sequence of actions—how it will feel, what you will be thinking and so on. Of course, in the extreme this could become ruminating, a symptom of obsessive-compulsive disorder, but in that case the anxiety, provoked by imagining something threatening, is what drives the images. Otherwise known as mind power or positive thinking, this cognitive-behavioral technique makes use of our human ability to construct alternative scenarios in our minds and how we might achieve them. Fantasy is a related idea.

Our imaginations are a gift from God. However, they can be used for good or ill. Christians throughout the centuries have had some ambivalence regarding our ability to imagine things. For instance, in the King James Version of the Bible, the phrase "vain imagining" is used in Psalm 2:1 (repeated in Acts 4:25) and Romans 1:21. Other translations use different concepts, but the negative connotation of the imagination has persisted. In English we see remnants of this view in synonyms such as "fantasy" or "conjuring up ideas." It is rooted in the second of the Ten Commandments (Ex 20), which tells us not to make images or idols and not to worship them. Making an image in our mind is akin to making an idol and so could be considered idolatry.

However, the complete biblical teaching regarding imagination is considerably more complex. Several points can be made:

1. Our imagination, like everything else about us, is affected by the fall:

   - "The LORD saw how great the wickedness of the human race had become on the earth, and that every inclination of the thoughts of the human heart [imagination] was only evil all the time." (Gen 6:5)

   - "Thus says the LORD of hosts, 'Do not listen to the words of the prophets who are prophesying to you. They are leading you into futility; they speak a vision of their own imagination, not from the mouth of the LORD.'" (Jer 23:16 NASB)

2. But, our imaginations, like all of who we are, can be redeemed:

   - "We demolish arguments and every pretension that sets itself up against the knowledge of God, and we take captive every thought [imagination] to make it obedient to Christ." (2 Cor 10:5)

   - "Therefore, prepare your minds for action [imagination]; be self-controlled; set your hope fully on the grace to be given you when Jesus Christ is revealed." (1 Pet 1:13 NIV 1984)

   - "So I tell you this, and insist on it in the Lord, that you must no longer live as the Gentiles do, in the futility of their thinking [imaginations]." (Eph 4:17)

   - "Do not conform any longer to the pattern of this world, but be transformed by the renewing of your mind [imagination]. Then you will be able to test and approve what God's will is—his good, pleasing and perfect will." (Rom 12:2)

3. Our imaginations are known by God:

   - "And you, my son Solomon, acknowledge the God of your father, and serve him with wholehearted devotion and with a willing mind [imagination], for the LORD searches every heart and understands every desire and every thought. If you seek him, he will be found by you; but if you forsake him, he will reject you forever." (1 Chron 28:9)

4. There are things we cannot imagine (but maybe should try to!):

- "We cannot imagine the power of the Almighty, and yet he is so just and merciful that he does not destroy us." (Job 37:23 TLB)

- "Yes, dear friends, we are already God's children, right now, and we can't even imagine what it is going to be like later on. But we do know this, that when he comes we will be like him, as a result of seeing him as he really is." (1 Jn 3:2 TLB)

5. While the imagination is tainted by the fall, and prone to misuse and sinful focus, it can be used for God's glory:

- "You will keep in perfect peace those whose minds [imagination] are steadfast, because they trust in you." (Is 26:3)

- "A rich man's wealth is his strong city, and like a high wall in his own imagination." (Prov 18:11 NASB)

- "Don't imagine that I came to bring peace to the earth! No, rather, a sword." (Mt 10:34 TLB)

- "Finally, brothers and sisters, whatever is true, whatever is noble, whatever is right, whatever is pure, whatever is lovely, whatever is admirable—if anything is excellent or praiseworthy—think [imagine] about such things." (Phil 4:8)

- "Now to him who is able to do immeasurably more than all we ask or imagine, according to his power that is at work within us, to him be glory in the church and in Christ Jesus throughout all generations, for ever and ever! Amen." (Eph 3:20-21)

Adapted by Fred Gingrich from an unknown source (1999). For additional thoughts about the use of imagination in Christian counseling, see Wright (1986).

REFLECTING APPARENT DISCREPANCIES

Instead, speaking the truth in love, we will grow to become in every respect the mature body of him who is the head, that is, Christ.

EPHESIANS 4:15

CHAPTER FOCUS

SKILL: confronting

PURPOSE: to reflect the apparent discrepancies within the counselee's story

FORMULA: "On the one hand, _____, but on the other hand _____."

*W*HAT DO YOU THINK OF when you hear the word *confrontation*?

» Write down the words, pictures or emotions that come to mind:

Now, think about the last time you were involved in a confrontation, either on the giving or receiving side of the confrontation.

» Write down what happened that led to the confrontation. What was the confrontation itself like? How are things now between you and the other person?

We (Heather and Fred) once had a young woman, Noreen, renting a room in our house for several months while she was between apartments. Prior to her moving in, we had known her casually, and although we were not close, we were on friendly terms. One day Noreen came home from work and, not responding to our greetings, walked right past us into the kitchen. We got the message that something was wrong, but we had no idea what. So we attempted to initiate a conversation again, but to no avail; she looked straight ahead and walked on by. This time her nonverbal communication made it even clearer that she was not just upset but that it had something to do with our relationship.

What were we to do? We could have just ignored her, but neither one of us wanted to live in such a hostile atmosphere for the weeks remaining in her stay with us. We decided that we needed to confront Noreen, but neither one of us wanted to. Thinking that Noreen might feel less defensive if another woman confronted her (at least, that was Fred's excuse!), we decided that I (Heather) would talk with her. What followed changed my perspective on confrontation forever. This is what happened:

Knock, knock, knock. No answer at her bedroom door. Knock, knock, knock.

Heather: Noreen, I know you're there. I'd just like to talk to you for a few minutes.

Noreen *(through closed door)*: I'm tired. I don't want to talk.

Heather: I'd really appreciate it if you'd open the door so we could talk. I won't take long.

The door opens a couple of inches, and Noreen peers through.

Heather: Thanks, Noreen. It's pretty obvious that you're upset with us, but Fred and I don't have any idea why . . .

Noreen: I'm not upset.

Heather: Well, could I come in so that we could talk about it more?

Noreen: *(grudgingly opening the door wide)* I guess.

Heather: Thanks, Noreen. On the one hand, I know that you just said that nothing is wrong, but when you went past us twice without speaking, you were communicating loud and clear that you are upset about something to do with us!

At this point Noreen acknowledged that she was indeed angry at us. I do not remember what the issue itself was; I know it was a relatively minor misunderstanding that was resolved rather quickly once we talked about it. What I *do* remember clearly is Noreen telling me at the end of the conversation that she could not believe that we were able to talk the issue through and have our former relationship intact.

Heather: Well, what has happened when you've had disagreements with people before?

Noreen: I just never talk to them again!

Heather: So that's the end of the relationship?

Noreen: Yes. I guess that's why my friendships don't end up lasting. Thanks for showing me that there's a different way.

I left this conversation astounded. Was it really possible that some individuals had such poor relational skills that they did not ever resolve even simple issues? How very sad! I realized in a new way how essential confronting is. We became even closer to Noreen after I gently confronted her and she responded. Seeing the great impact that confronting made in this situation motivated me to no longer shy away from appropriately confronting counselees when confronting had the potential to help counselees grow or, conversely, when *not* confronting would be detrimental to their continued growth. Just as Noreen learned firsthand that a relationship can not only survive a confrontation but thrive when an issue is resolved, so, too, your counselees can experience what it is like be confronted and have your counseling relationship deepened as a result.

WHAT IS CONFRONTATION?

A lot of times confrontation gets a bad rap. Many people dread confrontation, avoiding it at all costs. It is true that confrontation can be uncomfortable and that there is risk of damaging relationships when done with improper motive or poor timing, or without the necessary relational credibility. On the other hand, confrontation can be very enlightening, empowering and relationally connecting when done appropriately. As with any other advanced skill, confrontation is not always required; it may not be applicable to all counselees or all counseling relationships. However, learning how to confront well is an invaluable skill.

In common vernacular, *confrontation* often comes with a connotation of harshness, correction and even a challenge to the person on the receiving end of the exchange. For example, we often talk of needing to "confront the wrong" done by someone else. In a counseling setting, confrontation takes on a whole other meaning. Remember how, in chapter one, we talked about how the process of learning skills is often like learning a language? Well, let us go back to that analogy for a minute.

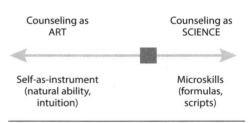

Figure 11.1. Art versus science: Confrontation

Often when learning a new language you stumble on a word in the new language that sounds like a word in your native language, but the words mean different (or even slightly different) things. It can get tricky because your brain hears a word it thinks it knows, but the meaning just is not the same. The skill of confrontation is like this in that it means one thing in everyday life but has a different meaning in counseling.

In counseling, confrontation is simply reflecting the *apparent* discrepancies within a counselee's story. It is not inherently a challenge, a rebuke or a correction, but instead is simply a reflection of two seemingly contradictory elements.

In a formula, this sounds like: "On the one hand, _____, but on the other hand _____."

Hammond, Hepworth and Smith (1977) identify three primary categories of discrepancies, which include:

- *Cognitive-perceptual:* Found within this category are apparent discrepancies related to irrational thinking, denial of reality or responsibility, overgeneralizations or stereotyping of self and others, self-deprecation and insufficient or inaccurate information.

- ◆ *Affective:* Apparent discrepancies in this category include incongruence between intensity of the expressed emotion and the situation, expressed and actual feelings, and verbally versus nonverbally expressed emotions.

- ◆ *Behavioral:* Behavioral discrepancies include absence of goals or direction, manipulative or passive aggressive behavior, incongruence between stated goals or values and behavior, and incongruence between expressed intentions or feelings and behavior.

It is important to remember that a confrontation reflects *apparent* discrepancies, always keeping in mind that the discrepancy may not actually exist but may be easily clarified and explained by the counselee. Examples of confrontation in a counseling setting may sound like:

- ◆ On the one hand, you want your mom to know what's going on in your life, but on the other hand, you're nervous to talk with her. (*behavioral discrepancy*)

- ◆ You just told me that you're not angry about your husband leaving you with your two-year-old for three weeks while he's away on a business trip, but as you're talking your teeth are clenched and your voice is raised. (*affective discrepancy; formula implied by the word* but)

- ◆ On the one hand, you want to be a professional baseball player when you grow up, but on the other hand, you don't want to practice. (*behavioral discrepancy*)

- ◆ On the one hand, you believe your friend who told you that you can't get pregnant the first time you have sex, but on the other hand, you're choosing to ignore your health teacher, who quotes medical research that you can get pregnant any time you have intercourse. (*cognitive-perceptual discrepancy*)

- ◆ On the one hand, you say you like your job, but on the other hand, you're saying you want to look for something new. (*behavioral discrepancy*)

- ◆ On the one hand, being honest is important to you, but on the other hand, you're not sure you want to tell your dad exactly what happened last night. (*behavioral discrepancy*)

- ◆ On the one hand, you feel really attracted to Ashley, but on the other hand, you're scared of getting into another relationship so soon after your recent break-up. (*affective discrepancy*)

- ◆ So you see yourself as really stupid, yet your boss just promoted you at work! (*cognitive discrepancy*)

Similar to the other skills in target 2, confrontation is meant to facilitate the counselee's depth and awareness of her story. By bringing attention to their apparent discrepancies, counselees are given the opportunity to clarify whether or not there actually is any contradiction and to reflectively look at why they may say or do one thing at one time but then say or do something different at another time.

The levels of confrontation. Similar to the empathy scale, the confrontation scale has five levels. The levels of confrontation range from missing or ignoring potential discrepancies to a deeply empathic and yet direct confrontation.

Confrontation Scale

Level 1:
✓ discrepancies are ignored or overlooked
✓ potentially productive areas for confrontation are neglected

Level 2:
✓ therapist does not overlook possible areas for confrontation but does not overtly identify them
✓ may respond with silence or reflection
✓ includes some premature and poorly timed confrontations

Level 3:
✓ therapist draws attention to discrepancy by overtly addressing it, but in a reflective or speculative way
✓ efforts to facilitate self-confrontation belong here
✓ timing is appropriate
✓ counselee is not demeaned

Level 4:
✓ therapist directly and specifically identifies discrepancies and inconsistencies
✓ timing is appropriate
✓ counselee is challenged to change behavior
✓ dignity and self-esteem of the counselee are protected

Level 5:
✓ therapist confronts directly
✓ keen sense of timing
✓ discrepancies may be further from the counselee's conscious awareness
✓ high level of respect for counselee's growth potential and self-esteem
✓ conveys caring

Care-frontation. I (Elisabeth) interned at a domestic violence treatment center during my master's program, working with men who were court-ordered to therapy due to their anger and violence in the home. My supervisor, Daryle, was a tall, fit, sixty-year-old retired military man with the biggest teddy-bear heart you have ever seen. Daryle taught me that confrontation was an integral part of the counseling process, particularly at our site, but he also taught me something deeper. Daryle rarely referred to this skill as "confrontation"; instead, he called it "care-frontation." He chose this language to remind himself and his counselees that the motive behind any challenging statement had to be a sincere care for the counselee. In keeping with this same conviction, we will be using *confrontation* and *care-frontation* interchangeably as we move forward as a way of remembering the heart and motive that should underlie this skill.

Empirical Support

In a study of substance abusers' perceptions of confrontation, Polcin, Mulia and Jones (2012) found that participants distinguished between helpful and unhelpful confrontations in the counseling process. A sample of their findings include:

Helpful Confrontations:
1. perceived as legitimate
2. offer hope and practical support
3. delivered by persons who are trusted and respected
4. delivered by persons who are very relationally important to the counselee

Unhelpful Confrontations:
1. hypocritical
2. overly hostile (angry)
3. occur within a tense or conflictual relationship

This study affirmed the importance of legitimacy, trust and caring, hope and practical support, timing and relationship in the counselee's ability to receive the confrontation and perceive it as helpful.

What makes a confrontation a "care-frontation"? There are multiple ways to implement a confrontation so that it is more likely to be received as a care-frontation. Consider the following tips when utilizing the skill of care-frontation.

◆ *Establish a good base relationship of mutual trust and caring.* As with any other advanced skill, a counselor must earn the privilege of speaking into the life of a counselee. Through the use of target 1 skills, patience and a sincere desire to help, motivations to punish, get even with or put down the counselee are mediated. Additionally, this helps establish a foundation of trust and mutual respect, allowing for a confrontation to be more easily heard and received by the counselee.

◆ *Be tentative.* While using vocal hedges is often discouraged in target 1, they can be helpful here in target 2. Specifically, prefacing a confrontation with "sometimes," "every once in a while," "perhaps" or "maybe" can soften a direct confrontation, allowing counselees to consider what has been said without feeling as if they need to defend or refute the reflection as an absolute in the story. For example, a counselor could say, "Sometimes I hear you say that you love your job, but every once in a while you come in here saying you're ready to quit."

◆ *Use humor.* Using humor can often take the pressure off an otherwise heavy situation and can make things more palatable. Albert Ellis, the founder of Rational Emotive Behavior Theory, recommended using humor within his highly

Diagnostic Implications

Some addiction literature, along with alcohol- and drug-abuse treatment manuals, are probably the most explicit about the need for confrontation in counseling. Some Christian approaches also gravitate toward confrontation as a primary counseling strategy (e.g., Adams, 1981; Backus, 2006; Backus & Chapian, 2014). It is understandable that helpers would gravitate toward confrontation, since a counselor can quickly become frustrated after providing sessions of nondirective empathy only to see the counselee return to previous unhealthy patterns of behavior. In addition, there are times when it appears that empathy not only does no apparent good, but it seems to reinforce addictive patterns and lead to relapse. Responding empathically about all of the difficulties people have and understanding how these led to the development of their addiction can simply make them feel bad again and prompt them to turn to their addiction to soothe their pain. The cycle needs to be broken, and so addiction specialists will readily use confrontation.

However, the research tells us that in general, confrontational approaches are not effective in counseling (Norcross, 2010). So it is important to reflect on several questions regarding confrontation. (1) What else is in your counseling arsenal when empathy has not seemed to be effective? (2) How do we know that empathy has been ineffective or that confrontation is effective? We often make pretty quick and superficial judgments regarding the effectiveness of our interventions. (3) How is the confrontation given? As mentioned in chapter seven, most skills can be used in combination with basic empathy. What matters the most is assessing how the confrontation, or whichever skill is being used, affects the counseling relationship.

To return to the topic of addictions, as Norcross (2010) argues, what is most effective in helping people with addictive behavior is motivational interviewing (see Rollnick & Miller, 1995). This is a specific approach to conducting a conversation with people who are caught in addictive patterns. It is focused, directive, goal oriented and aimed at resolving the counselee's ambivalence. Motivation to change must come from the counselee and is not imposed from outside. However, direct persuasion is not an effective method for resolving ambivalence. If confrontation, in the sense of persuasion, is used in counseling, it is likely to be ineffective with all types of counselees.

---

confrontational approach to therapy, including the use of humorous songs. (The Albert Ellis Institute has continued this practice, creating therapeutic songs to the tune of modern pop music. See http://albertellis.org/rebt-in-song-lessons-in-low-frustration-tolerance/# for examples.) It should be noted that sarcasm does not generally have a therapeutic role in the counseling relationship, as it can be interpreted as condescending, dismissive or demeaning when the proper relational foundation has not been firmly established.

◆ *Consider the spirit in which the confrontation is given.* Self-reflection and self-awareness on the part of the counselor are very important in the implementation of this skill. Every counselor encounters counselees that frustrate or annoy, or who simply do not make sense to the counselor. This does not make you a bad counselor; it means you are human! What is important is that you are aware of your motivations when confronting a counselee: Is the confrontation a backhanded way of expressing frustration or annoyance with the counselee? Or is the confrontation truly coming from a place of care, consideration and empathy for the counselee? If your motives are unclear or negatively clouded, consider seeking supervision before confronting a counselee.

- *"Sandwich" the confrontation with empathy.* In other words, make a level-three empathic reflection before you confront and after you confront so that the counselee feels understood throughout the process (Ivey, Ivey & Zalaquett, 2014). This helps the counselee receive the confrontation in the spirit in which it is given, as a care-frontation.

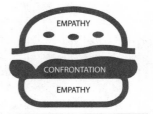

Figure 11.2. Empathy sandwich

- *Gradually and concretely.* No one really enjoys being confronted, and most people can become easily overwhelmed if they are presented with multiple things at one time that need to be changed in their life. Therefore a care-frontation approaches one topic at a time and addresses it concretely. For example, you have a counselee who struggles with personal hygiene, who invades the personal space of others in social situations and who does not always say appropriate things in professional settings. If you were to draw attention to each of these apparent deficits in the counselee all at one time, you would likely offend and overwhelm the counselee. Instead, you would need to choose one issue at a time, for example, personal hygiene, and provide specific and direct feedback on this issue. This might sound like, "Joe, you've told me that you want to improve your social relationships, but I've noticed that you often wear dirty clothes and smell as if you haven't showered in a few days. I'm wondering how you think this might be affecting your social relationships." The specificity of smelling as if he has not showered and wearing dirty clothes allows for what could be very concrete goals to emerge within the conversation: showering daily and wearing only clean clothes.

- *Deal with actions instead of just words.* Have you ever been caught in a conversation where "I didn't mean it like that" was an oft-stated retort? While it can be appropriate and therapeutically beneficial to confront a counselee based on two seemingly contradictory statements of any variety, it is often better to confront behavior. The reasoning behind this tip is that behavior is harder to refute or brush off, while words can often be explained away as being misunderstood or inaccurately stated. Additionally, a confrontation of one's actions can be experienced as slightly less personal by the counselee than a confrontation of one's words.

◆ *Use the least degree of directness and force necessary to accomplish the therapeutic objective.* It is often better to use a clear but gentle confrontation rather than confronting something in a bold or overly direct way. For example, it is better to say, "On the one hand, it sounds as though you'd prefer to stay home and avoid potentially stressful social situations, but on the other hand, you really wish you had more friends." Instead of, "On the one hand, you're terrified of social situations that can keep you stuck in your house, but on the other hand, you're tired of having no friends." When in doubt, start softer and then increase the directness if the counselee does not seem to pick up on the care-frontation. Emmanuel S. Hammer recognized the potential dangers of being too direct when he stated, "It's important not to get so used to tearing away people's masks that you no longer hear the rip" (as quoted in Hammond, Hepworth & Smith, 1977, p. 278). Remember that any confrontation has the potential to leave a counselee feeling vulnerable and exposed, so proceed gently.

◆ *Use what the counselee has said or done previously to contradict what the counselee is saying or doing now.* Whenever I (Elisabeth) have a counselee come into counseling to work on "relationship issues," one of my first activities is to have the counselee define and explain what they understand to be a "healthy relationship." This includes issues related to time together versus time apart, activities shared with the other person, physical and sexual expectations and boundaries, expectations for closeness, growth, affection, recreation and so on. With this explanation provided by the counselee at the very beginning, I now have a baseline to refer the counselee back to that is based on his or her own values, beliefs and language. This helps protect me as the counselor from imposing my values onto the counselee, and it serves to establish a caring and empathic foundation to any future confrontation.

A SAMPLE COUNSELING DIALOGUE WITH EMILY

Background on the conversation: I once had a counselee, Emily, who was seeking counseling for the stated goal of developing healthier romantic relationships. A single female in her mid-twenties, she had just ended a two-year affair with a man twenty-five years her senior, and her relationship prior to that was with a woman twenty years her senior. In one of our first sessions I asked Emily to define for me what she thought a healthy relationship was and what characteristics she wanted to have in any future relationship. Among a few other criteria, Emily provided me with a list that included goals or values such as, "male, no more than ten years older," "unmarried," "friendship before having a sexual relationship" and "a Christian."

About a year later in therapy, Emily came into counseling wanting to talk about a potential person of interest at her work. Our dialogue went something like this:

Emily:	*Okay, so I don't know what you're going to think, I don't even know what I think. But, I've been flirting back and forth with this person at work. Her name's Becky, and I think I like her.*

Counselor:
(Elisabeth)
You're interested in someone named Becky at work, and you're not quite sure what you think about the situation yet.

SKILL	reflecting content

Emily:
Yeah, it's just fun. I mean, nothing's really happened yet. We're just flirting.

Elisabeth:
This is the first time in almost a year that I've heard you talk about being interested in someone. I'm wondering whether you're simply attracted to her, or whether you're considering starting a relationship with her.

SKILL	reflecting content, prompt

Emily:
I know, and it's weird. I don't really know how to determine what I want. I know I like the attention and the flirting, but I don't know if I want more from Becky or not. While I think she's super cool, when she talks about what she and her friends do on the weekend, I couldn't imagine hanging out with them. They sound like total partiers, and that's just not me. I don't know if we could really be friends outside of work. The flirting is super fun though.

Elisabeth:
On the one hand, you think Becky is pretty cool and you like flirting with her, but on the other hand you aren't sure about her friends or your ability to be friends with her outside work.

SKILL	care-frontation—level three, cognitive discrepancy

Emily:
Yeah, that about sums it up.

Elisabeth:
I'm wondering whether you remember when we first started meeting together, and you created a list of values that you said were important to you, things that you saw as nonnegotiables if you were to get into a relationship again.

SKILL	prompt—used to confirm counselor and counselee were on track to move forward together

---

Emily:
Oh, yeah, I completely forgot about that list! I don't totally remember what's on it, but you kept a copy in my file, right?

Elisabeth:
I did keep a copy. I'm wondering whether it would be helpful for us to take a look and see how what you said previously helps you in your decision about Becky.

SKILL	prompt

Emily: *That sounds like a good idea. Let's do it.*

I pulled out the list and read it aloud without commentary, and then said:

Elisabeth: *I'm wondering what stands out to you about the list in comparison to the situation you just described with Becky.*

SKILL	prompt

Emily: *Well, one thing that's the same is that I said I wanted to date someone who was within ten years of my age, and Becky is only seven years older than me! I also said I wanted to date someone who wasn't currently married, and Becky fits both criteria. That's a first!*

Elisabeth: *Way to go, that is an improvement to be interested in someone closer to your age and not already taken! Now, on the one hand, you also said that you wanted to date someone who was male, a Christian, and that you were friends with first, but on the other hand, you're saying that you're interested in Becky, who is female, not a Christian and doesn't hang out with people you want to be around. I'm wondering how you make sense of those two pieces, or whether the list no longer represents the values that are important to you.*

SKILL	
Authenticity (which will be described in chapter twelve), provided that I am not just saying something without meaning it. In this case my spontaneous response serves as an encourager. Encouragement, although not a microskill in and of itself, it is often very important to affirm the small steps or realizations that counselees make within the journey. Care-frontation—level three; perceived discrepancy between stated goals or values, and affect. Prompt—invites the counselee to comment and leaves an opening for the counselee to say she has changed her mind and that the list is no longer reflective of her values.	

Emily: *No, those are all still important values to me and, at my core, I don't want to compromise on them. It's just been such a long time since I felt interested in someone and they truly seemed interested in me. I guess I like the attention, but I also know this probably isn't a relationship I should get involved in.*

Elisabeth: *Even though this relationship has some pieces that are different from past relationships, and those feel like growth and progress to you, you also feel uncomfortable compromising your earlier goals.*

SKILL	empathy, level 3
feeling = uncomfortable content = compromising earlier goals for possible relationship	

Emily:	A part of me says, "Forget about it, just do it!" But the bigger part of me says I shouldn't. I can't promise that nothing will happen, or that we'll totally stop flirting, but I do want to keep using counseling to help me stay committed to my earlier list.

One of the things I appreciated about working with Emily is that she was always quite direct. Notice that she did not just take the care-frontation and bounce out the door, never to struggle with healthy relationships again. Instead, she honestly stated that she was not sure whether she could live out her values but wanted to try. In the end, she did continue to flirt with and even kiss her coworker, but she cut off all contact shortly thereafter. We celebrated her success in not engaging in a sexual relationship with this coworker as well as her ability to put boundaries in place far earlier than she had been able to do in previous relationships. Her growth in pursuing and having healthy relationships grew out of a confrontation that asked her to examine her current behavior in light of past statements she had made about what she valued and wanted in life.

Clinical Tips

1. Confrontation is considered a specialized skill. This means that it is necessary for all counselors to know what it is and how to use it well but that it will not be applicable in all counseling situations.

2. When in doubt, empathize first.

3. Empathy-sandwich any confrontation: whenever possible, make an empathic statement before and after each confrontation.

CHRISTIAN FOUNDATION FOR CONFRONTATION

Throughout the Bible we see examples of people confronting one another, drawing attention to seeming contradictions between actions and professed faith. In 2 Samuel 12, Nathan confronts David through the use of story, showing David the underlying theme in what he had done by murdering Uriah. This method was truly experienced as a care-frontation, serving to soften David's defenses and connect him empathically to the consequences of his sin. In John 21:15-19 Jesus' care-frontation of Peter, after Peter's denial, is more direct and concrete in its delivery but still is overflowing with relational connection. In his interaction with the woman at the well (Jn 4) and with the rich young ruler (Mk 10), Jesus again uses a softer, less direct form of confrontation to bring awareness to the recipient regarding the incongruence in his or her behavior (living with a man who was not her husband, and prizing money and financial security over obedient service to God, respectively). In each of these one-on-one examples, a model of care-frontation is used. Each example mirrors Jesus' instructions for how we are to confront the sin we see in one another, by going to the individual first and then proceeding to include extended levels of community if the individual is unresponsive (Mt 18:15-17).

Evangelism Versus Confrontation in Counseling

There is a very big difference between reflecting apparent discrepancies to someone and trying to convince them that their way of thinking, feeling or believing is "wrong." Counseling is not about convincing but about listening and facilitating growth. As such, confrontation does not seek to prove anything to the counselee but simply strives to facilitate counselees' better understanding of their thoughts, feelings or actions in a given situation.

Evangelism, in contrast, is the process of communicating the gospel message to someone who does not yet believe. It can, at times, involve offering proofs and seeking to convince someone else that what you believe is what they too should believe. While evangelism is part of the Great Commission (Mt 28:19-20), it is not appropriate to use a counseling context to proselytize. Additionally, pointing out discrepancies between someone's current behavior and the biblical standards for behavior will not be helpful to someone who does not acknowledge the Bible as the Word of God (1 Cor 2:14).

Jesus provides us with other examples of confrontation in Scripture that, on the surface, appear much more like *confrontation* than they do like *care-frontation*. For example, take Jesus confronting the Pharisees for being "whitewashed tombs," among other things (Mt 23). This public and collective confrontation is much more direct and seemingly harsh. It is still rooted in a love for humanity and a desire to see all people come into relationship with the Father (1 Tim 2:4-6). It seems as though Jesus often made a distinction between how he confronted individuals one on one (i.e., using care-frontation) and how he confronted a group of people publicly (more directly and even harshly). In any situation his motive was the same, but exactly how he confronted varied with the context and the nature of the sin being confronted.

In each instance of confrontation we see in Scripture, the goal and purpose of the confrontation is to restore the confronted individual into fellowship and to facilitate her on a path toward healing, growth and wholeness in Christ. Any confrontation in counseling should carry this same goal and be motivated by a heart of compassion and a desire to see the confronted individual restored and whole (Prov 3:12; Heb 12:6).

Check Your Understanding

For the following exchanges, identify the "best" *care-frontation*. Rate each response on the confrontation scale and provide an explanation as to why that response earned that rating. Author ratings and explanations can be found in appendix A. *Note: It is possible for there to be more than one response at each rating level.*

1. Adolescent counselee: It's just not fair! I thought Erin and I were friends, but then she goes and talks about me behind my back to Stephanie. I mean, fine, if she wants to be that way, I don't want to be her friend either!

Counselor:
Sounds like normal junior high stuff to me.

Rating: _____

Explanation: _____

_____

On the one hand, you want to be friends with Erin, but on the other, you're hurt and want to walk away.

Rating: _____

Explanation: _____

_____

What a jerk! I bet that makes you super mad.

Rating: _____

Explanation: _____

_____

I can tell you're really hurt by Erin gossiping about you rather than coming to you directly about what's bothering you, but I'm also kind of confused, because just last week you told me you were angry at Stephanie and talked to Erin about it, but you didn't let Stephanie know how you felt!

Rating: _____

Explanation: _____

_____

2. Counselee: UCLA has always been my dream school. Who wouldn't want to go to school in LA? But, while I've been accepted, I just found out that I didn't get any scholarships, and I just don't know that I can afford out-of-state tuition. I don't know what I'm going to do.

Counselor:

On the one hand, you really want to go to UCLA, but on the other hand, it's outside your budget.

Rating: _____

Explanation: _____

_____

Wow, Josh, that is a tough spot to be in. Going to UCLA could be a dream come true for you, but weighing the financial wisdom of such a decision seems to have taken away some of the initial excitement of getting accepted.

Rating: _____

Explanation: _____

_____

On the one hand, you got accepted to UCLA, but on the other hand, you didn't get a scholarship.

Rating: _____

Explanation: _____

_____

I'm really sorry, Josh, I know you really wanted to go to UCLA.

Rating: _____

Explanation: _____

_____

3. Counselee: So here's my dilemma. I have two amazing job offers on the table, which is a blessing in and of itself. One job lets me stay here, near my extended family, but pays less and doesn't offer quite the growth possibilities. The other job requires that I move out of state but pays more and has more opportunities for advancement. I love my family, but I just don't know that I can pass up this opportunity out of state.

Counselor:

It can be really difficult to navigate major life transitions when you're confused about where you're going and what God wants for you.

Rating: _____

Explanation: _____

_____

What is it about taking the job out of state that feels so appealing to you?

Rating: _____

Explanation: _____

_____

On the one hand, your family is really important to you, but on the other hand, so is your professional growth.

Rating: _____

Explanation: _____

_____

Josh, it sounds as though you're really conflicted about this situation. You are excited about the possibilities for advancement at the out-of-state job, but I'm a little confused because last week you told me that you wanted to prioritize spending more time with your family.

Rating: _____

Explanation: _____

_____

WHEN TO USE CARE-FRONTATION

Care-frontation is a skill that is best used in specific situations and to accomplish very specific therapeutic goals. The list below is not exhaustive but is intended to help get you thinking about the types of situations where confronting might be appropriate. Care-frontation may be appropriate when the counselee:

◆ *Fails to own the problem.* "On the one hand, you're unsatisfied with your relationships, but on the other hand, you think everyone else needs to change."

◆ *Fails to identify the problem in solvable ways (AKA "I can't").* "On the one hand, this is a problem you want to solve, but on the other hand, you feel helpless and aren't sure there's really anything that you can do."

◆ *Fails to interpret critical experiences, behaviors or feelings.* "On the one hand, you're crying as you tell me about this really hurtful breakup, but on the other hand, you're telling me that it wasn't a big deal and you've moved on."

◆ *Fails to identify or understand consequences of behavior.* "On the one hand, you don't understand why you were put in detention, but on the other hand, you're saying you shoved Jacob on the playground."

◆ *Hesitates or is unwilling to act on new perspectives.* "On the one hand, you just came up with a really creative solution to your problem at work, but on the other hand, you aren't sure you want to go through with it."

◆ *Uses evasions, distortions or game playing.* "On the one hand, you say you want to fix this problem in your life, but on the other hand, you dismiss and refuse to try every possible solution we've come up with."

◆ *Is misinformed.* "On the one hand, you believed what your classmate told you about the requirements for the major paper in the course, but on the other hand, the course syllabus states requirements that are different from what your classmate described."

◆ *Is demonstrating behavior that goes against counselee's stated values.* "In your job interview you told me that you valued working hard, but every time I've passed your cubicle this week I've seen you on Facebook."

It is important to remember that just because a counseling situation might meet one of the above criteria, it does not obligate the counselor to use confrontation. This is always an optional skill that requires the counselor to use discernment, patience and empathy when it is employed.

Reluctance and resistance. Even though many people come into a counseling relationship with the expressed goal of gaining insight, getting help or making changes in life, there are plenty of scenarios in which counselees can appear less than cooperative with the process. Sometimes this lack of cooperation is due to the counselee being required to be in counseling by a family member, significant other or the court system. Other times a counselee may have started counseling voluntarily, but as the process unfolded he felt overwhelmed, vulnerable or unprepared and began to put up walls in order to self-protect and slow the process down. Although care-frontation may seem like the best approach to dealing with an uncooperative counselee, a counselor's best resources are to first go back to target 1 skills (reflecting content, reflecting feeling and empathic reflection) in order to remain present in the here and now with the counselee, seeking to solidify trust and the therapeutic relationship. There are two primary types of uncooperativeness in counseling: reluctance and resistance.

Reluctance. Reluctance is when a counselee is still moving forward in the therapeutic process but is doing so with hesitation, apprehension or hedging. This is often seen in an adolescent counselee who may push back, argue, stonewall or refute the suggestions and solutions made in the counseling relationship, but who ultimately still makes progress and slowly implements change. With reluctant counselees, it is important for counselors to see the big picture, noting change across meetings and not just from the beginning to the end of a single conversation.

Resistance. Resistance is a stronger form of uncooperativeness in the counseling relationship. A resistant counselee appears to be truly stuck and either unable or unwilling to engage in the therapeutic process, thus preventing any forward movement.

Most of the time that you encounter a truly resistant counselee, it is often connected to their being mandated to counseling in some way or to their being unprepared or unequipped for the direction taken in counseling.

A key principle to remember within any counseling relationship is that *behavior is purposeful*. If a counselee is uncooperative in the counseling process, there is likely a reason behind her lack of forward movement. Some possible reasons for both reluctant and resistant behavior include but are not limited to:

◆ *Ability:* Sometimes a counselee does not have the emotional, cognitive, social or systemic resources needed to proceed in counseling. If this is the case, it is best that the counselor back up and slow down the counseling process, potentially working with the counselee to develop other skills and resources before moving forward again.

◆ *Emotion:* The counseling experience can bring up a lot of powerful emotions within a counselee, such as shame, fear, anxiety and doubt. When counselees experience high levels of these and other negative emotions, they can become flooded and unable to proceed until those emotions are better mediated or attended to.

◆ *Motivation:* There are times in which a counselor's desire to see growth and change in a counselee is higher than the counselee's desire. Low desire or motivation for change in the counselee often indicates that something in her present way of living is providing a benefit or reward that she is unwilling to give up quite yet, or that the

Biblical/Theological Connections

In the history of pastoral care, confrontation has been frequently referred to as an effective form of guidance and direction. For an example, see Oden's (1987) chapter in which he refers to admonition as a "pastoral duty" (pp. 160-62). There is some scriptural support for the use of confrontation in people helping (e.g., Mt 18:15-17; Col 1:28; 1 Thess 5:12, 14). Furthermore, it is easy to understand how people helpers gravitate toward telling counselees what they should and should not do, since change is difficult and in our concern and frustration we can become confronters rather than counselors.

In contemporary models of Christian counseling, nouthetic counseling (sometimes called biblical counseling; Adams, 1970, 1981; Powlison, 2010) tends toward a directive and confrontational style as a primary approach to producing change in counseling. *Noutheteo/nouthesia* is used thirteen times in the New Testament and is variously translated as "confront," "exhort," "teach," "instruct," "admonish" and "restore" ("bring into line with"). Adams and his followers utilize confronting and teaching as primary counseling methodologies, and Adams (1981) writes that personal, verbal confrontation is the means used to effect change (p. 11). In the contemporary context of empirically validated theories and techniques, is this an effective technique for producing change in counseling relationships?

discomfort of change is perceived by the counselee to be worse than the discomfort they currently experience.

◆ *Counselor conflict:* Sometimes a counselee's reluctance or resistance is not because of something in them but something in the counselor. No one clicks or gets along with everyone, and just as certain people can rub you the wrong way, sometimes a counselor is not the best fit for the counselee. This lack of fit may be due to a personality conflict of some sort, or it can be because the counselor is pushing the counselee too hard, leaving the counselee feeling pressured and overwhelmed by the counseling process. Whenever a counselor encounters a reluctant or resistant counselee, one good first question is to ask whether the counselor could have been perceived by the counselee as pushy or having not listened to the underlying messages within a counselee's story.

◆ *Environment:* Many counselees possess an internal desire and drive toward change, but their social or cultural surroundings limit what is actually available to them. For example, I (Elisabeth) have a friend whose parents are Chinese immigrants. She is a brilliant individual with multiple Ivy League degrees. If she were to have met with a counselor to discuss her career plans in high school or college, the counselor would have likely experienced her as reluctant or even resistant to any career-counseling process that focused on her personal interests or aptitudes. This would not have been because she was uninterested in career exploration but because her family's culture limited her options to medicine and law. Understanding a counselee's culture, social supports and environmental limitations is an important part of the counseling puzzle.

CAUTIONS WHEN USING CARE-FRONTATION

Care-frontation, even in its best form, can still be a risky skill to implement. As with other advanced skills, the greater the potential a skill has to provide insight to the counselee, the greater the potential for harm to the counselee and the therapeutic relationship. Therefore a few cautions are in order when utilizing this skill. These are not meant to dissuade you from using this skill but to remind you of the gravity and importance of using confrontation appropriately.

◆ *Do not assume that confrontation is to be used in all counseling relationships.* Confrontation is a specialized skill that will be fitting in some counseling relationships and not in others. Not every counselee comes in with apparent discrepancies that need to be examined, and even when discrepancies are clear to you, the counselee may not be ready to have them pointed out. This skill should be implemented only after attempts at empathy and clarifying have still left the counselee stuck.

◆ *Do not confront early in the counseling process.* If you jump into confrontation without building a relationship first, the counselee will likely feel unsafe. In a worst-case scenario, counselees may not come back for future sessions, if they cannot summon the courage to tell you face to face that they do not want to make another appointment. Remember, you *earn the privilege to use confrontation* through the use of empathic listening and reflection. Using confrontation too early in the counseling process risks sounding like a verbal villain: detached from emotion and only focusing on content or action.

◆ *Do not expect drastic changes from one confrontation.* Think about a time in your life when someone confronted you, pointing out an inconsistency in your life or story. How quickly or dramatically did you change after that interaction? It is true that sometimes a confrontation can provide so much insight, awareness and conviction that we change immediately. But, more often than not, change comes slowly, in small increments over time. Extend the same patience and grace to your counselee as God has extended to you in areas needing confrontation.

◆ *Do not ignore small changes and improvements along the way.* Change is difficult and can often be discouraging when it does not happen quickly or dramatically. It is important that a counselor look for even the smallest changes and improvements made by counselees, affirming and encouraging them in the progress they *are* making.

RELATIONSHIP APPLICATION

Care-frontation is an important part of any healthy and growing relationship. Although it can be uncomfortable, there is some truth to the idea that those who really love us care enough to point out when what we are doing is hurtful or counterproductive to our goals in life. But no relationship can sustain if it is only care-frontation or correction. This skill requires a healthy deposit within the relational bank to already exist, based on empathy, understanding and support over time.

Gottman & Silver (2000) make the claim that the ratio of positive to negative comments in a healthy relationship should not drop below five to one. The ratio of five positive comments (or more) to one negative comment is essential for marital success and satisfaction. Less than a 5:1 ratio means that there is a 94% certainty that the couple will not remain together or will not be satisfied. To the degree that care-frontation is experienced as a criticism or complaint in the relationship, this ratio probably applies to counseling relationships as well.

MULTICULTURAL APPLICATION

Confrontation is always tricky, because if not done with sensitivity and care, you run the risk of your counselee becoming defensive and perhaps more resistant to the helping process. When you are working crossculturally the danger is increased because cultures vary greatly with respect to how confrontation is regarded and what is considered appropriate. Writing for an international business audience, Meyer (2014) titled chapter seven of his book "The Needle, Not the Knife: Disagreeing Productively."

European North Americans often see certain cultural groups as highly confrontational and other groups as nonconfrontational, or avoidant of conflict and disagreement. For example, Germans and French are in general better able to separate an idea from the person expressing it and can objectively critique an idea without threat or harm to the relationship (Meyer, 2014). If you find confronting difficult, you will be at a disadvantage with respect to some counselees from cultural backgrounds for whom direct expression is expected, and you may need to force yourself to confront more readily in order to help effect change.

On the other hand, Chinese, and even more so Japanese and Thai, cultures are very reluctant to disagree or express contrary views in relationships. The cultural values of honor and group harmony are higher principles that direct expression. For some people this tendency would be labeled as avoidance of conflict. When your counselee is from this type of culture, your confrontations will need to be more indirect. One form indirect confrontation can take is to be extremely tentative, allowing the counselee a lot of room to disagree with you and still save face. For instance, you could begin by saying something like, "I'm really confused about what you just said. It sounded like you were blaming your coworker for the project not going well, yet I thought you indicated earlier that you knew you had not put your best effort toward this project. Perhaps I misunderstood . . ." Notice that the counselor is admitting to potential weakness on his own part through addressing the confusion. Also, using the phrases "it sounded like" and "I thought you indicated" as well as "perhaps I misunderstood" gives counselees a way to deflect full responsibility and not experience self-deprecating shame if they are not yet ready to own up to their part of the difficulty. When such counselees feel safe enough within the helping relationship, they may be increasingly able to accept confrontation.

If you do not know how a particular counselee will respond to confrontation, your safest bet is to begin with an indirect, tentative confrontation. If this attempt does not get picked up, then try being more and more direct until it is clear that your message is being heard. Of course, just as with any skill, you can also broach discussion of it with your counselee. For example, "As you know, I don't have much experience with individuals from your cultural group. I'm wondering whether you'd be willing to talk with me about how people confront or have disagreements with each other in your culture."

MINISTRY APPLICATION

Matthew 18 is very clear that we, as Christians, are not to simply let one another continue on in sin but are to address our concern with them directly. Depending on the church or ministry you are a part of, chances are you have experienced either one extreme or another on this topic—either extreme legalism and excessive rebuking of one another, or extreme passivity for fear of being "judgmental." As humans we struggle to find balance in life and in relationships, and this topic is one place where that imbalance can be easily seen.

Go back to chapter two and the discussion of priests and prophets. Some of you who are more priest-like may struggle with confrontation, tending to feel as if your words are going to be too harsh no matter how they are delivered. Your natural tendency is to want to empathize and find ways in which a counselee's seeming contradictions could actually make sense. On the other hand, those of you who are on more of the prophetic end of the spectrum will likely need to remember that care-frontation must exist in the context of relationship and must not be the primary method of intervention. Whether you tend to be more priest-like or more prophet-like, confrontation and empathy must go hand in hand as you walk with others in their journey toward health and wholeness.

A SAMPLE COUNSELING DIALOGUE WITH JORDAN

Skills used: reflecting content, empathic reflection, open question, prompt and care-frontation

Background on the conversation: Jordan is a fifteen-year-old male whom you have been seeing in a counseling setting for the last six weeks. Jordan came to counseling because he was regularly getting into verbal and physical fights with his parents and frequently skipping school, and had been arrested for marijuana possession. For the last two months Jordan has been living with his Aunt Susan and Uncle Mark in the hope that a new environment will allow Jordan to address his anger and behavioral issues. Jordan is not mandated by the court to be in counseling, but his aunt and uncle have told him that it is a condition of him living in their house.

Counselor: *Hey, Jordan, it's good to see you again. What's been going on in your world since I saw you last week?*

Jordan: *Not much, I guess. School's okay. I still really hate Mr. Anderson, my math teacher. I just don't see why I need to take algebra if I'm going to be an artist when I grow up.*

Counselor: *You still feel aggravated by your math class and your math teacher.*

SKILL	empathy, level 3
feeling = aggravated content = math class and teacher	

Jordan: *Yeah, but I guess that doesn't really matter today. It is what it is. At least I don't have to go back for another couple weeks—maybe by then Mr. Anderson's attitude toward me will get better. He just doesn't like me.*

Counselor: *Tell me more about not going back to math class for a couple of weeks.*

SKILL	prompt
This is new information to the counselor and he/she is unaware as to the reasoning behind Jordan's break from math class.	

Jordan: *Oh, it was stupid. I got suspended for a couple weeks because I got up in Mr. Anderson's face last Friday. It really wasn't my fault. He wanted me to sit down and do my homework, but I'd already done my homework and wanted to go out in the hall to get a drink from the drinking fountain. He wouldn't listen, so I got real close to him to make sure he heard me. I thought it was funny.*

Counselor: *You got suspended for getting in Mr. Anderson's face.*

SKILL	reflecting content

Jordan: *Yep. Pretty stupid, huh? He should have just let me go get a drink.*

Counselor: *In what ways do you see this situation being like other situations we've talked about in here?*

SKILL	open question

Jordan: *Hmmm, I hadn't thought about that. I mean, I guess this is kind of similar to when my mom and I got in a fight over the iPad. Remember, I was going to bed and I wanted to take the iPad up to my room with me, but she told me I had to leave it downstairs. I tried to explain to her why I wanted to take it with me, but she wouldn't listen. So I got up real close to her face and explained real loud that it was my iPad and I would take it upstairs if I wanted to. I was grounded from technology for a week after that.*

Counselor: *In both situations you felt unheard because the other person wasn't agreeing with your request.*

SKILL	empathy, level 3
feeling = unheard content = others weren't agreeing with you	

Jordan: *Totally! I mean, it's not like I wasn't speaking English! I'm almost an adult, and I should be able to make my own decisions. Especially when I explain why I want something, they should respect that.*

Counselor: *On the one hand, you want to be respected like an adult, but on the other hand, you're still getting in other people's faces when you want something.*

SKILL	care-frontation

Jordan: *Well, yeah, I guess that's all true. I mean, what would you have done? I just wanted Mr. Anderson to treat me like an adult and let me go get a drink if I wanted a drink.*

Counselor: *I'm wondering how you've seen other adults in your life ask for what they want or need.*

SKILL	prompt

CONCLUSION

An advanced skill that is not appropriate for all counseling situations but is necessary for all counselors' toolboxes, confrontation reflects apparent contradictions within a counselee's story. As with any other skill in target 2, the goal of confrontation is to help counselees develop greater clarity, insight and understanding of themselves and their situation. As for the counselor, self-reflection and self-awareness are critical in making sure that any confrontations are delivered from a place of care, empathy and respect for the counselee.

REFLECTION QUESTIONS

1. How would you describe your feelings and reactions around confrontation in your personal relationships with friends, family, colleagues, etc.?

2. On a scale of one to ten, how comfortable are you with the idea of using care-frontation with a counselee? Explain your score.

3. Who is someone in your life who uses care-frontation well? How do they approach confrontation? How do you feel after being confronted by them?

4. Describe a time in which you were involved in a confrontation that went poorly. In light of what you learned in this chapter, what could have made the confrontation a care-frontation, and how might that have changed the experience?

USING THE HERE AND NOW

When Jesus saw her weeping, and the Jews who had
come along with her also weeping, he was deeply
moved in spirit and troubled. . . . Jesus wept.

JOHN 11:33, 35

SKILL: authenticity, self-disclosure and immediacy (contextual and relational)

PURPOSE: to make good use of the here and now within the helping relationship

FORMULA: "Right now I'm experiencing _____."
"You are (crying, smiling, etc.)."
"When you _____, I feel _____."
"That reminds me of (counselor's personal experience)."

*T*HINK **ABOUT AN INSTANCE** when an individual attempted to be helpful to you by sharing an incident from his or her own life, but you did not perceive it as beneficial. What made it not helpful? What would you rather he or she had done?

» Write down your responses.

Now reflect on a time when the result was the opposite; what was shared was helpful in some way. What in particular affected you positively?

» Write down the thoughts that come to mind.

As a young adult, I (Heather) was sharing with my counselor some struggles I was having in my relationship with my father. My counselor had a daughter about my age and proceeded to tell me how he and his daughter had worked out issues in their relationship. I felt too intimidated to tell him how I was feeling about his self-disclosure, but in actuality I was really frustrated! I remember thinking, "I know he means well, but I couldn't care less about his problems with his daughter! I want him to understand *my* problem with *my* father!"

In this chapter we will be looking at the here and now of the helping relationship, that is, what is happening in the moment with you as the counselor (authenticity and self-disclosure), the counselee (contextual immediacy), and in the relationship between you and the counselee (relational immediacy).

Empirical Support

Emotions, experienced in the here and now, are powerful, visceral responses to life circumstances. The research on emotion and emotional regulation (Gross, 2014) suggests that there is a fine, and maybe undefinable, line between the experience of an emotion and how we assess and ultimately control our responses. We are in a situation, then give attention to the emotion that emerges, then appraise it and respond. However, this all can happen in a moment, and the attention and appraisal elements might not be conscious or intentional, resulting in what might be called an emotional reaction, not a response. The literature on emotion differs widely regarding the degree to which we can control or regulate emotion, with most agreeing that while the raw, emotional experience might not be under conscious control, people can learn to gain some measure of control by attending to

emotion as it emerges, utilizing strategies to appraise the experience and reflect on the outcomes of the experience.

The concept of emotional regulation incorporates the idea that the process involved is learnable, teachable and transferable to others. However, it suffers from the implication, pervasive in the history of Western civilization, that emotions should be regulated; it suggests that emotion is suspect, might lead us astray and might be maladaptive or immature.

However, Thompson (2010) writes, "Life is fundamentally about emotion. If you do not attune to it, you will eventually respond to it anyway, but in forms of thought, feeling, and behavior that bring you closer to shame than to glory" (p. 104). This is a more balanced and helpful perspective on the central role of emotion in life and faith.

WHAT IS AUTHENTICITY?

Authenticity has to do with the level of genuineness that counselors exhibit within the helping relationship. The term Rogers (1957/1992) used to describe counselor authenticity was *congruence*. Congruence is one of the core counselor conditions that Rogers purported was essential in order for counselees to grow. He states that

the therapist should be, within the confines of this relationship, a congruent, genuine, integrated person. It means that within the relationship he is freely and deeply himself, with his actual experience accurately represented by his awareness of himself. It is the opposite of presenting a façade, either knowingly or unknowingly. (p. 282)

Being authentic, then, does not mean that you as the counselor can do or say whatever comes to mind, nor does it look the same in the helping relationship as it does within a mutual friendship or intimate relationship. It does have to do with being a real person in the moment, not hiding behind a professional, expert mask. According to Rogers, authenticity also has a lot to do with self-awareness, particularly in terms of our internal reactions to what is happening here and now within the helping relationship. If we ourselves do not know who we are, how can we possibly genuinely be ourselves in the counseling role?

Biblical/Theological Connections

The belief that emotions should be closely regulated characterizes the history of the church as well as Western civilization in general. Christians take a verse such as Galatians 5:22-23 (cf. Col 3:12), which lists the fruit of the Spirit (italicized below), and emphasize the last one, self-control. Christians often overlook that in many ways these fruit are closely related to emotions. Note the emotional nuance of these words and synonyms found in alternate translations. Are these entirely under our control?

> But the fruit of the Spirit is *love* (sincere appreciation, affectionate high regard, deep concern), *joy* (gladness, great happiness), *peace* (completeness, soundness, well-being; freedom from worry), *forbearance* (patience, longsuffering, restraint; emotional calm), *kindness* (lovingkindness, benevolence), *goodness* (resistance of evil, generosity), *faithfulness* (devotion, loyalty, adherence, trustworthiness, dependability), *gentleness* (meekness, humility) and *self-control* (temperance; control over desires and actions). Against such things there is no law. (Gal 5:22–23)

The passage continues: "Since we live by the Spirit, let us keep in step with the Spirit" (Gal 5:25). We are essentially encouraged to live a life characterized by these fruit, suggesting that it is possible to grow into and develop them. Colossians 3:12 tells us as "God's chosen people" to "clothe" ourselves with compassion, kindness, humility, gentleness and patience.

The specific strategies by which this can be done are numerous, but we will mention a few. Praying about an area of emotional struggle is an obvious one. Another would be immersing ourselves in contexts that encourage these fruit of the Spirit and surrounding ourselves with others who exhibit them. This is ideally what Christian community is. In psychology, the recent emphasis on mindfulness (cf. Tan, 2011b) is helpful for learning to become a nonjudgmental observer of one's own emotions as they are experienced while resisting the urge to evaluate, intensify or deny the emotional experience. As we extend and focus more intentionally on the process of experiencing emotion, we are then better able to respond in new and less reactive ways.

This is a helpful example of the convergence of biblical teaching and psychological technique, as they affirm similar approaches to understanding and working with emotion.

CHRISTIAN FOUNDATIONS OF AUTHENTICITY

We have found that in some evangelical circles there is a misunderstanding that Christians should "have it all together." When struggles come their way, they expect that their relationship with Christ will carry them through, helping them to meet every personal difficulty with peace and hope. Unfortunately, when such individuals find themselves experiencing inner turmoil, they may feel compelled to hide their confusion and pain so that they are not labeled by others in their faith community as unspiritual.

This view is not biblical. The psalmist often cries out to God in his anger, fear, pain and confusion. For example, Psalms 10, 28 and 55 each describe anger that is so intense that a desire for revenge is clearly expressed. Other psalms (e.g., Ps 42) reveal emotions of despair and hopelessness.

Authenticity also calls people to be honest about positive emotions, times of confusion and doubt or moments of excitement and extreme joy. Too often "Christian maturity" is perceived to mean stoicism or emotional neutrality. Just as David openly expresses his anger in the Psalms, he too expresses delight, praise and joy (e.g., Ps 98). The father of a miraculously healed boy authentically communicated to Jesus his tension between belief and doubt (Mk 9:24). And Paul expresses his appreciation and joy for the relationship he has with the Philippians with genuine delight (Phil 1:3-8).

Christ, too, offers us a model of how to be authentic. For instance, his agony is clear in the Garden of Gethsemane as he wrestles with his immanent crucifixion (Mk 14:32-36). Jesus even wept publicly when he was among those grieving for the death of Lazarus (Jn 11:35). The biblical example, therefore, is one of authenticity.

While the skill of authenticity refers to congruence on the part of the counselor, moment by moment in the counseling relationship, as Christian counselors our authenticity should go further; we should be authentically ourselves within all of our relationships. If we are incongruent outside counseling relationships, we are not living as Christ called us to live; we are called to live with integrity.

LEARNING THE SKILL OF AUTHENTICITY

The skill of authenticity is far more art than science (figure 12.1) and therefore has no formula. Instead it relies on the counselor to incorporate an accurate sense of self into her verbal and nonverbal responses to a counselee. In all reality, no one can be completely authentic all the time, and we all will likely need to be engaged in a lifelong exploration of what it means to be genuine in any given situation. Striving for a level three on the authenticity scale is sufficient and appropriate for most

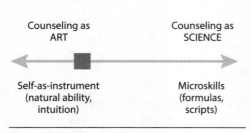

Figure 12.1. Art versus science: Authenticity

counseling situations. Be aware that in the early phases of learning counseling, many students struggle to maintain a level three, as the new "language" of counseling does not yet feel genuine to them. Be encouraged that it will come. Keep practicing!

The levels of authenticity (adapted from Hammond, Hepworth & Smith, 2002). Just as reflecting content, reflecting feeling and empathic reflection can be used at varying levels, so it goes for authenticity. The scale goes from extreme inauthenticity (e.g., duplicitous, manipulative, withholding) at one end, to authenticity to the point of confrontation at the other end.

Authenticity Scale

Level 1: This response will likely be harmful to the therapeutic relationship. It is characterized by marked discrepancies between the counselor's internal thoughts or feelings and his stated responses, or marked discrepancies between the counselor's nonverbal communication and her stated responses. The counselor's response could be any of the following:

✓ outright lies about how he is feeling
✓ artificial in verbal responses
✓ guarded, defensive or evasive responses
✓ irrelevant or inappropriate self-disclosures
✓ withholding of self-disclosure that would benefit the counselee

Level 2: This level of authentic response indicates some lack of genuineness that could still be damaging to the counselee. Counselor responses are empty or sterile, sounding "professional" but lacking personal connection. Responses in this category often sound canned, pre-scripted or cliché.

Level 3: At this level the counselor is not explicitly revealing her thoughts, feelings or reactions but is not hiding behind a mask. Unlike level one, there is no defensiveness, guardedness, or insincerity, but the emotions that the counselor does show are shallow or communicated vaguely. Counselor responses, whatever their intended purpose, should seek to never fall below level-three authenticity, and the vast majority of counselor responses will be at this level.

Level 4: At this level the counselor does explicitly reveal his genuine reactions but tends to still be cautious or hesitant in his disclosure, particularly in the sharing of negative emotions. In a level-four response, the counselor is able to use both positive and negative self-disclosure of his personal feelings and reactions in a way that is facilitative to the therapeutic relationship. The counselee experiences the therapist as being genuine and present.

Level 5: In this final level of authentic response, the counselor is freely herself, able to interact spontaneously, without hesitation and consistent with her own inner feelings and sense of self. The counselor is able to honestly and sincerely share positive, negative and ambivalent feelings when they are relevant and beneficial to the counselee's process. The counselor's ability to openly share her emotional reactions facilitates a constructive exploration of the counselee's process and/or the therapeutic relationship.

Diagnostic Implications

The diagnostic process walks a fine line between focusing on the past versus focusing on the here and now. Many counseling theories take the counselee's past seriously and argue that the past predicts, at least to some degree, the present. Psychoanalytic, object relations, Gestalt, existential and to some degree cognitive-behavioral theories are examples of theories that intentionally explore the past. However, there are other theories (e.g., experiential, person-centered, brief and solution-focused, emotion-focused) that focus almost exclusively on the current experience of the counselee in the room.

The here-and-now experience of the counselee in the room with you, the counselor, is an essential focus. Yet, when considering diagnosis, Morrison's (2014) principles include the following suggestions about the counselee's history versus current reports of here-and-now experience:

✓ Family history can guide diagnosis, but counselee reports cannot always be trusted.

✓ A history of symptoms is more preferable than the current appearance of symptoms.

✓ Recent history is more helpful than ancient history.

✓ Collateral reports of the counselee's behavior are at times more helpful than the counselee's here-and-now report of her condition.

✓ Signs that you observe here and now in the session are a better guide than symptoms that the counselee reports to you.

✓ Be careful of crisis-generated information; it is easily distorted.

✓ The best predictor of future behavior is past behavior.

From a Christian biblical perspective, this same tension is present. The past is seen as an important reminder of how God and humanity interacted, recognizing both the ways in which God rescued people (e.g., the people of Israel from Egypt) and how God was angry with his people (e.g., the people of Israel wandering in the desert). The Jewish Passover is a heavily symbolic retelling of how God and his people interacted. On the other hand, verses such as Isaiah 43:18 suggest the opposite: "Forget the former things; do not dwell on the past" (cf. 2 Cor 5:17; Eph 4:22-24; Phil 3:13-14).

In other literature we see the same tension. C. S. Lewis (1950/1977), in *The lion, the witch and the wardrobe*, has Aslan (the God figure in the story) say to Edmund's sisters, "There is no need to talk to him about what is past" (p. 126). Yet a Congolese proverb says: "Life is lived forwards but understood backwards" (Press, 2011).

Obviously, we are not recommending, either in diagnosis or in counseling relationships in general, that counselors only focus on the here and now. However, to the degree that real, currently experienced emotions and thoughts can be brought into the session, the less likely we will be to get lost in the past stories of hurt and harm. The balance is important.

Most of the time, a level-three response is what you as the counselor are aiming for. As long as you are aware of what is going on inside you and you are not being artificial in your demeanor or in how you state your response, you will be at a level three with respect to authenticity while you are also reflecting content, reflecting feeling, using empathic reflection, asking clarifying questions and confronting. With most counselees, higher levels of authenticity are to be avoided early on in the relationship. The danger of levels four and five is that in revealing what you think or feel about a situation, your value system is being made explicit. Counselees who are insecure in themselves, or who are uncertain of their relationship with their counselor, may end up making decisions that are unduly influenced by what their counselor shared, in their desire to please their counselor or even to avoid judgment and potential rejection. Later on in the process, after the relationship has been firmly established and counselees exhibit a more solid sense of self, the risks of using high levels of authenticity are reduced.

A SAMPLE COUNSELING DIALOGUE WITH WANDA

Let us look at the case of thirty-five-year-old Wanda, who is being battered by her husband. Consider the skills used by the counselor as well as their appropriateness or inappropriateness.

Wanda: *This weekend Frank really scared me. I guess he'd been yelling for me because he wanted me to bring him a tool. He likes to save money by changing the oil on our vehicles, so he was under the car. But I was in the kitchen making lunch and didn't hear him. I guess I should have been listening better, or I should have thought of keeping the door from the garage into the house open so that I could hear him if he called.*

Counselor: *Wanda, it sounds as though, in addition to being afraid, you're also feeling guilty about not having been able to anticipate Frank's needs. You know, Wanda, it really isn't your responsibility to figure out what Frank might want from you.*

SKILL	reflecting feeling; intuitive empathy, level 4; authenticity, level 5
feeling = afraid intuitive empathy = guilty. Wanda never stated this emotion, but it was inferred through how she told the story. Authenticity is demonstrated by the counselor's reminder to Wanda to remember what is and is not her responsibility.	

Wanda: *Yeah, I realize that Frank is the one who should have communicated his expectations. But he's not very good at doing that and I'm left to face the consequences.*

Counselor: *What happened when you didn't come running when Frank called?*

SKILL	clarifying—open question

Wanda: *I was at the stove, so my back was turned, and I didn't hear him come in. But he grabbed me by the shoulders and spun me around. I had been about to drain the pasta and had the pot in my hand, so when he grabbed me the boiling water splashed onto my arm.*

Counselor: *That's why you're wearing the bandages?*

SKILL	clarifying—closed question

Although normally to be avoided, in this case a closed question was appropriate to clarify that the bandages were relevant.

Wanda: *Yes. But when I screamed from shock and pain, Frank got really angry and shoved me hard. I fell and hit my head on the edge of the table. I wanted to go to urgent care because I was really dizzy and thought I might have a concussion, and my arm was really burning, but Frank told me I just wanted attention and he didn't want us to waste money paying for urgent care.*

Counselor: *I'm really worried about you Wanda. It looks as though Frank's violent behavior is escalating. I think it's time for you to leave him before things get worse.*

SKILL	authenticity, level 4; authenticity, level 5

The counselor's first sentence falls at a level four on the authenticity scale, as it reveals some but not all of the counselor's emotions and reactions. The final sentence is a level five because of the level of honesty, spontaneity and sincerity in the counselor's statement.

Before we dissect the above exchange and inform you what we think are good and not-so-good examples of counselor authenticity, we invite you to take a few minutes to read over the dialogue again. This time ask yourself:

» Which responses are examples of higher levels of authenticity that are used well?

» When was the counselor's use of authenticity potentially problematic?

Now that you have asked yourself these questions, we will tell you what we see in the transcript! We believe that the counselor made a valid point when he told Wanda that anticipating her husband's needs was not primarily her responsibility. However, just as higher levels of empathy are confrontational in nature, so too are high levels of authenticity. Whether or not this particular use of level-four authenticity is appropriate depends on the strength of the helping relationship as well as Wanda's overall level of defensiveness. In this instance Wanda's response is not overly defensive, indicating that the therapeutic relationship was strong enough to handle it. It may also have helped that the counselor reflected feeling and used intuitive empathy prior to making the highly authentic response.

Authenticity in Psychoanalysis

Attention to the here and now is fundamental to the therapeutic process in psychoanalytic approaches. While psychoanalysis has often been stereotyped as being a theory largely concerned with the counselee's past, that past is continually manifest in the present moment and relationships, particularly the therapeutic relationship. This is why psychoanalysis has traditionally focused on the transference/countertransference matrix that is created between the therapist and client.

The myth of the inauthentic analyst putting forward a total "blank screen" began to be challenged early in the development of psychoanalytic theory. In the early twentieth century, Hungarian analyst Sándor Ferenczi posited that the "fundamental honesty of the relationship constitutes the curative difference" in therapy (Goldstein & Suzuki, 2015, p. 452). Contemporary psychoanalytic approaches have more explicitly deconstructed this myth and focused on the need for a "genuinely truthful encounter" (Buechler, 2002, p. 277) in the therapeutic relationship. Authenticity in this relationship is letting the counselee know that "You affect me, and I affect you, and this is how I am experiencing our relationship." This authenticity generally involves some degree of spontaneous "disclosures of immediacy" (Knox & Hill, 2003, as cited in Goldstein & Suzuki, 2015, p. 453) for the purpose of what Stark (1999) would term a corrective relational experience. These disclosures contribute to insight of relational dynamics and enactments emerging from the transference/countertransference matrix.

In fact, Stark (1999) considers authentic relationship one of the three primary modes of therapeutic action in psychoanalytic approaches. While analytic therapists often provide interpretation to help the client gain insight and to provide a corrective emotional experience through empathic attunement, it is in the authentic relationship that the therapist is vulnerable to the client, providing opportunity in the here and now to grow through "engaging, and being engaged by an authentic real other in real relationship" (p. 110). This is a two-person psychology, involving two subjectivities affecting one another and coming together with "authenticity, spontaneity, mutuality, reciprocity, and collaboration" (p. 111).

Chris Stanley, PsyD
Plena Vita Psychological Services
Adjunct professor, Denver Seminary

It is clear that the counselor has justifiable concerns about escalating violence. Therefore the high level of authenticity the counselor expressed when he said he was worried for Wanda's safety is justified, given the seriousness of the incident. He would have to make sure he carefully perceived what Wanda's response was to his statement about being worried, because victims of intimate partner violence are often in a lot of denial. The counselor's expression of worry may therefore either surprise Wanda or make her defensive.

Where the counselor makes a large error is in advising Wanda to leave her husband. If Wanda leaves Frank primarily because her counselor tells her to, her problems could actually get bigger. For example, statistics show that a victim of spouse abuse is actually in increased danger of being killed by her partner after she leaves (Miles, 2011). While his intentions are good, by advising Wanda to leave her husband the counselor may inadvertently be placing Wanda at greater risk of abuse or even death. In addition, he is also not empowering Wanda to make her own decisions but may be inadvertently creating unhealthy dependency by telling her what to do. In this case it would be appropriate for the counselor to use level-four authenticity in expressing his concern, but rather than give Wanda advice, it would have been better to explore with her various options for helping her to stay safe, allowing her to choose a course of action.

Check Your Understanding

For the following exchanges, rate each response on the authenticity scale, provide an explanation for why you gave it that rating and identify the counselor response that best exemplifies appropriate use of *authenticity*. Our ratings and explanations can be found in appendix C. *Note: It is possible for there to be more than one response at each rating level.*

Counselee: I studied really hard for my midterms and got the results back yesterday. I got As in all five of my exams! Can you believe it?

Counselor:
That's great, Dennis! I'm really proud of you!

Rating: _____

Explanation: _____

_____

That's terrific, Dennis! It's wonderful to see you so excited about the results of your hard work!

Rating: _____

Explanation: _____

_____

It's about time you actually put some effort into your studies!

Rating: _____

Explanation: _____

_____

Now that you've proven you can do it, maybe you should apply to that graduate program you said you were interested in!

Rating: _____

Explanation: _____

_____

SELF-DISCLOSURE

While all higher levels of authenticity ultimately disclose something about the counselor, the term *counselor self-disclosure* refers more specifically to the counselor explicitly sharing some aspect of her personal story for therapeutic purposes. Therefore, while authenticity and self-disclosure are not identical concepts, there is overlap between them (see figure 12.2).

Figure 12.2 illustrates how the skills that are the focus of this chapter are related. Authenticity should always be present at a minimum of three on the authenticity rating scale and encompasses the other skills. Contextual immediacy is the broader category of immediacy and includes any intervention that explicitly focuses on the here and now. Relational immediacy is a subset of contextual immediacy that focuses on the here and now of the counseling relationship. Self-disclosure is a particular form of authenticity that can at times overlap with relational immediacy and contextual immediacy.

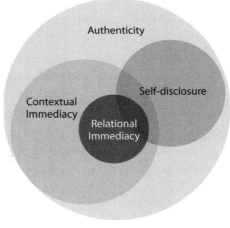

Figure 12.2. Skills that use the here and now

We have noticed that nonprofessionals tend to use self-disclosure a lot, as they talk about life experiences they have had in an attempt to identify with others' difficulties. In mutual relationships this practice can at times be helpful, although as part of the exercise at the beginning of this chapter, you likely identified times where you were on the receiving end of someone else's self-disclosure and felt that the focus switched from you to the other person.

In helping relationships self-disclosure should be used only sparingly, because there is the potential for damage (Barnett, 1998) when used incorrectly or inappropriately. Like salt in cooking, there are some dishes that are perfectly delicious without any salt added, while other dishes need salt to bring out the fullness of flavor. However, once you have added too much salt you cannot take it back, and the dish can be ruined. The rule of thumb is to use the least amount of self-disclosure necessary to accomplish your goal. For example, if a counselee is discussing her grief at the death of her mother, and you too have lost your mother, it may be appropriate to say something like, "My mother died a year ago. I know what it's like to question whether life will ever be normal again. I'm wondering what feelings the loss of your mother is evoking for you?"

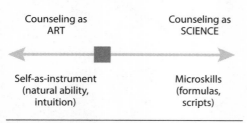

Figure 12.3. Art versus science: Self-disclosure

Social Media and Unintentional Self-Disclosure

Social media, such as Facebook, can be a way that your counselees may obtain information about you without your permission or even your knowledge. Such unintentional self-disclosure can greatly affect the helping relationship. Counselors should consider the following (adapted from Cook, 2011):

✓ Do not have a Facebook, Twitter, Instagram or other social media account.
✓ If you do have a social media account:
  • Be aware of the privacy settings and restrict access to all personal information.
  • Do not allow yourself to be "tagged" by other people (because you have no control, otherwise, of photos, etc., that people share of you).
  • Only post what you would be comfortable disclosing with your counselees.
  • Remember that what gets posted on the web is always there, even if you "delete" it.

Notice that the details of the death and grieving process that the counselor experienced are not introduced because they may be distracting rather than helpful. Whether more is shared would depend on the response of the counselee. If, for instance, the counselee responded with, "Really? You've gone through this too? How did you get through those first few months?" the counselor has a number of options. One would be to answer the question directly and share some specifics of what had been helpful, that is, continue to self-disclose. Another might be to redirect the conversation with a response such as, "Everyone is different, so there is no one right way to grieve. What's worked for me may not be particularly helpful to you. But would you be interested in the names of some books that give many practical suggestions for how to survive the grieving process? You could then try those that appeal to you."

Notice also the question that directly follows the counselor's self-disclosure. It serves as a kind of hand-off, bringing the focus from the counselor back to the counselee. This helps decrease the risk that the self-disclosure will result in attention staying on the counselor's experience instead of returning to the counselee's situation.

As with any intervention, counselors need to be assessing whether the use of self-disclosure at a particular point in a session will benefit the counselee rather than meet their own needs. If you decide that self-disclosure could be helpful, you need to continually assess your own motivations for sharing. If you do decide to self-disclose, you then need to perceive the counselee's verbal and nonverbal responses to what you are sharing in order to evaluate whether your self-disclosure is having its intended effect or whether you need to revamp your approach.

IMMEDIACY

The skill of *immediacy* explicitly makes use of counselors' *perceiving* skills to enable them to address a specific issue in the here and now of the session. We are going to distinguish between two types of immediacy: *contextual immediacy* and *relational immediacy*. Contextual immediacy is termed just *immediacy* by some authors (e.g., Evans, Hearn, Uhlemann & Ivey, 2011). However, we thought it would clarify the confusion that we have seen our students struggle with by making a clearer distinction between it and relational immediacy.

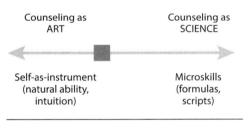

Figure 12.4. Art versus science: Immediacy

Contextual immediacy. Contextual immediacy encompasses anything that a counselor perceives a counselee is portraying nonverbally in a given moment and that the counselor decides to make explicit, with the exception of material that pertains specifically to the therapeutic relationship. For instance, if you see tears welling up in a counselee's eyes, you could either choose to use intuitive empathy and say, "You seem to be feeling really sad," or you could use contextual immediacy and state, "I notice the tears in your eyes," and then wait for the counselee's response. The two responses could be combined into "I notice the tears in your eyes—you seem to be feeling really sad," which would be making use of both skills.

As with any skill, just because you perceive what is happening does not mean that you necessarily act on, or draw attention to, what you observe. Similar to high levels of authenticity, both intuitive empathy and use of contextual immediacy contain confrontational elements in the sense that counselees may not even be aware of their behavior, or even if they are, they may be trying to hide it from you. Therefore choosing the appropriate time to use contextual immediacy is important.

Gestalt Therapy

Gestalt therapy makes extensive use of both contextual immediacy and relational immediacy. Gestalt therapists comment specifically on mannerisms and other behavior, often encouraging their counselees to exaggerate these in order to develop greater awareness of their experience (contextual immediacy). The relationship is also explicitly addressed in the here and now (relational immediacy). These principles are well illustrated by seeing Fritz Perls in action with Gloria in the old film "Three Approaches to Psychotherapy—Part II" (now available at www.youtube.com/watch?v=it0j6FlxIog).

Relational immediacy. Relational immediacy is making use of the here and now by explicitly addressing the therapeutic relationship. In chapter two we discussed the centrality of the person of the counselor and the power of the relationship between counselor and counselee in the process of change and healing for the counselee. By focusing specifically on the helping relationship itself, relational immediacy can be enormously instrumental in the change process.

A Spiritual Understanding of "Here and Now"

Henri Nouwen (1994) writes about the importance of living in the present moment without either focusing on guilt due to past mistakes or worrying about the future. He says that "real life takes place in the here and the now. God is a God of the present. God is always in the moment, be that moment hard or easy, joyful or painful. When Jesus spoke about God, he always spoke about God as being where and when we are" (p. 18). Nouwen's words can serve as a reminder to us to be fully present in the moment with our counselees and fully attuned to the therapeutic relationship.

Relational immediacy can be viewed as a special type of high authenticity because the counselor reveals her thoughts, feelings or reactions to something the counselee says or does (see figure 12.2). The context for the following scenario is that the counselee, Fran, has been ten to fifteen minutes late for her appointment three times in a row, and the counselor is now feeling frustrated.

Fran: I'm so sorry I'm late again! I was just about to leave the house when a friend dropped by, and I just couldn't get away! I hope you understand.

Counselor: Fran, I certainly understand that the unexpected can come up. Anyone can be late occasionally. But I must admit that I'm feeling frustrated! When we set a particular time to meet I'm watching out for you and can't really get involved in some other task. And this is now the third week in a row that you've come rushing in ten or fifteen minutes after we were scheduled to begin the session.

Fran: Oh! I hadn't really thought about how you'd be impacted! I'm sorry. You know it isn't just that I'm making excuses . . . there are always legitimate reasons that I've been delayed. But you're not really saying anything my husband hasn't already said! He says that I have a bad habit of being late and that it is disrespectful of other people. I always thought he was making too much of things, but maybe it's a bigger issue than I thought if you're pointing it out too! I hope you won't stop seeing me!

Counselor: Of course I am willing to continue to see you! Although our relationship is different from your relationship with your husband, or your friendships, there will still be issues to work out between us from time to time. Would you be willing to look more closely at what might be behind your chronic lateness and see whether together we can find some productive ways for you to work on it?

Fran: Definitely! I want to work on my friendships, too, and I think me being late isn't helping them at all. If I'm on time for meetings at work it may actually help my performance evaluations, too.

Counselor: That's great! I'm really glad you're willing to discuss this further. I appreciate that you took my feedback seriously and didn't react defensively. Six months ago it might have been a different story. The maturity with which you've handled this today shows how much you've grown.

The counselor had a couple of options here. She could have just brushed the incident off, but in doing so she would be inauthentic. In consequence, her frustration and resentment might then build to the point that it could have an adverse effect on the helping relationship. Alternately, the counselor also could still have made it clear that she was frustrated, but in expressing her frustration inappropriately she could have damaged the therapeutic relationship. This would be the case if, for example, the counselor had berated Fran by saying in an angry voice, "You realize this is the third time you've been late,

Clinical Tips

Awareness of your own emotions is essential for the counselor. Asking yourself the following questions can help you to use your emotions appropriately:

1. What am I feeling?
2. What triggered this emotion?
3. Are my feelings due to my own emotional baggage (which I need supervision about), or are they legitimate responses to what the counselee is saying or doing (and therefore can be used in the helping process)?
4. Are high levels of authenticity appropriate at this moment?
5. Is relational immediacy called for?
6. Should I remember this incident and see whether something similar comes up in the future?

don't you?! This is very inconsiderate of you!" The counselor may have been feeling genuine at the time, but such a response would be considered a one on the authenticity scale because it is disrespectful and ultimately not helpful or even destructive.

By being honest but in a way that furthered rather than hindered Fran's growth, the counselor was being highly authentic in her use of relational immediacy. Notice how the dialogue began with a discussion of the relationship, which then allowed for generalization to other people and situations. If the counselor had been unaware of her own frustration level, a productive therapeutic moment would have been missed.

RELATIONSHIP APPLICATION

In marriage and family counseling it is common to spend a lot of time recounting the stories of the past week—arguments, hurts, failures and miscommunications. The problem is that when counselors spend time rehashing conversations, it can be done quite factually without emotion or can become diluted because counselees can be ashamed of how they acted. So the countermeasure to this distorted recollection of events is to ask the couple or family to replay the discussion they had at home in the session, here and now. This is called an enactment (Treat & Hof, 1987), a dialogue that the family (or subgroup of the family) has that the therapist orchestrates in order to aid the family in improving family communication. Enactments encourage families to talk *with* each other rather than *about* others.

The challenge in this here-and-now focus is that the counselor never knows where the enactment is headed. This out-of-control feeling is often why counselors resist encouraging the family to enact a conversation. However, the advantage is that the counseling is dealing with real emotions in real time; authenticity, self-disclosure and immediacy are all in play.

MULTICULTURAL APPLICATION

Cultures vary in the extent to which they value authenticity. Some Asian cultures, for example, more highly value an outward sense of harmony over the potential conflict that could ensue from being more open. For example, in the Philippines, the common usage of the acronym SIR (smooth interpersonal relationships) illustrates the value Filipinos ascribe to not making relationship waves in order to preserve harmonious relationships (Jocano, 1997).

While use of higher levels of authenticity and relational immediacy may still be necessary, counselors should use greater caution when giving feedback that could be assessed as negative so that a shame response is not elicited. High levels of authenticity that are more affirming may be somewhat less risky but should still be used carefully because they, too, could elicit a negative, shame-based reaction in individuals from cultures that value group achievement but frown on attention being drawn to individual achievements.

MINISTRY APPLICATION

In more informal ministry settings, you are more likely to have multiple roles with your counselees so that they see you in more than just a counseling role and likely know more about you than a counselee in a more formal setting would. This means that increased levels of self-disclosure, or higher levels of authenticity, may be more appropriate earlier on in the counseling relationship or in a pastoral care role. In youth ministry greater use of self-disclosure may be particularly helpful for building rapport. Keep in mind, however, that these skills can still be overused in these settings.

Try It Out

Below are two scenarios between a counselor and counselee. Putting yourself in the position of the counselor, create your own response that is a level three or four on the authenticity scale. Include self-disclosure and/or immediacy as it seems appropriate. Then explain the rationale for your response.

Scenario 1: You are the small group leader for a Bible study. Part way through the year a new person, Taylor, joins the group. You notice that Taylor often acts like the class clown, using jokes to draw attention away from deeper topics and to engage other participants. In an attempt to get to know Taylor, better you meet for coffee. You notice that Taylor continues to use a lot of humor in conversation with you.

How do you experience Taylor? What thoughts, feelings or reactions get stirred up in you?

_____

_____

Do you assume Taylor is male or female? How old is Taylor? What in your past contributes to these assumptions?

_____

_____

How might you respond to Taylor with authenticity, immediacy and/or self-disclosure?

_____

_____

Scenario 2: Charlie started coming to counseling with you a few months ago. Charlie is talkative, intelligent and generally likeable. Over the past few weeks you have noticed that Charlie's communication patterns have started to change with you. Where previously Charlie would listen and then respond thoughtfully to your comments and reflections, he now interrupts frequently, is dismissive of your input by the use of the phrase, "Yes, but . . ." and is fidgety whenever the topic of his wife or his work is brought up.

How do you experience Charlie? What thoughts, feelings or reactions get stirred up in you?

_____

_____

How do you make sense of the change in Charlie's behavior? What insecurities does his response style evoke in you? What hypotheses do you consider regarding his current emotional situation?

_____

_____

How might you respond to Charlie with authenticity, immediacy and/or self-disclosure?

_____

_____

CONCLUSION

The here-and-now skills of authenticity, self-disclosure and immediacy are potentially the most artful of all the microskills. Relying on the person of the counselor and the counselor's self-awareness within the counseling session, these skills are highly susceptible to what is going on in and with the counselor at a given moment. Valuable in small and well-timed doses, here-and-now skills serve to personally connect the counselor and counselee in the experience of counseling as well as the broader experiences of life.

REFLECTION QUESTIONS

1. On a scale of one to ten, with one being completely uncomfortable and ten being completely comfortable, how comfortable are you when others self-disclose in a conversation? Why?

2. Think about the relationships in your life. With whom do you find yourself the most authentic on a regular basis? What contributes to your sense of being able to be genuine with this person?

3. What are some things (fears, barriers, apprehensions, etc.) that keep you from being more authentic in your relationships?

4. Is there any indication from the reactions of others to you that you are sometimes too authentic (e.g., scaring others off by being too blunt/opinionated or sharing too deeply too quickly)? Or that you are too guarded or inauthentic (e.g., others can't read you or figure out what you really think or feel)?

5. Who is someone in your life that you consider to be authentic? What about them contributes to this assessment? What do you admire about them? How do you *feel* when you are in conversation with them?

STRATEGIES
FOR GROWTH

*Whatever you have learned or received or heard from me, or seen in
me—put it into practice. And the God of peace will be with you.*

PHILIPPIANS 4:9

SKILL: implementing change

PURPOSE: to help counselees identify tangible ways to implement change for long-lasting growth

FORMULA: "How can I help you put (the changes you desire) into reality?"

*T*HINK OF SOME NEW YEAR'S RESOLUTIONS you have made.

» Were you able to keep them?

» If not, what got in the way of your succeeding? If you were successful, what helped?

As failed New Year's resolutions can attest to, lasting change is difficult. If new patterns are going to develop and change is going to stick over the long haul, intentional strategies for continued growth need to be implemented.

When we talk about "implementing change" in this chapter, we are not merely talking about behavioral change, but tangible change in one of several domains. For example, implementing change might be changing an attitude or working through a difficult emotion, as well as finding another job or implementing a regular exercise regimen. Just as a change in physical behavior may be as subtle as blinking an eye, or as obvious as jumping over a hurdle, the kinds of changes we are describing in this chapter may be small, inner changes, noticeable primarily to the counselee, or they may be huge, externally observable changes that have significant effects on relationships or the counselee's external world. Either way, implementing change involves a decision by the counselee to take action in some area of their internal or external being. Target 3, "Growing," focuses specifically on skills that help counselees take everything that they have learned up to this point and make lasting changes that help them to grow in significant ways.

WHAT IMPLEMENTING CHANGE IS ALL ABOUT

As discussed in the introduction to targets 2 and 3, some counselees feel relief at just being able to unload on someone who feels safe. Once their sense of emotional overload abates, making them less symptomatic, such individuals may feel that they have gotten what they wanted out of counseling and will not continue. Counselees who actually do make it this far in counseling have reached a point where they understand that permanent change is different from temporarily diffusing symptoms and are prepared to do the hard work that target 3 requires.

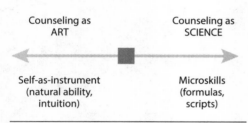

Figure 13.1. Art versus science: Implementing change

The goal in aiming for target 3 is to pull together all the pieces that have been gathered thus far in the counseling relationship in order to be able to effect permanent change and growth. Target 3 involves creativity, intuition and collaboration between the counselee and the counselor and is usually guided by specific counseling theories. As such, skills used to accomplish target 3 are equally art and science.

EXAMPLES OF CHANGE STRATEGIES

A complete overview of possible change strategies for counselors to use is beyond the scope of this book. However, to provide a sense of the kinds of counseling foci that have been suggested over the years, here is a partial list:

- experiencing emotional release
- gaining insight
- making choices
- deepening spirituality
- stopping behaviors
- initiating new behaviors
- thinking through
- coping with emotions

- building identity
- facing shame and guilt
- forgiving the past
- forgiving self and others
- strengthening relationships
- grieving losses
- improving life skills
- caring for physical health

We suspect that students enter counseling training with some automatic assumptions regarding how people change. Often these assumptions are based on personal experience with how change has occurred in our own lives or the lives of people we know. The danger is that counselors focus on "favorite" change modalities while downplaying or ignoring other change strategies. Often this is not helpful to our counselees. Having an overarching theory of change that guides our work with counselees is essential.

PROCHASKA'S STAGES OF CHANGE

One of the most popular and empirically based theories of change is Prochaska and DiClemente's (1983) five-stage model, revised to a six-stage theory (Prochaska & Norcross, 2013). Prochaska and Norcross argue that these stages represent a transtheoretical model that can be used as a template from which to analyze all counseling theories, which they do thoroughly in their 2013 text.

Change may appear to be a simple concept, but it is rarely an easy one. Particularly with large life changes or changes to long-standing life patterns, counselees are likely to go through various, somewhat predictable stages. Where a counselee is at in regard to stages of change can affect the strategies for growth that are implemented within the counseling relationship. The stages of change and related growth strategies are:

1. *Precontemplation:* This is an important stage to acknowledge and not overlook. In this stage counselees are not yet even considering change. They are unaware of or unwilling to address the possible changes that could be made in their life or in a given situation. "Consciousness raising" and "dramatic relief" are strategies Prochaska and Norcross identify (2013, p. 465) as helpful in moving counselees to begin to consider change.

2. *Contemplation:* Counselees in this stage may be aware that change could, or even should, occur in their life at some point, but they are unwilling or unable to actively pursue change at this time. They are likely open to exploration of what change *might* look like *if* they were to pursue it, but it generally remains only a cognitive exploration. Environmental (situational) reevaluation and self-reevaluation are the two change strategies highlighted in this stage.

3. *Preparation:* In this stage, counselees are beginning to test the waters, so to speak, regarding change. They are gathering resources and support, developing a plan for change but not yet implementing that change on a significant level. Self-liberation or willpower is a requirement of this stage. Belief in one's autonomy and power to change (also called self-efficacy) open up new possibilities, an increasing awareness that change is possible and would greatly improve one's life.

4. *Action:* This is where counselees begin to actively make change in their lives, implementing the plans that have been made and practicing their new behavior, thoughts and feelings. Action, in this stage, has a broader meaning than simply

doing something. New thoughts, emotions and behaviors are possible. Technically, contingency management, counterconditioning and stimulus control are the change processes identified in this stage and the next.

5. *Maintenance:* In the maintenance stage, whatever change has been implemented is now a part of "normal" life. Continued commitment to the new behaviors, thoughts and feelings is cultivated and sustained. Prochaska and Norcross (2013) identify the process as a cycle in which earlier stages are recycled through, perhaps a number of times, before the change is permanent. Relapse prevention, understandably a major concern in the addictions field, is a focus of this stage.

6. *Termination:* The final stage, also more important than is often imagined, ends the active, intentional effort to produce change. Endings require attention to feelings, thoughts and behaviors that accompany the ending of relationships.

The Prochaska stages of change are a helpful backdrop to our understanding of how people change. While not as explicitly phase or stage focused, our phases and targets overlap with many of the concepts identified by Prochaska, though we recognize that our model diverges significantly from Prochaska's model.

THE ABCS OF MOVING FORWARD: DOMAINS OF GROWTH

At its core the counseling process involves helping a counselee discover new ways of approaching life. In many ways counseling is a creative endeavor, with counselor and counselee seeking to think outside the box. Even in the most creative forms of art, there are guidelines, or even rules, that inform the legitimacy of the artistic expression.

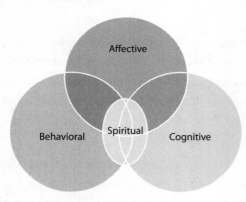

Figure 13.2. Domains of growth

Counseling is no different. The possible interventions one could collaboratively develop with a counselee are endless, but each potential intervention is ultimately guided by theory.

One way to look at growth is through the lens of four domains: behavioral, affective, cognitive and spiritual (see figure 13.2). Whether or not the counselee is a Christian, or acknowledges any type of spirituality as important, we see the spiritual domain as core. Sometimes growth will happen as a result of directly working through the spiritual domain. This could be the case, for example, with spiritual direction, or when a counselee's spiritual concerns are made an explicit part of the counseling session. However, the spiritual domain is most often accessed through our thoughts, emotions or behavior. Real change in any one of the domains will affect the others.

An argument could be made that a relational/social domain could also be included. However, the four domains we have included all affect the relational/social aspect of our lives, and we deal with relational systems in detail in the next chapter.

Various counseling theories tend to emphasize some domains more than others, but counselors using any theory will attempt to bring about change in how the counselee feels, thinks or behaves. While we will discuss each domain as a separate entity, in many counseling situations the domains overlap, and a counselor draws from two or more in order to effectively facilitate the counselee's forward movement (see McHenry & McHenry, 2015, for a succinct overview of foundational therapeutic skills and interventions). It is important to remember that the domain selected should be chosen based on the needs of the counselee and not simply on the theoretical preference of the counselor.

The current book is a counseling skills book rather than a counseling theories book (see Jones & Butman, 2011; Tan, 2011a, for Christian overviews of the key secular counseling theories). Therefore prior to this chapter we have mentioned theoretical approaches only in passing in some chapters. However, we thought it would be helpful to point out how various theoretical approaches relate to the specific domains of growth because ultimately you will use these skills within a particular theoretical framework.

Some Words of Wisdom (adapted from Garland [1999], pp. 460-62)

✓ Don't try to convince people that change will be easy.
✓ Change occurs more effectively when it is supported by personal relationships than when it is carried out by rational decision-making processes alone.
✓ Change needs to be introduced in language that relates to the counselee's experience.
✓ We change more easily when others can show us the way.
✓ Change sometimes requires leaps of faith (stepping out beyond common sense).
✓ Change can be "catalyzed," but the results cannot always be predicted or controlled.

Affective domain. This domain of growth looks primarily at helping counselees change the emotional responses within their story. This domain also seeks to build counselee self-awareness as well as the counselee's awareness of other people's feelings (Okun & Kantrowitz, 2015). Focusing on affective growth is particularly important for counselees who struggle to express their feelings. It is also recommended for counselees who lack awareness of how their behavior affects other people or who refuse to take responsibility for themselves. The focus may be on increased awareness of feelings in the present, including the here and now of the counseling relationship, or it may be on working through feelings connected to events in the past.

Affective theories. The affective domain of growth is built primarily from psychodynamic, humanistic and existential theories. These theories include psychoanalytic, person centered, existential, Gestalt and some elements of Adlerian. Foundational theorists connected with these theories include Sigmund Freud, Carl Jung, Alfred Adler, Carl Rogers, Fritz Perls, Rollo May, Viktor Frankl and Irvin Yalom.

Affective techniques. When functioning primarily out of the affective domain with a counselee, much of what is implemented as movement toward growth is helping counselees to increase awareness of their own emotions and/or apply empathy, intuitive empathy, immediacy and self-disclosure within their interpersonal relationships as well as within their own self-talk. Specifically focusing on the here and now, and encouraging the counselee to use "I" and "you" statements rather than globalizing, are foundational to working within this domain for counselors using some of these theories. Psychodynamic approaches also look at how past events affect current symptoms. Additional techniques of imagery, sensory awareness, free association and dream analysis are used to promote growth in this domain (Okun & Kantrowitz, 2015).

It is important to acknowledge that for Rogers (1957/1992), the facilitative conditions referred to in earlier chapters were seen as necessary and sufficient for change to occur. When implemented skillfully and sensitively, the skills discussed in previous chapters will move a counselee forward without techniques from the other domains. While many would suggest that Rogers' conditions are insufficient in many counseling situations, the power of these affective skills, competently used, should not be underestimated.

When pursuing affective spiritual growth, similar techniques can be applied that draw the counselee's focus onto the emotions that guide their spiritual life. Contemplative disciplines such as praying the Psalms, *lectio divina* (Benner, 2010), the practices of silence and solitude, and the practice of slowing (Ortberg, 2015) can all be affective spiritual techniques.

Behavioral domain. This domain of growth focuses on physical action and answers the question, "What are you going to *do* about it?" A widely applicable domain, behavioral strategies appeal to our most basic functions as human beings; a counselor using a behavioral approach does not ask counselees to think or feel differently but simply to do (Corey, 2013). Like any other learned skill, behavioral strategies are about repetition and practice. This domain is particularly useful with children, individuals who struggle with verbalizing emotions or cognitions, those with cognitive or developmental delays, and people with extreme fears or phobias (Antony, 2014; Wilson, 2005).

Behavioral theories. Behavioral therapy, and theorists such as B. F. Skinner, J. B. Watson and Albert Bandura, lay the foundation for this domain of growth. In current practice, most behavioral counselors also incorporate at least one other domain of growth into their case conceptualization and their interventions. It is most common to pair behavioral approaches with cognitive ones, such as in cognitive-behavioral therapy.

Behavioral techniques. Growth strategies within the behavioral domain include assertiveness training, reinforcement, punishment, contracting, modeling, systematic desensitization, role-playing and modeling. Behaviorally focused growth strategies place higher emphasis on action than on understanding the motives, thoughts or feelings behind the behaviors being looked at.

Spiritual growth strategies within the behavioral domain focus on the implementation of spiritual disciplines and emphasize the importance of engaging in the discipline even if one's heart or mind is distracted by other things. Common behavioral spiritual interventions include acts of service, Scripture reading and prayer, and the practice of celebration and remembrance (Ortberg, 2015). Scripturally, this domain focuses on the instruction in Colossians 3:17, which states, "And whatever you do, whether in word or deed, do it all in the name of the Lord Jesus, giving thanks to God the Father through him."

Cognitive domain. Changing the way counselees think about themselves, their problems and their stories provides the structure for using growth strategies within the cognitive domain. This domain is particularly effective when counselees are seeking to engage in a problem-solving process, or when it is evident that their cognitive world is impeding their ability to engage in the physical world in a way that is consistent with their goals. Within this domain the counselor is seeking to help the counselee identify thoughts and thought processes that are distorted, inconsistent or self-defeating and to provide a new framework or perspective from which counselees can make sense of themselves and their story.

Cognitive theories. Similar to behavioral theories and approaches, cognitive strategies can be used exclusively but are often integrated with other domains of growth. Theories such as cognitive therapy, cognitive-behavioral therapy (CBT), rational emotive behavioral therapy (REBT) and choice theory (also called reality therapy), along with their respective theorists, such as Aaron Beck, Donald Michenbaum, Albert Ellis and William Glasser, provide the framework for the cognitive domain of growth.

Cognitive techniques. Change strategies and techniques within this domain include confrontation, cognitive restructuring and reframing, shame attacking, thought stopping, bibliotherapy, open questions and homework (Okun & Kantrowitz, 2015). Cognitively focused spiritual growth places priority on what counselees know or think about regarding their spiritual life. Specific techniques may include an inductive Bible study, research on a specific spiritual topic, Scripture reading and memorization, or journaling (depending on the prompts and focus this could also be an affective strategy; Foster, 2002; Ortberg, 2015). Theophostic prayer ministers make use of the cognitive domain when they attempt to expose the lie behind a troubling memory, considered an essential aspect of the healing process (Smith, 2005). Paul's instructions in Philippians 4:8 to think about "whatever is true, whatever is noble, whatever is right, whatever is pure, whatever is lovely, whatever is admirable," and his instruction in Romans 12:2, "Do not conform to the pattern of this world, but be transformed by the renewing of your mind," provide the underlying foundation for cognitively focused spiritual growth strategies.

Biblical/Theological Connections

The book of James in the New Testament, perhaps more explicitly than anywhere else in the Bible, addresses the common human problem of hypocrisy—saying one thing and doing another. Duplicity, insincerity, having a double standard—this is not just a Christian problem, it is a human problem. Many times in our lives we are confronted with the challenge of believing and saying one thing and acting in a different way. James says:

> Do not merely listen to the word, and so deceive yourselves. Do what it says. Anyone who listens to the word but does not do what it says is like someone who looks at his face in a mirror and, after looking at himself, goes away and immediately forgets what he looks like. But whoever looks intently into the perfect law that gives freedom, and continues in it—not forgetting what they have heard, but doing it—they will be blessed in what they do. (Jas 1:22-25)

While this is as true for counselors as it is for counselees, we want our counseling efforts to result in changed attitudes, emotions, thoughts and behaviors. The Bible suggests many ways to move in this direction of consistency between our internal world and our actions. One window into what this means is to look at the biblical concepts of righteousness and holiness. Rather than simply focusing on right or holy behavior before God in a legalistic way, these concepts focus on healthy, honest relationships. To be righteous or holy is to be dedicated to God and others—to be in relationships that have been put right. Of course, this implies that we act in ways that genuinely respect and honor one another.

The ability to do this is a gift from God. From the foundation of Jesus' righteousness, sustained by the work of the Holy Spirit in our lives, we are able to put into action the changes we come to in counseling relationships. This makes sense for Christian counselees, but what about non-Christians? On what basis are they able to put into action the changes they desire? Theologically, the concept of common grace, the grace of God given to all people regardless of their beliefs, tells us that while God's saving grace is given to those who believe, grace—including the ability to make changes in our lives and rooted in the *imago Dei*—is freely given to all.

With regard to the focus of this chapter, the overarching theological lesson is that "Whatever you have learned or received or heard from me, or seen in me—put it into practice. And the God of peace will be with you" (Phil 4:9). Peace, healing and wholeness result when we put into practice what we have learned and received. "'I will restore you to health and heal your wounds,' declares the Lord" (Jer 30:17).

Both/and. In reality, very few counseling approaches or growth strategies are purely within one domain of growth. As figure 13.2 demonstrates, there is often a fair amount of overlap, and it can serve counselees well when growth strategies engage multiple domains of their selves and their lives. Cognitive-behavioral approaches (CBT and REBT) tend to be the best-known examples of growth strategies and approaches that combine domains.

THE PROCESS

The process of implementing change in a way that promotes lasting growth follows three primary guidelines. Promoting growth is:

- **Collaborative.** Developing a course toward growth should be a process that is jointly engaged by both the counselee and the counselor. This does not mean that the contributions to this collaborative experience are necessarily equal. The responsibility of final decision making should always fall to the counselee, as should the majority of the weight of the evaluation of positive and negative consequences. Depending on the situation and on the personalities of both counselor and counselee, the primary responsibility for brainstorming and creative solution development could fall to either participant. When the problem has been identified and the counselee has been able to state the goal of counseling moving forward, it can be helpful to intentionally draw out the counselee's ideas about how she could move forward. Some possible prompts and open questions that facilitate collaborative approaches when target 3 is the focus include but are not limited to:

  - What could be done about this?

  - What aspects of your current dilemma are similar to situations we've worked through before?

  - How does your new understanding of _____ affect how you are going to deal with this new challenge?

  - How could this become more a part of your life?

- **Attentive to the counseling relationship.** It is tempting for some counselors to step into fix-it mode once they get to discussing growth strategies, but it is important to resist this temptation and remain in a facilitative role. The counseling relationship is still essential to the change process and so needs ongoing attention even when you are aiming for target 3. Utilizing the target 1 reflective skills and target 2 deepening skills will help minimize the risk that you are jumping ahead of the counselee and that the counseling relationship remains strong.

- **Intentional.** As seen in the discussion of the three domains of growth strategies, theory can and should inform the growth stage of the counseling process. Therefore, plans to promote growth are not simply random, creative ideas that have no grounding to them but are instead creative ideas informed by the therapeutic process, the counselee's goals and a theoretical conceptualization of the counselee's situation.

Operationalizing the growth process. It is important for counselors to have some basic structure for how they approach the exploration and implementation of potential growth strategies. Whether implicitly or explicitly utilized, the following seven steps can help to provide a framework for target 3 work (Okun & Kantrowitz, 2015). In some situations, particularly those in which affective strategies are implemented, some of these steps may be combined or even removed from the process, due to their inapplicability.

These seven steps would normally be viewed as a problem-solving or decision-making approach most relevant to the behavioral domain of growth, in that the language used implies a discrete problem and a counselee and counselor who are able to follow and implement a sequence of steps. However, by interpreting these steps more broadly, they can be applicable to working within the affective, cognitive and spiritual domains as well. The theoretical orientation of the counselor and the related domains of growth, as well as the issues a particular counselee presents with, will affect all of these steps.

Step 1: Identify the problem. As a basic formula, this sounds like the counselor reflecting to the counselee, "The issue you want to pursue growth in, or change, is _____." This process begins from the first session as the presenting problem is discussed. However, once target 2 skills are utilized, the deepening process allows for core issues to be identified that then become the main focus of interventions when aiming for target 3. It is important that counselor and counselee identify the problem in the same way, or they may be working at cross purposes.

In a theoretical orientation based on an *affective* domain of growth, the problem is likely to be perceived as connected to the counselee's emotions. For example, counselees may be viewed as not being aware enough of their emotions or as not being able to regulate or process their emotions. Within theoretical approaches that make use of the *behavioral* domain, the problem will be identified as a need to change a particular behavior. For instance, within the behavioral domain, a counselee who loses his temper would not be seen as someone who has difficulty processing his anger (affective domain) but as someone who needs to develop anger management skills. Similarly, for counselors who practice primarily from the *cognitive* domain of growth, the problem of this same counselee would be framed as a difficulty with how he thinks about situations that end up leading to anger responses.

Certainly what is identified as a problem is potentially influenced by the *spiritual* domain, particularly when a moral issue is involved or when the counselee perceives that his or her religious community would disapprove of where he or she currently is with respect to a specific issue. For example, an evangelical Christian may identify lack of forgiveness of a perpetrator as a problem because of their interpretation of Bible verses that point to the importance of forgiveness. Counselees with a different worldview may not see lack of forgiveness as a problem, although they may wish they could stop obsessing about what happened to them.

Step 2: Identify the desired outcome(s). It is not enough just to identify the problem or issue; the counselor and counselee must also identify the desired outcome for which they are working. For example, if a counselee says that her husband has been cheating on her, the course of therapy looks very different when her desired outcome is reconciliation versus when she wants is a divorce. Theoretical orientation will also affect the desired outcome. Whatever the theoretical orientation, however, the goal of step two is to make sure that both counselor and counselee are in agreement as to what is the desired outcome.

Given the above example, a counselor focused on the *affective* domain of growth might see the counselee's increased ability to be aware of how she feels about her husband cheating on her, and perhaps her ability to understand her husband's emotional state, as a desirable outcome, whether or not the relationship itself is salvaged.

A counselor utilizing a theory that makes use of the *behavioral* domain might focus on specific coping behaviors or communication skills that might help to resolve some conflictual areas within the marriage. The ability to learn such behaviors could be considered a desirable outcome.

Utilizing the *cognitive* domain, a counselor could help this distraught wife not to catastrophize the affair, helping her to change her thinking patterns so that whatever happens with respect to the marriage or her husband's behavior, she can remind herself that God cares for her and that she will be okay. This would overlap with the *spiritual* domain.

Step 3: Brainstorm possible ways of reaching the desired outcome(s). This process can take moments to multiple sessions. Just like in elementary school when you learned to brainstorm with thought webs and a near stream-of-consciousness thinking process, all ideas are welcome in this process. This is a collaborative element within the growth stage, drawing from the ideas, skills and personality of both counselor and counselee. At the same time, a counselor must be attentive to how dependent a particular counselee could be and gauge the counselor's role in providing input appropriately. It may be therapeutically beneficial for a particular counselee to simply write down his ideas, while another counselee may benefit more from the counselor also contributing to the list of options. This step is most applicable to the *behavioral* domain, although brainstorming with respect to ways of looking at how to correct distorted or inaccurate ways of thinking (*cognitive domain*), or brainstorming possible ways of processing feelings (*affective domain*)—for example, journal writing, dream work or in-session roleplays—are also possibilities.

Such brainstorming could involve interventions that are explicitly spiritual. For example, meditating on a passage of Scripture, singing worship songs or writing a letter to God are examples of interventions that are part of the *spiritual* domain of growth.

Step 4: Identify and evaluate the positive and negative consequences of the most likely growth strategies. Once a sufficient list of options has been developed, we recommend that the counselee identify the two or three growth strategies that appeal to them the most. The counselor then facilitates the counselee in exploring the potential positive and negative consequences of each strategy. Among other things, consequences could be relational or interpersonal, emotional, spiritual, physical, financial, social, familial, legal or ethical. If applicable, identification and evaluation of a plan needs to also include a possible step-by-step outline for the counselee's "real world" implementation.

The risk of negative consequences is likely going to be greater when working with the *behavioral* domain, simply because the counselee's explicit behavior often affects other people and systems, resulting in potential relational fallout. The potential negative fallout of any specific growth strategy within the *affective* or *cognitive* domains is more likely to primarily affect the counselee herself, at least in the short term. For example, a Gestalt two-chair technique intended to increase self-awareness about how a counselee feels about her relationship with her mother could be beneficial in providing some emotional release from emotions that have been pent up. However, if the intensity of the emotion that is surfaced is more than the counselee can handle and she becomes suicidal as a result, obviously the technique could be dangerous to her mental health as well as indirectly affecting her husband and children.

The *spiritual* domain would likely only come into play if some potential growth strategies were deemed unacceptable for moral or religious reasons. For example, some Christians might be uncomfortable with interventions that involve acknowledging feelings of anger and expressing them because they feel that anger is sinful.

Step 5: Choose a growth strategy to implement. The counselee then chooses a strategy to help promote growth around the desired issue or problem. The choice should rest fully with the counselee, without coercion, manipulation or pressure from the counselor. The counselee is the one who will ultimately have to live with the plan he puts into place.

Again, *behavioral* strategies will likely be more straightforward, and so the counselee may be better able to make such a choice. In the *affective* and *cognitive* domains, the counselee may not have ever attempted a particular growth strategy and may have to rely on the expertise of the counselor in assenting to try a particular strategy. However, it is important that the counselee does not feel coerced under these conditions and is free to withdraw consent at any point. The choice of a particular strategy could be influenced by religious beliefs in ways similar to what has been described above as part of our discussion on the *spiritual* domain.

Step 6: Implement growth strategy. In most *behavioral* situations, implementation will take place outside the counseling relationship and within the counselee's real-world experiences. But for *affectively* and *cognitively* focused strategies, implementation may first take place in the counseling relationship with the facilitative help of the counselor. Role-playing (a behavioral strategy) the selected strategy is often helpful in preparation for real-world implementation.

Step 7: Evaluate positive and negative consequences of implemented plan. If satisfied with outcome, explore plans for maintaining growth. If dissatisfied with outcome, go back to step 1 or to target 2 of the counseling process. Evaluation of the implemented growth plan can take place by the counselee alone, outside the counseling relationship, but it can also take place between the counselee and the counselor. If the growth strategy proved helpful and effective, it can be important to then discuss with the counselee how he plans to maintain this growth in his life moving forward. When a growth strategy proves ineffective or serves to stir up other issues that the counselee would like to address, it may be best to circle back to target 2 work and further explore areas in the counselee's story that may now have a new sense of relevance or importance. While with some situations such evaluation can take place fairly quickly, at other times several weeks or months may need to pass before being able to assess the degree of success of the strategy. Regardless of outcome, the counselor's role is to continue to affirm and encourage the counselee's autonomy (ability to make her own decisions) and to facilitate the counselee's growth process and forward movement.

WHAT IMPLEMENTING CHANGE IS *NOT*

While we have been discussing how to facilitate the counselee in implementing change, we must also address what moving forward in growth is not. Many individuals come into counseling with the preconceived idea that they will meet with a counselor, pastor, chaplain or spiritual adviser and that individual will simply tell them what to do, much like a doctor writing a prescription and sending a patient on his or her way. Recall from chapter two that simply spouting off a "prescription" and telling a counselee what to do without attending to the counselee's process and emotions is considered a verbal villain in counseling. Reminding yourself, and reminding your counselee, what your role is and is not will help keep you from paying inadequate attention to targets 1 and 2 and jumping prematurely into a focus on target 3. As a foundational principle of target 3, it is important to remember that growth is *not*:

- *Only doing.* Growth, or moving forward, does not just involve behavioral change. While some growth is about doing something differently than has been done before, such as a recovering alcoholic taking a different route home from work to avoid the liquor store, some aspects of implementing change are more internal. This is more representative of the *affective* and *cognitive* domains.

- *Telling a counselee what to do.* Do not take the bait! Every counselor, at some point in his or her career, has a counselee who says, "So what do you think I should do?" As appealing as this question may be to your ego (who does not like it when someone values our opinion?), you must remember that it is not your question to answer. The counselee is the one who lives with the consequences, both positive and negative, of the implemented growth strategies. Therefore the decision of what to do must be theirs. There may be elements to the story that you are unaware of, such as relational dynamics, limitations in resources or conflicting cultural values that could make your recommendation impractical or even harmful to the counselee.

If you are wrestling with the idea of counselors not giving advice, the reflection at the end of this chapter provides further information on this topic. It outlines the pros and cons of counselors giving advice using four scenarios with possible outcomes for the counselee and the counseling relationship. This exercise can also be used to explore the implications of using homework or reading as a primary growth strategy in the counseling process. The scenarios suggest outcomes that are not our desire as counselors but unintentionally affect the counseling relationship. The core of the issue is counselee autonomy and who is responsible for change. The conclusion of the discussion regarding this frequent issue in training counselors is that regardless of how one looks at it, giving direction or an opinion, telling a counselee what to do or giving homework that a counselee may or may not do typically affects the counseling relationship negatively. While a counselee may be frustrated by not getting advice from the counselor, it is ultimately for the counselee's benefit to be encouraged to take ownership for her choices and whatever consequences are the result of those choices.

◆ *Giving the counselee more growth strategies than they know what to do with.* It is tempting to believe that giving a counselee a greater number of options in how to move forward is best. While this may be true for some counselees, the majority will thrive best with a small number of practical and realistic options that emerge as they collaboratively work with their counselor. Fight the temptation to come up with even more ideas that only serve to clutter the mind or confuse the counselee. Instead, explore the small handful of possible growth strategies that emerge, weighing the positive and negative consequences before embarking on a new brainstorming activity.

◆ *Shaming or guilting (instilling guilty feelings) the counselee into trying a particular growth strategy.* Decisions in life have natural logical consequences, including decisions to not decide or not take action. As a counselor, there will be times in which you believe a counselee would be best suited to engage in a particular growth strategy, but the counselee chooses not to follow this same path. It can be tempting for a counselor to use persuasive methods such as shame and guilt to convince the counselee to go in the direction that the counselor thinks is best. Instead, a counselor should help facilitate the counselee's awareness of the positive and negative consequences of each growth strategy available to the counselee.

◆ *Blaming the counselee for his or her current situation.* Implementing growth strategies is all about moving forward, not about looking back at what *should* have been done. While there is a time and place for counselees to reflect on what they could do next time to prevent such a situation and thus indirectly identify what could have been done differently in the past, the focus of implementing change needs to be on moving forward.

Diagnostic Implications

One of the characteristics of the DSM (APA, 2013) is that diagnostic criteria for disorders are often described as symptoms that are present for a specified period of time. For instance, to diagnose adjustment disorder, emotional and behavioral symptoms must develop within three months of a significant stressor. Furthermore, once the stressor is no longer present, the symptoms do not continue for more than an additional six months. This type of description of symptoms suggests that problems in living occur in patterns—absence of symptoms, increasing symptoms, reduction or removal of symptoms. Embedded in the DSM is the recognition that growth, change and healing typically occur over time.

The ebb and flow of symptoms over time suggests that growth tends to occur in more of a wavy-line pattern than a straight-upward trajectory.

This is an important realization for both counselors and counselees. Sometimes counselors should remind counselees that it may get worse before it gets better. Not all sessions are fun, pleasant, entertaining experiences; some are hard and deep work. Despite the need for, and frequent counselee requests for, briefer forms of counseling, it is helpful to take a longer-range perspective of pre-, mid- and postcounseling and acknowledge that change more often comes slowly and in waves.

Growth is not a straightforward process; it is a journey with hills and valleys, imperfect reactions and meaningful change in personal and interpersonal growth.

A SAMPLE COUNSELING DIALOGUE WITH ELENA

Skills used: reflecting content, empathic reflection, care-frontation

Background on the conversation: You are thirty minutes into your fourth session with Elena. Elena is twenty years old and is an Airman First Class who has come to talk with you, her chaplain, about her fears and apprehensions surrounding her deployment next month. You spent the first few meetings building rapport with Elena, getting to know her, her background and her interest in the Air Force. You have learned that Elena and her family emigrated from Russia when she was a young child, at which time they gained US citizenship. Elena explained that she enlisted in the Air Force as a way to give back to the country that provided solace to her family and as a way to pay for college. She states she will be deploying at the end of the month to a potential war zone and that her commanding officers have informed her that she is of particular value to the team because of her bilingual abilities.

Elena:	*I'm glad that my speaking Russian will actually be good for something, but I'm also nervous about what that'll mean when deployed. I knew enlisting could mean deployment at some point, I just never thought I'd actually go into battle.*
Chaplain:	*On the one hand you're glad your skills can be used, but on the other hand you never expected them to be used in war.*

SKILL	care-frontation

Elena: *That's exactly right. Ever since I got my orders I've had bad dreams, not quite nightmares, about what it's going to be like over there. What worries me most is that in the last week I've started getting caught up in daydreams as well where my mind just spins and spins about all that could go wrong while we're deployed. When they were just dreams I could handle that—it made sense that my brain needed somewhere to work things out. But, now they're interrupting my daytime too, and I'm afraid it's going to affect my ability to do my job. Then we'd be in even more danger!*

Chaplain: *You're terrified that your anxious daydreams will compromise your safety and effectiveness on the job.*

SKILL	empathy, level 3.5
feeling = terrified content = daydreams will compromise safety and effectiveness	

Elena: *I'm so terrified! I know you can't get me out of deployment, and I don't actually want out of deployment. I just want to be able to cope with my anxiety and fear and get through like everyone else. I don't expect it to all go away; I just want to be able to manage it so that I don't feel so overwhelmed by fear all the time.*

Chaplain: *So the problem you're trying to solve is how to mitigate your anxiety and get it to a level that you can cope with it and still do your job well.*

SKILL	reflecting content, possible bridge to target 3

Elena: *Yes, that's exactly right. What can I do?*

Chaplain: *Well, I think that collaboratively we can come up with some ideas that might help you feel more in control of your fear. Specifically, I'd like to talk about how you think about deployment, as well as what you can physically do to help lessen your anxiety. Does that sound to you like a good place to start?*

SKILL	
While there is no specific title for this skill, the chaplain is effectively trying to cast vision for where the counseling process is now going to head. This invites the counselee to agree with or alter what the chaplain has proposed. Although the final question is closed, it is a necessary question in order to confirm or reject the counselee's agreement with the proposed path.	

Which growth strategy is actually implemented to help Elena with her anxiety will vary depending both on the chaplain's theory of counseling and what Elena reveals as the conversation continues. For example, the chaplain could teach Elena some relaxation techniques, which fit within the behavioral domain. Or the chaplain could help Elena look at her cognitive processes, discovering that Elena was telling herself, "If I'm deployed it means I'm going to die."

If Elena is open to looking at the spiritual domain, the chaplain may be able to help her look at her relationship with God and how that affects her sense of readiness or lack of readiness to face death. On further discussion of Elena's story, the chaplain may discover some past trauma that triggered her terror at deploying (affective domain). For example, perhaps Elena witnessed a terrible car accident as a child and saw the mutilated bodies of the victims, instilling in her an unconscious fear of injury and death. In this situation relaxation techniques (behavioral domain) and refuting the irrational belief that deployment means a certain death sentence (cognitive domain) may help to some degree, but they will not be likely to be successful until the traumatic incident is worked through. Therefore the growth strategy taken could potentially look very different depending on the specific circumstances, Elena's motivation to work within certain domains, the chaplain's theoretical orientation and the chaplain's skill at perceiving Elena's core issue.

Try It Out

Using the following exchanges, identify the domain that best encompasses the counselee's problem and explain why you would go in that direction. Authors' answers and explanations can be found in appendix A. *Note: It is possible for there to be more than one possible domain for each scenario.*

1. Counselee: Gabriel has come to see you because he "feels angry all the time." He says the anger started when he did not get into the college he wanted and had to settle for a state school in his hometown. Gabriel says that "ever since college, nothing has gone my way. It's like the world is out to keep me down."

Domain(s) of growth: _____

Rationale: _____

_____

2. Counselee: Laura is the mother of fifteen-year-old Grace. Laura is "fed up" with Grace's continued delinquency from school and her disrespectful attitude at home. Laura has come to you for recommendations on what to do next.

Domain(s) of growth: _____

Rationale: _____

_____

3. Counselee: Take the previous scenario, but this time fifteen-year-old Grace is your counselee. She is angry with her mom for "micromanaging" and wishes Mom would just "leave me alone to do my own thing." Grace claims her choices should only affect her and it shouldn't matter to her mom because it's Grace's life.

Domain(s) of growth: _____

Rationale: _____

_____

_____

4. Counselee: Diane is a thirty-eight-year-old single female who has never been married. She's come to counseling because her most recent relationship just ended after three years. She tells you that she just can't seem to find joy or meaning in life anymore and feels as if God doesn't care about her or her happiness. She denies any suicidal ideation but feels like her life is a waste of pointless monotony.

Domain(s) of growth: _____

Rationale: _____

_____

_____

5. Counselee: Andrea has come to counseling because she has struggled to feel connected within her community and her marriage. She speaks in absolutes like "never," "always," "no one" and "everyone." Specifically, she states that "I have to do *all* the work in my marriage" and "I won't have *any* friends here after Joy moves this summer, and I don't want to have to start over again." Throughout her story, you hear instances where her husband, although seemingly passive, does make attempts at connection with Andrea, and Andrea does have a variety of other social connections and friends within driving distance.

Domain(s) of growth: _____

Rationale: _____

_____

_____

6. Counselee: My boss just informed me that I have to go on a business trip at the end of the month. I am deathly afraid of flying, but there's no other way to get to this out-of-state meeting. I don't know what I'm going to do.

Domain(s) of growth: _____

Rationale: _____

_____

_____

RELATIONSHIP APPLICATION

Research has shown that relationships outside counseling have significant impact on counseling efficacy, specifically the support of friends, family and other community support resources (Lambert & Barley, 2002; see chapter fourteen). Specifically, 40% of counselee improvement is from extratherapeutic factors, 30% is attributed to the therapeutic relationship, 15% from the specific techniques used, and 15% is from the placebo effect (Lambert & Barley, 2002, p. 18). What that means for you as a counselor is that it *does* matter what you do in the counseling room, as 45% is about what you bring or do to help a counselee. But almost equally as important are the support and resources that a counselee has access to outside the counseling relationship (40% of change). As people, we are more likely to persist in making difficult changes in our lives when we feel that we have the support of those closest to us and we have the tools to implement the identified changes.

Some counselees may need to strengthen their support system before they are able to engage in other desired changes that emerge in the counseling process. Friends and family are not always able to help a counselee think or see outside the box in the way that an outside person (such as a counselor) can. However, friends and family can offer a supportive context of care and attention, providing a kind of secure base that can enable counselees to test the waters of change, knowing that their support system is there for them between counseling sessions. After all, you as the counselor are likely only part of a counselee's life for an hour or two a week at most. You cannot possibly meet all of your counselee's emotional and relational needs, nor should you.

In noncounseling relationships we often discover which domain we are most comfortable living in. For example, I (Elisabeth) prefer to work out of the cognitive and behavioral domains of action because that is where I am most comfortable. As such, when friends or family are going through rough times, my natural tendency is to listen for apparent contradictions, help cognitively reframe the situation and develop a new course of behavioral action. In contrast, the people closest to me in my life tend to be most comfortable in the affective domain and focus on empathy and facilitating self-awareness. We need each other. Having people in our lives who understand us but can also help move us into domains that are less natural for us can be of great benefit in the growth process.

MULTICULTURAL APPLICATION

When working crossculturally, not only do we need to pay close attention to the way in which we develop the counseling relationship (reading nonverbals, use of vocabulary, etc.), but we also need to recognize that change occurs differently in different cultures. In fact, the way we typically conduct counseling in the West (time-limited, private location, one-on-one, etc.) may be so foreign to some that our best counseling efforts will be ineffective. At a deeper level, how change occurs and the strategies we use to move counselees forward in their healing process may be alien and alienating.

As Christians we need to affirm that God is at work in people's lives and in all cultures, regardless of whether we can see it. Indigenous forms of providing care and counsel can be discovered through careful and sensitive questioning and listening. Growth strategies exist in all cultures; the West does not have a monopoly on how change occurs. Gingrich and Smith (in press) address this concern in depth in their forthcoming book.

A vivid example of this is seen in the following example (a Rwandan talking to a Western writer, Andrew Solomon, about his experience with Western mental health and depression; Solomon, 2008):

> We had a lot of trouble with western mental health workers who came here immediately after the genocide and we had to ask some of them to leave. They came and their practice did not involve being outside in the sun where you begin to feel better. There was no music or drumming to get your blood flowing again. There was no sense that everyone had taken the day off so that the entire community could come together to try to lift you up and bring you back to joy. There was no acknowledgement of the depression as something invasive and external that could actually be cast out again.
>
> Instead they would take people one at a time into these dingy little rooms and have them sit around for an hour or so and talk about bad things that had happened to them. We had to ask them to leave.

MINISTRY APPLICATION

Just as counselees may need to change the way they think, feel or act in other domains of life, the same can be true for their relationship with God. It is important that the counselor not impose his theological perspectives onto the counselee but listen for where the counselee expresses incongruence or dissatisfaction with the way her spiritual beliefs are intersecting with the rest of life.

Let us look at a case example. Bob is a fifty-year-old male who grew up in a conservative evangelical church. He struggles with anxiety on a regular basis and has a history of both physical and spiritual abuse (i.e., using religion to coerce, shame or punish) at the hands of his stepfather. Bob comes to see you, stating that he is afraid he committed "blasphemy against the Holy Spirit" years ago when he got very angry with God for the abuse he suffered. He states that he has been obsessing over this fear for the past couple of weeks, so much so that it is both waking him up and at times keeping him up at night. As the counselor, and depending on your own faith tradition, it could be tempting to dismiss the counselee's fear, trying to reassure him that the very fact that he is worried about committing this sin means he has not actually committed it.

Another route that you could take would be to utilize behavioral techniques to help mediate Bob's anxiety, or cognitive techniques to refute apparent contradictions in logic within his story. An affectively focused approach may encourage Bob to explore and really experience all the emotions that come along with the anxiety in order to better connect with his own sense of self moving forward. A spiritual approach may actually incorporate all of these domains and approaches. For example, you could facilitate Bob's exploration of his own belief system, asking Bob to provide evidence from within his own faith system for and against his fear that he has committed such a sin. Additionally, you could inquire as to the spiritual disciplines Bob is comfortable with and ask him which ones he has already implemented in seeking to mediate his anxiety. Given Bob's stated faith background, it would be appropriate to inquire as to the role that Bible reading, Scripture memory and prayer play in his life currently, and to discuss ways in which such spiritual disciplines could both help and hurt him in this process. When utilizing spiritual techniques or interventions, it is important that you still conceptualize the counselee's problem in light of the other three domains of growth. You should be all the more attentive to letting the counselee take the lead in the collaborative brainstorming process, taking into account the counselee's faith system without imposing the counselor's beliefs.

CONCLUSION

Implementing changes for long-lasting growth can be a very challenging and yet very exciting part of the counseling process. When target 3 is the focus, counselors seek to collaboratively, therapeutically and strategically work with counselees to develop specific strategies. Identifying which domain of growth is of primary importance will help guide both the counselor and the counselee, allowing for both creativity and structure in this process.

REFLECTION QUESTIONS

1. Which domain of growth do you most naturally gravitate to? Why?

2. Think about the three people closest to you in your life. What domain(s) of growth does each of them gravitate to? How does this help and hurt your own personal growth process?

3. If you have taken a counseling theories course, what counseling theories are you most drawn to? How might that inform the domain(s) of growth that you utilize in counseling?

4. Think of a time in your life when you needed to make a change of some sort in regard to your thoughts, feelings or actions. What was the process like for you? How long did you spend focusing on each target area? What role did the Holy Spirit play in your change process? Can you identify the ways in which the Holy Spirit was gracious and patient in your change process?

Table 13.1. Why giving advice is usually unhelpful

Counselor's advice is:	Counselee's action	Who is responsible (blamed or credited)?	Is the counselee helped?	Impact on the counseling relationship
Bad (wrong, misleading, poorly communicated)	Doesn't follow it	Counselee is blamed (because they did not follow it) Counselor is blamed (because it was bad advice)	No	• counselee fears displeasure of counselor • perhaps counselee knows it was bad advice and now distrusts counselor • relationship is tenuous at best
	Follows it	Counselor is blamed	No	• perhaps feels angry at counselor for bad advice • perhaps pretends it was good advice to maintain a smooth relationship • relationship is at best damaged or even worse, deceptive
Good (correct, on target)	Doesn't follow it	Counselee is blamed	No	• counselee feels guilty for not following advice or resentful for counselor being right • perhaps counselor feels frustrated (angry) that counselee is not doing his or her part and following the advice • relationship is negatively affected
	Follows it	Counselor is credited	Yes, but no	• the counselee gets no credit • the counselee is temporarily helped but not empowered to grow, change and take more responsibility for him- or herself • the therapist is seen as the expert, which produces distance in the relationship • symptom relief at best

Any way you look at it, the counselee is not helped significantly.
Source: Adapted by Fred Gingrich from comments by Dr. Bruce Narramore, 2004.

EXPANDING THE COUNSELING SYSTEM

There are many parts, but one body.

1 Corinthians 12:20

SKILL: thinking systemically and using the relational system

PURPOSE: to recognize that all counseling situations involve both intrapsychic issues and relational contexts, and to use the support and power of those relational systems to help create change

FORMULA: "What you are experiencing internally might relate to (aspects of your relational system)."

*H*AVE YOU EVER SUCCUMBED TO PEER PRESSURE, even if it went against your value system? Or have you gone along with someone else's suggestion or followed their advice, even if you sensed that it was not best for you?

» Describe one of these situations.

Conversely, perhaps someone else's influence actually kept you from making a grave mistake or affected your beliefs or values in a significant way.

» Describe one of these situations.

The reality is that we all live in a complex web of positive and negative relationships. We are rarely if ever completely isolated from the influence of others, and our ability to influence them. Scripture affirms this perspective from the book of Genesis (created in God's image for relationship) to Revelation (being in relationship with God and others within the new creation). Both the Old Testament focus on the people of Israel and the New Testament focus on the community of God's people, the church, tell us through many stories and teachings how we are to live with one another and with God. This systemic, relational emphasis is central to understanding people and how they change.

WHAT IS A SYSTEM?

Building on chapter ten's inclusion of metaphor within the counseling process, we thought we would begin this chapter with a metaphor or proverb fitting for the current topic: *The chain is only as strong as its weakest link.* If you have ever worked with chains, you know this to be true. But does this apply equally well to groups of people, to families, to business teams, to the church?

An analogy to football will be helpful. The effectiveness of an American football team (though it applies to all team sports) depends on the overall, collective performance of the team. Winning teams do not win because they have some very strong links and few weak links. The Super Bowl champions win because each player has a role, a position (lineman, running back, punt return specialist, quarterback, etc.) for which they have been specifically trained and have effectively performed, and the team members are able to masterfully coordinate their efforts. Even the team's superstar cannot win the game for the team that cannot function together.

This is the concept of a system. Systems are more than just a group of people; they are a group of people *plus* their relationships with each other. People riding to work on the bus are not a system unless something unusual like an accident occurs. At that point the people might begin to function as a system, albeit likely a chaotic system. With a system the overall outcome is important (are we achieving our goals?), and the relationships between the parts of the system are important. A fact of human nature is that we are all parts of systems. We either contribute to or detract from their effectiveness, and the systems reciprocally affect us. We are changed by the systems in our lives just as we change the systems.

The majority of counseling sessions that occur in Western countries involve a counselor and an individual counselee in the room. This makes perfect sense, and for many of us this would feel "normal." The problem with this scenario, however, is that the counselor has no objective basis on which to evaluate the accuracy of the counselee's story, the truth of his or her statements, and the additional factors that might be playing a part in the problem situation. The counselor sitting in a room with the counselee has limited knowledge and access to other resources that may help in understanding and promoting change in the counselee's life. In fact, to be blunt, counselees lie, not necessarily consciously but at the very least unconsciously, painting a picture of themselves, their circumstances and others that is a distorted view of reality (Prov 18:17). Distortions can be either favorable (self-promoting) or unfavorable (self-demeaning) in terms of the impression a counselee gives her counselor. As we alluded to in chapter two, image management is an issue for both counselor and counselee. However, in this chapter the focus will be on ways in which a counselor can moderate the distortions counselees present, and how other systems can become a resource for change.

Basic counseling skills include the ability to focus on a counselee within his or her relational networks. These relational and organizational networks are referred to in the counseling field as *systems*. However, working directly with systems in counseling (i.e., bringing the other systems into the counseling room as in marriage counseling) requires additional skills that are beyond the scope of this chapter and this book. The focus here will be on the counselor developing the capacity to think systemically about counselees and utilizing counselees' resources beyond themselves for change. If this is an area of interest to students, we encourage you to pursue future study in the areas of marriage and family therapy and systems counseling, which will focus more on the skills of creating interactions (enactments) between the counselees, identifying patterns of behavior and communication, working with relational processes versus discussing content, and creating new experiences in relationships that can open up possibilities for new relational patterns to emerge. Regardless of whether you want to work with systems directly or you plan to only work with individuals, you need to be able to think systemically and understand how counselees interact within the relational systems in their lives.

The Body Is a System (1 Cor 12:12, 15-27)

Just as a body, though one, has many parts, but all its many parts form one body, so it is with Christ. . . .

Now if the foot should say, "Because I am not a hand, I do not belong to the body," it would not for that reason stop being part of the body. And if the ear should say, "Because I am not an eye, I do not belong to the body," it would not for that reason stop being part of the body. If the whole body were an eye, where would the sense of hearing be? If the whole body were an ear, where would the sense of smell be? . . . If they were all one part, where would the body be? . . .

The eye cannot say to the hand, "I don't need you!" And the head cannot say to the feet, "I don't need you!" On the contrary, those parts of the body that seem to be weaker are indispensable, and the parts that we think are less honorable we treat with special honor. And the parts that are unpresentable are treated with special modesty, while our presentable parts need no special treatment. But God has put the body together, giving greater honor to the parts that lacked it, so that there should be no division in the body, but that its parts should have equal concern for each other. If one part suffers, every part suffers with it; if one part is honored, every part rejoices with it.

Now you are the body of Christ, and each one of you is a part of it.

In Scripture, the apostle Paul's description of the body of Christ clearly illustrates that people exist and function within a complex web of relationships that are mutually interdependent and interconnected. Paul understood this clearly. His discussion of unity and diversity in the church by making the analogy to the human body and Christ's body is a poignant description of a system.

WHAT IS A RELATIONAL SYSTEM?

I (Fred) remember the tropical fish mobile that hung above our son's crib. A slight breeze or nudge moved one fish on the mobile, and the movement rippled through the entire mobile. Likewise friendships, groups, marriages, families, classrooms and the church are all relational systems. To understand each individual part of the system (if that were even possible) does not add up to knowing the system; a system is always more than the sum of its parts because the relationships among the parts are a huge factor in how the system operates.

Figure 14.1. Fish mobile

One implication of this perspective is the idea that if you affect any part of the system, you potentially affect, to some degree, the whole system, just like with the mobile mentioned above. This is the crux of the systems theory of change. In individual counseling, for instance, producing change in the individual you are seeing (i.e., producing change in one part of the system) will produce change, positive or negative, in other parts of the system (e.g., the counselee's family, circle of friends, work relationships). Let's look at the example of Terry, a wife and mother who enters counseling because she is depressed. It soon becomes apparent that Terry focuses most of her time and energy on meeting the wants and needs of her husband and children to the detriment of her own needs. When Terry starts to become more assertive as a result of her counseling sessions, her depression begins to lift, and she feels as though she is gaining a new lease on life. However, her husband and children may resent these changes because they now have the responsibility to do some things for themselves that Terry previously did automatically. Terry will now either bow to the pressure, taking on her former role as their servant, or persist in her new behavior until the system shifts, settling into a new state of equilibrium.

The danger is that we cannot always accurately predict what change will occur in the system. So getting the system in the room, such as having an entire nuclear family in the counseling office, allows us to observe directly what impact efforts to change are having on the whole system, that is, the other family members and their relationships with each other. In the absence of other parts of the system in the room, we rely on the counselee to report on how the system is responding to the counselee's efforts to change.

A FAMILY SYSTEMS APPROACH TO THE SMYTHE FAMILY

There is a language associated with systems thinking and family therapy that is different from that of more individually focused approaches. While we do not expect you to fully understand these concepts after reading this chapter, we do think that it is important that you are somewhat familiar with these ideas. Following are some key principles and terms associated with a systems approach to counseling, illustrated with the case of the Smythe family.

The Symthe family consists of Lynne (mom); Jack (stepdad); Kevin (twenty-year-old), who is going to college out of state; Josh, who is a junior in high school; and Kristy (thirteen-year-old).

The whole system is more than the sum of its individual parts (i.e., wholeness). The Smythe family is made up of a number of separate individuals, each with their own personalities and characteristics. Mom is a devout Christian who is involved in her church and prioritizes personal devotions. The stepdad works hard at his blue-color job, striving to provide for his fairly new family. Kristy is a bubbly, pretty girl but struggles with low self-esteem because of some learning disabilities she has that make school difficult. Josh only cares about the rock band he plays in and the friends he does drugs with, while Kevin is focused on his studies and life at college. As a family there are significant relational dynamics that cannot be explained by knowing each one as an individual. For example, because Lynne was single for so long, she relied on her oldest son, Kevin, for feedback about how to deal with his problem brother, Josh. There is now unspoken, subtle competition between Jack, the new stepdad, and Kevin for Mom's ear. Another dynamic is that Mom desperately wants her husband and children to come to church with her, but only Kristy complies. Tension is thick whenever Lynne brings up the subject of God or church. But just when that situation is about to explode, Josh gets arrested for drug possession or breaks curfew, and the focus goes back on him. The family as a whole is an entity that cannot be explained by looking at each individual separately. This could become a problem if, for instance, Josh ends up in a rehabilitation program without any attention being given to the family as a whole.

Any change in one part will affect the other parts (i.e., equifinality). Being in rehab may impact Josh so profoundly that when he is released and comes home he may be able to impact the family. Or, with Josh out of the house, and more time and attention being given to each other, the issue of church attendance might erupt. Lynne and Jack might get into so much conflict that they reach out for help from their pastor. Or, with her mom and stepdad fighting more, Kristy may start to become more withdrawn and sullen, raising concerns from her school counselor. Any of these entry points into the system may result in changes. One approach is not obviously better, since any of them might initiate change in the whole family.

The counselor does not need to know all parts of the system to instigate change (i.e., equifinality). Lynne was so distressed that she started to see a Christian counselor. Her counselor was masterful at empathic reflection and was able to develop a strong therapeutic alliance relatively quickly. Making use of the strength of the relationship, the counselor gently confronted Lynne with the discrepancy between her desire for her husband to come to church with her and her nagging behavior, which was developing increased hostility toward the things of God rather than drawing her husband closer. Over the next week Lynne apologized to her husband for pushing him so hard. She expressed that she missed him when she went to church alone and would love to have him join her anytime but that she would leave the decision up to him. Lynne was not totally successful at not guilt-tripping him, but she caught herself doing it and apologized right away. After a number of weeks her husband initiated a conversation about church for the first time. He said he was not ready to go to worship services but he was willing to go to any church social events or get to know some of the other couples their age.

It really does not matter whether the counselor gets the intervention "right"; any intervention has the potential to alter the system (i.e., equifinality). It is difficult to predict how an intervention will affect the system. It is not so much a matter of whether getting Josh into rehab, or Mom going to see a counselor, or the couple seeking marital counseling, is the best intervention. Any of these options can be powerful and appropriate. But we also cannot predict exactly what a particular intervention will produce. In rehab Josh might meet a couple of people who become new friends, and under the guise of AA meetings, they begin to party as wildly as Josh ever did before. In marital counseling other issues between Lynne and Jack might be triggered, and they realize that church attendance is only the tip of the iceberg.

Systems exist on a continuum from open and chaotic to closed and rigidly structured (open or closed systems). Healthy systems provide structure for people's lives and provide enough flexibility for new experiences to change the system. The Smythe family is likely on the more structured and inflexible end of the continuum. Change will not come easily. Or perhaps change will initially come easily but will not last. There are pros and cons to both ends of the continuum.

> » Would you describe your family of origin as being more *open*: flexible in its rules and roles, at times lacking in structure, or *closed*: rigid in its rules and roles, resistant to change or outside input? Explain.

Systems tend to resist change (homeostasis or equilibrium). There is a lot of pressure and momentum in systems to have them stay the way they are. This means that counselees will often experience a lot of resistance (negative feedback) from outside or even from inside themselves to keep things the way they are. Unfortunately, no change happens in many situations. Lynne was ultimately successful in getting the tension around church attendance to dissipate, but she found that she had to make a concentrated effort to not nag her husband to attend, even though she knew it was destructive. For a few weeks after she began to back off, her husband began picking fights by expressing religious views that he knew would get a reaction from his wife. When she realized what was happening, Lynne stopped reacting. Without support from her counselor she likely would have taken the bait, and the tension around church would have continued to escalate.

The fear of change (the unknown), of conflict (tension, hurt) and of failure (it didn't work) help keep systems from changing (negative feedback). Risking new behaviors, new interactional patterns and new emotional connections can change the entire system (positive feedback). Often members of a system will uncon- sciously sabotage the family's efforts to change. Various unspoken fears or worries, of which members may not be aware, can keep things from changing. For example, by the family keeping the attention on Josh, the other children's behavior is not scrutinized as closely. Or, Lynne and Jack do not have the mental or emotional capacity to look at their relationship because they are focused on Josh's delinquency.

The counselor's power to influence change is limited by many factors, but the coun- selor does have the power to create new experiences and interactions between parts of the system (enactments). New experiences result in new emotional, cognitive, be- havioral and relational interactions occurring. These new experiences can result in long-term changes in relationships. In complex systems counselors may feel as if they have no power to effect change in the individuals or the system. However, counselors can encourage and orchestrate new experiences for the system. With new experience (i.e., an enactment) new information can emerge, new learning can take place and change can happen. For example, in a family session at the rehab center, Josh could ask some pointed questions of his mom, such as why her relationship with his father ended. His mom could respond honestly, sharing a previously held secret (e.g., that their father had been involved in an affair), and all three children might learn new information about their mom, father and stepfather that has the potential to change relationships and internal emotional worlds. Whether this change is perceived as good or bad is of less concern than the system's ability to tolerate and then integrate the change.

Ignoring the power of the system in a counselee's life can be very detrimental to counselees. Destructive communication patterns, lack of secure attachment, family secrets, abuse and addictions are all examples of ways in which family members can be negatively affected by the systems of which they are a part. In the Smythe family it is clear that some of what they are experiencing is related to the nature of their relationships with each other. Not everything that goes wrong is a result of systemic patterns; we also contribute our own levels and types of pathology. This interplay of individual and systemic dysfunction makes meaningful change difficult to experience in counseling and yet very worth the effort.

THE "WITHIN" AND "BETWEEN" DYNAMIC OF CHANGE IN COUNSELING

On the left-hand side of figure 14.2 is the typical conception of change in counseling: help counselees shift, modify, eliminate or add something inside themselves. Systems thinking suggests that making changes internally (within the person) may actually affect relationships and situations on the outside, or that some external change be-

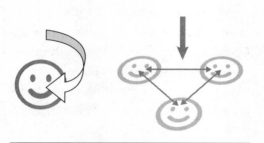

Figure 14.2. The "within" and "between" approaches to change

tween people in relationship or between a person and a situation may change the inside. Thus change in our lives is often circular (within the self to outside the self, or between the self and others) and not linear (as in one thing causes the change to occur). Figure 14.3 graphically illustrates the difference between linear and circular causality.

An example of the left-hand side of figure 14.3 goes like this: I'm stressed at work (A), I'm late getting home (B), my wife yells at me (C) because the dinner is ruined, and I explode (D). We therefore get into a fight all because I'm stressed at work (E). Typically in individual counseling, either I have an anger problem or my wife is insensitive (she has a problem), rather than *we* have a problem to work out.

With circular causality, which is represented by the diagram on the right-hand side of figure 14.3, it is easier to work with the system, seeing that events in a relationship and life are caused by multiple factors. Simply blaming one person does not explain or help change

Figure 14.3. Linear versus circular causality

the situation; the pattern needs to change. What is happening between people may sometimes be easier to access and alter than changing the inside of people—we can choose to respond differently even if we do not feel different yet. This is particularly true of marriage and family but applies to all systems—organizations, churches, groups and so on. This means that some of the skills that counselors need are to be able to identify, explore, access and utilize the systems of which the counselee is a part.

What systems, for example? For the majority of people, the most significant systems over their lifespan are their families of origin: "God sets the lonely in families" (Ps 68:6). For those who marry, the marital system should become their primary system and focus of loyalty and emotional investment (Gen 2:24). However, we know that the dual families of origin present in marriage continue to affect spouses long after the wedding. Having children broadens and complicates the marital system, with the birth of the first child being on average the most stressful time for couples (Gottman & Gottman, 2007). This relational dynamic is very often the focus of counseling, which is why marriage and family therapists have emerged as a distinct, specialized profession in the mental health field.

Diagnostic Implications

A mental disorder is defined as a "clinically significant disturbance in an individual's cognition, emotion regulation, or behavior" (DSM-5, p. 20). Notice the language: *in* and *individual*. The implication is that counseling would focus on exploring and changing what is occurring within an individual. The DSM, however, does add that "mental disorders are associated with significant distress or disability in social, occupational, or other important activities" (p. 20). But again, notice the language: *associated with*. There is little acknowledgment in the DSM that serious problems can be caused by relational distress and conflict. In fact, the DSM specifically adds that "socially deviant behavior (e.g., political, religious, or sexual) and conflicts that are primarily between the individual and society are not mental disorders unless the deviance or conflict results from a dysfunction in the individual" (p. 20).

In the DSM-IV axial format, axis IV was labeled "Psychosocial and environmental problems," so a counselee's relational problems were identified as part of the diagnosis, though not a required part. In DSM-5, these factors are now listed as V codes (p. 16; pp. 715-27; ICD-10-CM calls them Z codes, pp. 895-96). These are not disorders but associated with disorders. Notice, however, how many of these V codes are directly related to relational difficulties (e.g., problems with spouse, partner, child, sibling, health and housing services, education, employment, prison, abuse, acculturation, etc.). These issues are called "Other conditions that may be a focus of clinical attention."

The problem with this predominant conceptualization in the mental health field is that it downplays both the causal and change role of the counselee's extended and external systems. This is summarized well by Beck and Demarest (2005):

> The [DSM] criteria sets for a large number of disorders specifically require the presence of impairments in occupational or social functioning (the schizophrenias, manic episodes, dysthymia, bipolar I and II disorders, cyclothymia, the specific phobias, social phobia, obsessive-compulsive disorder, post-traumatic stress disorder, plus many others). Even if theorists are unwilling to concede interpersonal causal factors underlying psychopathology, they do recognize that mental illness has interpersonal consequences. (p. 359)

But the impact of systems does not end with family. Again, from the research we know that friendships (peer relationships), particularly in adolescence, in conjunction with social media, can be the most powerful external force in a counselee's world (Killen & Coplan, 2011). In addition, sibling relationships are forms of peer relationships with some different dynamics from other family relationships, which are typically hierarchical to some degree.

From figure 14.4, we see that Bronfenbrenner's model of development explicitly acknowledges that growth over the lifespan happens within numerous systems, which he conceptualizes as a series of concentric circles. Beyond one's immediate networks of family and friends, counselees exist within systems such as educational institutions, employment, health, economic and political systems. Of decreasing importance in Western culture are the religious systems that in previous generations deeply affected the majority in society. In many parts of the world and in many cultures, beyond family, religious systems are often the most significant systems in people's lives.

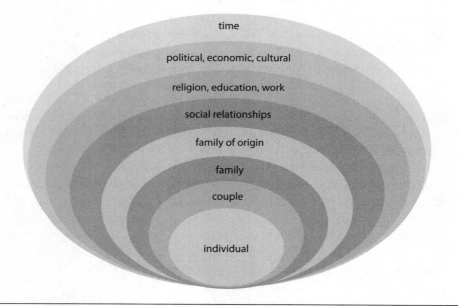

Figure 14.4. Adapted from Bronfenbrenner's (1999) framework for human development

Another way to describe the systems involved in a counselee's life is through the use of eco-maps. An eco-map is a visual diagram of the major participants in a counselee's life. The eco-map in figure 14.5 is of a counselee who has some resources but also a lot of stress. The core issues of anxiety, abuse and addictions (Guernsey & Guernsey, 1991) provide a valuable lens for assessing the impact of this counselee's system on his or her functioning. In the current situation the counselee derives strength and positive relationship from a strong educational background, financial stability, a good supportive faith community and recreational pursuits. However, the counselee has a poor employment and housing situation, inadequate health care, conflict with extended family and no relationship with community or friends. The counselee derives support from a relationship with God and expends a lot of energy on spouse and children but derives little support from them.

An eco-map is particularly useful in working with complex families from different cultural contexts from your own (www.strongbonds.jss.org.au/workers/cultures/ecomaps.html). For example, an eco-map could help in working with immigrant families, where it is difficult to get a detailed picture of the social and family relationships that are often more significant in non-Western cultures than in Western ones. In such families, mapping areas of isolation or disconnection may also be important.

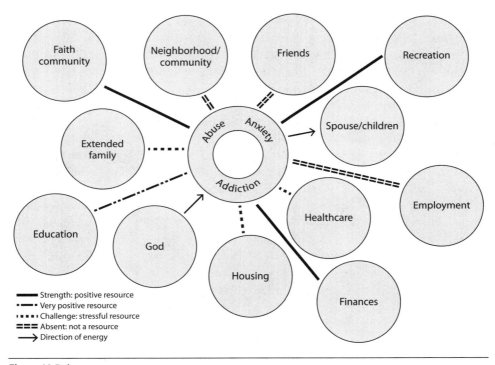

Figure 14.5. An eco-map

THE BUILDING BLOCKS OF SYSTEMS: TRIANGLES

People have best friends, dyadic romantic relationships and special one-on-one relationships that sustain them throughout life. However, life experiences in families, school and work show us that dyadic relationships tend to become triadic ones. Triangular relationships come in many forms. For example: mom, dad and baby; brother, sister and parent; mother-in-law, husband and wife; boss, employee and customer; pastor, elder and ministry leader; me, you and God. Whenever disagreement, tension or conflict enters the system, we all tend to try to resolve the tension by pulling in a third thing or person to try to decrease the tension, typically by trying to get the other person or thing on our side of the issue. Another way of thinking about this is that relationships are like a two-legged stool: it will support you but is less stable than a three-legged stool. Dyadic relationships are intrinsically less stable. As Foley (1979) points out, "Whenever the emotional balance between two people becomes too intense or too distant, a third person or thing can be introduced to restore equilibrium to the system and give it stability" (p. 462).

Empirical Support

There is an enormous amount of empirical evidence for the relationship between the quantity and quality of social support people have and their ability to cope with life.

Duru (2008), using the Adjustment Difficulties Scale, the UCLA Loneliness Scale, the Social Provision Scale and the Social Connectedness Scale, found that not only do lower levels of social support and social connectedness and higher levels of loneliness correlate with adjustment difficulties, but that the relationship between these variables is predictive. Lack of social support/connection leads to loneliness and to adjustment difficulties. Furthermore, Chao (2011) studied the relationship between managing stress, maintaining well-being and problem-focused coping versus avoidant coping. He found that they were all affected by social support.

Applied specifically to traumatic events, Shallcross, Frazier and Anders (2014) found that while insecure attachment (anxious or avoidant) prior to a traumatic event results in poorer post-

traumatic adjustment (distress), strong social support (or less social withdrawal or less negative support) increases people's capacity to handle traumatic events in life.

Leibert, Smith and Agaskar (2011) add another interesting dimension to the relationship between social support and adjustment. It appears from their research that "extratherapeutic" factors (e.g., external social support), as well as within-session factors (e.g., the quality of the counseling relationship) correlate with better counseling outcomes. However, when counselees had lower external social support, the quality of the counseling relationship became even more important in producing positive outcomes. In this sense, counseling, pastoral care and mentoring themselves provide an important source of social support for counselees, but these helping relationships *plus* strong social support beyond the counseling relationship are even more powerful. Helping counselees build support systems is itself a helpful intervention.

The counseling relationship as a system. One of the fascinating aspects of counseling and systems theory is that individual counseling is, in essence, a dyadic (two-person) system. In couple or marital counseling it becomes a triadic (three-person) system. From two people and one relationship (2+1) it increases exponentially to three people and three relationships (3+3). By the way, add a child to the session and it becomes a system of four people and six relationships (4+6); add another child and it becomes a system involving five people and ten relationships (5+10).

The point is that counseling is a relational system that functions according to systemic principles.

In marital counseling, one such systems dynamic is that to some degree both partners in counseling are trying to convince the counselor to be on his or her side. If the counselor agrees with me, then you are wrong, and I am the victim of your mistreatment. But it happens in individual counseling as well. When a counselor challenges or in some other way sets a boundary in the relationship with the counselee, it is not unusual for the counselee to try to align with someone or something else (e.g., a spouse or parent; an expert who wrote a book, article or website; God; Scripture). A common example in Christian contexts is some variation of a counselee who refers to Jesus' intense ministry, his suffering and death on the cross to counteract the counselor's suggestion that self-care is an important and valid activity. Encouraging the counselee toward self-responsibility and reducing blame on the other parts of the system is an ongoing aspect of counseling. Encouraging self-responsibility is also a significant theme in the New Testament (Mt 7:1-5).

Detriangling: A core counseling tool when working systemically. When a two-person relationship experiences external challenge, internal tension, disagreement or conflict, we "triangle in" a third person or thing to try to stabilize the relationship. For a couple, this might be a child, a mother-in-law, the house, a job, the car, a friend or any number of either helpful or destructive third parties. Relationship counseling is by definition an intentional triangle in which a couple asks a counselor to help them resolve issues in their dyadic relationship. But this is a temporary triangle. Similarly, two employees at work might ask a colleague or boss to mediate a conflict. But whenever this happens, there is a danger that the triangle will be seen as a permanent solution that keeps the two parties dependent and locked into relationship with the third. Remember that the counselor's role is to temporarily enter the triangle in order to point them toward resolving their dyadic relationships. This is true of pastoral counseling and spiritual direction as well. The counselor does not become a mediator between the counselee and God but helps the counselee talk to and listen to God—to strengthen the counselee's dyadic relationship with God.

We do our counselees no favors when we take their side on any issue. Being understanding, expressing empathy and showing support for them as people who are struggling are not the same as agreeing with them and their perspective. Staying balanced, not taking sides and setting interpersonal boundaries regarding what your role is and is not are core skills in counseling. Think about how Jesus interacted with many people. Did he agree with the life choices of the woman at the well, Zacchaeus the tax collector or the rich young ruler? No! Yet he came alongside and supported them. He did not align with the person against others (i.e., form a triangle of two against one). He allowed them to take the responsibility for their lives, their past relationships and their future decisions.

Try It Out

For the following exchanges, identify what you think is the "best" way to respond. The natural inclination when you want someone to expand his or her systemic awareness is to ask a question, such as, "What people in your life might be able to help?" While a question may be appropriate, try to reflect empathy and then gently prod them to consider other possibilities or resources that may be helpful. In the explanation space, give a rationale for your response.

Example: Counselee: I feel all alone in this. There really is no one for me to depend on!

Counselor: It's really hard to feel so isolated when you are going through such a difficult time. I wonder whether now might be a good time to begin working on finding a support person who could be with you through such situations?

Explanation: I wanted to ask "Really, no one?" but that might not have been as helpful. Continuing to be empathic allowed me to stay with the counselee in her loneliness. She might then be more open to my encouragement to find a solution.

1. Counselee: I want to be able to handle things on my own. I value my independence. I'm tired of having to rely on others.

Counselor: _____

Explanation: _____

_____

2. Counselee: She won't budge. I have tried to get her to change. What can I do?

Counselor: _____

Explanation: _____

_____

3. Counselee: I just can't handle him anymore. He's only two, and it is already too much.

Counselor: _____

Explanation: _____

_____

4. Counselee: I know there are programs that could help me, but I just can't get motivated to find out about them.

Counselor: _____

Explanation: _____

_____

5. Counselee: I feel like there are barriers, something getting in the way that keeps me from moving forward. Can we talk about what that might be?

Counselor: _____

Explanation: _____

_____

ADVOCACY: AN ESSENTIAL ROLE FOR ALL COUNSELORS

Another way in which counselors engage the systems of their counselees is through advocacy. The ACA Code of Ethics (2014), along with most people-helping professional codes of ethics (e.g., marriage and family therapy—AAMFT; social work—NASW), define one of the roles for counselors as identifying, exploring and initiating contact with the broader systems of a counselee's life. The section in the code of ethics is brief, however, it represents a multitude of ways of engaging with external systems, particularly as they are barriers to a counselee's growth. Counselors might think this is only the work of social workers, or pastors might think this is the job of social service organizations. However, biblical examples and teaching (e.g., Jas 2:15-17) make it clear that this is the responsibility of everyone. Housing, employment, finances, education, medical and social service systems, and government functions (e.g., immigration, taxation, licensing) are complex to understand and negotiate. Even well-educated, intelligent professional people can have difficulty and may need assistance.

It is an interesting study to look at the various codes of ethics regarding advocacy and related responsibilities and vocacy and related responsibilities and

> **Advocacy** (ACA Code of Ethics, 2014)
>
> *A.7. Roles and Relationships at Individual, Group, Institutional, and Societal Levels*
>
> *A.7.a. Advocacy*
> *When appropriate, counselors advocate at individual, group, institutional, and societal levels to address potential barriers and obstacles that inhibit access and/or the growth and development of clients.*
>
> *A.7.b. Confidentiality and Advocacy*
> *Counselors obtain client consent prior to engaging in advocacy efforts on behalf of an identifiable client to improve the provision of services and to work toward removal of systemic barriers or obstacles that inhibit client access, growth, and development.*

dual or multiple relationships with counselees. It would appear on the one hand that counselors need to protect the integrity of the counseling relationship and not get into relationships that overlap (e.g., counselor role and teacher role with the same counselee). This also raises confidentiality concerns. On the other hand, the role of advocacy appears to suggest that counselors need to get involved with counselees outside the boundaries of the office. There is a paradox in this—both are important therapeutic guidelines. The tension is resolved by another guideline, informed consent. With your counselee's agreement (in some situations and relationships written consent is required), a counselor can become involved in situations outside the office. But notice this is "informed" consent, not just a passive agreement to whatever the counselor suggests. For instance, a counselor, with consent, could call a school guidance counselor or teacher, or find out information about a medical procedure or medication. However, in our culture, which is highly attuned to privacy rights, it can get complicated when another professional requires written consent from the counselee before talking with you. Regardless of the challenges encountered when advocating for counselees, it will likely be worth it, and it is part of our responsibility.

Toporek, Lewis and Ratts (2010) outline some helpful dimensions regarding advocacy in counseling. One dimension is the macro to the micro level. For example, social/political advocacy would be at the macro level, whereas individual counseling would be at the micro level. Advocating for a counselee in his or her immediate context, for instance with an educational institution, would be an in-between level. Another dimension of advocacy is a counselor *acting with* a counselee, or a counselor *acting on behalf of* a counselee. Collaborating with (or acting with) counselees can be empowering for the counselee. For example, helping a counselee find out whom to contact at a social service organization and planning how to make the contact would encourage a set of valuable counselee life skills. As a matter of principle, it is likely rare that a counselor would need to act on behalf of counselees. However, it is at times necessary, since counselees can legitimately be unable for a variety of possible reasons to act on behalf of themselves. These situations require some careful assessment and discernment regarding the degree of involvement a counselor will have, as well as obtaining explicit and clear consent from counselees.

LEVERAGING EXTERNAL SYSTEMS FOR CHANGE

Another way to involve systems outside the counselee's individual, in-session discussions with you is to bring other people into the session. Again, with your counselee's consent, spouses or partners, parents, friends, pastors, teachers and so on can be asked to join a session. In such a case the added person is not the counselee; you have no agreement to enter into a counseling relationship with them. However, the added person comes into the session to consult with you and your counselee, to provide additional information, clarify situations and offer perspective. Additional people could become counselees as well, such as in the case of marriage and family counseling. However, there are complicated ethical concerns about moving from individual to couple or family therapy that are beyond the scope of this chapter.

Getting more of the system physically into the counseling room is a mantra that I (Fred) use frequently in my teaching. The benefits are numerous: adding additional perspectives, being able to work on communication between people in the session, and seeing and working with relational patterns right in front of you rather than talking about what happens outside the office. The power for change is greatly increased, but the anxiety of the counselor often goes up and maintaining "a non-anxious presence" (Friedman, 1985) in the room is a challenge that can easily get in the way of being objective and helpful.

According to Bowen (1978), a well-known family therapist, the goal of counseling is to help people differentiate. Differentiation should not be confused with becoming more independent, self-sufficient or autonomous. Rather, differentiation refers to becoming clearer and better defined in our own sense of self. As relationships become more emotionally intense, we tend to lose our sense of self; we take on aspects of others in relationships (become like them), be what others want us to be or react to others by disagreeing (become the opposite of them). Rather than responding from who we are and what we believe and desire, we become something else that will hopefully be less potentially challenging in the relationship. Counseling can help people understand these tendencies and explore ways of choosing alternative responses that are more in line with who they are.

There are many cautions in working with the impact of a counselee's external system on him or her. We will highlight two here.

1. As the counselor you can easily become angry with how other people or systems have hurt and abused your counselee. This is particularly difficult in clear cases of injustice such as abuse, domestic violence or crime. While our anger at injustice, like God's anger (Hab 2:12), may be justified, we can quickly lose perspective regarding what counseling response will truly be helpful to the counselee. Perhaps railing with him at injustice will be helpful; perhaps not. Our compassionate hearts can at times get in the way of challenging counselees to develop a clearer and stronger sense of self and what they want from their relationships and life.

2. The second caution involves short-circuiting the forgiveness process with our counselees out of a desire to either avoid conflict or see the counselee "feel better" faster. This happens when the counselor helps the counselee prematurely patch up hurt relationships rather than helping him or her do the tougher work of dealing with conflict in healthy ways. For instance, counselees may bypass deeper and more heart-based work when the counselor avoids posing challenging questions such as, What has the counselee done to understand his or her relationship conflicts? What has he or she done to try to resolve the situation? Or, What would be necessary to help someone prepare to enter into a reconciliation process? The biblical principle is clear: if counselees have not talked directly about their concerns with the person who has offended or sinned against them, the first step is to go to the person (Mt 18).

If counselees have tried to have conversations to resolve problems, encourage them to again go to the other party to try to resolve the conflict. If they have tried and failed, if they are afraid to go alone or if the person with whom they have a broken relationship is no longer accessible, develop a safe plan for how they could have the conversations and/or role-play possible scenarios. A further step, and many times the hardest step in the forgiveness process, is to develop understanding and empathy for those who have hurt you. This is necessary work in the forgiveness and reconciliation process (Worthington, 2001). Attempts to short-circuit the forgiveness process ultimately serve to ignore or dismiss the reciprocal impact a counselee has on and with their system.

Sometimes we as counselors fail to remind our counselees of the hard work of resolving conflict. The focus of counseling is preparing counselees emotionally and cognitively to have these kinds of conversations with the people in their lives and helping them to find ways to express their concerns, enabling them to engage their systems in healthier ways. Depending on the degree of a history of violence in the counselee's relationship, this may not be possible without bringing others (e.g., law enforcement) into the situation. Of course, ethically, regardless of our helping role, we have the responsibility to protect our counselees from harm.

Clinical Tips

1. Counseling can become gossip when the focus becomes complaining and not trying to change or help improve the situation. Gossip is included in lists of very serious and destructive sins in Romans 1:29-31 and 2 Corinthians 12:20.

2. Sometimes by being too empathic you may aggravate the problem. Remember that your individual counselee is only able to give you one perspective—empathy does not mean agreement.

3. Stay balanced—your agreement does not matter as much as your understanding does.

4. Self-responsibility is what we all resist; ownership must precede assigning responsibility to others (blame).

5. Altering your counselee's side of a relationship pattern will produce a change in the other side of the pattern (though the outcome is not always predictable).

6. When stuck, do something different.

7. Look for small changes (exceptions to the usual), rather than the big change; small changes open up possibilities for big ones.

8. Role-play possible conversations in counseling—with a parent, a partner, a friend or even God in order to explore other ways of interacting.

9. Patiently reflect empathy or ask questions to help your counselee see things more clearly or to gently confront her with alternative perceptions (Prov 25:12, 15).

MINISTRY APPLICATION

In our efforts to help people change, if we only rely on our own expertise or put the responsibility for change solely on the counselee, we might be surprised that getting stuck or being unproductive is a common outcome of counseling relationships. As Christians, we know we have limits and must rely on the Holy Spirit to guide us, the Father to love us and Jesus to walk with us.

But is this enough? A New Testament theology points clearly and repeatedly to the fact that the body of Christ, the church, is essential for life and spiritual and mental health. Admittedly, many are hurt by their experiences in church, but the church is much more than local congregations filled with imperfect people; it is the global body of fellow Christ-followers who collectively provide for one another. In addition, there are many resources outside the church. While these resources may be dismissed as "secular," the fact is that God is revealed through his creation (Rom 1:20). So government assistance, social service organizations, community resources all reflect as in a mirror darkly (1 Cor 13:12) God's rich provision for the poor, widows and orphans (Jas 1:27; 2:5). Relying on the resources that God has provided is how he wants us to live.

Biblical/Theological Connections

The "one another" passages in Scripture provide instruction as to how we are to relate with others. Specifically, we are called to:

✓ love	✓ bear burdens	✓ pray for	✓ teach
✓ serve	✓ carry burdens	✓ prefer	✓ admonish
✓ forgive	✓ submit to	✓ be united to	✓ refresh
✓ edify	✓ encourage	✓ supper with	✓ be truthful to
✓ accept	✓ confess to	✓ rejoice with	✓ spur on
✓ comfort	✓ pray with	✓ restore	✓ give to

. . . one another.

A study of the passages in the New Testament that instruct us in how to relate with "one another" clearly points to the many ways we need and can assist each other (see "Biblical/Theological Connections" sidebar). In ministry contexts, programs that provide opportunities to build interpersonal support and community life by being involved in one another's lives are examples of being the body of Christ on earth. Many of us who have grown up in church or who have been exposed to churches have experienced the downside of small groups and judgmental aspects of community life. However, a robust theology of the church (ecclesiology) acknowledges that local congregations of believers are filled with sinful people, people who are broken, damaged and needing grace. Churches are hospitals for sick people, so it should not surprise us when relationships are hurtful and less than we hoped for.

Helping counselees work through this paradox is part of their sanctification process. Churches are places where pain and suffering gather and are played out, but they are also, potentially, the safest, most healing place on earth (Crabb, 1997, 1999).

> *It's time we turned our chairs toward one another and learned how to talk in ways that stir anorexics to eat, multiples to integrate, sexual addicts to indulge nobler appetites, and tired Christians to press on through the dark valleys toward green pastures and on to the very throne room of heaven.*
>
> **Crabb, 1999, p. 20**

In the church we glimpse the healing power of community, where the Spirit is experienced.

In church and parachurch ministries the small group emphasis of recent decades, with groups like Celebrate Recovery (celebraterecovery.com) and Redemption Groups (redemption groups.com; cf. smallgroups.net), has restored an essential dimension of healing available to Christians. Group spiritual direction (Dougherty, 1995; Fryling, 2008; Pretchel, 2012; Webb & Peterson, 2009) has a power for transformation that individual spiritual direction may not have, at least for some people. These church-based community life groups, where Scripture is applied to our lives together, are an indispensable tool for the Christian counselor. Do not let any negative experiences with groups that we may have rob our counselees of this gift of the Spirit for edification and healing.

MULTICULTURAL APPLICATION

It has often been observed that Western cultures tend toward self-sufficiency, independence and autonomy, while Eastern cultures tend toward communal sufficiency, interdependence and group cohesion (e.g., Nisbett, 2003). Others have defined the differences between "hot" and "cold" climates and the impact that has on culture (Lanier, 2006). In increasingly globalized cultures, the distinctions are becoming less stereotypical but not any less vital. How important systemic thinking is, that is, understanding individuals within the context of their relationship networks, varies greatly worldwide. With broad strokes, it may be accurate to say that Westerners do not as naturally look at people within their relational systems (i.e., with others as external resources to rely on) but view the individual as being ultimately rational, resourceful and resilient (i.e., with his or her own internal resources viewed as more essential than what can be obtained through others).

Hence expanding the system may be easier for those from more collectivist cultures to naturally turn to. However, we think it is also fair to say that to only depend on one's external resources overlooks a potentially powerful source of change: one's internal emotional, cognitive, spiritual and behavioral resources. This paradoxical tension in our understanding of the nature of personhood and change, like many things in life, is complex. The goal is not to fall into either extreme—becoming too focused on the self or becoming too focused on relationships as the source of motivation and energy in the change process.

CONCLUSION

While the counselee in your office may only be one person, it is important to learn as much as you can about the systems within which she resides. No counselee is an island; he is connected and interconnected with others, and those others can be critical to the success (or failure) of the counseling process. As you sit with counselees, listen for the role that others play in the story and leverage those systemic resources for the counselee's benefit. Listen for circular causality and embrace the complexity of counselees' lives. Question the effect that the counselee's relational network has on the counselee's motivation and direction in counseling. Explore who or what in the counselee's relationship system can be a valuable resource and advocate for the counselee's growth, health and sanctification.

REFLECTION QUESTIONS

1. Go back to figure 14.4. Describe the relative impact each sphere has had on you over your lifetime. Which ones have had the most positive and most negative impact?

2. Take five to ten minutes to reflectively journal about the role your family of origin currently plays in your everyday life. In what ways do you see the influence of your family in your life? Is this more or less influence than you would prefer? What role do you play within your family of origin? What would happen if you stopped playing that role for a month, six months or a year?

3. At the center of the eco-map (figure 14.5) are the three concepts of anxiety, abuse and addiction. To what degree were these behavioral and emotional patterns part of your relationships growing up? Your counselees will frequently relate stories of the three *As*. How will you respond, and to what degree will their experiences intersect with your own?

4. Describe a relational triangle in which you are currently a part. Is it an unhealthy triangle or a functional one? Are any dyadic relationships in the triangle being avoided?

5. Reflect on the tension between encouraging counselee autonomy and advocating for a counselee. What might be some ways you can recognize unhealthy autonomy in a counselee? What might be some examples of times when advocating for a counselee would be appropriate?

APPRECIATING
THE SACRED

*For where two or three gather in my
name, there am I with them.*

MATTHEW 18:20

SKILL: attuning to the Holy Spirit and spiritual themes

PURPOSE: to be aware of and draw attention to God's presence within and between the counselee and the counselor

FORMULA: "I'm wondering whether there is something (spiritual, sacred, about God) in what you experienced?"
"What might (God, Jesus or the Holy Spirit) be saying to you and us?"

*T*HINK ABOUT A TIME WHEN YOU went to someone for help, were given a Bible verse that felt like a simplistic pat answer and left the conversation feeling frustrated.

» What about the way this Bible verse was used did not feel helpful to you?

Now think back to a situation in which someone suggested that you read a particular verse or passage of Scripture and you experienced it as helpful.

» What about the way Scripture was used in this instance made it helpful?

There is good science to support the incorporation of spirituality into the counseling process, and there is an increasing amount of research to provide evidence of its positive impact on the counseling process. Yet, the use of spirituality and spiritual interventions in counseling does significantly relate to the person of the counselor with respect to his or her beliefs and values, as well as to the counselee's beliefs and values. Therefore determining the appropriate attention that should be given to spiri-

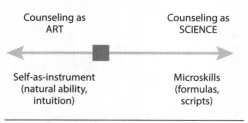

Figure 15.1. Art versus science: Appreciating the sacred

tuality as part of the counseling process is often a matter of discernment and wisdom rather than skill. As can be seen in figure 15.1, this aspect of counseling is more an art than a science. However, as with all of the skills, appreciating the sacred should be considered both.

THE "CHRISTIAN" PART OF CHRISTIAN COUNSELING

The following two scenarios illustrate this tension as well as differing ways of dealing with the sacred in counseling. You will see that both situations involve Christian counselees who are seeing Christian counselors. But what each counselee gets out of the counseling relationship is greatly affected by the approach the counselor takes to incorporating spirituality into the counseling sessions.

Empirical Support

The research support for a biblically integrative approach to counseling is substantial (see Koenig, 2011, 2012; Koenig, King & Carson, 2012). Rather than citing numerous studies detailing the positive effects of religious/spiritual (R/S) beliefs and practices, it is important to note that the effects of R/S involvement have been studied with numerous populations, including medical and psychiatric patients as well as numerous other diverse subgroups within society.

The positive impacts on mental health include positive outcomes for well-being, happiness, hope, optimism and gratefulness; negative outcomes (i.e., decreasing the negative effects) for depression, suicide, anxiety, psychosis, substance abuse, delinquency/crime and marital instability; and both negative and positive effects on personality traits.

The impact on physical health includes decreasing negative effects of heart disease, hypertension, cerebrovascular disease, Alzheimer's disease and dementia, immune functions, endocrine functions, cancer, overall mortality, physical disability, pain and somatic symptoms; and a positive influence on response to treatment.

The impact on physical health behaviors includes increase in physical activity, decrease in cigarette smoking, greater weight loss when dieting, positive sexual experiences and greater avoidance of risky sexual practices.

Results of studies have been reported in peer-reviewed journals in medicine, nursing, social work, rehabilitation, social sciences, counseling, psychology, psychiatry, public health, demography, economics and religion. By far the majority of studies report significant relationships between R/S and improved health outcomes.

Scenario 1. Ben is enrolled in a counseling program in a secular graduate school that requires that students have a certain number of counseling sessions before beginning internship. Ben is a Christian and sought out a counselor who is a Christian, recognizing that some of the issues he is struggling with are affecting his relationship with God. Ben really connected with his counselor.

But during the second session something happened that Ben found puzzling. Ben began talking about his relationship with Christ, and after a slight pause the counselor asked him a question that was pertinent to his presenting problem but had nothing to do with what Ben had just shared about his spiritual life. Although the counselor did not explicitly say, "This isn't the place to talk about your relationship with God; counseling is for dealing with the emotional/psychological aspects of life," this is the implicit message that Ben picked up on. Disappointed, Ben briefly thought about finding another counselor but then assumed that all Christian counselors would be the same. As a result he got some good help from his counselor but continued to wrestle alone with how his relationship with Christ was affected by his struggles.

Scenario 2. Denise is thirty-five years old. Her husband, Roy, was suddenly killed in a car accident six months previously. She has a nine-month-old, a two-year-old and a five-year-old who just began kindergarten. Denise comes into counseling totally overwhelmed with single parenting, going back into the work force after being a stay-at-home mom for the past five years, and still grieving the loss of Roy.

Denise's counselor uses a lot of empathic reflection, which helps Denise to feel understood. "My friends have been great," Denise tells her counselor, "but I don't want to overburden them by talking about the same things over and over again. I'm so glad that you are here and that you understand." Denise's counselor knows that Denise is a Christian because it was mentioned in the intake form. But Denise has not initiated any discussions about her relationship with God, so her counselor waits until the relationship is well established before she brings up the topic.

"Denise," the counselor says, "on your intake form you identified yourself as a Christian. You haven't said anything about your relationship with God, and we don't have to discuss it if you don't want to, but it isn't unusual for someone to have a crisis of faith when a tragedy like this happens. I'm just wondering how your relationship with God has been affected by everything you are going through?"

Denise begins to cry and then opens up about how abandoned she feels by God, yet how guilty she feels for these feelings. "I was afraid you might judge me because I know you're a Christian counselor. And I know that the Bible says that 'God will never leave us or forsake us.' But I can't help it. I feel like God *has* left me." This was the beginning of many discussions that Denise and her counselor had about God, discussions that Denise found very helpful because her counselor respected Denise's pace and did not preach at her. Scripture was utilized but not offered as a quick fix. Rather, the counselor helped Denise wrestle with what made it so difficult for Denise to embrace the truth of Scripture. In time, after her anger at God had been worked through, Denise was able to once again receive solace from reading the Bible. She found reading the Psalms aloud particularly helpful. She commented, "David railed at God, too, but God didn't condemn him for it. I want to be as honest before God as David was."

Was the sacred appreciated? Denise's counselor appreciated the sacred by broaching the topic of spirituality respectfully and waiting for the appropriate time to do so. Ben's counselor, on the other hand, did not allow the sacred into the counseling hour even when Ben initiated the topic. Some might suggest that Ben would be better off seeking the help of a spiritual director, and that may be exactly what he needs. However, what a tragedy that Ben's counselor did not take advantage of the opportunity to talk with Ben about the interconnection between the psychological/emotional and spiritual aspects of his struggles! Ben's counselor was obviously not familiar with the extensive literature on the integration of psychology and theology, or counseling and spirituality, which illustrates the importance of paying explicit attention to the religious and spiritual (R/S) values of the counselee.

OUR ORIENTATION TO SPIRITUALITY IN COUNSELING

We cannot possibly summarize all of this integration literature in one chapter. However, we want to at least expose you to some of the key concepts so that you can begin to lay a foundation for the interventions you will use with your counselees. We believe that in order to appreciate the sacred in the counseling process you need to be aware of the complexities involved. For those of you who are particularly interested in this topic, we have included some additional academic and theoretical considerations in appendix D at the end of the book.

A Clarification

Technically, *religious* refers to aspects of behavior connected to organized faith systems (e.g., religions, denominations, churches and practices associated with a group of fellow adherents). *Spiritual* refers to the individual, personal aspects of experience related to beliefs, values and behaviors. The abbreviation R/S is used in the literature and here to refer to combined religious and/or spirituality aspects.

In chapter two, on the role of the counselor, we discussed the person of the counselor and what we as counselors bring to the counseling relationship. But there is a much more significant component that we did not discuss in depth in that chapter. In our view, counseling is foundationally a sacred space and a spiritual relationship. It is easy to forget in the professionalism of contemporary life that the counseling room is not unlike the holy ground where an angel appeared as flames of fire in a burning bush, and God and Moses had a conversation (Ex 3). It is our belief that in the counseling relationship, whether explicitly faith based or not, the Holy Spirit is both present and active.

While some readers may welcome the previous paragraph, rejoicing that we finally have reached the guts of the counseling process, other readers may be feeling a little uncomfortable. Either way, suspend your judgments as we delve into this complicated and easily misunderstood topic.

OUR THEOLOGICAL FOUNDATION

Our theology affirms the Trinity, which encompasses the Father, Son and Holy Spirit. God the Father is present in his sovereignty and providence (Gen 28:15); the Son is our redeemer and exemplar of what humanity can be (Gal 4:4-7); and the Spirit graces us with wisdom, knowledge, direction and the fruit of the Spirit (Gal 5:22-23). All are present and active, and we severely limit the potential of counseling if we do not attune to how God is already at work in our counselee's life, in our own life and in the relationship between us.

WHAT IS SACRED ABOUT COUNSELING?

We have adopted the word *sacred* (Pargament, 2011) to describe the many aspects of life and experience that point to a transcendent dimension. Biblically the word *sacred* is related to the concept of holy and holiness, technically meaning set apart for God. However, unlike some interpretations of what is meant by being holy or sacred, we do not mean to imply that being sacred means being disconnected from the world or reality. Sacredness refers to how the divine is deeply connected to the everyday, common stuff of life. We consider counseling to be sacred in that in the counseling room we touch something that is part of our everyday lives yet is also beyond human understanding. As such God is part of the relationship, and it is a sacred encounter. Counseling, as with other ministry relationships, involves sacred spaces, sacred time or moments, sacred patterns or rhythms of life, and sacred relationships and conversations.

Sacred spaces. Scripture frequently refers to specific physical locations as sacred. Previously we referred to the incident where Moses encountered God in the burning bush and it was called "holy ground" (Ex 3, and repeated in Acts 7). Moses is asked to remove his sandals, signifying that this is a unique and supernatural encounter. In the Old Testament the ark of the covenant and the temple are sacred places. In the New Testament the focus is not so much on specific places endowed with spiritual significance but that in the presence of Jesus places can become holy. The mount of transfiguration (Mt 17) and the place from where Jesus ascended into heaven (Acts 1) are also considered sacred places. We believe that it is possible that a counseling office, or a place where conversations of spiritual and ultimate significance occur, becomes sacred because, when invited, God is present (Mt 18:20).

Sacred seasons. Many religions refer to sacred times of the year or sacred seasons. Again, the New Testament identifies that any time dedicated to encountering the Spirit in our midst becomes sacred. Moments in time when God is sought, Jesus is acknowledged and the Spirit is present take on the significance of defining moments—moments when God, who is beyond time and space, enters our time and space to affect the lives of people.

Sacred patterns or rhythms. The spiritual formation literature refers to another aspect of the sacred when it describes sacred rhythms of life, or what some spiritual formation writers have called the "rule of life" (Barton, 2006). This is the recognition that spiritually and emotionally healthy people have chosen repeated patterns in their lives that they have discovered aid them to grow in faith and maturity. Such rhythms occur in counseling when we teach and model to counselees patterns of attention to their inner life, habits of meditation or what is frequently referred to in the contemporary psychological literature as mindfulness (see Tan, 2011b, for a Christian review). In counseling, while we may not frequently be specifically addressing the following patterns, in one form or another these activities may punctuate counseling sessions: solitude and companionship, sabbath (rest) and work, Scripture reading (knowledge) and worship (experience), prayer and service, and many others. The rhythm of active and passive spiritual practices seems to reflect the active and more passive elements of a counseling relationship as we encourage counselees to embrace the patterns of activity, such as work, creativity and caring for others, as well as more passive patterns of reflection, meditation and rest (Palmer, 1999).

Sacred relationships. Furthermore, relationships that are dedicated to God, whether or not both parties acknowledge it, become consecrated relationships. Sacred relationships involve sacred companions (Benner, 2004) on our journey toward healing and wholeness together.

Sacred conversations. Last, the conversations that occur in counseling are frequently sacred in the sense that they touch on our deepest wounds, our greatest longings and hopes, and the meaning or lack thereof that we encounter in life. These are the themes of the lifelong process of sanctification, a growing in Christlikeness, whether or not the counselee has acknowledged God in this process.

IDENTIFYING THE SACRED

If one takes the perspective, as we do, that everything is psychological/sociological and spiritual at the same time, then every conversation in counseling has psychological, emotional, cognitive, behavioral, relational and spiritual dimensions. The struggle many of us have, even those of us familiar with the Christian subculture and the language and ethos of the church, is how to link our psychological and spiritual knowledge and experience together. Rather than viewing them as integrally related, we instead tend to draw lines of distinction between our psychological worlds and our spiritual worlds. We categorize some things as being R/S and others as not.

The challenge is that most Christians working in the people-helping professions are not dually trained in psychology/counseling and theology/ministry. Thus the vocabulary and concepts of theology are not as familiar to most counselors. However, we would encourage all Christians in the helping professions to make use of opportunities to study theology and the Bible in order to become better able to translate the rich and meaningful content of our faith to the experiences in our work (e.g., Entwistle, 2010; McMinn, 1996; McMinn & Campbell, 2007).

Just as counselors are usually not experts in theology, similarly our counselees are often not very knowledgeable about what is actually spiritual in nature, let alone being well versed in theology. Benner (1988, 1998) makes the point that Christian helpers of all varieties have a tendency to define spirituality too narrowly and so may miss opportunities to help individuals navigate their spiritual journeys. He views existential concerns such as questions about the meaning of life, anxieties about mortality or struggles to make sense of suffering as ultimately spiritual in nature. Identifying the sacred, then, is not merely about listening for a counselee's use of religious vocabulary; it is about tuning in to the underlying spiritual quest behind many of the issues that counselees present. This is one aspect of the skill that is the focus of this chapter, that of attuning to spiritual themes.

Identifying the sacred also means looking for where God is working in an individual's life. If the Holy Spirit is ultimately behind all healing, then it is important for us as counselors to acknowledge that God is working, whether or not the counselee is aware of it and whether it is appropriate to explicitly point it out to the counselee. This is part of what we mean by attuning to the Holy Spirit, which is another dimension of the skill we are addressing in this chapter.

"GENERIC" SPIRITUAL INTERVENTIONS

Despite the long tradition of honoring spirituality in Western and non-Western societies, we now live in a world that is very ambivalent if not outwardly hostile to Christians. Younger generations, in particular, have little trust or respect for the church, its leaders and those connected to it. This is clearly described by Kinnaman and Lyons (2012) in their book *unChristian,* where they suggest that Mosaics, or the millennial generation (those born from the early 1980s through the early 2000s), consider Christians to be hypocrites, sheltered, too political, judgmental and often unable to relate to people who do not believe what they believe. For this cohort, Christians are perceived as being arrogant, self-righteous and uncaring when interacting with people who are culturally or morally different from themselves. Some view Christians as only concerned about getting people converted and not about building a genuine relationship with others.

Those of us committed to Christ and to helping people are likely to encounter many who are skeptical or even hostile to spirituality and especially organized religion. Yet as people of Christian faith we need to graciously and nonreactively engage such negative perspectives, and affirm and advocate for the role spirituality plays in mental, emotional, relational and physical health. We need to take the opportunities we are given to allow the Spirit to work in the lives of our counselees whether or not they profess Christian faith and values.

As mentioned above, spirituality can be identified in the counseling process without it necessarily being explicit. In addition, there are various ways in which spirituality can be explicitly addressed in counseling, but in ways that are more generic or less sectarian in the sense that they are not tied to a particular religion or religious tradition. Such uses of spirituality can bypass a lot of resistance to traditional religious language and concepts.

For example, a basic list of questions that are appropriate for counseling relationships in which spirituality is being considered is provided here. You will notice that the word *beyond* is used to allude to the idea of deity without reference to a particular god. Some twelve-step programs (e.g., Alcoholics Anonymous, 2002) use the phrase "power greater than ourselves" (step 2) in a similar fashion.

Religious/Spiritual Counseling Questions

✓ What do you call your relationship to what is beyond yourself and the physical world?
✓ What do others call it? Do others see it the same or differently than you?
✓ How are other people involved in your relationship to that which is beyond?
✓ How do you think the beyond is involved in your life?
✓ How is the beyond related to the good things and bad things that happen in life?
✓ Does the beyond help you understand and cope with suffering?
✓ How is the beyond involved in your current struggles in life?
✓ Most of the time, do you primarily fear, live in awe of, worship, love, obey or ignore the beyond?
✓ What are the main ways the beyond is involved in your life? How does the beyond help or hinder you?
✓ Overall, how important is the beyond in yours, your family's and your community's life?

I (Heather) have found that spiritual issues inevitably surface when dealing with counselees who have suffered intensely, such as survivors of complex relational trauma (e.g., child abuse, torture, ritual abuse/mind control). With counselees who do not identify as Christian or those who have been victims of spiritual abuse, Christian terminology may need to be avoided. Nonetheless, when we discuss what meaning their lives have despite or perhaps because of the trauma they have experienced, I believe that we are actually dealing with a theology of suffering even if the discussion is not couched in Christian language.

Avoiding theologically laden language can be particularly challenging, however, when the sense of an ongoing spiritual battle is very palpable. A group of colleagues who specialize in complex trauma but who represent a multivariate spectrum of religious traditions (e.g., atheists, Eastern religions, New Age spirituality, shamanism, nominal Christian as well as evangelical) have been helpful in coming up with alternate terminology to use in such circumstances.

I have found one of the most beneficial concepts to be the analogy of a war between light and darkness. While I conceptualize light and darkness as Light and Darkness, (that is, God and Satan), I have seen evidence of the battle becoming less intense as my counselees consciously choose the side of light. One of my counselees actually visualized shining a strong flashlight into the evil-laden darkness that threatened to engulf him. This same counselee took a verbal stand "for" light and "against" darkness but would have reacted extremely negatively to any implication of personalized good/ God or evil/Satan. This is an example of both attuning to very real spiritual themes while also attuning to the Holy Spirit for guidance as to how to address these spiritual themes in respectful, nonthreatening ways.

EXPLICITLY CHRISTIAN SPIRITUAL INTERVENTIONS

When counselees identify as Christians, the opportunities for identifying the sacred in the counseling process can be expanded to include specific Christian language and use of spiritual resources associated with Christianity. This does not mean, however, that any spiritual intervention can be used at any point in the counseling process with any counselee.

The dilemma. I (Fred) have heard numerous conference presentations on the use of spiritual resources in counseling. Many have been excellent in their efforts to present a balanced approach. We know that counseling is loaded with implicit, if not explicit, spiritual values, and we also know that counseling is not evangelism or a form of indoctrination. However, in the seminars I have attended I have often felt that there was a war in the room but that no one knew exactly which side anyone else was on. Loosely, the sides of the battle were the pro–spiritual forces and the perceived anti–spiritual forces. If one person affirmed the use of spiritual resources, it seemed as though someone else would say, "Yes, but be careful." Then someone would follow up with something like, "Of course we need to be careful, but we need to make sure to harness the power of the Spirit in our ministry." My guess is that most of us are actually on the same side, believing that spirituality in counseling is not only important but that it is essential.

Of course the particular ministry context a counselor serves in is very relevant to this issue. Evangelism, or explicit sharing of the gospel, while not generally considered ethical in professional counseling contexts, may be very appropriate for pastoral counselors, spiritual directors and spiritual mentors. Similarly, explicit use of spiritual resources may be almost expected in certain Christian helping contexts. Even in these settings, though, their use may not always be beneficial.

Examples of R/S Interventions in Counseling (adapted from Doherty, 1999)

✓ acknowledge spontaneous counselee statements
✓ ask questions about beliefs and practices
✓ inquire about the integration of the spiritual into other aspects of life
✓ affirm their spiritual yearnings
✓ articulate counselee's spiritual struggles
✓ point out contradictions
✓ challenge how counselees manage spiritual beliefs

One of the errors that Christian helpers can make is a tendency to assume that counselees are more mature psychologically and/or spiritually than they may actually be. Thus we may use an intervention that does not take seriously the developmental psychosocial stage, or faith stage (see Demarest, 2009; Fowler, 1984) of the counselee. To illustrate, Monroe (2005) gives this example: A counselee's current status is characterized by immaturity and anxiety/fear. The biblical teaching clearly is "don't be afraid," "trust the Lord." The danger in counseling is to use these Scripture verses or to pray with counselees in order to point them to where they should be as if they were more mature and able to "hear" the spiritual advice. The counselee's lack of spiritual development may in fact be the block to the effectiveness of the spiritual resources. In this case the psychological/emotional reasons behind the counselee's anxiety and fear may need to be addressed before the counselee is able to find encouragement rather than condemnation in these Bible verses.

What do we mean by Christian spiritual interventions? Authors vary on what activities are included as R/S resources and interventions. In the sidebar "Examples of R/S Interventions in Counseling" are some examples of such interventions. A much more extensive list of possible spiritual interventions from a range of authors and perspectives is provided at the end of this chapter. Some are more complex interventions requiring a counselor to follow specific protocols; others are quite straightforward in how they might be utilized.

At the end of this chapter you will find table 15.2. The left-hand side of this table refers to a list of healing gifts from God, loosely divided into three categories: healing words, healing experiences and healing relationships. As Job 33:14-30 describes, God speaks to us in many different ways. Following the first column are several columns representing a number of authors who identify various spiritual interventions and approaches. While perhaps overwhelming to read and think about, the point is that God has many ways to relate to us, help us grow and heal us. Latching on to any one approach and applying it to all counselees limits the possibilities for how God brings his light to shine on us. Despite the amount of information that is included on the chart, it is not by any means exhaustive.

Using explicitly Christian resources well. Whether or not Christian counselors are aware of the complexity of the issue, it is our guess that most Christian counselors will likely use spiritual interventions to some degree, even if it is simply praying for a counselee outside the counseling session. But while attuning to the Holy Spirit as to if, when and how specific spiritual interventions should be used is essential, McMinn (1996), Tan (1994, 1996) and Chapelle (2000) offer some helpful suggestions for making these decisions.

McMinn's questions. McMinn (1996), in his discussion of the use of prayer and Scripture in counseling, suggests a very helpful approach to the use of any spiritual resource in counseling. To paraphrase McMinn, the best question in not "Should I use this spiritual intervention in counseling?" but "Which spiritual intervention should I use with which counselee under which circumstances?" Some counselors might never use a particular spiritual intervention (e.g., deliverance prayer), and other counselors might have a favorite go-to intervention in most situations (e.g., journaling). Nevertheless, decisions about which interventions to use when and with whom should be made on an ongoing case-by-case basis.

McMinn (1996) then goes on to outline three additional questions that can serve as helpful guidelines in addressing the overarching question posed above:

1. *Will using this intervention help to establish a healthier sense of self for the counselee?* In other words, will this intervention build the counselee's sense of who she is and what her purpose in life is? If we truly believe that God created us (Gen 1:26-27), that his creation is very good (Gen 1:31) and that he loves us sacrificially (Jn 3:16), then this should have a positive impact on our identity. This is the strength of Anderson's (1990; Anderson, Zuehlke & Zuehlke, 2000) "steps to freedom in Christ." Anderson provides an explicitly spiritual intervention that seeks to help the counselee firmly establish her identity derived from a set of biblically based statements regarding our relationship with God.

2. *Will this help establish a healthy sense of need for the counselee?* If one's identity is from God, we are ultimately dependent beings. It is not pathological to be dependent, which is affirmed in both Scripture (e.g., Gen 2:24; Jn 15:4-5; Acts 17:28; Phil 2:1-2; Col 3:14; 1 Pet 4:10) and attachment theory in developmental psychology (Bowlby, 1988). Healthy dependency is the foundation of mental, emotional and spiritual health (Cloud & Townsend, 2001).

3. *Will this help establish a healing relationship between the counselee and the counselor?* If the power of the helping relationship is one of the most significant aspects of effective counseling, then any intervention that strengthens a healthy relationship and produces healing for the counselee is worthwhile. Alternatively, misusing

spiritual interventions can be damaging to the point of being abusive (see the following for examples of ways in which spiritually based relationships, based on false assumptions regarding faith, can become abusive and ultimately toxic: Arterburn & Felton, 1991; Cloud & Townsend, 1994; Enroth, 1992, 1994; Orlowski, 2010).

Tan's suggestions for use of explicit spiritual interventions. Following is a list of suggestions adapted from Tan (1994, 1996) regarding the ethical use of spiritual interventions in counseling. They cover some of the same ground as McMinn's questions but also add significantly to the discussion. Tan is both a psychologist and a pastor and carefully mediates the tension between the two sides of this issue.

◆ *Respect the counselee's freedom.* Any hint of the counselor imposing religious beliefs or values on the counselee must be avoided. However, what constitutes "imposing" when the very nature of the counseling relationship is one in which the counselor holds more expert and positional power than the counselee and can easily, sometimes without even realizing it, be influencing the counselee? It is like the parent who silently models values to a child, who picks them up simply because the parent is the parent. One way this can be done unwittingly is for the counselor to focus on (i.e., pay closer attention to, be more responsive to) spiritual comments the counselee shares, even when the goal of the counseling is not specifically spiritual in nature.

◆ *Assess our own competence.* As the people in the expert role, it is easy to start believing that we know more than we do. The counselee does not know our level of competence, and it is relatively easy to persuade a counselee in ways that alter his or her values. We can be unethical by claiming competence in R/S issues that we do not have, by not sharing clear information, by not encouraging counselees to do their own research and so on. Even more problematic is to adopt ecclesiastical authority and perform ecclesiastical functions if we are not qualified to do so, particularly if a specific helping relationship is not a church-related relationship. Referral to church leaders may be warranted instead.

◆ *Be aware of our triggers.* We all have our trigger topics. For me (Fred), views regarding roles of women and men in ministry and marriage are things I feel strongly about. In counseling, or when teaching, I can easily get pulled into a conversation or even an argument if someone does not agree with me. While discussing certain theological understandings may be appropriate in a classroom setting, in a counseling session arguing over doctrinal issues is never appropriate; our role is to help counselees clarify these sorts of issues for themselves.

◆ *Do not use spirituality as a way to avoid pain or confrontation.* A subtle but highly problematic tendency for Christian counselors, and those in pastoral and spiritual direction roles, is to use spiritual resources, such as prayer and Scripture, to avoid dealing directly with a counselee's painful issues. This is a case of countertransference in which the counselor's own limitations regarding how much he can handle emotionally or what topics he can or cannot listen and respond to interfere with the counseling process. Staying superficial, never challenging, is an understandable response for a counselor who is struggling personally or is feeling vulnerable, but when this becomes the typical way of working it quickly falls into the category of an "impaired" therapist (Sanders, 2013).

◆ *Do not overspiritualize.* A further concern is utilizing only religious interventions with situations and problems that may require more specialized psychological intervention or even medical intervention or medication.

◆ *Be cautious with psychotic individuals.* The use of spiritual interventions with more seriously disturbed or psychotic counselees can aggravate or at least confuse both the counselee and the counselor. For example, someone with psychotic episodes can easily become lost in their R/S delusions.

◆ *Be careful with those from legalistic backgrounds.* Finally, the use of spiritual interventions, especially spiritual disciplines, with counselees from very harsh and legalistic religious backgrounds can trigger obsessive-compulsive symptoms and increase levels of shame.

Modification of Chapelle's model. Figure 15.2 outlines an intentional, step-wise process based on Chapelle's (2000) model. While it may seem burdensome to work through these steps in every situation, they can be a useful guide and reminder,

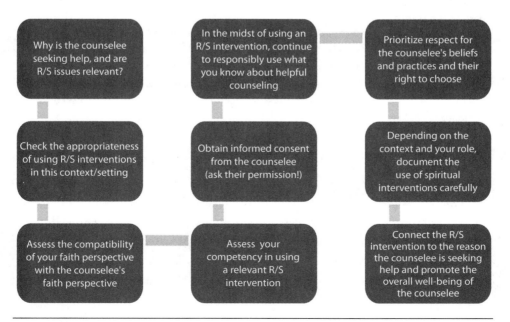

Figure 15.2. A suggested process for applying R/S interventions in counseling

Diagnostic Implications

The DSM does not help us much in appreciating the sacred. A summary of the DSM perspective on the spiritual dimension of mental disorders is:

✓ Religion/spirituality (R/S) is only handled as a component of cultural issues.

✓ R/S is not seen as a unique core component of personality.

✓ R/S is not seen as a significant component of mental disorders.

✓ In contrast to the Freudian legacy, spirituality is not completely negative, but essentially the DSM avoids it or minimizes its impact.

✓ R/S Is recognized as a component in psychotic symptoms (e.g., hallucinations and delusions), manic episodes, nightmares, obsessive-compulsive behaviors, OCPD, dissociative disorders, tic disorders, sexual disorders, etc.

✓ Exploring a counselee's religious history in a diagnostic interview is encouraged.

✓ R/S can be a V-code (a focus of clinical attention) labeled religious or spiritual problem. Examples include distressing experiences that involve loss or questioning of faith, problems associated with conversion to a new faith, or questioning of spiritual values that may not necessarily be related to an organized church or religious institution.

The ASERVIC competencies (2009) state: "When making a diagnosis, the professional counselor recognizes that the counselee's spiritual and/or religious perspectives can a) enhance well-being; b) contribute to client problems; and/or c) exacerbate symptoms." While an affirmation of the potential positive role of faith in mental functioning, this statement continues to suffer from the overwhelming negative bias against religion and spirituality in the history of treating mental illness. To be fair, this is not completely unjustified. Many disorders, across many cultures, tend to express religious ideation and symbolism, religious beliefs and religious practices as part of their symptomatology. Ritual hand washing, veneration of saints and beliefs about the afterlife, for example, are common among those with mental illness.

However, why wouldn't people with mental illnesses express their symptoms in terms of some of the most powerful concepts and beliefs within a culture? The challenge is distinguishing between symptoms that are a distortion of a person's reality and the healthy, life-giving, community-based resources of many faith communities. Unfortunately, the strong bias in the field leaves the impression that faith is at least partially related to dysfunctional beliefs.

particularly in more complicated scenarios. What we have discussed above with respect to McMinn and Tan's work can be incorporated into this overall procedure. As with all interventions in counseling, there needs to be careful consideration of the appropriateness of using specific techniques. In appendix D at the end of the book we extend the model and outline it in more detail as well as include some reflections and case examples.

THE HOLY SPIRIT AND COUNSELING

We have discussed this topic to some extent earlier in the book; however, we believe it is crucial to the counseling process for Christians and so deserves additional attention. This is not to say that the other persons of the Trinity are not also integrally involved; God the Father, Jesus the Son and the Holy Spirit all are relevant to counseling. Reminders of the love of Father God, his sovereignty and his provision for us, are pertinent to counselees who are not feeling cared for. In chapter seven we discussed how Jesus experienced exactly what we experience yet is also God and so becomes the perfect model for how to empathize. But it is the Spirit, the sanctifier, the healer, who is called the wonderful counselor (Is 9:6).

How the Spirit works in counseling. Tan (2011a), in his text on counseling theories from a Christian perspective, affirms the importance of the Spirit in counseling. The Bible talks about the Spirit's power, which gives Christians the gifts of exhortation, encouragement, healing, wisdom, knowledge, discerning of spirits, mercy, teaching, faith and intercession (Rom 12:6-8; 1 Cor 12:8-10, 28; Eph 4:11). Several of these gifts are particularly applicable in counseling; specifically mercy (compassion for those who are in need or suffering), wisdom (understanding of the complexities of life) and exhortation (encouragement for others to persist) come to mind.

The Holy Spirit in Counseling

✓ Gives spiritual gifts
✓ Produces the fruit of the Spirit
✓ Conveys truth
✓ Informs and energizes the counselor
✓ Provides hope
✓ Works in the counselee's life.

✓ Offers quiet guidance for the counselor
✓ Is present in the counseling relationship.
✓ Produces personality growth and change
✓ Heals

The Spirit conveys truth, particularly truth about ourselves, moral behavior and the ethical aspects of counseling. In addition, the Spirit produces the fruit of the Spirit in our lives: becoming Christlike in love, joy, peace, patience, kindness, goodness, faithfulness, gentleness and self-control (Gal 5:22-23). The Holy Spirit informs and energizes the counselor, is at work in the counselee's life whether acknowledged or not and is an ever-present third person active in the counseling relationship. Tan (2011a) also suggests that the Holy Spirit provides hope for the counselee, quiet guidance and inner promptings of knowledge and wisdom for the counselor, and direct healing for the counselee and the counselor. Several authors have added significant reflections on this topic (e.g., Averbeck, 2008; Beck, 2009, Egan, 2010; Kim-van Daalen, 2012), including reflections on the role of the Spirit in Christian community and formation, the role of the Spirit in suffering and in the development of moral conscience. In 1999 the

Journal of Psychology and Christianity dedicated an entire issue of the journal, with a number of helpful articles, to the topic of the Holy Spirit in counseling.

In 2002 Decker, in his review of published articles on the Holy Spirit and counseling, suggested that the Spirit takes us beyond relationality with the Spirit to union with the Spirit, what some denominations would call being "filled with the Spirit" (Acts 9:17). This allows the counselor to move into an increased openness to the movement of the Spirit within the counseling relationship. Further, Decker argues that the Spirit plays a central role in personality development and change. Recognizing the Holy Spirit's impact on adult religious experience is another important benefit. Decker also acknowledges the need for counselors to be attentive to cultural differences in attunement to the Spirit; some cultures—and we would add denominations (or subcultures)—are much more conversant with how the Spirit affects their lives.

How can I recognize the Holy Spirit's voice? How you think about the work of the Holy Spirit will be to some degree influenced by the theological tradition you espouse. Those from more Pentecostal/charismatic backgrounds or those who practice contemplative spirituality may be more familiar with listening for the Spirit's prompting. However you think about the Holy Spirit at this point in your spiritual journey, we encourage you to seek to further refine how you listen for the Holy Spirit's voice in your day-to-day life. It will be more difficult for you to recognize the Spirit's voice in the midst of a counseling session if you do not recognize it in other circumstances! Here are some suggestions for discerning the voice of the Spirit:

- Identify how you currently see the Holy Spirit working in your life and amid personal circumstances.

- Reflect on how in the past you have responded to the Spirit's prompting, and evaluate the results of following the Spirit.

- Consider whether the Spirit's voice is consistent with or in contrast to what Scripture, properly interpreted, says.

- Intentionally listen for the Holy Spirit at different points in your day with respect to situations in *your own* life that do not directly affect someone else. Do the same with regards to how you interact *relationally* with a friend or family member.

- Invite the Holy Spirit to make his voice more recognizable to you. Ask him to confirm himself through other means (e.g., a wise colleague or supervisor).

- Make use of your spiritual community for guidance and confirmation.

- Make use of professional guidance and supervision.

- If you are unsure, delay acting on the promptings you sense until you receive further assurance that you should proceed.

- As you become more confident in your ability to discern the Holy Spirit's voice, make use of those inner promptings in counseling.

Training, intuition, countertransference or the Holy Spirit? Many counselors relate that they have experienced moments in counseling when they did not have a clue where to go and have shot up a quick inner "Help!" prayer to God. While sometimes these kinds of prayers go seemingly unanswered (i.e., the counselor continues to feel as though he or she is stumbling along without any clear idea of what to do next), at other times it is not unusual to sense a flash of inspiration that has led to a therapeutic breakthrough. So what was the source of such inspiration? Did the counselor's training eventually come to his aid? Did intuition kick in? Did the Holy Spirit speak directly to the counselor's mind?

We introduced this topic in a sidebar in chapter three, but we want to expand on it here. As mentioned previously, our suggestion is that perhaps it is not necessary to differentiate one from the other; the Holy Spirit can use our training and intuition, as well as speaking to us more directly. But doing our part to get good training and hone our intuition by testing it out can only help in the overall discernment process.

What is more problematic is confusing the Holy Spirit's voice with our own. In other words, we can mistakenly assume that our own emotional reactions to a specific counselee (i.e., countertransference) are promptings from the Holy Spirit.

A tragic example of this error was a situation that arose when a colleague was consulting with me (Heather) about a particularly difficult case. I agreed with my colleague's assessment that her counselee was potentially at a high risk of being revictimized by former perpetrators. What alarmed me was her solution to this problem.

My colleague had taken her counselee into her home in order to protect her. These days this kind of boundary violation would be grounds for a professional counselor to be grieved and perhaps lose his or her license to practice counseling. But while at this particular time in the history of counseling such ethical standards were not as well established as they are today, I knew that having her counselee live with her and her family was not a good idea, and I told her so. However, my colleague had convinced herself that the Holy Spirit had told her that this is what she should do.

Unfortunately, things ended badly. The counselor became so severely burned out within a short period of time that she not only had to ask her counselee to leave her home, but she also ended up having to end the counseling relationship altogether. Therefore, rather than protecting her counselee from harm, she actually became the source of much emotional damage to her counselee in the form of rejection and abandonment.

Not only was this particular counselee affected, but as a direct result of this misguided decision my colleague ended up having to leave the counseling profession altogether. Many years later I had a chance to reconnect with my former colleague, who told me that her countertransference in the form of fear for her counselee's safety was so intense that she ignored the cautions of others, baptizing her decision to go against advice with her perception that "the Holy Spirit told me to do it."

IMPROVING RELIGIOUS AND SPIRITUAL
COMPETENCIES IN COUNSELING

If counseling practitioners truly desire to be attentive to diversity and multiculturalism, broadly defined, then we clearly need to include religion in the list of topics that we claim to attend to and respect in terms of competence training. Plante (2014) suggests that ethical and competent counselors will find it useful to follow the following four steps in their efforts to increase their competence as it pertains to religion and spirituality. These include (1) being aware of biases, (2) considering religion like other types of diversity, (3) taking advantage of available resources in both the psychological and religion fields, and (4) consulting colleagues, including clergy. In addition, the ASERVIC competencies (see appendix D) are a more detailed resource on increasing competence.

Another way to increase competence is to simply become more aware of interventions specifically inspired by Scripture (see the examples at the end of the chapter). One caution is that, as people who respect science and research, we should not be afraid to study our interventions so that empirical validation (outcome or effectiveness studies) is attained.

MULTICULTURAL APPLICATION

Are R/S issues in counseling just one dimension of multicultural or crosscultural diversity issues? Anthropology, the study of humanity, and particularly cultural groups, in terms of their social, linguistic and historical expressions, typically includes religion as an essential element of any culture. Some counseling-related discussions of culture approach the topic with minimal acknowledgment of the religious underpinnings of the culture.

In American society this is becoming increasingly common; we can describe European American culture with little reference to the religious heritage and ongoing role of religion in the society. This is true of many European cultures and of both Francophone and Anglophone cultures in Canada. However, for much of the remainder of the world, religion continues to be a dominant cultural force. For example, in the Middle East it continues to spark ongoing cultural and national battles; it is at the core of decades of violence in Ireland; it is a renewed focus within Chinese and Russian culture despite decades of repression and claims of the success of purely secular societies; it is stronger than ever in African and Latin American cultures, where it is deeply embedded in almost every aspect of the cultures; it is at the foundation of decades of increased terrorism worldwide; and due to immigration in many Western nations, various religions and a spiritual perspective on life are alive and well in the immigrant and ethnic subcultures that make up a growing percentage of the American cultural mosaic. With regard to spiritual and religious perspectives on life, the gap between mainstream Western culture and most other parts of the world is wide and increasingly challenging for Western, secular-trained mental health professionals to navigate.

Crosscultural Counseling Questions

✓ What do you call your problem? What name does it have?

✓ How do others see your problem?

✓ How are other people involved in your illness?

✓ What do you think has caused this problem?

✓ Why do you think it started when it did?

✓ What does your sickness do to you? How does it work?

✓ How severe is it? Will it have a long or short course?

✓ How is your illness understood in term of the supernatural?

✓ What do you fear most about your sickness?

✓ What are the chief problems your sickness has caused for you?

✓ What kind of help do you think you should receive?

✓ What are the most important results you hope to receive?

Source: Kleinman, Eisenberg and Good (1978).

Well-known in the world of cultural psychiatry, Kleinman, Eisenberg and Good (1978) developed a set of questions to use crossculturally that make fewer assumptions from a Western perspective yet get a sense of a psychological problem (see "Crosscultural Counseling Questions" sidebar). This kind of careful cultural analysis is equally as valid as a template for the spiritual and religious understanding of counselees (see "Examples of R/S Interventions in Counseling" sidebar).

Thus religion and multiculturalism are intricately tied together. One cannot consider the cultural background of a counselee without also reflecting on the religious context of the counselee. The danger is that in our efforts to understand the complexity of our counselees we end up with what Dueck & Reimer (2009) call "thick" counselees and "thin" counselors. Thin cultural analysis involves a focus on clothing, language, customs and information about the culture, whereas thick analysis extends that to include symbols, meanings, worldviews, relationships, spirituality and a person's perception of reality.

We acknowledge that cultural analysis is always incomplete because it is always in transition both within the culture and within our individual counselees. However, we need to do our work to more deeply understand the nuances of our counselee's worldview and how his view of reality differs from our own.

MINISTRY APPLICATION

Spiritual interventions are an expected resource in most ministry, church and parachurch contexts. For instance, in one study (Weld & Eriksen, 2007), 82% of *Christian* counselees desired audible prayer in counseling. Even in a secular society that largely rejects formal religion and Christian values, when wrestling with personal life problems,

R/S practices become increasingly important. In Christian counseling we would expect that the use of spiritual interventions would be common. Obviously, in secular contexts the expectations of usage will differ and vary depending on counselor, counselee and context.

Some authors/practitioners would argue that spiritual direction, pastoral counseling and counseling are distinct roles with different training, emphases and goals. However, others would suggest that they form a continuum with many overlapping aspects. A helpful reflection on the different emphases is Tisdale, Doehring and Lorraine-Poirier (2004) in their chapter, "Three voices, one song; Perspectives on the care of persons from a psychologist, spiritual director and pastoral counselor" (cf. Hall & McMinn, 2003).

Another helpful explanation is adapted from Sperry (2003, p. 7), who contrasted the functions of spiritual direction and psychotherapy (see table 15.1). Pastoral counseling would likely float somewhere in the middle. Whether one agrees with each of his points or not, the significance of the helping relationship is similar, including transference (what the counselee transfers or projects onto the counselor) and countertransference (what the helper projects on to the counselee).

Table 15.1. Spiritual direction compared to psychotherapy

Spiritual Direction	Psychotherapy
Spiritual assessment	Initial psychological evaluation
Differentiating spiritual experience from psychopathology	Differential diagnosis between disorders
Transformation	Symptom reduction, increasing functioning, personality or character change
Explicit triadic relationship	Dyadic therapeutic alliance
Advisement (guidance)	Therapeutic interventions (e.g., cognitive restructuring)
Discernment	Mutual collaboration
Spiritual resistance	Psychological resistance
Transference and countertransference dynamics	Transference and countertransference dynamics

Source: Adapted from Sperry, 2003, p. 7.

CONCLUSION

The role of the sacred in the counseling relationship cannot be ignored and should be pursued and understood as something central to the identity of a counselee. Whether you are working with a Christian counselee or not, the Holy Spirit is present and active in the counseling process and in that individual's life. Creating sacred spaces, honoring sacred seasons and utilizing interventions that allow for counselees to step more fully into their spiritual identity can be both professionally ethical and theologically grounded. The work of the counselor is sacred work, which requires each one of us to attend to our own spiritual growth and well-being so that we may walk with others in respect and grace.

REFLECTION QUESTIONS

1. How important do you think empirical validation is, as well as the appropriateness of applying research criteria and methods, to the study of R/S interventions? Why?

2. How do you believe God works in counseling-type relationships to achieve healing? What is the unique role of the counselor in facilitating God's healing in people's lives?

3. How would you describe the role of Scripture, prayer and the Holy Spirit in counseling to (a) a fundamentalist Christian, (b) a "New Age" spiritual person and (c) an adherent to a different religion?

4. How would you currently describe the role of religion or spirituality in your own life? In what ways might your own spiritual journey help you as you counsel others? In what ways might your own spiritual journey hinder you as you counsel others?

5. In light of chapter two's discussion of self-as-instrument, combined with this chapter's discussion of the sacred in counseling, what steps might you take to further your own growth, skill and competence in the integration of religion and spirituality in the counseling relationship?

RELIGIOUS/SPIRITUAL INTERVENTIONS:
A SAMPLING AND REFLECTION

In the following table, column one is not specifically a list of spiritual interventions; it addresses the broader issue of how God "speaks" into our lives. Broadly based on Job 33:14-30, it lists a multitude of ways that God brings healing into our lives so "that the light of life may shine" on us (Job 33:30). Categorized into healing words, healing experiences and healing relationships, many of these can be used as counseling interventions or the focus of reflection in counseling conversations. A detailed description of each of these is beyond the scope of this book, but many are fairly obvious, and references are provided for further descriptions.

Reviewing the entire chart of R/S interventions is a bit overwhelming. However, this is only a sample of authors addressing this topic. The list could be much longer. The main point is to expand possibilities for addressing spirituality in counseling relationships. Our God is creative, and his options for healing are multitude.

Table 15.2. Comparison of various authors' examples of R/S interventions

Healing Gifts (Gingrich, F.)	Spiritual Disciplines in Counseling (Moon et al., 1991)	Self-Reported Spiritual Practices (Ball & Goodyear, 1991)	Christian Counseling Approaches (Gingrich, F.)
Healing Words: • study of Scripture • meditation on Scripture • prayer (many types) • preaching of the Word • teaching (wisdom, knowledge) • stories • identity in Christ • reading • journaling **Healing Experiences:** • faithful Christian walk (perseverance) • observing others • worship and music • celebration • being prayed for by others • solitude • creation (cultures, nature, animals) • renewal (play, relaxation, rest, sleep, sabbath) • everyday routines (habits) • following one's vocation • deliverance (spiritual warfare, exorcism) • spiritual experiences • dreams • inner healing (healing of memories) • miracles of healing • Lord's Supper **Healing Relationships:** • fellowship (community) • service • small groups • discipleship/mentoring • spiritual direction • friendships • marriage • confession (and forgiveness) • self-care in relationships • pastoral care • counseling/psychotherapy • marital or family therapy	**Meditation: (contemplation or reflection):** • concrete meditation • abstract meditation **Prayer:** • intercessory • contemplative • listening • praying in the Spirit **Scripture:** • didactic • study • memorization • homework • confession • worship • forgiveness • fasting • deliverance • solitude/silence • discernment • journaling • obedience • simplicity • spiritual history • healing (including laying on of hands and anointing with oil)	• prayer • teaching of concepts • reference to Scripture • Scripture memorization • relaxation techniques (with guided imagery, meditation and reference to spiritual concepts) • forgiveness • use of self as technique • homework assignment • use of outside resources • secular techniques (with a religious reference, e.g., biblical dream interpretation or role-playing God) • anointing with oil • confrontation (what does God say about that?) • screening/intake assessment (regarding spiritual history and values)	• Nouthetic Counseling (J. Adams et al.) • contemporary biblical counseling (Kellemen et al.) • dialogue counseling (Tournier) • discipleship counseling (Collins) • biblical counseling (Crabb) • Christian psychology (Johnson et al.) • spiritual direction • spiritual disciplines • spiritual gifts • pastoral counseling • identity in Christ (Anderson) • deliverance/spiritual warfare • inner healing/healing of memories (e.g., Seamands, Tan) • Theophostic prayer ministry (Smith)

Spiritual Practices (Plante, 2009, p. 33)	Transformative Encounters (Appleby & Ohlschlager, 2013)	R/S Interventions (summarized from Cashwell et al., 2013)	Evidence-Based Practices in Christian Counseling (Worthington et al., 2013)	Other Examples
• prayer • meditation • meaning, purpose and calling in life • bibliotherapy • attending community services and rituals • volunteerism and charity • ethical values and behavior • forgiveness, gratitude and kindness • social justice • learning from spiritual models • acceptance of self and others (even with faults) • being part of something larger than oneself • appreciating the sacredness of life	• inner healing • Theophostic prayer ministry • deliverance • biblical counseling • spiritually oriented cognitive-behavioral therapy • Christian holism (Holy Spirit and counseling) • contemplative prayer • Christian emotion-focused therapy • formational counseling • transformational group counseling • counseling and forgiveness • praying the Scriptures within cognitive-behavioral therapy • visualization and EMDR • Christian cognitive-behavioral therapy for depression and anxiety • counseling for sex addiction • addiction recovery groups • counseling unwanted sexual attraction and behavior • human flourishing in life coaching	• use R/S metaphors/ analogies • co-construct therapeutic goals related to R/S beliefs • refer to someone who can more effectively work with R/S perspective • draw on R/S texts that are consistent with beliefs • identify R/S themes by initiating the topic, responding to questions and expressing interest and respect • discuss how R/S beliefs support or impede psycho-social functioning • use formal and informal spiritually oriented assess-ments and include in case conceptual-ization • consider R/S development across the lifespan • self-disclose own R/S beliefs when requested • determine when own R/S biases could be detri-mental and avoid imposing own R/S perspectives • pray with them in session and/or for them outside session • talk about God, good and evil, forgiveness, R/S practices, twelve-step principles, and compare and contrast the concepts of spirituality and religion • encourage to deepen their R/S commitments	• devotional meditation for anxiety • Christian-accommo-dative (CA) cognitive therapy for depression • CA trauma-focused cognitive-behavioral therapy for children and adolescents • principles for psychodynamic and process-experiential psychotherapies • preparing couples for marriage: the SYMBIS model • Christian PREP (Prevention and Relationship Enhancement program) • hope-focused couples approach • relationship conflict restoration model • couples and forgiveness • CA group for-giveness	• spiritual assessment (Greggo & Lawrence, 2012) • holy name repetition (Oman & Driskill, 2003) • spiritual self-disclosure (Denney, Aten & Gingrich, 2008) • differentiating spiritual experience from psychopathology (Sperry, 2003) • dealing with spiritual resistance (Sperry, 2003) • practicing the presence of God (Tan, 1996) • mindfulness, ACT and cognitive-behavioral therapy from a Christian perspective (Tan, 2011b)

Following are some reflection questions regarding this chart:

1. What might be some of the reasons that different authors have such different perspectives regarding what is a spiritual intervention? Their definitions are often implied but result in diverse lists.

2. What additional spiritual interventions might be added?

3. What ultimately distinguishes an R/S intervention from a so-called secular intervention?

4. Is there any inconsistency and problem with becoming skilled in the application of a particular approach or theory of counseling (e.g., cognitive-behavioral therapy) and adapting spiritual interventions for use within that theoretical framework?

5. If competency is required in the use of specialized techniques (see the ASERVIC competencies in appendix D of this book), to what degree and in what ways is this possible with such a diverse list?

6. This list spans over two decades of publications. In recent years the issue of empirically validated techniques and models has emerged, and it is now expected by licensing agencies, insurance companies and researchers. In order to justify the use of a particular technique, it should have a body of research verifying its validity, that is, does it accomplish what it says it will? The problem is that there is a lot of resistance in some religious circles to the idea that anything spiritual in nature should be forced into a scientific mold and subjected to research verification. Our view of integration is that effective spiritual interventions will ultimately be validated by good scientific research. This is also the position of Worthington et al. (2013) and their effort to begin the process of examining the empirically validated Christian counseling practices. The theoretical foundation for this view of the relationship of science to religion is given in Worthington's (2010) book. To what extent do you believe that spiritual interventions should be judged by empirical research standards? Why?

7. Ultimately the question is, how does God bring healing into our lives? How do you believe God works in counseling-type relationships to achieve this, and what is your unique role in facilitating God's healing in people's lives?

CONSOLIDATING

AND ENDING

*T*HE LAST AND OFTEN THE MOST OVERLOOKED phase of the counseling relationship is the late phase, in which target 4, "Consolidating and Ending," is the focus. The aim of target 4 is for counselor and counselee to work together so that the counseling process ends well.

Consolidation of learning and change is an essential aspect of target 4. It is exciting for both counselee and counselor to recognize that the strategies for change that were implemented using target 3 skills are bearing fruit. The danger at this juncture is moving too quickly toward termination of the counseling relationship. If initial changes are not solidified and fully integrated into a counselee's person and life, regression to old patterns is a very real possibility. Therefore time and attention should be given to ensuring that the desired changes are permanent so that the danger of relapse is minimized. The rest of target 4 involves tying up any loose ends, reflecting back on what has been learned, and creating a plan for launching the counselee out into life without the ongoing support of the counselor.

Sometimes growth takes place so gradually that it is easy to lose sight of just how far an individual has come. That is why it is so important to look back and reflect on what is different now compared to when the counselee began her journey. This process is done collaboratively, with the counselee and counselor both identifying themes and patterns of growth. The counselor not only seeks to affirm the counselee for the growth that has already occurred but also encourages the counselee to look at areas that she might desire to pursue in the future. In figure T4.1 the dashed line on the right-hand side of the figure illustrates that the growth process continues after counseling stops.

Finally, we look at termination and how the end of counseling should also be a growth experience that can actually be viewed as the beginning of something new and exciting for both the counselee and the counselor. Recognizing that one counselor cannot provide for all the needs of a counselee, the use of community resources and referrals is also discussed so that the counselee can connect to additional forms of support within his or her larger system.

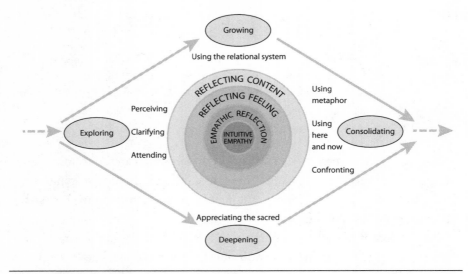

Figure T4.1. The targets, skills and process of counseling

In a parallel process we will also examine the ending that takes place for you who are reading this book as you reach the end of your microskills training and transition into the next stage of your growth process in people helping. We seek to affirm and celebrate the growth you have made throughout the microskills training process as well as cast vision for the ways in which you can bring all that you have learned through your training into your future counseling experiences.

ENDINGS AND NEW BEGINNINGS

Forget the former things;
do not dwell on the past.
See, I am doing a new thing!
Now it springs up; do you not perceive it?
I am making a way in the wilderness
and streams in the wasteland.

Isaiah 43:18-19

SKILL: consolidating and ending

PURPOSE: to help counselees and counselors end counseling well; facilitating counselees' abilities to take their progress and continue its application after counseling has formally ended

FORMULA: The changes you have seen in yourself are _____.
These changes can become permanent by _____.
You will know you are ready to end counseling when _____.

WHEN YOU THINK ABOUT THIS microskills training coming to an end with this chapter, what thoughts and feelings are evoked in you?

» Thoughts:

» Feelings:

When you think about working with a real counselee, what thoughts and feelings are evoked in you?

» Thoughts:

» Feelings:

My counselor told me today that she thought that I was doing so well that soon we would have to talk about when we bring our counseling to an end. I totally panicked! My counseling sessions have been my lifeline; I've been able to get through difficult days because I know that if I can just hang in there I'll be able to talk to my counselor on Wednesday. I just can't imagine not having her there!

As I listened to my friend Rita, I could see and hear her anxiety. Rita obviously was not yet ready for counseling to end, yet within a few weeks I saw hints that she was closer to being ready for termination. "You know," she said, "Vicki asked me to have lunch this week and Wednesday was her only option. If only I didn't have my counseling appointment on Wednesday, we could have gotten together!" After another two weeks, Rita mentioned how nice it would be to have the extra money to spend that currently went for counseling. At that point she caught herself, expressing to me, "You know, I never thought it was possible to feel this way, but I think my counselor was right. . . . I am actually beginning to look forward to some aspects of not going to counseling!"

CONSOLIDATING

In our understanding of the counseling process, target 4 includes both consolidating and endings. As discussed in the introduction to target 4, the consolidation aspect involves making sure that the changes implemented have become fully integrated into who the counselee is as a person and how the counselee interacts with his or her world. Some of this will occur naturally over time as long as there is a mechanism with which to check whether progress has been maintained. Initially the counselor can serve to provide this type of accountability while the counseling relationship is in the late phase. As the process comes closer to the end, the counselee will need to have developed ways in which he can continue to be aware of indicators that relapse may be immanent. This may involve other people in his relational system, such as spouses, friends, a mentor or an accountability group. Or the counselee may have put internal checks and balances in place through intentional use of spiritual resources, journaling or mentally taking inventory of how he is doing in areas of potential risk.

Another relapse prevention strategy is for you as the counselor to provide education about what the counselee can expect in the future. I (Heather) often use the analogy of an alcoholic "falling off the wagon" at some point after his or her recovery. The tendency of those who have struggled with addictions is often to give up once they realize that they have not stayed abstinent and tell themselves, "I've blown it now because I've already had two drinks. So I guess I'll just keep drinking because I'll never be able to change!" This is a crucial decision-making moment, because if the individual continues to drink, old patterns may once again take over.

However, it actually is not too late. All of the changes that have been implemented up to that point, in this instance all of the days, months or years that an individual has managed to stay sober, place her at a very different point in recovery than she was at previously. The key is to catch the mistake as quickly as possible. Using the analogy of the alcoholic, if after two drinks the individual realizes that she has made a mistake but does not want to go back to an alcoholic lifestyle, the choice can be made to stop drinking immediately and seek help.

I tell counselees that they can count on there being times in the future where they will fall back into old patterns, particularly when under a lot of stress, in crisis, fatigued or sick. I want them to know that they do not have to give up at these times but that they instead become aware of increased risk under such circumstances and do what they can to keep from falling over the proverbial cliff or, if they are already on their way down, that they stop their fall as soon as they can. Coming up with specific strategies for what they could do if they relapse could help them at some point in the future.

Another aspect of consolidation involves simply reflecting on the progress made to date. As sessions begin to wind toward the end, either the counselee or counselor, or both, begin to make statements that pull the various strands of the counseling process together. For instance, "I'm noticing that over the sessions we have looked at (particular areas of growth), and I feel like some good progress has been made." Such a statement might even come as a surprise and initiate an explicit discussion that summarizes the process.

In other situations, consolidation might be intentionally initiated by either party, by making a statement or asking a question that points to summarizing the relationship. These are important moments in the process that can easily be short-circuited by the emotions that are triggered by the anticipation of ending. It is worthwhile to intentionally review the progress, perhaps by consulting session notes, by recalling early statements about goals and expectations, by asking specifically about the progress made toward early goals and by asking about the counseling relationship. Jumping too quickly to how and when to end can overlook significant opportunities to solidify changes and to make contingency plans for times of future stress and difficulty.

ENDINGS AND NEW BEGINNINGS

Like parents who seek to launch their children into the world as self-sufficient adults, the goal of counseling is to launch healthier and more equipped counselees back into the world. It is normal for parents to have mixed feelings when their children strike out on their own. While there is often a sense of excitement and feelings of fulfillment to see their children enter the adult world, there is also often an accompanying sense of grief and loss. Similarly, the end of the counseling relationship is what each counselor has in mind as a goal when the counseling process begins. It is the task of every counselor to work himself or herself out of a job by passing on insight, skills and abilities to the counselees with whom they have the privilege of working. Even if the goal is and always has been to get to a place where the counselee no longer needs to be in counseling, there is often still sadness in the ending of such a personal and profound relationship for both counselors and counselees.

This chapter marks the end of your microskills training but the beginning of your ongoing growth and development as a counselor. As such, it is important that we take some time to explore what you as students are feeling about the end of this process and at the beginning of whatever clinical training awaits you. We will also explore the complex elements that contribute to the termination of a counseling relationship and the role of supervision and outside referral sources to the counseling process.

The counseling process is like training for a marathon. At the beginning of training, you gather a bunch of information about running and about marathon training in particular. Then you set out actually running as part of your training, slowly building up to the 26.2 miles that make a marathon. Counseling is similar in that throughout the counseling process counselees are practicing, or training, for life outside counseling. Counselees may test-run various interventions or techniques, but they get to come back to the safety of the counseling relationship, able to check in with their counselor and modify the counselor's suggested techniques or approaches to life. When counseling is over, counselees are set on the path to run themselves, implementing all the knowledge, training, encouragement and skills they have developed for this very moment. While there may be sadness that the training phase is over, there is also great rejoicing in the arrival of the finish line. This is what all the hard work was for!

The counseling student. Your own journey through this microskills training process has its own bittersweet ending and new beginning. It is a time to celebrate all that you have learned and accomplished through this process, the self-awareness you have gained and the growth you have made as a counselor in training. Way to go! It is also time to look excitedly toward the future and what it may hold for you as a counselor, chaplain, pastoral counselor, spiritual director or other type of helper. The options are endless.

At the same time, we have found that many students reach this point in the process and encounter various levels of anxiety, self-doubt and apprehension. The reality that your next step in a training process is likely going to include working with real counselees strikes many students with a heavy sense of responsibility and insecurity. The sweetness of the excitement and hopeful anticipation of what is to come is also often met with the bitter tastes of fear, uncertainty and self-doubt. Both the positive and the negative emotions are normal and are to be expected at the end of this process, although they will vary in intensity for each student.

◆ What about this training process are you happy or relieved to leave behind? Why? _____

_____

_____

◆ What about this training process will you miss? Why? _____

_____

_____

◆ Thinking back to who you were at the beginning of this book, what have you learned about yourself in this process? _____

_____

_____

◆ Thinking back to the beginning of this book, what have you learned about the counseling process? _____

_____

_____

◆ What is something that you want to be sure to remember about yourself or the counseling process as you move into the next stage of your journey? _____

_____

_____

The counselor and counselee. The beginning of the end of the counseling relationship can come in various forms, some sudden and others more gradual. In an ideal world the counseling process comes to an end gradually and with mutual agreement between the counselor and the counselee. In reality, this generally only happens when the *counselee's goals have been attained* or *reasonable progress has been achieved* and both counselor and counselee agree that the counselee no longer needs the ongoing support of the counselor. But there are different kinds of endings to the counseling relationship. Each type of ending generally brings with it a different type of reaction within the counselor. It is likely that, at some point in your career, you will encounter all of these endings.

The timing is right. The end that every counselor hopes for is one in which counseling goals have been met, and both counselor and counselee are ready to see the counselee launched out on their own. These terminations are times of celebration and hope and are usually filled with both happiness at what has been accomplished and sadness to part ways.

Biblical/Theological Connections

At various points throughout the book we have developed a theology of emotion. This is not intended to diminish reason and rationality but to counter the cultural tendency to elevate reason and rationality and diminish emotion. It is a myth that emotions operate independently of volition (will), cognition (thinking) and action (behavior). As with all aspects of ourselves, our wills can be stubborn, weak or beneficial; cognition can be distorted, illogical or renewed; behavior can be damaging, apathetic or helpful; and emotions can be either adaptive, seeking personal connection, or maladaptive, pushing away relationships.

For Paul, "a Christian's emotional life is all rolled up in and with and around how we should behave and how we should think. For Paul, it's no different to 'cry with the grieving' than to say 'don't lie.' Duty is there, but not devoid of passion and true emotion. It's all one. So feel. And feel deeply" (Elliott, 2014, p. 25).

So it is with endings in counseling. Counseling relationships are real life, deeply personal and interpersonal relationships. Ending such relationships should evoke emotions in both the counselee and the counselor. There is no healthy way to avoid or downplay the emotionality of endings. Loss, grief, joy, satisfaction and even a taste of anger or depression are all understandable responses to the ending of a relationship. While "moving on" is the mantra of our society, counseling relationships need to carefully model what relationships can and should be. But whereas other relationships in life are often not necessary endings, counseling relationships do have to end, at least on this side of heaven.

The well-known passage in Ecclesiastes 3:1-11 is a fitting reminder that from God's perspective "There is a time for everything, and a season for every activity under the heavens." Among the examples given in this passage are several that metaphorically refer to relationships:

a time to be born and a time to die,
a time to plant and a time to uproot,
a time to weep and a time to laugh,
a time to mourn and a time to dance.

The passage continues: "He has made everything beautiful in its time. He has also set eternity in the human heart." For the Christian, endings are not forever, because we carry a longing for forever within us.

It's not time yet! One of the hardest goodbyes in counseling is when the termination feels premature. In these scenarios the counselee often self-selects out of counseling before the counselor feels the goals have been reached. Sometimes this happens because the counselee feels that he has gotten enough support, resources or skills to move on—even if the counselor believes there is more work that could be done. At other times counselees may want to end counseling because they encountered something in the journey that they are not yet ready to work through. Or it may be that finances or other family pressures move counseling down the counselee's list of priorities, resulting in termination of the counseling relationship.

At times a *counselee decides to quit* without input from the counselor and may or may not even discuss this decision with the counselor. Whenever possible, the counselor should follow up with a counselee who stops counseling suddenly to confirm the counselee's well-being and possibly encourage the counselee to return to counseling.

Sometimes counselees or counselors wonder whether counseling should end because it feels as though a *plateau has been reached.* It is possible, however, that the plateau signifies the end of the early phase of counseling, that it is actually a form of resistance to doing the hard work of the middle phase. Skills from target 2 should be utilized in order to reevaluate goals and options. If new goals cannot be determined, it may be necessary to terminate counseling either permanently or temporarily.

Finally, it is sometimes the *counselor* who prematurely ends the counseling relationship. This is often the case for counseling interns, who must move on due to the end of an internship. But even graduation from a counseling program, the end of an employment contract or other circumstances within the counselor's life, such as relocation, maternity leave or other personal or familial responsibilities, can result in having to bring the counseling relationship to a close before the goals have been fully accomplished.

Whew! There are the times when a counseling relationship ends and the counselor, at least, gives a sigh of relief. In these scenarios, the counselee has likely been particularly challenging to the counselor either due to having a particular personality or a presenting issue that stretches the counselor's areas of expertise. When counseling ends with a "whew!" it may also be a premature termination by the counselee, who still has more work to do but is not willing or able to continue that work with that particular counselor. As will be discussed later, providing appropriate referral options becomes incredibly important for this type of counselee.

It is what it is. While everyone likes to assume that each counselor and counselee will have a deep and meaningful relationship, this is just not the case every time. There will be situations in which the end of counseling is neither a sad nor a joyous experience, it simply is the end. In these scenarios, counseling often has not been a longstanding relationship, or it did not delve into particularly deep or vulnerable territory. Goals were met, tasks were accomplished, and both the counselor and counselee leave the relationship on neutral to good terms.

Time to refer. Finally, a counseling relationship may end when there is a need to *refer* the counselee out to another helper. The need to refer to can arise for a variety of reasons:

- The counselor has recognized and come to the limits of her expertise as a helper.

- The counselee needs help in a specialized area such as hospitalization, addiction treatment, sexual issues, trauma therapy or medication.

- A counselor of the opposite sex from you would be more helpful with the counselee's current issues.

- Transference or countertransference issues are too strong and unable to be resolved.

- You are involved with the person in multiple roles—e.g., the counselee is a board member and you are the pastor. (Note: We realize that pastors are constantly juggling multiple roles, but there are times when you may sense that with a particular parishioner the multiple roles may interfere with a beneficial outcome for the counselee.)

- The person is related to you, in which case the referral should take place prior to the commencement of any helping relationship.

- You or the counselee are making a geographical move.

- One of you is ill for an extended period of time, you are on parental leave or the counselee needs support while you are on vacation.

Just as the end of the training process brings mixed emotions for you as a student, a similar experience will likely take place for you and your counselees as you come to the end of your time together. The reaction to the end of counseling can be different for each counseling relationship and depends on timing, personality and the relationship that exists between the counselor and the counselee. Regardless of why the counseling relationship is ending, it is important that counselors go through some self-reflection with respect to their role in the counseling relationship (see "Reflection Questions" at the end of this chapter).

In any counseling relationship, separating out what you as the counselor are responsible for from what God and what the counselee are responsible for will promote your growth, health and longevity as a counselor.

Clinical Tips

Consider referring a counselee to another helper when:

1. The counselee requires more advanced or specialized help than you can offer.

2. A counselor of the opposite sex from you would be helpful to the counselee's process.

3. Transference or countertransference becomes too problematic.

4. You are related to or serve multiple roles within the counselee's life.

5. You are going to be inaccessible for an extended period of time due to vacation, illness or other life circumstance.

6. The counselee is moving away.

THE TERMINATION PROCESS

All good counseling must come to an end. While it is not always possible, the termination of counseling is ideally a process rather than simply a momentary event. Just as the counseling relationship was built over time, slowly growing in depth, the termination process should function as the gradual separation between counselor and counselee.

When a counselor collaboratively works with a counselee to determine the goals for counseling early on in the process, what he is essentially doing is identifying when both participants will know that they have reached the end of counseling, that counseling has accomplished its purpose in this season. These are the goals that begin to surface during the early phase of counseling, using target 1 skills, and then are refined in the middle phase as part of the target 2 deepening process and finally are implemented when aiming for target 3. Now, as target 4 is predominant, it is time to refer back to these earlier discussions. Below is an excerpt from a dialogue between a counselor and counselee that illustrates a target 4 discussion.

> **Counselor**: Amy, we have been working for several months now on your relationship with your mother, and it seems to me that things have vastly improved!
>
> **Amy**: You're right! I actually enjoy spending time with her now . . . well . . . at least in small doses!
>
> **Counselor**: So you not only don't dread time with her, you actually like spending time with your mother!
>
> **Amy**: Yeah, pretty amazing, isn't it?
>
> **Counselor**: It's a big change for sure. Amy, do you remember our discussion back in the fall when it first became clear that the relationship with your mother was what you most wanted to focus on in counseling? I asked you questions back then like, "How would you know that things have improved?" and "What would the indicators be that you might not need to continue on in counseling anymore?"
>
> **Amy**: Oh no! I see where this is going! You're not going to kick me out of counseling, are you? I'm not ready for that!
>
> **Counselor**: Relax, Amy! You can continue to come and see me as long as you feel the need, if there are things you want to continue to work on. But I sense you may be closer to being ready than you think. That's why I wanted to at least bring up the topic.
>
> **Amy**: You know, I was just thinking the other day about what a nice time I'd had with Mom over the weekend. I mean, she still tried to get me to cut the tomatoes her way and offered parenting advice I didn't ask for, but rather than get into a big argument about it I just laughed and said, "Mom, I've been cutting tomatoes this way for 20 years!" and then I just changed the subject. She looked kind of surprised, but she let it drop.

Counselor: Even four months ago, I'll bet you never imagined that you could stand up to her that way.

Amy: You're right. I would have either bitten my tongue and chopped the tomatoes the way she wanted me to but then resented it for days afterward, or I would have tried to stand my ground but end up totally overreacting and coming across like a rebellious teenager! This is really new.

Counselor: I made some notes on what you said would be indicators that things had changed with you mother, and being able to be appropriately assertive with her, without feeling a lot of inner turmoil afterward, was the main thing you mentioned. And now you're doing it! This wasn't the first time, either. You've actually told me about several incidents over the past month where you didn't let your mother run over you and you felt okay about it.

Amy: That's true. I just hadn't realized how frequently that has actually happened. Maybe that's why I'm actually starting to look forward to her visits rather than dreading them.

Counselor: It will still take a while for this to become an ingrained change. What might help with that process?

Amy: Maybe if I plan on taking at least one opportunity every visit to actively address something I disagree with, it will become easier and easier.

Counselor: That makes sense. I think that when it starts to become second nature to interact with your mother in this new way, we could talk more seriously about ending our counseling sessions. One thing we could do is space our sessions out so that you have more time in between sessions to practice. What would you think about meeting every other week for a while to kind of test it out? You can always call and set up an appointment for the off week if you're having a hard time. We could look at it as a kind of experiment.

Amy: Hmm. Well, it's a little scary, but if I knew that I had the option of coming to see you if I really needed to, then it feels a little more manageable. I am doing a lot better . . . I just don't quite trust it yet.

Counselor: A lot of people feel that way at this point in their growth process. It sounds as though you just need a little more time to prove to yourself that these changes are permanent.

Amy: Okay. What if we try it for the first two weeks and then reevaluate if I want to continue on the every-other-week schedule?

Counselor: I can live with that!

Notice how the counselor refers back to early discussions of the counseling goal related to Amy's relationship with her mother and then draws attention to ways in which that goal is currently being accomplished. Note, too, how the counselor makes suggestions that will help consolidate the changes that have already been implemented. Sometimes beginning counselors see the first signs of change and assume that the goal has been accomplished, moving too quickly to terminate counseling. However, old patterns have often been years, if not decades, in the making and do not shift easily. Once the new changes are more consistent over time and feel natural to the counselee, you know it is time to draw the relationship to a close.

Just as in the example above, as you begin to notice movement toward resolution of the counselee's concerns and movement toward the accomplishment of their goals, it is the counselor's responsibility to begin exploration of the termination process. With that being said, counselees can also be the ones to broach the subject of termination, often saying something like, "I don't know that I need to keep coming anymore." Regardless of who initiates the conversation, it is the counselor's responsibility to continue the therapeutic nature of the relationship through the final session, facilitating the counselee's self-exploration and self-awareness regarding the termination process.

Ward (1984) provides a good overview of the concepts and strategies related to termination. Specifically, he discusses three key strategies within the termination process, to which we have added a fourth. While each strategy is important, not every strategy will require the same amount of time or attention with every counselee.

1. *Evaluation of counseling goals.* When using this strategy, you will begin to explore what the goals of counseling were, how they were pursued and what the counselee perceives as the current status of that goal. You saw an example of this in the dialogue above. While this strategy may be initiated by the counselor, it is important that it is primarily assessed or determined by the counselee. The reason for this is that, once counseling does end, it will be up to counselees to remember the gains they made in counseling. The counselor will no longer be around to help with this reminder. This process is incredibly important and affirming for the counselee and should not be taken for granted by the counselor. Because most personal growth takes time, counselees often do not recognize the growth they have made. It is helpful if the counselor can provide specific examples back to the counselee or have the counselee complete a stem such as, "Early in counseling, I said/did/felt _____. I've noticed a change in that I now _____." Reflection on growth should focus on any domain of life in which change may have occurred for the counselee. Domains of life may include but are not limited to counselees' internal processes (thoughts and feelings), behavior, interpersonal relationships, social interactions, spiritual life, self-concept and self-efficacy. In the counseling dialogue Amy was focused on her interpersonal relationship with her mother, her own behavior (i.e., more assertive) and her internal processes (feelings about her mother and about her own attempts to implement change).

2. *Closure of issues within the counseling relationship.* This strategy becomes an exploration of the relationship between the counselee and the counselor. Namely, it asks counselees to reflect on their feelings about and toward the counselor, the counseling relationship and termination of the counseling relationship. When appropriate, it can be very beneficial to the counselee's process if the counselor also shares his or her feelings about the counseling relationship. This is particularly beneficial when the counselor can genuinely affirm and encourage the counselee, at times even expressing the sadness felt by the counselor to see the counselee depart. Counselees will sometimes ask whether the relationship can continue but in a different way. Some may ask you whether developing a friendship after the counseling relationship ends is a possible option. Others may suggest occasionally getting together for coffee. While it may be tempting to acquiesce to these requests, particularly if you really like the counselee, it is not a good idea. Even if you have worked collaboratively, the reality is that there is a power differential between the counselor and counselee that does not just disappear once the counseling relationship ends. For this reason professional associations have ethical guidelines that prohibit sexual relationships, if not any type of relationship, between mental health professionals and their former counselees for specific periods of time. If your helping role is more informal, you may not be restricted by the same ethical codes. However, you do need to be aware that it is unlikely that you will be able to develop a fully mutual friendship with someone when she is used to being the sole focus of your times together. You also need to keep in mind that your opinions and suggestions will likely continue to hold a lot more weight because of the previous counseling role you have had.

   3. *Preparation for self-reliance and postcounseling life application.* This is more a category of strategies than a single strategy. Here is where counselees begin to identify practical ways in which they can expect to transfer what they have learned in counseling into their "real life." Similar to the marathon-training analogy at the beginning of the chapter, counselees will likely have already begun to implement some of these ideas throughout the course of counseling. The difference now is that they begin to consider how they will continue implementation and application without the ongoing presence of the counselor in their life. Helping the counselee to create a specific list or plan is a good place to start. Amy's suggestion that she make a point of practicing assertive behavior with her mother at least once a visit is an example of such a plan.

   Other important elements within this strategy are collaboratively helping counselees to (1) identify key people who can support them in their continued growth, (2) identify other internal or community based resources that could foster continued growth in the counselee and (3) identify possible roadblocks to their continued growth along with a specific action plan or resource to counter each roadblock. Remind counselees that returning to counseling is always an option and does not indicate failure or a lack of growth in the counselee. Instead it simply means that additional resources and skills are needed. Sometimes even a single session at some point in the future can be helpful in getting unstuck or working through a specific issue. For some counselees, titrating out of counseling is a great adjustment strategy in which sessions move from once a week to once every two weeks to once a month over the course of a few months. This can help to ease counselees into doing life without the counselor and to see firsthand how well they have learned to apply all the growth they have made in counseling while having the built-in safety net of a session coming up. Amy would not have been ready to end counseling at the point at which the excerpt was taken, but experimenting with increasing the length of time between sessions felt more manageable to her.

4. *The final session.* Final sessions should be preplanned and collaboratively set by the counselor and counselee. Generally about three weeks (or sessions) prior to the final session discussion between the counselor and counselee should begin. This discussion may start simply by the counselor asking whether there is anything that the counselee still wants to have covered before counseling ends. For example, the counselor might ask, "We have about three more meetings together. Is there anything you want to make sure we cover between now and then?" Questions regarding the counselee's feelings about the imminent end of the counseling process are also important. For instance, "I'm wondering what feelings get evoked in you as we discuss only having three (or two, or one) sessions remaining together?" could be an appropriate question. Checking in with the counselee about the upcoming final session may or may not take much time, but nonetheless it serves to honor the counselee, their journey and the vulnerability they have shared in the counseling process.

Your last session together should be memorable in some way. You can ask counselees what might be most meaningful to them in that last session, something that might help them reflect on and remember all that they have accomplished in counseling. Counselees can be amazingly creative. One of my counselees (Heather) brought in two garbage bags full of balloons that we tied to the office furniture, as well as a cake that we shared. She thought that a party was the perfect way to celebrate the progress that she had made in counseling, progress that she had never thought was possible. As we ate we talked about what had changed since she first began to see me and what goals she had for the future.

For the final session, I (Elisabeth) have written notes to counselees that summarize their progress and strengths, or I have found a stone or a small figurine that somehow represents the counselee or his journey. In our final session we discuss the progress counselees have seen in themselves. They write their observations on a card as we reflect together, and they then leave with both my note and their own self-reflected card. At other times I have had counselees create their own memento during the final session, such as a drawing, to wrap up the counseling experience. While I am not artistically creative in the slightest, I have drawn pictures alongside a counselee and at other times have had them use the art project as the springboard for the verbal discussion of what they take away from our time together. The creative options are endless. In group settings, I often have participants write words of affirmation and encouragement to other group members on index cards so that each group member leaves with some specific feedback about who they are and what they have contributed to the group. Words, pictures and tangible mementos can be used later by a counselee to remember and be inspired (1 Sam 7:12; Josh 4).

Markers of Remembrance

The Old Testament in particular is filled with examples of how the people of Israel used tangible mementos to help them remember the work of God in their lives. For example, in 1 Samuel 7:12, Samuel used a stone as a long-standing tangible reminder of the Lord's help in battling the Philistines. In Joshua 4, Joshua had one man from every tribe of Israel gather a stone to build a memorial to remind themselves and future generations of God's faithfulness in leading Israel across the Jordan.

WHEN TERMINATION DOES NOT GO ACCORDING TO PLAN

Not every counseling relationship ends pleasantly or with the opportunity to terminate over time. Sometimes counselees just stop showing up; sometimes a family, medical or financial emergency prevents them from returning; and sometimes a third party (the courts, insurance company or guardians of a minor) steps in and halts any further meetings. There can be myriad reasons why endings may not go smoothly. When this happens, there are a few key things that a counselor must do. Whenever possible, a counselor needs to try to make final contact with the counselee, even if that is by phone because the counselee is unable to come in to meet face to face. This final contact should attempt to see whether the counselee is in need of any further referrals (see below) or whether there is anything further that the counselor can provide that is within his or her scope of practice. The principle behind this practice is *continuity of care* (ACA, 2014). This final contact may not be possible due to screened calls, counselee illness or death, or other impeding issues. Nonetheless, contact should be attempted when possible and documented within the counselee's file.

While ultimately the decision about whether or not to continue in counseling rests with the counselee, you as the counselor need to be aware that a counselee's stated desire to stop counseling may not be what he or she really wants. It may be that you are at a point in counseling that is particularly difficult and it seems easier to the counselee to run away than to face core issues. Or perhaps the counselee is angry at you but does not yet possess the relationship skills to communicate anger directly. For these reasons it is always best to have a final session that both parties *know* is the last session.

I (Heather) feel so strongly about the importance of having this opportunity to debrief the counseling experience with the counselee that I make it a part of the contract (written or verbal) of counseling. I tell counselees that if they wish to stop counseling

Diagnostic Implications

Our final diagnostic reflection again considers a personality disorder. Counselors may find that they have trouble "getting rid" of certain counselees. In fact, this is a frequently cited critique of counseling—it goes on and on and never ends. And this is sometimes the case, especially when a counselor is able to respond empathically and provide support that is missing from the counselee's relationship network. Due to the length and depth of their pathology, some counselees need ongoing help and care, perhaps even lifelong support.

Diagnostically, there is a connection between counselees with this need and dependent personality disorder (DPD). DPD is characterized by a pervasive and excessive need to be taken care of, leading to submissive and clinging behavior and fears of separation.

Apart from counselees who fit this diagnosis, there are some with less severe tendencies toward this interpersonal style. These individuals latch onto their counselor and the counseling process and seem to require it as a regular part of their life. Rather than counseling being for a season of life, they become what I have heard some counselors call "suction-cup" or "Velcro" people. It is easy to start labeling such people, since they tend to generate frustration and eye rolling on the part of counselors.

If we take an attachment view of this phenomenon (see attachment references at the end of the chapter), it is well accepted that everyone needs relationships (i.e., attachments). For some, relationships may provide the safe haven to retreat to and the secure base from which to move back out into the world (i.e., secure attachment; Bowlby, 1988). For others, relationships are to be avoided, and the autonomous self is seen as sufficient (i.e., avoidant attachment). For others, relationships are characterized by anxiety (i.e., anxious attachment) in which the person is chronically worried that the other person will end the relationship or is not as committed to the relationship, resulting in a state of constant anxiety. It is this third category who would have the greatest difficulty in ending counseling. Despite a long-term relationship with a counselor, this person will become anxious about whether he can handle life without the counselor.

Of course, the obvious question is, what does a counselor in this kind of relationship do? First, with a relationship moving toward ending, it is hopefully not the first time in the relationship that the counselor is aware of this tendency toward anxious attachment. Second, the counseling should have been at least somewhat geared toward this tendency of the counselee and the need for the counselee to build a healthy support network. With such counselees it is necessary at times to take quite a while to prepare them for ending a relationship. It can be helpful to repeatedly remind yourself and the counselee that the need underlying this dynamic is healthy. Endings are hard; they should be. But the nature of the counseling relationship, as with the parenting relationship, is that the relationship will end, or at the very least change, and the baby bird needs to launch. Having a job in which you are consciously working yourself out of job sounds kind of self-defeating, but it is the nature of most helping relationships.

A final point: Is it the counselee who is hanging on or the counselor? Examining our own reactions as people helpers to endings is essential.

that will always be their decision, but that my policy is that we have a final face-to-face session. In other words, I ask them to agree to not communicate their intention to stop counseling via an email, phone call, text message, voice mail message or by simply not showing up for sessions. Months later counselees may not remember this agreement, but on being reminded they generally agree to come in. My experience has been that the majority of the time counselees agree to continue counseling once we have openly discussed their reasons for wanting to prematurely end the process.

One counselee balked at seeing me for a final session, saying that he did not see why he had to pay for a session he did not want! He had been obviously angry about something I had said or done, which made it all the more important that we have an opportunity to process what was going on. So I agreed to waive the fee for service, and he came for the session. While he did not want to continue counseling, this final session allowed us to discuss his grievances, and we parted on much better terms.

The counselor should keep in mind that a counselee abruptly ending counseling does not necessarily mean that the counselor did a poor or insufficient job (although it is wise to bring the matter to supervision to see whether you could have done anything to prevent the premature termination). Instead, spend some time answering the reflection questions at the end of this chapter. Behavior is purposeful, and a counselee's decision to leave counseling should be respected and seen as purposeful in some way within the counselee's worldview.

Sometimes a counseling relationship ends before it even begins because you immediately know that you are not the best counselor for a particular counselee. At other times you may have seen a counselee for a period of time and then realize that it would be better to refer her out to someone else. It is not possible for a counselor to be all things to all counselees or even everything to one counselee. You have a unique set of skills, abilities, gifts and personality characteristics that will allow you to work better with some counselees than with others. It is important that counselors learn to recognize their limitations and develop a network of other professionals who are better equipped in the counselor's areas of limitation. This is called a referral list. For example, I (Elisabeth) have only basic clinical training regarding trauma, posttraumatic stress disorder and dissociative disorders; it is not an area in which I have much, if any, expertise. Heather, on the other hand, is a leading expert in the field of trauma therapy. In light of this, when I get a call from prospective counselees who are wanting counseling for past abuse and trauma, I refer them out to Heather and other trauma specialists in our area. Likewise, when I have had counselees who start therapy with one presenting issue (e.g., problems in school) but discover along the way that they actually have bipolar I disorder and could benefit from psychotropic medication, I have referred the counselee to a psychiatrist for a medical and medication evaluation in conjunction with continuing talk therapy. As a counselor I am not trained or legally able to advise a counselee regarding medication; that is the job of a medical doctor.

Referral lists should be made up of individuals and resources in your community that you trust, either through direct knowledge or due to community reputation. Referral lists should contain the names and contact information (i.e., phone number, website, email, address, etc.) of other professionals who specialize in various domains of helping. Possible referral list categories include:

◆ *Addictions counselor and treatment centers:* Addictions counselors, depending on state regulations, can be either bachelor's- or master's-level counselors who specialize in treating chemical or behavioral addictions. Treatment centers can include both detox facilities and addiction rehabilitation facilities. Having contact numbers for local chapters of Alcoholics Anonymous (aa.org), Narcotics Anonymous (na.org), Over-Eaters Anonymous (oa.org), Sexaholics Anonymous (sa.org) and Celebrate Recovery (a Christian twelve-step recovery group, celebraterecovery.org) is also recommended.

◆ *Chaplains:* Chaplains are often provided by a particular organization (e.g., the military, hospitals or corporations) to attend to the spiritual and emotional needs of their constituents. They are often great frontline resources within their given organization.

◆ *Medical doctors:* Maintaining a list of physicians in the area who can address medical concerns of counselees that could directly or indirectly affect counseling is of particular importance when a counselee does not have a primary care physician. Whether it is an endocrine or hormonal imbalance, a chronic illness, chronic pain or any variety of health concerns, getting counselees connected with proper medical care can drastically improve their chances of success in counseling.

◆ *Professional counselors:* Professional counselors are generally licensed, master's-level clinicians. They are usually trained to work with individuals but may work with couples and families as well. Counselors tend to focus on prevention and wellness in addition to psychopathology. They also give particular attention to multicultural counseling and see part of their role as advocacy. Even if you are a professional counselor yourself, having a handful of other clinicians in the area that you respect and trust is important, as no two counselors are the same and you will not always have the time or skill set needed to take on every counselee who calls you.

◆ *Marriage and family therapists:* While both marriage and family therapists and professional counselors may see individuals, couples and families, marriage and family therapists have been trained from a family systems perspective (see chapter fourteen) instead of being taught to view problems as residing within the individual. Particularly for counselees who are struggling in their relational system, a referral to someone who works from a systems perspective may be helpful.

◆ *Psychiatrists:* Psychiatrists are medical doctors who specialize in mental health care, generally through the use of psychopharmaceuticals (i.e. antidepressant, antianxiety and antipsychotic medications). A counselee's primary care physician is generally the first stop in being prescribed such medications, but a psychiatrist has greater knowledge and training regarding these medications and should be used over a primary care physician whenever possible.

◆ *Psychologists:* Psychologists are licensed, doctoral-level clinicians who have been trained in individual and sometimes couples and family counseling. Their training often includes more neuropsychology and psychological assessment than a professional counselor or marriage and family therapist.

◆ *Rehabilitation counselor:* Rehabilitation counselors are generally master's-level clinicians who specialize in working with individuals who have emotional and physical disabilities, helping them to live independently and overcome social and institutional barriers to their disabilities.

◆ *Religious leaders:* This should include individuals of your own faith as well as those of other faiths in your community who are able to work with counselees who have questions about faith, religion or spirituality that are beyond what you can or should offer. Some possible titles for individuals within this category include pastors, rabbis, imams, priests, deacons or other lay ministry leaders.

◆ *Social worker:* A social worker is generally a bachelor's- or master's-level provider and can be a licensed master's-level clinician (Licensed Clinical Social Worker). Social workers are generally best equipped to help counselees with social system concerns such as food, housing, transportation and advocacy, although some master's-level social workers are specifically trained to do therapeutic work as well.

◆ *Spiritual directors:* These individuals are often found within churches or religious organizations. They have specific training in discipleship, spiritual growth and faith development.

Depending on your geographic area and the type of counselees you regularly work with, other referral sources may be more or less pertinent to you.

SUPERVISION

If you are currently studying in a counseling program, one of the new beginnings that awaits you is being part of a supervision process. An important part of any counselor's development is his or her involvement in supervision, both during and after a training program. Most helping professions have an ethical, and sometimes a legal, mandate for trainees and early professionals to work under a more experienced professional for a set period of time. In this way, training as a counselor is much like apprenticeship. It is ideal when a counselor (or supervisee) can identify a supervisor he wants to work under for the purpose of learning specifically from that individual. With that being said, there are plenty of times where supervisors are assigned without input from the supervisee, and much can still be gained by the supervisee in the process.

The supervisor. A supervisor is generally someone within the same or a similar field of counseling or helping as the supervisee. It is the supervisor's responsibility to monitor the work being done by the supervisee, provide guidance in the course of case development and assist the supervisee in both skill development and professional identity development. In some situations a supervisor will watch recorded video of the supervisee with their counselee and provide input, noting counselor strengths and areas for improvement. (It is important to note that both audio- and video-recording of counselees cannot ethically or legally be done without the counselee's written consent. Counselors should consult state law and their professional organization's code of ethics for more details.)

In other situations supervision is a verbal process by which the supervisee recounts the significant elements of the conversations she had with counselees, highlighting areas of strength and areas in which she would like further input or guidance from the supervisor. The supervisor's goal is to ensure that their supervisees' counselees are getting adequate care by monitoring the work of the counselor and continuing the training process. While there will come a time that the counselor has reached a professional level of competency so that regular ongoing supervision is no longer required, there will always be times when a counselor can benefit from consulting another professional on particular cases.

At times a supervisor will focus on teaching or training a supervisee skills or interventions that the supervisee may not have learned in his training program but are relevant to the counselees with whom he is working. At other times a supervisor will focus on the person of the counselor, helping the supervisee gain awareness as to how her unique personality, skills, giftings, emotions and thought processes affect and are affected by the counseling process. At other times the supervisor will serve more as a consultant, taking on a collegial role in case assessment and development. Each role serves a different purpose and has a different place in a counselor's developmental process (see Bernard & Goodyear, 2013, for further discussion of counseling supervision theory). In other words, supervision is a process that serves to expand and develop the counselor's perspective and skills within the counseling relationship.

Empirical Support

Bernard, Clingerman and Gilbride (2011) examined the role that gender and personality type play in supervision interventions. All supervisees in this study were in their first semester of clinical training. The authors discovered, using the language of the Myers-Briggs Type Indicator, "that regardless of supervisor or supervisee personality type or gender, clinical supervision interventions were primarily reported as Intuitive and Perceiving" (p. 166). Beyond this general pattern within supervision, supervisors often chose to engage "in interventions that challenged their supervisees' proclivities" (p. 166).

The supervisee. A supervisee is anyone working under the ongoing instruction and guidance of a more experienced professional. It is the supervisee's responsibility to be open, honest and teachable within the supervisory relationship. Just like counseling, supervision is a collaborative process, and supervisees have a responsibility to share the goals they have for supervision along with the specific areas of growth that they become aware of in themselves as a counselor. This may include various skills or interventions, including more attention to microskills than was given in this initial process.

If a supervisee has the luxury of choosing a supervisor, we recommend two primary methods for supervisor selection. Early in the counselor development process it can be helpful to choose a supervisor who embodies or represents the type of counselor the supervisee thinks she would like to be. In this situation the goal is a supervisor to whom you are similar in theoretical approach, personality or relational style. This allows the supervisee to more easily see what she might be like as a more advanced clinician, drawing from similar personality traits, theoretical orientations and ways of relating. Later in the counselor's developmental process, we recommend finding a supervisor who differs from the supervisee either in theoretical orientation or in his ability to provide more advanced training and guidance in an area of specialty that is of interest to the supervisee. For example, I (Elisabeth) did my initial supervision under an advanced counselor who worked mostly from a rational emotive behavioral therapy approach, like I did. Working with this supervisor allowed for an "at home" feeling in supervision, as he was able to understand, validate and help refine the approach I was naturally wanting to take with counselees. Later in my supervision experience I intentionally chose a supervisor who took a more psychodynamic and attachment theory approach to counseling—two theories that I had very little background or experience in and that are very different from my traditionally cognitive approach. This experience challenged me to see counselees from a new perspective and allowed me to deepen and enrich my own counseling approach, taking the foundation I had and adding to its resources from a completely different way of thinking about a counselee's case. Perhaps the following questions will help you think about your own supervision process.

» What do you hope supervision will be like?

» What about the idea of supervision leaves you anxious?

» From what you know of yourself today, what kind of supervisor would you initially like to look for? Describe his or her personality, style, possible theoretical orientation or primary domain of action and any other characteristics that may be important to you.

RELATIONSHIP APPLICATION

Many counselees have a history strewn with severed relationships that have ended abruptly without ever having been resolved. Therefore ending the counseling relationship well is crucial in helping counselees realize that it is actually possible to end a relationship in a healthy way. This is one reason to not give up easily on having a last session. If counselors do not go the extra mile to ensure that the counseling relationship ends well, they have lost an opportunity to model a valuable relationship skill.

MULTICULTURAL APPLICATION

A collaborative approach to planning for the final session may be particularly important when working crossculturally. We encourage you to find out how goodbyes are said in your counselee's culture. For example, are there particular rituals involved, food shared or tokens exchanged? This discussion can then serve as the foundation for brainstorming about possible meaningful ways for the counseling relationship to end.

If you are an international student or a member of a minority group, or you regularly work with counselees who fit one of these descriptions, it will be important for you to seek out a supervisor who is able to address cultural issues with you. Of particular importance will be the ability of your supervisor to help you determine how your cultural background affects how you perceive your counselees' behavior as well as how to best attend to what you may be communicating to someone of a different cultural group.

If you have studied in a different cultural context than you will ultimately be practicing in, you may need help in modifying your counseling skills to fit the new cultural context. I (Heather) have talked to a number of graduates from programs in Western countries who have attempted to transfer their skills directly to counselees in Asian contexts and have been discouraged when it has not worked well. Finding a supervisor who can help you take the principles you have learned as a student but also help you modify their use in a new context can be immensely valuable.

MINISTRY APPLICATION

In many ministry contexts, termination of the counseling relationship does not necessarily mean that you will not have an ongoing relationship of a different kind with your former counselees. For example, if you are a church-based counselor or pastoral caregiver, you may have contact with them in Bible study groups, church committees and so on. The boundaries are much less clear in informal counseling contexts. But while you may not be saying goodbye for good, there still will be a change in your relationship. It is important that these changes be acknowledged and discussed.

Many years ago I (Heather) I worked at a small Christian undergraduate college where I had multiple roles. In one of my ministry roles I saw some students for counseling. However, I knew that I would run into them in chapel and in the hallways, and perhaps even sit at their table in the dining hall. Some of the debriefing we did in our last session was to discuss such things as, "What will it be like if we are at the same table in the dining hall? How comfortable will you be having more casual conversations after the in-depth issues we have discussed in counseling?" The reality is that the question "How are you?" is a very different one in a counseling context versus a brief exchange on a campus walkway.

CONCLUSION

The end of one season is the beginning of another, and this is where you now find yourself. You have endured through this microskills training process, learning the new language of counseling, growing as both a person and as a future counselor. Well done! As you close this chapter and begin embarking on one that likely includes real-life counselees, we bless you and trust that both you and your counselees will benefit from this journey. May you never stop learning, exploring and growing in all areas of your life.

REFLECTION QUESTIONS

1. What about working with counselees is exciting to you?

2. What about working with counselees feels anxiety provoking to you?

3. How do you handle goodbyes in your life? How might this affect your approach to termination in counseling?

4. How do you feel about this counseling relationship coming to an end? Why?

5. What did you like about working with this counselee?

6. What did you learn from this counselee?

7. What was challenging or difficult for you about working with this counselee?

8. What is something you did in your role as a counselor that could be viewed as a strength or an asset within this counseling relationship?

9. What is something you wish you had (or had not) done to make this counseling relationship better?

10. What is something this counselee did that could be viewed as a strength or an asset within this counseling relationship?

11. What is something this counselee did (or did not) do that hindered this counseling relationship?

12. Where did you see God working in the life of this counselee?

13. How did God use this counselee to affect your growth as a counselor and as a person?

ATTACHMENT REFERENCES

Bartholomew, K., & Horowitz, L. M. (1991). Attachment styles among young adults: A test of a four-category model. *Journal of Personality and Social Psychology, 61*, 226-44.

Bowlby, J. (1988). *A secure base: Clinical applications of attachment theory*. New York, NY: Basic Books.

Clinton, T., & Sibcy, G. (2002). *Attachments: Why you love, feel and act the way you do*. Brentwood, TN: Integrity.

Cooper, M. L., Albino, A. W., Orcutt, H. K., & Williams, N. (2004). Attachment styles and intrapersonal adjustment: A longitudinal study from adolescence into young adulthood. In W. S. Rholes & J. A. Simpson (Eds.), *Adult attachment: Theory, research, and clinical implications* (438-66). New York, NY: Guilford.

Eckert, K. G., & Kimball, C. N. (2003). God as a secure base and haven of safety: Attachment theory as a framework for understanding relationship to God. In T. W. Hall & M. R. McMinn (Eds.), *Spiritual formation, counseling, and psychotherapy* (105-23). New York, NY: Nova Science Publishers.

Johnson, S. M. (2004a). Attachment theory: A guide for healing couple relationships. In W. S. Rholes & J. A. Simpson (Eds.), *Adult attachment: Theory, research, and clinical implications* (367-87). New York, NY: Guilford.

Levine, A., & Heller, R. (2010). *Attached: The new science of adult attachment and how it can help you find—and keep—love*. New York, NY: Tarcher.

Reinert, D. F., Edwards, C. E., & Hendrix, R. R. (2009). Attachment theory and religiosity: A summary of empirical research with implications for counseling Christian clients. *Counseling and Values, 53*, 112-25.

POSTSCRIPT

WE TRUST THIS BOOK HAS BEEN OF HELP in developing your skills for ministry to hurting people. After reading about the skills, the research and the technical aspects of counseling, I (Fred) would like to offer a conclusion to this book, not in the form of a summary or highlighting main points but in the form of a reflection on what motivates me in my vocation of counseling and training counselors.

Early on in my development as a counselor I had the chance to read Henri Nouwen's (1972) classic book *The wounded healer*. The book itself was well worth the investment in time and reflection, but it is the title that has stuck with me over the decades since. My calling as a counselor has been and continues to be to bring healing through the graces of the Holy Spirit from a deep place of woundedness and healing within my own life.

Biblically, Nouwen (1972) roots the image of being wounded healers in the prophetic messianic passage in Isaiah 53, specifically verse 5:

> But he [the Messiah] was pierced for our transgressions,
>> he was crushed for our iniquities;
> the punishment that brought us peace was on him,
>> and by his wounds we are healed.

Jesus, our Messiah, did exactly this. He took our mistakes, failures and wounds, both self-inflicted and caused by others, onto himself and became our healer so that out of our experience of wounding and healing we can become that for others.

David Augsburger (1986), a deeply insightful counselor and wonderful storyteller, reflects on the idea of wounded healers. Drawing from his reflections, I would like to encourage all counselors and would-be counselors who read this to deeply consider these thoughts.

We are all wounded by our own sin and sinfulness (Rom 3:23), and by being sinned against by others. In the midst of and sometimes deeply buried beneath the pain and suffering of life, as creations of God, we reflect God's image (Gen 1:27; 9:6). Through the life, death and resurrection of Christ, the gifts of the Spirit and the healing community around us, we experience some healing moments in life.

However, when I take this into the counseling relationship I soon realize that I cannot heal you any more than you can heal me. Healing comes from God through his Spirit. Thus I, as healer, cannot approach you in your woundedness and be of help.

Perhaps I can show some compassion, but that is all. If we meet "healer" to "wounded," I risk becoming a rescuer, taking full responsibility for you. My helpfulness, my intervention, may actually decrease your ability to heal and may cause you to focus on me instead of God.

Nor can I approach you from my woundedness and help you with your woundedness; in this situation we are likely to only harm each other. If we meet "wound" to "wound," I share and relive my woundedness as I respond to your pain. Our identification with each other may only intensify our pain as I pour my woundedness into your wound and vice versa.

When we meet "wounded" with "wounded" and "healer" to "healer," we will not infect one another, but can stand in each other's presence with understanding and support. We do not rush to rescue each other but call forth God's healing power into each other's lives.

It is only when I, in my awareness of my own woundedness and my acceptance of God's healing in my life, am able to approach you in your woundedness, as well as your capacity to heal, that the Spirit is released to work in and through our relationship for our mutual healing. To try to bring healing any other way will ultimately fail.

It is when my woundedness and capacity to heal connect with your woundedness and capacity to heal that we experience healing. It is when "deep calls to deep" (Ps 42:7) that healing occurs. This is our hope for you in your ministry of healing to others.

A phrase from a Celtic morning prayer captures our prayer for you, and perhaps you can say it as you begin a day of counseling: "That I may be well in my own soul and part of the world's healing this day" (Newell, 2000, p. 41).

ANSWERS TO CHAPTER EXERCISES

CHAPTER 3

Try It Out

1. Counselee: Before I sit down and dive in to what's happened this week, I really need to use your restroom. Where is it?

Request type: *request for information*

2. Counselee: Oh my goodness, you won't believe it! I found out this week that I got a full-ride scholarship to my dream school! I am so excited!

Request type: *request for understanding and involvement*

3. Counselee: I have got a killer migraine today. Could you turn the overhead light off and only have the table lamps on?

Request type: *request for action*

4. Counselee: I don't even know where to begin, this week has been so awful! My babysitter just up and quit last night. I don't know what I'm going to do next week. She was supposed to watch the kids Wednesday through Friday while my husband and I were both away on business trips!

Request type: *request for understanding and involvement*

5. Counselee: Ugh, I just met the other counselor down the hall. I don't know how you work with her. She seems really mean and rather snooty too.

Request type: *request for inappropriate interaction*

6. Counselee: My son just got diagnosed with ADHD. I know that's one of your specialties. Can you tell me a little bit about it?

Request type: *request for information*

7. Counselee: My mother just got diagnosed with Alzheimer's, and I'm just so overwhelmed. I don't know anything about how to care for someone with dementia, and there's just so much to take in. I wish there was an *Alzheimer's for Dummies* book I could read.

Request type: *request for understanding and involvement*

CHAPTER 5

Try It Out

Counselee: Last night was my final dance recital for the year. My dad said he was going to come, but at the last minute he texted my mom to say he wasn't going to make it. It's the third time this month that he's promised to be somewhere but then didn't come. I didn't find out that he wasn't there until after the recital, which was good because I really did do a good job and I'm afraid I would have messed up more if I'd known he'd bailed again.

What's the Content? Identify all of the following that you can:

Who (who is involved in this story? list them all): *the counselee, her dad and her mom*

What (what took place?): *last dance recital of the year, Dad texted to say he wouldn't make it, counselee found out after the recital*

When (when did these events occur?): *last night*

Where (where did this story take place?): *unknown*

How (how did these event take place or come to be?): *Dad texted Mom, counselee found out after the recital*

Check Your Understanding

1. Counselee: I am just swirling with so many different emotions. My brother got arrested for drug possession last night. It's the third time he's been arrested, and I just don't know that he'll ever turn his life around.

Counselor:
a. Your brother got arrested last night for the third time.

Rating: *comparable*

Explanation: *In regard to content, this reflection captures the major elements of the counselee's story. The only thing left out is that it is the brother's third arrest, and depending on the counselee and the context, that may or may not be of great significance.*

b. You're worried about your brother getting arrested.

Rating: *additive*

Explanation: *This response includes a reflection of the counselee's potential emotion and is therefore additive, as reflecting content does not include any explanation or affective reflection.*

c. Your brother has a serious problem with his drug use.

Rating: *additive*

Explanation: *This statement makes an assumption and an evaluative judgment about the counselee's brother, who may or may not be using the drugs he is accused of having within his possession.*

d. Yesterday was a hard day.

Rating: *subtractive*

Explanation: *This reflection is subtractive because it fails to reflect back to the counselee the facts of the story, leaving the counselee to wonder whether the counselor actually heard any of the details.*

2. Counselee: You won't believe everything that happened since I saw you last! My best friend decided to move from out of state to just down the road from me; plus, I got a promotion at work, and I won a vacation from the radio station! It's like every area of life is perfect right now.

Counselor:

a. What I'm hearing you say is that a lot's happened since I saw you last.

Rating: *subtractive*

Explanation: *While accurate, this reflection misses out on the opportunity to reflect that a lot happened for the counselee across multiple domains of life.*

b. In other words, in a very short period of time something wonderful has happened in multiple areas of your life!

Rating: *comparable*

Explanation: *The statement accurately reflects the multiple elements that are of importance to the counselee.*

c. A lot of good things happened since I saw you last, but you still don't have a boyfriend.

Rating: *both additive and subtractive*

Explanation: *Aside from simply being mean, this statement is additive in that it adds content that the counselee has not included themselves, and it is subtractive in that it does not reflect the significant events or facts that are present in the counselee's story.*

d. Your life is perfect.

Rating: *both additive and subtractive*

Explanation: *This statement is additive in that it generalizes the counselee's content about specific life arenas to include her entire life, and it is subtractive in that it neglects to reflect the important details that the counselee did communicate.*

Anytime Activity

Find the Facts

Vignette 1:

Counselee: Oh my goodness, you would not believe the weekend I've had! It was just the best! On Friday my best friend surprised me and flew into town for my thirtieth birthday. We went to my favorite restaurant for dinner, and then Saturday we got to go to breakfast before spending the day hiking. Then in the evening my best friend had arranged for a group of friends to all meet at my favorite restaurant for dinner and karaoke. It was just an amazing weekend!

Counselor: *In other words, you had a really eventful weekend when your best friend made a surprise visit to celebrate your birthday.*

Vignette 2:

Counselee: I just don't know what I'm going to do. I found out yesterday that my company is downsizing. My boss informed me yesterday that at least half of our department will be without a job by the end of the year. I don't know what to do.

Counselor: *What I'm hearing you say is that you recently found out that half of your depart-ment could be without a job by the end of the year.*

Vignette 3:

Counselee: Prom is in two weeks, and I'm *so* excited! Jack asked me to be his date, and I couldn't be happier. I bought this beautiful blue dress with sequins. It makes my eyes really shine. Jack and I are going to double-date with my friend Kate and her boyfriend, Zach. It going to be the best night ever!

Counselor: *In other words, prom is coming up, you have a great blue dress, and you get to go as a double date.*

Vignette 4:

Counselee: Tomorrow's football game is going to be really important. My coach has said that scouts from three major universities are coming to check me out. This game could mean the difference between a college scholarship or working through school.

Counselor: *What I'm hearing you say is that the scouts who are coming to the game tomorrow night could offer you a scholarship.*

Vignette 5:

Counselee: Next week I'm going to China on a business trip. I've never been to Asia before, and I'm kind of nervous. I'm not quite sure what to expect. Plus this is a really big deal for our company, and I want to make sure everything goes to plan.

Counselor: *In other words, you're heading to China next week for business, and this trip is significant for multiple reasons.*

CHAPTER 6

Try It Out

Scenario 1:

Counselee: I'm so disappointed. Last night was my final dance recital for the year. My dad said he was going to come, but at the last minute he texted my mom to say he wasn't go-ing to make it. It's the third time this month that he's promised to be somewhere but then didn't come. I didn't find out that he wasn't there until after the recital, which was good because I really did do a good job and I'm afraid I would have messed up more if I'd known he'd bailed again.

Explicit emotions: *disappointed (-)*

Implicit emotions: *hurt (-), let down (-), relieved (+), rejected (-), unimportant (-)*

(Note that other implicit emotions may be present but are likely to fall within the same broad categories of those listed)

Reflection of feeling, option 1: *You feel disappointed.*

Reflection of feeling, option 2: *You feel hurt.*

Reflection of feeling, option 3: *You feel let down.*

(Note that any of the options given would be equally as appropriate. The response is likely to depend on the personality of the counselor, the relationship with the counselee and the surrounding context.)

Scenario 2:

Counselee: Oh my goodness, I am so excited I can't even stand it! I just found out that I got accepted to my top choice for college *and* I got a scholarship too! I feel like I'm in a dream. I never thought this would actually become a reality. There is so much to do between now and August, my head is spinning with excitement!

Explicit emotions: *excited (+), dreamy (+), spinning (+)*

Implicit emotions: *ecstatic (+), surprised (+), overwhelmed (+)*

(Note that for both "spinning" and "overwhelmed" the emotion could be either positive or negative depending on the context.)

Reflection of feeling: *You feel ecstatic!*

Check Your Understanding

1. Counselee: I am just so pissed, I can't believe my brother pawned my drum set!

Counselor: Whoa. I can't believe he did that. What did he pawn it for?

Rating: *subtractive*

Explanation: *This response has no affective reflection and therefore is subtractive. It uses inappropriate counselor commentary and asks a question that is not relevant to the counselee's process.*

Counselor: You feel kind of upset.

Rating: *subtractive*

Explanation: *While "upset" may be an accurate reflect feeling, adding "kind of" to the reflection serves to minimize the relevance or acceptability of the counselee's feeling.*

Counselor: You feel irate.

Rating: *comparable*

Explanation: *The word* irate *is a comparable synonym for the counselee's use of the slang word* pissed.

Counselor: Your brother pawned your drum set.

Rating: *subtractive*

Explanation: *While this is a well-formulated content reflection, it includes no emotion and is therefore subtractive.*

2. Counselee: I can't believe it! I got accepted to Harvard for law school!

Counselor: You feel ecstatic!

Rating: *comparable*

Explanation: *The counselee's use of exclamatory statements, coupled with her statement of disbelief, communicate her high level of excitement.*

Counselor: You're excited because you got into Harvard.

Rating: *additive*

Explanation: *While the emotion in this reflection ("excited") is comparable and accurate, the inclusion of an explanation as to why the counselee feels excited makes this reflection additive. Remember this for chapter seven, as it is a perfectly formulated empathic reflection.*

Counselor: What kind of law do you want to practice?

Rating: *subtractive*

Explanation: *This response has no affective reflection and therefore is subtractive. It asks a question that is not relevant to the counselee's process at this time.*

Counselor: You feel shocked.

Rating: *comparable*

Explanation: *Given the counselee's exclamation of disbelief, this may be a very accurate feeling reflection.*

3. Counselee: I just don't get it. I studied and studied and studied. How did I fail that midterm?

Counselor: You feel betrayed.

Rating: *additive (if accurate)*

Explanation: Betrayed *is a very strong word that goes beyond what the counselee explicitly states. If the counselee agrees that the word* betrayed *is a good fit for what the counselee is actually experiencing, it is additive. If the counselee was not trying to imply that her failing the test was due to someone else's deception or manipulation, then* betrayed *significantly adds to what is likely disappointment, discouragement, confusion or anger.*

Counselor: You feel really confused.

Rating: *comparable*

Explanation: *The use of the modifier of* really *adds weight or emphasis to the affective word con-fused. This amplifier reflects the level of confusion or disbelief that is expressed by the counselee.*

Counselor: Man, that's really disappointing.

Rating: *subtractive*

Explanation: *While the counselee may be feeling disappointment, this reflection places the emotion in the situation rather than within the counselee.*

Counselor: You feel confident.

Rating: *subtractive*

Explanation: *While the counselee was feeling confident before the exam, she is not currently feeling confident. As such, this feeling reflection misses the counselee's current emotion and is therefore subtractive.*

CHAPTER 7

Check Your Understanding

1. Counselee: Every day at school Jayden takes my lunch. I don't want to be a tattletale, but I get really hungry.

Counselor: Dude, that's totally a bummer.

Rating: *empathy level 1*

Explanation: *While the response minimally acknowledges the negative quality of the counsel-ee's situation, the response is unprofessional, minimizes the counselee's emotion and does not actually reflect an affective word or the content of the counselee's situation.*

Counselor: You feel confused about what to do when Jayden takes your lunch.

Rating: *empathy level 3*

Explanation: *Depending on the counselee's personality, demeanor and delivery, the affective word here could be* confused *(truly doesn't know what to do),* angry *or* frustrated. *This re-sponse accurately reflects the counselee's feeling and content without making it bigger or smaller than the counselee communicated*

Counselor: What a jerk! I bet that makes you super mad.

Rating: *empathy level 1.5*

Explanation: *In this response, the affective word may be accurate, but it is stated in a way that "tells" the counselee how to feel rather than reflecting how the counselee feels. It also is highly inappropriate to place value on or call the third party a name.*

Counselor: I remember when I was in third grade and this kid, Tyler, always took my lunch. Finally, one day, I just punched him, and he never took my lunch again!

Rating: *empathy level 1*

Explanation: *This response completely ignores the feelings of the counselee and makes the exchange about the counselor, utilizing the verbal villain of the historian.*

2. Counselee: Pastor Tim, I really want to go on the high school camping trip this weekend, but because I broke curfew last week my parents said I can't go. It's just not fair!

Counselor: It sounds like you're angry that something you did last week is affecting what you want to do this week.

Rating: *empathy level 3*

Explanation: *Both the feelings and content of the counselee's statement are reflected, and done so without judgment, agreement or taking sides.*

Counselor: Well, I guess you did it to yourself, huh? If you hadn't broken curfew you'd get to come. Maybe next time you'll think ahead a little more.

Rating: *empathy level 1*

Explanation: *This response utilizes the hangman verbal villain, blaming the counselee for his/her feelings.*

Counselor: I'm really sorry, Kaitlyn, I know you wanted to come camping with everyone. Maybe next time.

Rating: *empathy level 1.5 or 2*

Explanation: *This response has no affective reflection and attempts to rescue the counselee from her negative emotion.*

Counselor: Maybe you should talk to your parents again and see whether they can move your punishment to another weekend.

Rating: *empathy level 1*

Explanation: *This response has no affective reflection, attempts to tell the counselee what to do and potentially undermines the parent-child relationship.*

3. Counselee: I just don't know what to do. It's my senior year of college, and all my friends know exactly what they want to do with their lives, and many of them already have jobs lined up, but I feel just as confused as I did before I began college. I wish I knew what God wanted for my future.

Counselor: It can be really difficult to navigate major life transitions when you're confused about where you're going and what God wants for you.

Rating: *empathy level 2*

Explanation: *This response implies that the counselee may be confused but does not directly reflect it, thus distancing the counselee from the emotion of the situation.*

Counselor: I wonder who you've talked to about this dilemma and what kind of suggestions they've had for you.

Rating: *empathy level 1*

Explanation: *This response jumps to problem solving without any reflection whatsoever. It also places responsibility for the dilemma outside the counselee.*

Counselor: Well, Jacob, I think I know you pretty well, and I've always wondered whether God was calling you into missions work. You love people, you enjoy learning about new cultures and you pick up languages easily. I don't know, but maybe it's something you should consider.

Rating: *empathy level 1*

Explanation: *This response does not reflect content or emotion and goes straight for giving advice.*

Counselor: As you look at your life after college approaching you feel really uncertain as to what's next.

Rating: *empathy level 3*

Explanation: *This response accurately reflects the feeling of "uncertain" and the content of what to do after college.*

4. Counselee: My husband and I just can't seem to get on the same page! I can't keep having this same fight over and over again. It's maddening!

Counselor: You feel exasperated by the ongoing conflict between you and your husband.

Rating: *empathy level 3*

Explanation: *This response accurately summarizes the content of the counselee's statement while also reflecting the intensity of the counselee's emotion (exasperated).*

Counselor: You're aggravated because you and your husband can't seem to find resolution on this topic.

Rating: *empathy level 3*

Explanation: *This would also be an appropriate response, as it accurately reflects content and* aggravated *is within the same category of emotion as* maddening *and* exasperated, *although slightly on a lesser level.*

Counselor: Man, that's really annoying. I hate it when my spouse and I can't come to an agreement. I don't know how you've put up with it for so long.

Rating: *empathy level 1*

Explanation: *This response completely turns the conversation onto the counselor and also adds judgment to both the counselee and her spouse.*

Counselor: At least your husband is talking to you. That's an improvement from last month. I know it would be nice if you could come to an agreement, but look on the bright side.

Rating: *empathy level 1*

Explanation: *This response negates the counselee's emotion and attempts to put a flowery bandage over the situation by telling the counselee how she should look at the situation.*

5. Counselee: I'm really sad. My daughter, her husband and their three children are moving away at the end of next month. Our family has always lived so close together, and now they're moving halfway across the country. I know it's the right decision, and it's in their best interest as far as personal and professional growth, but I'm just so sad to see them go.

Counselor: I completely understand your sadness. It's hard to see family move far away.

Rating: *empathy level 2*

Explanation: *This response places the emotion (sadness) outside the counselee by making it something the counselor "understands" rather than reflecting it as an emotion the counselee possesses.*

Counselor: Why are they moving so far away? Did one of them get a really great job, or why couldn't they find something here in the area?

Rating: *empathy level 1*

Explanation: *The detective verbal villain dominates this response, asking curiosity details to appease the counselor rather than facilitate the counselee's process. There is no reflecting feeling or content.*

Counselor: It feels bittersweet to see your children make good choices for themselves when those same good choices take them away from you.

Rating: *empathy level 3*

Explanation: *The affective word* bittersweet *accurately captures the conflicted nature of the counselee's statement. The content reflected here accurately summarizes the whole concept rather than simply the details.*

Counselor: I know it's sad, but think of how much fun you'll have getting to visit them in their new home and all the great memories you guys will make exploring their new city!

Rating: *empathy level 1.5*

Explanation: *While the emotion is in the ballpark, this response places the emotion on the situation ("it's sad") rather than placing it within the counselee. This response also seeks to tell the counselee how they should look at the situation rather than reflecting how they do see the situation.*

Try it Out

Section A:

1. Female counselee: I cannot believe it, I was so shocked this weekend when David proposed! It was the best birthday present ever!

Feeling: *elated, overjoyed*

Content: *David's unexpected marriage proposal*

Counselor: You feel elated because of David's unexpected marriage proposal.

(Note: While a word like surprised *or* stunned *could be a synonym for* shocked *or the feelings behind "I cannot believe it," the overall sense of what is being expressed is elation, or joy.* Excitement *is possibly subtractive; one could say "very excited.")*

2. Counselee: I just don't know what I'm going to do. My babysitter canceled for tonight, and I have this work dinner that I absolutely cannot miss. If I'm not there I could literally lose my job, and now I only have an hour to find a new babysitter.

Feeling: *frantic*

Content: *it's essential that you find childcare and you don't know how that will be possible in such a short period of time*

Counselor: You feel frantic because it's essential that you find childcare and you don't know how that will be possible in such a short period of time.

3. Counselee: I just found out I didn't get into the college I wanted. I am really, really disappointed, and now I have no idea what I'm supposed to do come next fall.

Feeling: *saddened, discouraged, upset*

Content: *your plans to get into the college you had your heart set on have been thwarted, and you don't have a plan B*

Counselor: You feel discouraged because your plans to get into the college you had your heart set on have been thwarted, and you don't have a plan B.

4. Counselee: I was convinced I lost my wallet this morning on the bus, but this amazing person found my wallet with my business card inside and brought the wallet to my office before lunch. I don't know what I would have done if he hadn't been so kind.

Feeling: *amazed, grateful*

Content: *someone went to a lot of trouble to get your wallet back to you*

Counselor: You feel so grateful because someone went to a lot of trouble to get your wallet back to you.

5. Counselee: I work so hard, and my boss never seems to notice. I stay later than everyone else, I volunteer more than anyone else, and all I want is a simple recognition that I'm an asset to our team. Is that too much to ask?

Feeling: *discouraged, deflated*

Content: *all your efforts to please your boss seem to have been for nothing*

Counselor: You feel discouraged because all your efforts to please your boss seem to have been for nothing

Section B:

6. Counselee: Oh my goodness, last night was horrific! I was walking up on stage to sing my solo and completely tripped over *nothing*! My sheet music went everywhere as I landed on my hands and knees. It was awful!

Feeling: *embarrassed, humiliated*

Content: *you fell last night as you got up to perform*

Counselor: You feel embarrassed/humiliated because you fell last night as you got up to perform.

7. Child counselee: It's just not fair, every other kid in school gets a new backpack every year, but not me. My mom says mine is still in good shape and I don't need a new one. I know it looks fine, but I want a new one like everyone else!

Feeling: *upset, disappointed, ticked off*

Content: *you wanted a new backpack and your mom wouldn't get you one*

Counselor: You feel ticked off because you wanted a new backpack and your mom wouldn't get you one.

8. Adolescent counselee: I just moved here at the beginning of the semester, and I miss my old friends. It's really hard being the new person and not knowing anyone. I wish I had better friends here, or just some people I could hang out with on the weekends.

Feeling: *lonely, homesick*

Content: *you just moved and don't have a good social network here yet*

Counselor: You feel lonely because you just moved and don't have a good social network here yet.

9. Student Counselee: I just got my grade back from my statistics midterm and found out I made an A! I studied so hard for that exam, I can't believe it actually paid off!

Feeling: *excited, elated, thrilled*

Content: *your efforts resulted in such a good grade on your statistics exam*

Counselor: You feel thrilled that your efforts resulted in such a good grade on your statistics exam.

10. Counselee: I feel unbelievably sad after this morning. I had to take my dog to the vet and have him put down.

Feeling: *sorrowful, depressed*

Content: *you had to have your dog put to sleep this morning*

Counselor: You feel sorrowful because you had to have your dog put to sleep this morning.

CHAPTER 8

Check Your Understanding

Counselee 1: Today was the best day ever! From beginning to end it was just amazing. I truly couldn't have asked for it to go better.

Prompt: Tell me more about this amazing day.

Open question: What was it about today that felt so amazing?

Signpost: Amazing!

Counselee 2: I don't know what I'm going to do. I am just so devastated by the fact that I didn't get the promotion at work that I was up for. I mean, I just don't understand how that happened.

Prompt: Tell me more about feeling devastated.

Open question: What is it about not getting the promotion that feels so devastating?

Signpost: Devastated.

Counselee 3: I know I need to have this conversation with my mom, but it's just tricky.

Prompt: Tell me more about it being tricky.

Open question: What is it about having this conversation that feels tricky?

Signpost: Tricky.

CHAPTER 9

Check Your Understanding

Counselee: I don't know what I'm going to do! I can't believe my dad is making us move right before my senior year of high school. It's so unfair! I have lived in this house my whole life; this is where my friends are, where my church is and where all my memories are. How can they ask me to start over now? My parents should know that I don't like change, I don't make friends easily, and that I'm really shy. I wish we didn't have to move. I just want everything to stay the same.

Counselor: You feel angry because your family is moving.

Skill: *empathic reflection*

Empathy rating: *level 3*

Explanation: *Response includes the feeling (anger) and the content (moving) that the counselee has presented. It does not add or subtract from the counselee's story.*

Counselor: You feel scared.

Skill: *reflecting feeling*

Empathy rating: *level 2.5*

Explanation: *Depending on how the counselor uses nonverbal communication with this statement, it could be perceived as level 3 empathy as it accurately reflects the counselee's emotion. But it technically lacks connection to the counselee's content, making it a reflection of feeling and not a complete empathic reflection.*

Counselor: Moving is really hard. I'd be super upset too, if I were you.

Skill: *attempted empathy and attempted authenticity/self-disclosure*

Empathy rating: *level 1*

Explanation: *Empathy may have been attempted here, but the counselor does not use it appropriately. "Moving is really hard" is a commentary on the content rather than directly on the feelings of the counselee. Therefore it is unclear whether* hard *refers to emotionally difficult or physically difficult. "I'd be super upset too" is also unclear. The word* upset *could be an attempt at reflecting feeling, but because the counselor uses first person it sounds more like a self-disclosure. While we will discuss the role of self-disclosure in chapter twelve, this statement does not follow the guidelines for the skill of self-disclosure and only serves to draw attention to the counselor's emotions and to exacerbate the counselee. This is just not a good response any way you look at it!*

Counselor: You feel scared because stability is really important to you.

Skill: *intuitive empathy*

Empathy rating: *level 4.5*

Explanation: *The counselee has not directly talked about stability but has implied its importance in the other elements of his or her statement. Additionally, the emotion of scared has not been directly stated, but the way the counselee describes her objections to the move communicates an underlying fear connected to making friends, starting over, etc.*

Counselee: I got the job! I got the job! I got the job! I worked so hard for this, and I can't believe it all finally paid off. Ever since I was in high school I wanted to be a doctor. I'd watch movies and TV shows about people who had mysterious illnesses and would see how the doctors worked so hard to find ways to heal people. It was so amazing to me. And here I am now with a job at the Center for Disease Control. Being on the front lines of disease and death, but knowing I might be able to offer someone a chance at renewed health, there's no greater calling than that.

Counselor: Ugh, I get nauseous just thinking about anything medical.

Skill: *attempted self-disclosure*

Empathy rating: *level 1*

Explanation: *This statement goes completely off-script from any counseling skills available to you. This statement does not follow the guidelines for the skill of self-disclosure (see chapter twelve) and only serves to draw attention to the counselor's emotions and to minimize the counselee's interests and excitement.*

Counselor: You feel overjoyed at the opportunity to work for the CDC!

Skill: *empathic reflection*

Empathy rating: *level 3*

Explanation: *The emotion of "overjoyed" pulls together much of the counselee's stated emotions and descriptions. Rather than parroting back one emotion from the counselee, the emotion of "overjoyed" serves to reflect the cumulative feelings presented by the counselee. This does not add to the counselee's statement or understanding but serves as a mirror, thus making it a level 3 empathic reflection.*

Counselor: You feel invigorated working as a doctor because being able to care for the health of others is so important to you.

Skill: *intuitive empathy*

Empathy rating: *level 4*

Explanation: *This statement pulls together various elements of the counselee's statement but goes deeper into his or her motivations for being a doctor, not just his or her feelings about doing the job itself.*

Counselor: What is it about being a doctor that makes you feel alive?

Skill: *clarifying: open question*

Empathy Rating: *level 2*

Explanation: *While this is an accurate open question, the timing is inappropriate. The counselee first needs to know that counselor has heard the excitement about getting this new job and be present with the counselee in that moment of celebration. As such, even a well-formulated question can be contrary to empathy when asked at the wrong time. Despite the inappropriate timing, the counselor does reflect feelings accurately.*

Counselee: My dear Joe continues to decline. I've been able to care for him at home for the last year, but his Alzheimer's is getting so bad that I don't know how much longer I can keep him at home. After fifty-seven years of marriage, I can't imagine our home without Joe in it. But I also can't imagine how I can give him the level of care he needs right now. I've contacted various nursing homes in the area, and I think I know which one will be best for Joe, but I feel like I'm failing him. I'm his wife, I should be the one taking care of him, that's what I promised fifty-seven years ago. But maybe taking care of him means getting him better care than I can offer. Oh! I'm going to miss my Joe."

Counselor: Joe's Alzheimer's is getting worse, and you don't know what do to.

Skill: *reflecting content*

Empathy rating: *level 2*

Explanation: *This is not an inaccurate reflection, but while the counselee could perceive "you don't know what to do" as a reflection of her emotion, it is not actually an affective reflection. At the beginning of a session, this may be very appropriate as you build rapport with a counselee. But if there is a well-established relationship already, this content reflection may be perceived by the counselee as the counselor being "behind" the counselee or not "keeping up" with the emotional depth of the story.*

Counselor: You feel like a failure because you have to put Joe in a nursing home.

Skill: *empathic reflection*

Empathy rating: *level 2*

Explanation: *While the counselee has said she feels like a failure, it is not the underlying or even the most prevalent emotion in her story. For the counselor to focus on this emotion could serve as unintended affirmation to the counselee that she is in fact a failure. The focus of this reflection also communicates being "behind" the counselee, which can disrupt trust between the counselee and the counselor.*

Counselor: You feel torn because you want the best care for Joe, and that means putting him in a nursing home.

Skill: *empathic reflection*

Empathy rating: *level 3*

Explanation: *This statement captures the feeling (torn) and the two elements of content: (1) wanting good care for Joe and (2) putting him in a nursing home. It does not add meaning, motivation or values to the counselee's story, thus serving as a basic reflection.*

Counselor: You feel deep grief because Alzheimer's is taking your husband from you.

Skill: *intuitive empathy*

Rating: *level 4*

Explanation: *While this statement is not in perfect formula, it does capture the core element of intuitive empathy: going deeper and adding to the surface presentation of the counselee's story. Grief summarizes the underlying cause of the counselee's other, stated, emotions. Additionally, her grief is over the loss of relationship with her husband of fifty-seven years, both a literal and a figurative loss as he has not yet died but is changed by Alzheimer's.*

CHAPTER 10

Check Your Understanding

1. Counselee: I feel like I'm living in a soap opera!

Counselor: It's like things are spinning out of control!

Type of response: *creating and delivering*

Evaluation: *"Spinning out of control" is a different metaphor. Whether it is an accurate one or not would depend on how the counselee responds to it. For example, if the counselee enthusiastically agrees or expands on it, the counselee will have felt heard. If they respond, "Well . . . not really!" then the counselor has not received the message.*

Counselor: You just never expected that there would be so much drama in your life. It all feels unbelievable to you.

Type of response: *extending and explicating*

Evaluation: *Use of the word* drama *fits within the same metaphor as "soap opera," so the meaning is just being extended. The word* unbelievable *is a reflection of feeling that serves to make the implicit meaning of the metaphor more explicit.*

Counselor: What feels like the most important scene?

Type of response: *extending*

Evaluation: *Using the word* scene *is staying within the counselee's metaphor.*

2. Counselee: It's like he's just trampling me underfoot.

Counselor: You're feeling kicked around and ground into the dust.

Type of response: *extending*

Evaluation: *The response stays within the counselee's metaphor of being trampled.*

Counselor: What's it like to feel trampled underfoot?

Type of response: *explicating*

Evaluation: *The counselor is attempting to find out more about the meaning of the metaphor through clarifying.*

It's like you feel disregarded, and it hurts so much.

Type of response: *explicating*

Evaluation: *Empathic reflection is used to make the implicit explicit.*

3. Counselee: I feel like I'm drowning.

Counselor: The waves are just so huge that you're trying to stay afloat, but you keep getting pulled under.

Type of response: *extending*

Evaluation: *The counselor continues to use the metaphor of drowning.*

Counselor: You're feeling totally overwhelmed.

Type of response: *explicating*

Evaluation: *Empathic reflection is used to find out more about what the counselee is communicating.*

Counselor: It's like everything is crashing down on you.

Type of response: *creating and delivering*

Evaluation: *A new metaphor is used to describe the counselee's experience.*

CHAPTER 11

Check Your Understanding

1. Adolescent counselee: It's just not fair! I thought Erin and I were friends, but then she goes and talks about me behind my back to Stephanie. I mean, fine, if she wants to be that way, I don't want to be her friend either!

Counselor: Sounds like normal junior high stuff to me.

Rating: *level 1 confrontation; level 1 empathy*

Explanation: *Completely invalidated counselee's experience (level one empathy) and over-looked any potential discrepancies in the counselee's statement (level one confrontation).*

Counselor: On the one hand you want to be friends with Erin, but on the other you're hurt and want to walk away.

Rating: *level 3 confrontation; level 3 empathy*

Explanation: *Overtly addresses potential discrepancies using reflection; reflects counselee's feelings (hurt) and content (want to be friends and want to walk away).*

Counselor: What a jerk! I bet that makes you super mad.

Rating: *level 1 confrontation; level 1.5 empathy*

Explanation: *Does not address the potential discrepancies (level one confrontation); accurately identifies the emotion of "mad" but without content, and resorts to name-calling and siding with the counselee (level 1.5 empathy).*

Counselor: I can tell you're really hurt by Erin gossiping about you rather than coming to you directly about what's bothering you, but I'm also kind of confused, because just last week you told me you were angry at Stephanie and talked to Erin about it, but you didn't let Stephanie know how you felt!

Rating: *level 5 confrontation; level 4 empathy*

Explanation: *The counselee is not aware that her friend is exhibiting exactly the same behavior that she herself has done. The counselor pointing it out is, therefore, getting at something that is below her level of awareness (level five confrontation). The counselor saying "I'm also kind of confused" takes some of the sting out of the confrontation and will hopefully allow the coun-selee to receive it without getting too defensive. The counselee's surface feeling is anger, so re-flecting back "hurt" is intuitive empathy (level four empathy). The formula is implicitly there, although the words "on the one hand," etc., have not been actually used.*

2. Counselee: UCLA has always been my dream school. Who wouldn't want to go to school in LA? But, while I've been accepted, I just found out that I didn't get any scholar-ships, and I just don't know that I can afford out-of-state tuition. I don't know what I'm going to do.

Counselor: On the one hand, you really want to go to UCLA, but on the other hand, it's outside your budget.

Rating: *level 3 confrontation; level 2 empathy*

Explanation: *Accurately reflects the apparent discrepancies between the counselee's wants and his or her finances (level three confrontation); while tone and delivery could still be experi-enced as empathic by the counselee, the statement itself does not directly link emotions with content. However, "You really want to go to UCLA" implies emotion, even if affective language is not used (level two empathy).*

Counselor: Wow, Josh, that is a tough spot to be in. Going to UCLA could be a dream come true for you, but weighing the financial wisdom of such a decision seems to have taken away some of the initial excitement of getting accepted.

Rating: *level 5 confrontation; level 4 empathy*

Explanation: *The confrontation is direct and yet still communicates a high level of respect and caring for Josh and his process, pointing out the conflicting emotion that Josh is demonstrating between being excited about his acceptance to UCLA but also feeling conflicted or burdened by the financial decision. Intuitive empathy, level four, is demonstrated by the counselor's reflection of the initial feeling of excitement being in conflict with the feeling of needing to be financially responsible.*

Counselor: On the one hand, you got accepted to UCLA, but on the other hand, you didn't get a scholarship.

Rating: *level 1 confrontation; N/A empathy*

Explanation: *While the statement reflects two conflicting pieces of content, they are not apparent contradictions within the counselee's story, as they do not reflect discrepancies in behavior, affect or cognition. If the counselor had said, "On the one hand, you are excited you got accepted to UCLA, but on the other hand, you're disappointed that you didn't get a scholarship," then a level 3 confrontation would exist. So while the formula looks as though it has been used, it really has not been. Only content is reflected in this statement, without mention or connection to emotion (N/A empathy).*

Counselor: I'm really sorry, Josh, I know you really wanted to go to UCLA.

Rating: *level 1 confrontation; level 1 empathy*

Explanation: *Overlooked any possible discrepancies (level one confrontation); assumed conclusion that counselee will not be attending UCLA, which disregards his expressed emotion of tension or uncertainty as to what he should do (level one empathy).*

3. Counselee: So here's my dilemma. I have two amazing job offers on the table, which is a blessing in and of itself. One job lets me stay here, near my extended family, but pays less and doesn't offer quite the growth possibilities. The other job requires that I move out of state but pays more and has more opportunities for advancement. I love my family, but I just don't know that I can pass up this opportunity out of state.

Counselor: It can be really difficult to navigate major life transitions when you're confused about where you're going and what God wants for you.

Rating: *level 1 confrontation; level 1 empathy*

Explanation: *Does not address possible areas of confrontation (level one confrontation); over-spiritualizes response, given that counselee makes no mention of spiritual tension; and neglects to reflect the relational and professional tension that counselee is expressing (level one empathy).*

Counselor: What is it about taking the job out of state that feels so appealing to you?

Rating: *level 1 confrontation; level 1 empathy*

Explanation: *While this is a well-formed open question, it does not address potential discrepancies (level one confrontation), nor does it acknowledge the feelings or content that the counselee has already expressed related to taking the job out of state (level one empathy).*

Counselor: On the one hand, your family is really important to you, but on the other hand, so is your professional growth.

Rating: *level 3 confrontation; level 3.5 empathy*

Explanation: *Accurately addresses the possible discrepancies in the counselee's story (level three confrontation) and accurately identifies the counselee's high value on family (level 3.5 empathy).*

Counselor: Josh, it sounds as though you're really conflicted about this situation. You are excited about the possibilities for advancement at the out-of-state job, but I'm a little confused because last week you told me that you wanted to prioritize spending more time with your family.

Rating: *level 4.5 confrontation; level 4 empathy*

Explanation: *This is a direct confrontation that addresses an issue that has come up previously but was not part of the current discussion. In that sense the counselee does not seem aware of the blatant discrepancy (level 4.5 confrontation). Notice that the structure of the formula is there implicitly without the "on the one hand" phrase being used. The use of the word con-flicted is slightly additive. The counselee does not use an affective word, but excitement is im-plied (level 3.5 empathy).*

CHAPTER 12

Check Your Understanding

Counselee: I studied really hard for my midterms and got the results back yesterday. I got As in all five of my exams! Can you believe it?

Counselor: That's great, Dennis! I'm really proud of you!

Rating: *level 4*

Explanation: *The counselor is being authentic, expressing his or her feelings spontaneously. The "I'm really proud of you" comment could be a little problematic in that the counselee might want to continue to please the counselor rather than finding internal motivation for working hard in school. As an isolated comment this would not be a huge deal, but if there were a pat-tern of this kind of authentic response it could be counterproductive in the long run.*

Counselor: That's terrific, Dennis! It's wonderful to see you so excited about the results of your hard work!

Rating: *level 4.5*

Explanation: *This response is similar to the response above in that the counselor is spontane-ously sharing his or her feelings. However, it is a better response because when the counselor states "It's wonderful to see you so excited" he or she is sharing his or her own emotional response (i.e., "wonderful"), but the counselor's happiness is focused on the counselee's excitement about his exam results. Therefore, there is less likelihood that the counselee will continue to work hard in school in order to please the counselor.*

Counselor: It's about time you actually put some effort into your studies!

Rating: *level 1*

Explanation: *The response is judgmental, focusing on the errors of not having put effort into his studies in the past rather than focusing on the positives in the current situation.*

Counselor: Now that you've proven you can do it, maybe you should apply to that graduate program you said you were interested in!

Rating: *level 2.5*

Explanation: *While the counselor may be authentically stating his or her opinion, the response is indirectly giving advice. Advanced authentic responses will be more direct and more respectful in their delivery.*

CHAPTER 13

Try It Out

1. Counselee: Gabriel has come to see you because he "feels angry all the time." He says the anger started when he did not get into the college he wanted and had to settle for a state school in his hometown. Gabriel says that "ever since college, nothing has gone my way. It's like the world is out to keep me down."

Domain(s) of growth: *affective*

Rationale: *Gabriel seems to be lacking some self-awareness as to the role he plays in his own story.*

Domain(s) of growth: *cognitive*

Rationale: *The absolutist language that Gabriel uses in saying that "nothing" has gone his way leaves room to explore where there might be exceptions to this perception and to challenge the all-or-nothing thinking that Gabriel is demonstrating.*

2. Counselee: Laura is the mother of fifteen-year-old Grace. Laura is "fed up" with Grace's continued delinquency from school and her disrespectful attitude at home. Laura has come to you for recommendations on what to do next.

Domain(s) of growth: *behavioral*

Rationale: *While further counseling may uncover a need to address affective or cognitive domains, on the surface this involves a behavioral growth strategy in providing Laura with practical to-dos in how to talk with, set boundaries with and discipline Grace.*

3. Counselee: Take the previous scenario, but this time fifteen-year-old Grace is your counselee. She is angry with her mom for "micromanaging" and wishes mom would just "leave me alone to do my own thing." Grace claims her choices should only affect her and that it shouldn't matter to her mom because it's Grace's life.

Domain(s) of growth: *affective*

Rationale: *Grace appears to lack awareness as to how her behavior and attitude affect those around her. It may be beneficial to help Grace focus on developing greater self-awareness as to the motives and goals behind her behavior, as well as the implication of those behaviors on those around her.*

4. Counselee: Diane is a thirty-eight-year-old single female who has never been married. She's come to counseling because her most recent relationship just ended after three years. She tells you that she just can't seem to find joy or meaning in life anymore and feels as if God doesn't care about her or her happiness. She denies any suicidal ideation but feels like her life is a waste of pointless monotony.

Domain(s) of growth: *cognitive*

Rationale: *Similar to Gabriel, Diane's language is all on the "negative" side of the emotional scale. Utilizing skills in reframing and confrontation could prove helpful to Diane.*

Domain(s) of growth: *affective*

Rationale: *Diane may also lack the ability to express the totality of her emotions. Using empathy and intuitive empathy with Diane may facilitate the development of her own self-awareness and ability to remain in the present rather than catastrophizing all of life.*

5. Counselee: Andrea has come to counseling because she has struggled to feel connected within her community and her marriage. She speaks in absolutes like "never," "always," "no one" and "everyone." Specifically, she states that "I have to do *all* the work in my marriage" and "I won't have *any* friends here after Joy moves this summer, and I don't want to have to start over again." Throughout her story, you hear instances where her husband, although seemingly passive, does make attempts at connection with Andrea, and Andrea does have a variety of other social connections and friends within driving distance.

Domain(s) of growth: *cognitive*

Rationale: *Andrea uses a lot of absolutes in her language and seems to have some apparent contradictions in her story (having no friends versus losing one friend to a move). Care-frontation and removing absolutes from her language may prove beneficial to Andrea and increase her ability to cope with situations she finds undesirable.*

6. Counselee: My boss just informed me that I have to go on a business trip at the end of the month. I am deathly afraid of flying, but there's no other way to get to this out-of-state meeting. I don't know what I'm going to do.

Domain(s) of growth: *behavioral*

Rationale: *As stated in the chapter, behavioral strategies work best when dealing with fear or phobias.*

APPENDIX B

ADDITIONAL
LEARNING ACTIVITIES

CHAPTER 2

Hand in Hand. You will need one sheet of paper, unlined, and either crayons, markers or colored pencils. Place your left hand on the sheet of paper and trace its outline using your right hand. Then, next to that tracing, trace your right hand using your left. Which tracing was done with your dominant hand (i.e., if you are right handed, you would select your left-hand tracing)? In each of the fingers of that tracing, write a single adjective or short phrase that represents a strength about who you are as a person or as a counselor. Now, for the other tracing that was done with your nondominant hand, write a single adjective or short phrase that represents a growth area or potential weakness in your life. Color, decorate or creatively modify each tracing. Share your end result with a partner.

CHAPTER 3

I Don't Like Your Tone. With a partner, communicate each of the following sentences as if you were being genuinely complimentary to the receiver of the message:

1. That outfit looks great on you.

2. You are so smart.

3. This was the best fried chicken I've ever had.

Now, repeat each line, but choose a different underlying emotion, such as annoyance, sarcasm, insult or fear. What changes in your tone, rate of speech, inflection and pitch?

All in My Head. This activity asks you to bring your perceiving self into a public or social setting with the conscious intention of observing your own perceiving skills. For example, as you walk into your local grocery store, observe the people around you and really hone in. Who around you is wealthier? Poorer? Who has had a hard day? Who feels excited about life? What are the emotions that you read on the face of the cashier? On what do you base your perceptions?

This same activity could be done at a party or on a Sunday morning as you walk into church. To take it one step further, you could engage someone in your context and check out your perceptions with them, seeking confirmation and refutation of your observations.

Soap Opera Fun. Despite their often racy or immoral plot lines, soap operas are good for something: perceiving. Turn on a soap opera that has been recorded (or is available online) and watch just enough to get the gist of what is going on in the show, then mute the volume. What do you see? How does one character feel about the other? Is their conversation amorous, disdainful, grief-filled or suspicious? What do you notice about their facial expressions, body movements and use of space in the room? Unmute and play the scene back with volume this time. How accurate were your perceptions? What contributed to or detracted from your accuracy?

CHAPTER 4

Mirror, Mirror. This activity requires groups of three and will likely require participants to have the ability to move their chairs around. Identify who in your triad is going to play (1) the counselor, (2) the counselee and (3) the observer. Arrange your chairs so that the counselor and the counselee are facing one another and so that the counselor can sit in S.O.L.E.R. The observer should then sit next to and slightly behind the counselee, also facing the counselor. In this activity, the roles will be assigned as such:

Counselee: Tell your counselor about someone in your life whom you admire or consider to be your hero. Who is this person? What role has this person played in your life? What do you like or admire about this person? What is true about this person that you wish were true about you?

Counselor: Using only the skills discussed in this chapter, listen to your counselee's story. Remember to remain in S.O.L.E.R., to *not* speak and to monitor your facial expressions.

Observer: Facing the counselor, it is your job to mirror every physical movement, facial expression and nonverbal form of communication exhibited by the counselor. You are the counselor's human mirror.

Following this two- to three-minute conversation, debrief as a triad and discuss the following:

1. What was it like for the counselor to have no words?

2. What did the counselor notice about his or her own physicality? His or her comfort in the chair? His or her ability to remain focused on the counselee? His or her perceptions of his or her face and body while listening to the counselee?

3. What did the counselor observe in the "mirror"?

4. What was it like for the counselee to share his or her story without any verbal feedback from the counselor?

5. What did the observer notice about the counselor's presence and nonverbal communication?

Trade roles and repeat so that everyone is in each role at least once.

Try It Out: Verbal Villains. Review the verbal villains discussed in chapter four and answer the following questions for each one.

The Coach

1. Whom do you know that utilizes this particular verbal villain in their interpersonal or helping conversations? How do you feel when this person responds in such a way?

2. What is likely the positive intent of the counselor who approaches a counselee or a counselee's story from this perspective?

3. In what ways could this verbal villain be ineffective or harmful to a counseling relationship?

4. Provide an example of what this might sound like in a real-life conversation.

The Detective (aka the Journalist)

1. Whom do you know that utilizes this particular verbal villain in their interpersonal or helping conversations? How do you feel when this person responds in such a way?

2. What is likely the positive intent of the counselor who approaches a counselee or a counselee's story from this perspective?

3. In what ways could this verbal villain be ineffective or harmful to a counseling relationship?

4. Provide an example of what this might sound like in a real-life conversation.

_____

_____

The Diagnostician

1. Whom do you know that utilizes this particular verbal villain in their interpersonal or helping conversations? How do you feel when this person responds in such a way?

_____

_____

2. What is likely the positive intent of the counselor who approaches a counselee or a counselee's story from this perspective?

_____

_____

3. In what ways could this verbal villain be ineffective or harmful to a counseling relationship?

_____

_____

4. Provide an example of what this might sound like in a real-life conversation.

_____

_____

The Doctor

1. Whom do you know that utilizes this particular verbal villain in their interpersonal or helping conversations? How do you feel when this person responds in such a way?

_____

_____

2. What is likely the positive intent of the counselor who approaches a counselee or a counselee's story from this perspective?

_____

_____

3. In what ways could this verbal villain be ineffective or harmful to a counseling relationship?

_____

_____

4. Provide an example of what this might sound like in a real-life conversation.

_____

_____

The Florist

1. Whom do you know that utilizes this particular verbal villain in their interpersonal or helping conversations? How do you feel when this person responds in such a way?

_____

_____

2. What is likely the positive intent of the counselor who approaches a counselee or a counselee's story from this perspective?

_____

_____

3. In what ways could this verbal villain be ineffective or harmful to a counseling relationship?

_____

_____

4. Provide an example of what this might sound like in a real-life conversation.

_____

_____

The Guru

1. Whom do you know that utilizes this particular verbal villain in their interpersonal or helping conversations? How do you feel when this person responds in such a way?

_____

_____

2. What is likely the positive intent of the counselor who approaches a counselee or a counselee's story from this perspective?

_____

_____

3. In what ways could this verbal villain be ineffective or harmful to a counseling relationship?

_____

_____

4. Provide an example of what this might sound like in a real-life conversation.

_____

_____

The Hangman

1. Whom do you know that utilizes this particular verbal villain in their interpersonal or helping conversations? How do you feel when this person responds in such a way?

_____

_____

2. What is likely the positive intent of the counselor who approaches a counselee or a counselee's story from this perspective?

_____

_____

3. In what ways could this verbal villain be ineffective or harmful to a counseling relationship?

_____

_____

4. Provide an example of what this might sound like in a real-life conversation.

_____

_____

The Historian

1. Whom do you know that utilizes this particular verbal villain in their interpersonal or helping conversations? How do you feel when this person responds in such a way?

_____

_____

2. What is likely the positive intent of the counselor who approaches a counselee or a counselee's story from this perspective?

_____

_____

3. In what ways could this verbal villain be ineffective or harmful to a counseling relationship?

_____

_____

4. Provide an example of what this might sound like in a real-life conversation.

_____

_____

The (un)Holy Spirit

1. Whom do you know that utilizes this particular verbal villain in their interpersonal or helping conversations? How do you feel when this person responds in such a way?

_____

_____

2. What is likely the positive intent of the counselor who approaches a counselee or a counselee's story from this perspective?

_____

_____

3. In what ways could this verbal villain be ineffective or harmful to a counseling relationship?

_____

_____

4. Provide an example of what this might sound like in a real-life conversation.

_____

_____

The Magician

1. Whom do you know that utilizes this particular verbal villain in their interpersonal or helping conversations? How do you feel when this person responds in such a way?

_____

_____

2. What is likely the positive intent of the counselor who approaches a counselee or a counselee's story from this perspective?

_____

_____

3. In what ways could this verbal villain be ineffective or harmful to a counseling relationship?

_____

_____

4. Provide an example of what this might sound like in a real-life conversation.

_____

_____

*Your Personal Verbal Villain:*_____

  1. How might others feel when you respond in such a way?

  _____

  _____

  2. What is likely your positive intention when you approach a counselee or a coun-selee's story from this perspective?

  _____

  _____

  3. In what ways could this verbal villain be ineffective or harmful to a counseling relationship?

  _____

  _____

  4. Provide an example of what this might sound like in a real-life conversation.

  _____

  _____

CHAPTER 5

Just the Facts. Pair up. With a partner, take turns in the role of counselor and counselee.

Counselee: You are to share for three minutes about a vacation or trip you took or one you would like to take. Talk about where you went, how you got there, who was with you, what the trip was like, etc. Feel free to include as much description or detail as you would like.

Counselor: You are limited to attending skills and reflecting content. Listen to the counselee's story and reflect back the content that you hear using the formulas found in this chapter. Conclude the conversation with a summary reflection.

Three-Headed Counselor. In this activity one person (instructor or student) takes on the role of a fictitious character, utilizing character descriptions below. Three students collectively fill the role of counselor. In this activity the three students function as one counselor, able to play off the responses of one another and jointly approach the counselee's situation. *Only reflecting content may be used by the three-headed counselor in response to these scenarios.*

1. You are a freshman in college talking to your resident assistant. Your new roommate is playing music loudly and staying up until all hours. This is getting in the way of you being able to study and sleep.

2. Over the weekend you went to a family reunion. Talk about how it went, who was there and what happened. This can be based on your family, a fictitious family or some combination of the two.

3. You are a high school baseball/softball player who just made the varsity team as a freshman. You are telling your youth pastor all about it.

CHAPTER 6

A Story Without Words. Your instructor will find three pieces of instrumental music, preferably classical music or an instrumental track from a movie soundtrack. With the lights dim, listen to the first piece of music. Envision in your mind's eye what is happening throughout the song. Who is involved? What does the scenery look like? What is happening? What is the mood of the music, of the story? Does it stay the same throughout or change with different movements? What are the participants experiencing throughout the song? What emotions do you perceive, or get evoked in you, as you listen? After the song is over, quickly jot down your thoughts, feelings and impressions. Discuss with the class what you perceived.

Three-Headed Counselor. In this activity one person (instructor or student) takes on the role of a fictitious character, utilizing character descriptions below. Three students collectively fill the role of counselor. In this activity the three students function as one counselor, able to play off the responses of one another and jointly approach the counselee's situation. *Only reflecting content and reflecting feeling may be used by the three-headed counselor in response to these scenarios.*

1. You are a man who is unsatisfied with your job, although it provides very well for your family and has good benefits.

2. You are a twenty-one-year-old girl whose mother is always pressuring her to lose weight.

3. You are a male fourteen-year-old tennis star who is nationally ranked, but you would rather spend your free time with friends or playing chess or golf recreationally. Mom and Dad are planning to send you away for high school to "become a pro tennis player."

Expanding Affective Vocabulary. Take a look at the affective vocabulary chart at the end of chapter six. Choose one word from the list that you do not regularly use but that would not feel incongruent or inauthentic to who you are. Commit to incorporating that new word into your everyday conversations at least twice a day for the next week. Over time that new word will become a very natural and normal part of your affective repertoire.

Another version of this activity is to listen to other people as they use affective words in conversation. Does someone use a word that you like, appreciate or are intrigued by? Look it up in a dictionary to make sure you understand its true meaning and then begin incorporating it as described above.

CHAPTER 7

Three-Headed Counselor. In this activity one person (instructor or student) takes on the role of a fictitious character, utilizing character descriptions below. Three students collectively fill the role of counselor. In this activity the three students function as one counselor, able to play off the responses of one another and jointly approach the counselee's situation. *Only reflecting content, reflecting feeling and empathic reflection may be used by the three-headed counselor in response to these scenarios.*

1. You are twelve years old and have just found out you are being held back a grade.

2. You are an eighteen-year-old college freshman girl who just found out that she did not get into the sorority of her choice.

3. You are a sixty-five-year-old woman whose husband just died. She is alone now in a new community and has limited funds.

CHAPTER 8

Tell Me More. In each of the following scenarios, underline any elements in the counselee's story that seem vague or could use greater clarification. Then write two different clarifying statements or questions that a counselor could use to facilitate the counselee's deepening understanding of the story. Compare your answers with a partner's and discuss the similarities and differences you have in your responses.

Scenario 1:

Counselee: Oh my goodness! Oh my goodness! Oh my goodness! You will not believe what happened this week. I am beyond excited!

Counselor Clarifier 1:

_____

Counselor Clarifier 2:

_____

Scenario 2:

Counselee: Being a teenager sucks. I can't wait to be an adult, 'cause then I can do whatever I want without having to report to anybody. I'm so tired of my mom being all up in my business all the time.

Counselor Clarifier 1:

_____

Counselor Clarifier 2:

_____

Scenario 3:

Write your own counselee scenario. In pairs, trade scenarios and provide possible clarifiers for each other.

Counselee:

Counselor Clarifier 1:

_____

Counselor Clarifier 2:

_____

Three-Headed Counselor. In this activity one person (instructor or student) takes on the role of a fictitious character, utilizing character descriptions below. Three students collectively fill the role of counselor. In this activity the three students function as one counselor, able to play off the responses of one another and jointly approach the counselee's situation. *Only reflecting content, reflecting feeling, basic empathy and clarifying skills may be used by the three-headed counselor in response to these scenarios.*

1. You are a high school student engaged and planning to marry after high school. Your father is having difficulty accepting the engagement. There is a lot of fighting at home, and you are contemplating moving out and living with your fiancé.

2. You are a twenty-year old woman who is involved with a forty-year-old divorced man. Your friends are against the relationship.

3. You are a woman in her early forties who is unable to get pregnant. You and your husband are trying to decide between adopting or remortgaging your house to pay for fertility drugs.

CHAPTER 9

People in Your Life. Reflect on and then write down your responses to the following questions. When you have answered them, share with a partner.

♦ Have you ever known someone who seems to "see into your soul"?

♦ What type of person seems to know what you are thinking and feeling without being told?

- In what ways does this person demonstrate the use of intuitive empathy?
- What do you like about being around this person?
- What makes you uncomfortable around this person?
- How might that awareness benefit you as you develop your own skill in using intuitive empathy?

My Life in Song. If you could create a playlist of the five songs that best capture or summarize your life, what would they be? List them below. Then identify the main themes, motivations or values that are expressed in that song. When your list is complete, share with a partner or in small groups. Those listening may provide further observation about the possible underlying themes within your song selection!

1. _____

   Theme: _____

2. _____

   Theme: _____

3. _____

   Theme: _____

4. _____

   Theme: _____

5. _____

   Theme: _____

   How does this activity relate to intuitive empathy? Reflect here.

   _____

   _____

Three-Headed Counselor. In this activity one person (instructor or student) takes on the role of a fictitious character, utilizing character descriptions below. Three students collectively fill the role of counselor. In this activity the three students function as one counselor, able to play off the responses of one another and jointly approach the counselee's situation. *Only reflecting content, reflecting feeling, basic empathic reflection, clarifying skills and intuitive empathy may be used by the three-headed counselor in response to these scenarios.*

1. You are a male high school senior who has been sent by your soccer coach to meet with the school counselor because of aggressive behavior in last night's match. You are angry, guarded and defensive because you are afraid that the coach is going to bench you for tonight's game. Being benched would mean missing out on the college scouts that will be there and losing the opportunity to go to college on an athletic scholarship. No one knows how important college is to you so that you can help provide for your family in the future.

2. You have recently discovered that your partner has been unfaithful. You aren't sure whether you want to leave them or stay and make it work. You have a child together.

3. A businesswoman feels disrespected by her husband's family because she works outside the home, which requires the children to be in daycare.

CHAPTER 10

Minding the Metaphors. In small groups or as a class, collaboratively make a list of as many different metaphors as you can. You may use the ones provided in this chapter as springboards for your thought process. Make special note of the metaphors that have cultural or geographic nuance, taking time to explain unfamiliar metaphors to one another.

Messing Around with Metaphors. In small groups, have one individual in the group come up with a metaphor (or choose a metaphor from the previous exercise). The others in the group can then choose one of Strong's three strategies: (a) explicate, (b) extend or (c) create and deliver. The next person can then choose another one of Strong's categories, and so on, until all three have been used. Then have someone else deliver a metaphor and continue the process.

CHAPTER 11

Three-Headed Counselor. In this activity one person (instructor or student) takes on the role of a fictitious character, utilizing character descriptions below. Three students collectively fill the role of counselor. In this activity the three students function as one counselor, able to play off the responses of one another and jointly approach the counselee's situation. *Only reflecting content, reflecting feeling, empathy, clarifiers and confrontation may be used by the three-headed counselor in response to these scenarios.*

1. You are a student who is unsure about what major to pursue.

2. You have been working a job without any gratification for eight years and want to find something new, yet you fear the unknown and the effect on friends and family. Most of your friends are from your place of employment, and you provide primary financial stability for your family.

3. You are in a committed relationship (three years), but one of your exes has started to call you again. You never really got over him/her. Old and new feelings are starting to come up.

CHAPTER 12

In This Moment. For this activity you will need a magazine with a variety of different pictures or images. You could also compile a collection of at least five to ten pictures that include a variety of people, places, items, etc. With a partner, look at one picture or image at a time and write down the first descriptive word or phrase that comes to mind (e.g., *peaceful, gorgeous, snotty, obnoxious, jealous* or *happy*). The key to this is to not overthink or overexplain your response, just write it. When you have gone through the collection, go back and discuss with your partner what your reaction was and explain where you think that reaction came from within you. In many ways, this activity is one of authenticity, immediacy and self-disclosure all wrapped up together. Afterward, reflect on what images were easier or harder to be genuine about and why.

Three-Headed Counselor. In this activity one person (instructor or student) takes on the role of a fictitious character, utilizing character descriptions below. Three students collectively fill the role of counselor. In this activity the three students function as one counselor, able to play off the responses of one another and jointly approach the counselee's situation. *Only reflecting content, reflecting feeling, empathic reflection, clarifying skills, confrontation, metaphor, immediacy, authenticity and self-disclosure may be used by the three-headed counselor in response to these scenarios.*

1. You are a sixteen-year-old girl who comes to school smelling of a terrible odor. In the last week your mother was taken to jail, leaving you and your two siblings to sleep in a dirty backyard filled with trash.

2. You are a middle school girl or boy who is bullied consistently at school.

3. You are a wife and mother who has been living with an abusive husband for years. You are always complaining but can't leave that life.

CHAPTER 13

Keeping It Real. Think of three different real-life scenarios you have been a part of. Write each one up as a case study, changing identifying names and features as needed. Each case should be approximately one paragraph long and should provide enough information for a reader to be able to identify the main issues and possible goals for the potential counselee. When the case studies have been written, trade them with a partner. Now identify the domain of growth strategies that would be best suited for each scenario. Confirm your answers with your partner.

CHAPTER 14

Eco-Map. Following the model in figure 14.5, on a blank sheet of paper draw your own eco-map. The relative influence of different spheres can be indicated by drawing larger and smaller circles. Fill in the people or groups in each of the various spheres of your own life. Then add the various types of lines that describe the type of relationship you have with each sphere.

Explain your map to a partner, identify one area in which you would like to see change, and identify the resources that already exist within your system that could help facilitate that change. If no resources exist, consider what might need to be added.

Whose Role Is It Anyway? In pairs or teams, identify who will argue for "counselee's responsibility" and who will argue for "counselor's responsibility," and apply that perspective to the following scenarios:

- A counselee feels misunderstood by her family who keep pressuring her to "just get over it and move on." She has come to therapy for a history of trauma and abuse. Whose responsibility is it to advocate for the counselee with her family? Why?

- A counselee is in need of a referral to an addiction treatment facility. Whose responsibility is it to find treatment facility options? Why?

- A counselee just took a new job that puts a lot of stress and strain on him, as it requires a lot of travel and multiple late nights each week. The counselee is aware that this inconsistency of schedule can often serve as a trigger for his bipolar episodes. Whose responsibility is it to advocate for the counselee within the workplace? Why?

- An adolescent counselee is getting bullied at school and is afraid to tell her parents. Whose responsibility is it to advocate for the counselee with her parents? With the school? Why?

CHAPTER 15

Relating Theological Themes to Counseling. Systematic theology, the study of the doctrines of orthodox Christianity, describes a number of subtopics that relate to the study of God and how he interacts with his creation. There is so much richness in theology that it becomes a challenge to translate this rich vocabulary, biblical reflection and conceptual sophistication into language and meaning that enrich and challenge psychology, counseling and therapeutic dialogue. Here is a suggestion, with a few examples to get you started:

Table B.1. Theological concepts in counselee-friendly language

Theology's "ologies"	Biblical Concept	Social Science Concept	Counselee-Friendly Language
Pneumatology	Holy Spirit	Internal compass	Helper, guide
Sanctification	Christlikeness	Development, maturity	Growing up, changing
Ecclesiology	Christ's body, the church	Community, attachment	Relationships, intimacy
Eschatology	Christ's second coming	Delayed gratification, future	Expectations, hope, forever
Hamartiology	Sin, evil	Responsibility, dysfunction	Brokenness, suffering, wounds
(add your own examples)			

1. Identify other theological concepts and fill in the related biblical concept, social science concept and counselee-friendly language. Try to not force-fit the concept (eisegesis), but also do not get too worried about exact equivalence.

2. A theologian might chuckle (or be upset!) at the way in which this exercise diminishes the theological concepts. However, a concept is only as valuable as its ability to affect one's life in concrete ways. Do you agree or not? Why?

Identifying the Sacred. Utilizing the guidelines provided in this chapter, and taking into consideration all that you have learned thus far about microskills, craft a therapeutically appropriate response to the counselee's statement that might open up the conversation to include a spiritual dimension. Then identify the skill used and explain your rationale by indicating the direction you anticipate it taking the conversation. When complete, discuss your answers within small groups, providing feedback to one another. *Note: there is no right or wrong here; the goal is to get you thinking about the implications of a particular response.*

1. **Counselee:** It really doesn't make a lot of sense. I try to do the right thing and it always backfires. There's a piece missing; the formula I grew up with doesn't work.

   Counselor: _____

   _____

   Skill: _____

   Explanation: _____

   _____

2. **Counselee:** I went to synagogue as a kid. I even had my bar mitzvah. But I hated most of it. I don't get why my family continues to practice all those rules and old traditions.

Counselor: _____

_____

Skill: _____

Explanation: _____

_____

3. **Counselee:** I go to church, but I don't understand all of those words like *redemption* and *sanctification*. I guess since I don't understand them they don't really apply to me. But I enjoy my friends there, and the music is great!

Counselor: _____

_____

Skill: _____

Explanation: _____

_____

4. **Counselee:** Are you a religious person? The last thing I want is for someone to start trying to convince me that their faith should be mine.

Counselor: _____

_____

Skill: _____

Explanation: _____

_____

5. **Counselee:** What about all that supernatural stuff? Some of the TV shows with spirits and special powers are pretty good. It's not real, is it?

Counselor: _____

_____

Skill: _____

Explanation: _____

_____

6. **Counselee:** I'm a person who only believes what I can see for myself. Science makes sense. If there is research to back it up, I'm good with it. Everything else is phony.

Counselor: _____

_____

Skill: _____

Explanation: _____

_____

7. **Counselee:** My cousin is sort of nuts. He gets all worked up about God and what God wants him to do. He's even been in the hospital and has to take medication. He is really a religious fanatic. I hope it's not contagious.

Counselor: _____

_____

Skill: _____

Explanation: _____

_____

8. **Counselee:** I get so upset about all of the horrible stuff that happens to people. I can't imagine doing what you do, listening all day long to people and their pain.

Counselor: _____

_____

Skill: _____

Explanation: _____

_____

APPENDIX C

SMALL GROUP ROLE-PLAY EXERCISES AND TRANSCRIPT ANALYSIS ASSIGNMENT

*F*OLLOWING IS A SET OF NINE SMALL GROUP EXERCISES that can be used in conjunction with a course using this textbook. The exercises are aligned with the chapters of the text in sequence, beginning with chapter four. The exercises utilize groups of three students, each taking a turn in the role of counselor, counselee and observer. Students need to audio- or video-record the role-plays since they will be required to transcribe responses they give to the counselee. A detailed feedback template is provided for each chapter, which can be submitted and graded.

We suggest that the focus of grading not be on the students providing the best response but on students' ability to accurately assess their responses and to select better responses on the template. Especially nearer to the beginning of the exercises, student anxiety can be quite high, and responses are not expected to be always accurate or helpful.

A final transcript analysis assignment is provided as a helpful way to summarize the course and the small group exercises. This can also be used as a graded course assignment.

> **Note to instructor:** The templates included in this appendix are for informational purposes only. We have provided fillable forms that correspond to the answer template for each small group exercise on the website containing the Instructor Resources. Go to the website to download the templates, which you can make available to students (e.g., upload to your class website, email to students or add the writing spaces and photocopy) so that they will have whatever space they need to complete the form for a particular interview.

CHAPTER 4: ATTENDING BEHAVIOR

Instructions: For this and all small group exercises, you will need to be in groups of three. Take a few minutes to introduce yourselves to other members of your small group. *Before you begin*, take thirty to sixty seconds to jot down how you are feeling and what you are thinking before the session starts. Next, engage in brief interviews (a minimum of two to four minutes each), alternating the counselee, counselor and observer roles. Record each interview on a digital recording device that has both audio- and video-recording capabilities. Each student will need to take a turn in the counselor role.

In the counselor role, practice attending to the counselee's communication. Work on maintaining S.O.L.E.R. while taking in what the counselee has to say. You may *not* use any verbal responses or minimal encouragers.

In the counselee role, be cooperative and provide sufficient information for the counselor to practice. For this session, please describe a memory of an event or person that has been significant for you (positively or negatively). This memory should be something you can emotionally connect with and holistically communicate to the counselor.

In the observer role, operate the equipment and keep track of time. Look for whether the counselor shows appropriate eye contact, facial expression, gestures/ posture, verbal tone/pace and verbal responses.

After the interview, allow the counselor to begin the discussion by talking about how it felt to be in the counselor role with this counselee (using the questions below as a guide). Then allow the counselee to give feedback about how it felt to be in the counselee role with this counselor. Finally, allow the observer to provide feedback as to what they perceived about the counselee/counselor interaction. The discussion should be nonjudgmental and focus on positive as well as less effective responses. Possible prompts for small group debrief time include:

- As the counselor, I perceived the counselee making the following expressions with their face:

  _____

- As the counselor, I perceived the counselee using a tone of voice that expressed:

  _____

- As the counselor, I perceived the counselee's inflection and rate of speech as expressing:

  _____

- As the counselor, I perceived the counselee's use of space as expressing:

  _____

- As the counselee, I perceived the counselor making the following expressions with his or her face:

  _____

- As the counselee, I perceived the counselor's use of S.O.L.E.R. as being:

  _____

◆ As the counselee, I found the counselor's use of _____ to be _____ (helpful/distracting/etc.).

◆ As the observer, I perceived the counselee/counselor making the following expressions with their faces:

_____

◆ As the observer, I perceived the use of space by the counselee as expressing:

_____

◆ As the observer, I perceived the counselor's use of S.O.L.E.R. as being:

_____

CHAPTER 4: ATTENDING BEHAVIOR—WORKSHEET

Assignment Template

Name: _____

Other participants: _____

Written Assignment: Watch the recording of you in the counselor role. Write up your personal thoughts, feelings, reflections and observations from the session. Your reflection should be one to two pages in length.

Skill: reflection

Perception
✓ What did you hear in your counselee's story? Was what you heard based on their words, or their nonverbal, or both? Provide support from the recording.

_____

_____

Attending—S.O.L.E.R.
✓ Which parts of S.O.L.E.R. come more naturally to you? Which parts of S.O.L.E.R. are more challenging for you? Support your responses with evidence from your recording.

_____

_____

Self-as-instrument:
✓ What verbal villains were going through your head while listening to the counselee's story?

_____

_____

✓ What were you feeling *prior* to beginning this session? What were you feeling *during* this
   session? How did you feel *after* this session?

_____

_____

✓ What were your perceptions of the session when watching the recording in comparison
   to your perceptions during the session? What was similar? What was different?

_____

_____

_____

Overall skill evaluation: To be included in your one- to two-page write-up:
✓ What are you doing well in this session (particularly with regard to the targeted skill)?

_____

_____

✓ What do you need to continue working on?

_____

_____

_____

CHAPTER 5: REFLECTING CONTENT

Instructions: In your small groups of three, conduct brief interviews (a minimum of
three to five minutes, and at least four counselor responses), alternating the counselee, counselor and observer roles. Record each interview on a digital recording
device that has audio and video capabilities. Each student will need to take a turn in
the counselor role.

In the counselor role, practice paraphrasing the counselee's statements so that both
content and feeling are reflected. The last response in the series should summarize the
counselee's statements. *Do not ask questions or intervene in other ways. Focus only on the
targeted skill of reflecting content.*

In the counselee role, be cooperative and provide sufficient information for the
counselor to practice. It is important to use a real, current, personal issue that falls
around a four to a six on a scale of one to ten in terms of intensity level. For example,
a one would be someone who struggled that morning to decide whether to have cereal
or oatmeal for breakfast; a ten would involve discussing memories of a traumatic event.
A four to a six might be struggles with adjusting to graduate school, indecision about
one's major in school or career plans after graduation, or apprehension about being
with family over the next holiday break.

In the observer role, operate the equipment and keep track of time. Look for
whether the counselor is able to accurately identify the content of the counselee's story
and maintain appropriate attending behaviors. Provide constructive feedback following the session.

After the interview, allow the counselor to begin the discussion by talking about how it felt to be in the counselor role with this counselee. Then invite the counselee to share how it felt to be in the counselee role with this counselor: what the counselee appreciated and what the counselee found distracting or not helpful. The observer can then give feedback based on the guidelines provided in the text and anything else noticed. The discussion should be nonjudgmental and focus on effective as well as less effective responses.

CHAPTER 5: REFLECTING CONTENT—WORKSHEET

Assignment Template

Name: _____

Other participants: _____

Written Assignment: Watch the recording of you in the counselor role. Choose a section of the recording that includes four consecutive counselor responses and complete the following form. Make sure you include an alternate response even if you liked your original one.

Summary of what comes previous to this segment of recording (if transcript is not from beginning):

_____

_____

Counselee response 1 (exact words, not paraphrased):

_____

Counselor response 1 (exact words, not paraphrased):

_____

Evaluation (Was your response reflective or comparable, rather than additive or subtractive from the counselee's statement? If you mistakenly asked a question, etc., what made it difficult to stay on task?):

_____

_____

Better/alternate response, including evaluation (what makes this response a good or better response?):

_____

_____

Counselee response 2:

_____

Counselor response 2:

_____

Evaluation:

_____

_____

Better/alternate response with evaluation:

_____

_____

Counselee response 3:

_____

Counselor response 3:

_____

Evaluation:

_____

_____

Better/alternate response with evaluation:

_____

_____

Counselee response 4:

_____

Counselor response 4:

_____

Evaluation:

_____

_____

Better/alternate response with evaluation:

_____

_____

Overall Skill Evaluation:

✓ ***What I am doing well in this session*** (*particularly with regard to the targeted skill*)***:***

_____

_____

✓ ***What I need to continue working on:***

_____

_____

✓ ***Self-as-instrument reflection*** (*What was going in inside of my mind, emotions, body, etc.? What verbal villains was I fighting? What was distracting to me during this session?*)***:***

_____

_____

Proficiency Level (PL)

PL1: Does not use targeted skill appropriately.

PL2: Sometimes uses targeted skill appropriately.

PL3: Often uses targeted skill appropriately.

PL4: Regularly uses targeted skill appropriately.

PL5: Consistently and appropriately uses targeted skill.

In this exercise I feel I used *reflection of content* at PL _____.

Grader's Comments:

_____

_____

Student used reflection of content at PL level _____.

CHAPTER 6: REFLECTING CONTENT AND FEELING

Instructions: In your small groups of three, conduct brief interviews (a minimum of five to seven minutes, and at least five counselor responses), alternating the counselee, counselor and observer roles. Record each interview on a digital recording device that has both audio and video capabilities. Each student will need to take a turn in the counselor role.

In the counselor role, practice paraphrasing the counselee's statements so that both content and feeling are reflected. The last response in the conversation should summarize the counselee's statements. *Do not ask questions or intervene in other ways. Focus only on the targeted skills of reflecting content and reflecting feelings. Remember to keep them separate,* not *blending the two skills into one statement.*

In the counselee role, be cooperative and provide sufficient information for the counselor to practice. It is important to use a real, current, personal issue that falls between a four and a six on a scale of one to ten.

In the observer role, operate the equipment and keep track of time. Look for whether the counselor is able to accurately identify both the feelings and the content of the counselee and maintain appropriate attending behaviors.

After the interview, allow the counselor to begin the discussion by talking about how it felt to be in the counselor role with this counselee. Then invite the counselee to share how it felt to be in the counselee role with this counselor, what he or she as a counselee appreciated, and what was distracting or not helpful. The observer can then give feedback based on the guidelines in the text and anything else noticed. The discussion should be nonjudgmental and focus on effective as well as less effective responses.

CHAPTER 6: REFLECTING CONTENT AND REFLECTING FEELING—WORKSHEET

Assignment Template

Name:

Other participants:

Written Assignment: Watch the recording of you in the counselor role. Choose a section of the recording that includes five consecutive counselor responses and complete the following form. Make sure you include an alternate response even if you liked your original one.

Summary of what comes previous to this segment of recording *(if transcript is not from beginning):*

Counselee response 1 *(exact words, not paraphrased):*

Counselor response 1 *(exact words, not paraphrased):*

Evaluation *(Was your response reflective, rather than additive or subtractive from the counselee's statement? If you mistakenly asked a question, etc., what made it difficult to stay on task?)***:**

_____

_____

Better/alternate response, including evaluation *(What makes this response a good or better response?)***:**

_____

_____

Counselee response 2:

_____

Counselor response 2:

_____

Evaluation:

_____

_____

Better/alternate response with evaluation:

_____

_____

Counselee response 3:

_____

Counselor response 3:

_____

Evaluation:

_____

_____

Better/alternate response with evaluation:

_____

_____

Counselee response 4:

_____

Counselor response 4:

_____

Evaluation:

_____

_____

Better/alternate response with evaluation:

_____

_____

Counselee response 5:

_____

Counselor response 5:

_____

Evaluation:

_____

_____

Better/alternate response with evaluation:

_____

_____

Overall Skill Evaluation:

✓ ***What I am doing well in this session*** *(particularly with regard to the targeted skill):*

_____

_____

✓ ***What I need to continue working on:***

_____

_____

✓ ***Self-as-instrument reflection*** *(What was going on inside of my mind, emotions, body, etc.? What verbal villains was I fighting? What was distracting to me during this session?):*

_____

_____

Proficiency Level (PL):

PL1: Does not use targeted skill appropriately.

PL2: Sometimes uses targeted skill appropriately.

PL3: Often uses targeted skill appropriately.

PL4: Regularly uses targeted skill appropriately.

PL5: Consistently and appropriately uses targeted skill.

In this exercise I feel I used *reflecting content* at PL _____.

In this exercise I feel I used *reflecting feeling* at PL _____.

Grader's Comments:

_____

_____

Student used reflecting content at PL level _____.

Student used reflecting empathy at PL level _____.

CHAPTER 7: BASIC LEVEL EMPATHY (LEVEL THREE), REFLECTING CONTENT WITH FEELING

Instructions: In a small group, role-play brief interviews (a minimum of seven to ten minutes, with at least five counselor responses), taking turns in each of the roles (counselee, counselor and observer). Audio- or video-record each interview. Each person in the group needs to take a turn in the counselor role.

In the counselor role, practice empathic reflection, paraphrasing the counselee's statements so that empathy is reflected. You may also use any of the other skills that you have learned to this point (attending, reflection of content, reflection of feeling), but you are limited to the skills you have been taught to date, and the main goal is to attempt level three empathic reflections.

In the counselee role, be cooperative and provide sufficient information for the counselor to practice. It is important to use a real, current, personal issue. Choose an issue that is at an intensity level of four to six on a scale of one to ten.

In the observer role, operate the recording equipment and keep track of time. Look for whether the counselor is able to accurately reflect the feelings, the content and empathy for the counselee.

After the interview, the observer should facilitate the discussion, allowing the counselor to begin by talking about how it felt to be in the counselor role with this counselee. Then invite the counselee to share how it felt to be in their role with this counselor: What was appreciated? What was distracting or not helpful? The observer can then give feedback about anything he or she noticed that has not already been addressed. The discussion should be nonjudgmental and focus on effective as well as less effective responses.

Assignment Template

Name:
_____

Other participants:
_____

Written Assignment: Watch the recording of you in the counselor role. Choose a section of the recording that includes five counselor responses and complete the following form. Make sure you include an alternate response even if you liked your original one. If your response was something other than an empathic reflection, make your alternate response a level-three empathic reflection. If your response was lower or higher than a level-three empathic reflection, restate your response so that your better/alternative response is a level-three empathic response. *Note: Occasionally the counselee will not have expressed any emotion, in which case you may have to reflect content instead of an empathic reflection.* Under the "Evaluation" section, include how each counselor response rated on levels one to three of the empathy scale, or whether it was additive, comparable or subtractive if it was a reflection of feeling or content. If your response was above level three, just write "above level three." Also rate your "better/alternate responses" on the relevant scale.

Summary of what comes previous to this segment of recording (*if transcript is not from beginning*)***:***

_____

_____

Counselee statement (*exact words, not paraphrased*)***:***

_____

Counselor response (*exact words, not paraphrased*)***:***

_____

Evaluation (*What rating on which scale was the response? What makes it this level? If you mistakenly asked a question, etc., what made it difficult to stay on task?*)***:***

_____

_____

Better/alternate response with evaluation *(Come up with a level-three empathic reflection response that is different from the response you made. What makes this a level-three response?)*:

_____

_____

Counselee response 2:

_____

Counselor response 2:

_____

Evaluation:

_____

_____

Better/alternate response:

_____

_____

Counselee response 3:

_____

Counselor response 3:

_____

Evaluation:

_____

_____

Better/alternate response:

_____

_____

Counselee response 4:

_____

Counselor response 4:

_____

Evaluation:

_____

_____

Better/alternate response:

_____

_____

Counselee response 5:

_____

Counselor response 5:

_____

Evaluation:

_____

_____

Better/alternate response:

_____

_____

Overall Skill Evaluation:

✓ **What am I doing well in this session** (particularly with regard to the targeted skill)?

_____

_____

✓ **What do I need to continue working on?**

_____

_____

Proficiency Level (PL):

PL1: Does not use targeted skill appropriately.

PL2: Sometimes uses targeted skill appropriately.

PL3: Often uses targeted skill appropriately.

PL4: Regularly uses targeted skill appropriately.

PL5: Consistently and appropriately uses targeted skill.

In this exercise I feel I used *reflecting content* at PL _____.

In this exercise I feel I used *reflecting feelings* at PL _____.

In this exercise I feel I used *basic empathy* at PL _____.

Grader's Comments:

_____

_____

Student used *reflecting content* at PL _____.

Student used *reflecting feelings* at PL _____.

Student used basic empathy at PL _____.

CHAPTER 8: REFLECTIONS, BASIC EMPATHY AND CLARIFYING

Instructions: In your small groups, conduct brief interviews (a minimum of ten to thirteen minutes and at least *six* counselor responses), alternating the counselee, counselor and observer roles. Record each interview using a digital recording device that has both audio and video capabilities.

In the counselor role, practice reflecting content, reflecting feeling, reflecting basic empathy (level three) and clarifying (prompts, open questions and signposts).

In the counselee role, be cooperative and provide sufficient information for the counselor to practice. Please use a real situation from your own life that falls between a four and a six on an intensity scale of one to ten.

In the observer role, operate the equipment and make observations.

After the interview, allow the counselor to begin the discussion by talking about how it felt to be in the counselor role with this counselee. Then invite the counselee to share how it felt to be in the counselee role with this counselor: what he or she as a counselee appreciated and what was distracting or not helpful. The observer can then give feedback based on the guidelines in the text and anything else noticed. The discussion should be nonjudgmental and focus on effective as well as less effective responses.

CHAPTER 8: REFLECTIONS, BASIC EMPATHY AND CLARIFYING—WORKSHEET

Assignment Template

Name: _____

Other participants: _____

Written Assignment: Watch the recording of you in the counselor role. Choose a section of the recording that includes six consecutive counselor responses and complete the following form. Make sure you include an alternate response even if you liked your original one. Under the "Evaluation" section, include how each counselor response rated on the empathy scale. Also rate your "better responses" on the empathy scale. *You must include at least one level-three empathic response and one clarifying skill* (prompt, open question or signpost) in your "better responses."

Summary of what comes previous to this segment of recording:

_____

_____

Counselee response 1 *(exact words, not paraphrased):*

_____

Counselor response 1 *(exact words, not paraphrased):*

_____

Evaluation *(What level of empathy was the response? What makes it this level? If you asked a question, was it open or closed? What made it difficult to stay on task?):*

_____

_____

Better/alternative response with evaluation *(Try to come up with a level-three empathic reflection or use a clarifying skill. What level of empathy was the response? What makes it this level?):*

_____

_____

Counselee response 2:

_____

Counselor response 2:

_____

Evaluation:

_____

_____

Better/alternate response with evaluation:

_____

_____

Counselee response 3:

_____

Counselor response 3:

_____

Evaluation:

_____

_____

Better/alternate response with evaluation:

_____

_____

Counselee response 4:

_____

Counselor response 4:

_____

Evaluation:

_____

_____

Better/alternate response with evaluation:

_____

_____

Counselee response 5:

_____

Counselor response 5:

_____

Evaluation:

_____

_____

Better/alternate response with evaluation:

_____

_____

Counselee response 6:

_____

Counselor response 6:

_____

Evaluation:

_____

_____

Better/alternate response with evaluation:

_____

_____

Overall Skill Evaluation:

✓ ***What am I doing well in this session*** *(particularly with regard to the targeted skill)?*

_____

_____

✓ ***What do I need to continue working on?***

_____

_____

✓ ***Self-as-instrument reflection*** *(What was going on inside of my mind, emotions, body, etc.? What verbal villains was I fighting? What was distracting to me during this session?)***:***

_____

_____

Proficiency Level (PL):

PL1: Does not use targeted skill appropriately.

PL2: Sometimes uses targeted skill appropriately.

PL3: Often uses targeted skill appropriately.

PL4: Regularly uses targeted skill appropriately.

PL5: Consistently and appropriately uses targeted skill.

In this exercise I feel I used *reflecting content* at PL_____.

In this exercise I feel I used *reflecting feelings* at PL_____.

In this exercise I feel I used *basic empathy* at PL _____ .

In this exercise I feel I used *clarifying* at PL _____ .

Grader's Comments:

_____

_____

Student used *reflecting content* at PL _____.

Student used *reflecting feelings* at PL _____.

Student used *basic empathy* at PL _____.

Student used *clarifying* at the PL _____.

CHAPTER 9: REFLECTION, BASIC EMPATHY, CLARIFYING AND INTUITIVE EMPATHY

Instructions: In your small groups, conduct brief interviews (a minimum of fifteen to eighteen minutes, and at least six counselor responses) alternating the counselee, counselor and observer roles. Record each interview using a digital recording device with both audio and video capabilities.

In the counselor role, practice reflecting content, reflecting feeling, reflecting basic empathy (level three), clarifying (prompts, open questions and signposts) and intuitive empathy (level four to five) if applicable.

In the counselee role, be cooperative and provide sufficient information for the counselor to practice. Please use a real situation from your own life that falls between a four and a six on an intensity scale of one to ten.

In the observer role, operate the recording equipment and keep track of time. Look for whether the counselor is able to accurately identify both the feelings and the content of the counselee, maintaining appropriate attending behaviors, and utilize target 2 skills appropriately.

After the interview, allow the counselor to begin the discussion by talking about how it felt to be in the counselor role with this counselee. Then invite the counselee to share how it felt to be in the counselee role with this counselor: what he or she appreciated as the counselee, and what was distracting or not helpful. The observer can then give feedback as well. The discussion should be nonjudgmental and focus on effective as well as less effective responses.

Assignment Template

Name: _____

Other participants: _____

Written Assignment: Watch the recording of you in the counselor role. Choose a section of the recording that includes six consecutive counselor responses and complete the following form. Make sure you include an alternate response even if you liked your original one. Under the "Evaluation" section, include how each counselor response rated on levels one through five of the empathy scale. Also rate your "better responses" on the empathy scale. You must include at least one level-three empathic response, one clarifying skill (prompt, open question or signpost) and one intuitive empathy response in your "better responses."

Summary of what comes previous to this segment of recording:

_____

_____

Counselee response 1 *(exact words, not paraphrased):*

_____

Counselor response 1 *(exact words, not paraphrased):*

_____

Evaluation *(What level of empathy was the response? What makes it this level? If you asked a question, was it open or closed? What made it difficult to stay on task?):*

_____

_____

Better/alternative response, including evaluation *(Try to come up with a level-three empathy statement, a clarifying skill or an intuitive empathy statement. What level of empathy was the response? What makes it this level?):*

_____

_____

Counselee response 2:

_____

Counselor response 2:

_____

Evaluation:

_____

_____

Better/alternate response with evaluation:

_____

_____

Counselee response 3:

_____

Counselor response 3:

_____

Evaluation:

_____

_____

Better/alternate response with evaluation:

_____

_____

Counselee response 4:

_____

Counselor response 4:

_____

Evaluation:

_____

_____

Better/alternate response with evaluation:

_____

_____

Counselee response 5:

_____

Counselor response 5:

_____

Evaluation:

_____

_____

Better/alternate response with evaluation:

_____

_____

Counselee response 6:

_____

Counselor response 6:

_____

Evaluation:

_____

_____

Better/Alternate response with evaluation:

_____

_____

Overall Skill Evaluation:

✓ *What I am doing well in this session?* *(particularly with regard to the targeted skill)*

_____

_____

✓ *What do I need to continue working on?*

_____

_____

✓ **Self-as-instrument reflection** *(What was going on inside of your mind, emotions, body, etc.? What verbal villains were you fighting? What was distracting to you during this session?)*:

_____

_____

Proficiency Level (PL):

PL1: Does not use targeted skill appropriately.

PL2: Sometimes uses targeted skill appropriately.

PL3: Often uses targeted skill appropriately.

PL4: Regularly uses targeted skill appropriately.

PL5: Consistently and appropriately uses targeted skill.

In this exercise I feel I used *reflecting content* at PL _____.

In this exercise I feel I used *reflecting feelings* at PL_____.

In this exercise I feel I used *basic empathy* at PL _____.

In this exercise I feel I used *clarifying* at PL _____.

In this exercise I feel I used *intuitive empathy* at PL _____.

Grader's Comments:

_____

_____

Student used *reflecting content* at PL _____.

Student used *reflecting feelings* at PL _____.

Student used *basic empathy* at PL _____.

Student used *clarifying* at PL _____.

Student used *intuitive empathy* at PL _____.

CHAPTER 10: REFLECTION, BASIC EMPATHY, CLARIFYING, INTUITIVE EMPATHY AND USE OF METAPHOR

Instructions: In your small groups, conduct interviews together (a minimum of eighteen to twenty-two minutes and at least six counselor responses), alternating the counselee, counselor and observer roles. Record each interview using a digital recording device with both audio and video capabilities.

In the counselor role, practice reflecting content, reflecting feeling, making empathic reflections (level three), clarifying (prompts, open questions and signposts), using intuitive empathy (level four to five) if applicable and attempting to incorporate at least one metaphor.

In the counselee role, be cooperative and provide sufficient information for the counselor to practice. Please use a real situation from your own life that falls between a four and a six on an intensity scale of one to ten.

In the observer role, operate the recording equipment and keep track of time. Look for whether the counselor is able to accurately identify both the feelings and the content of the counselee, maintain appropriate attending behaviors and utilize target 2 skills appropriately.

After the interview, allow the counselor to begin the discussion by talking about how it felt to be in the counselor role with this counselee. Then invite the counselee to share how it felt to be in the counselee role with this counselor: what he or she appreciated as the counselee, and what he or she found distracting or not helpful. The observer can then give feedback as well. The discussion should be nonjudgmental and focus on effective as well as less effective responses.

CHAPTER 10: REFLECTION, BASIC EMPATHY, CLARIFYING, INTUITIVE EMPATHY AND USE OF METAPHOR—WORKSHEET

Assignment Template

Name:
_____

Other participants:
_____

Written Assignment: Watch the recording of you in the counselor role. Choose a section of the recording that includes six consecutive counselor responses and complete the following form. Make sure you include an alternate response even if you liked your original one. Under the "Evaluation" section, include how each counselor response rated on levels one to five of the empathy scale. Also rate your "better responses" on the empathy scale. You must include at least one level-three empathic response and one clarifying skill (prompt, open question or signpost), and identify one metaphor that could have been used in your "better responses." Although not required, you are encouraged to incorporate at least one intuitive empathy response within your "better responses."

Summary of what comes previous to this segment of recording:

_____

_____

Counselee response 1 (exact words, not paraphrased):

_____

Counselor response 1 (exact words, not paraphrased):

_____

Evaluation *(What level of empathy was the response? What makes it this level? If you asked a question, was it open or closed? What made it difficult to stay on task?):*

_____

_____

Better/alternative response, including evaluation *(Try to come up with a level-three em-pathic reflection, a clarifying skill or an intuitive empathy statement. What level of empathy was the response? What makes it this level?):*

_____

_____

Counselee response 2:

_____

Counselor response 2:

_____

Evaluation:

_____

_____

Better/alternate response with evaluation:

_____

_____

Counselee response 3:

_____

Counselor response 3:

_____

Evaluation:

_____

_____

Better/alternate response with evaluation:

_____

_____

Counselee response 4:

_____

Counselor response 4:

_____

Evaluation:

_____

_____

Better/alternate response with evaluation:

_____

_____

Counselee response 5:

_____

Counselor response 5:

_____

Evaluation:

_____

_____

Better/Alternate response with evaluation:

_____

_____

Counselee response 6:

_____

Counselor response 6:

_____

Evaluation:

_____

_____

Better/Alternate response with evaluation:

_____

_____

Overall Skill Evaluation:

✓ ***What I am doing well in this session*** *(particularly with regard to the targeted skills)***:**

_____

_____

✓ ***What I need to continue working on:***

_____

_____

✓ ***Self-as-instrument reflection*** *(What was going on inside of your mind, emotions, body, etc.?*
   *What verbal villains were you fighting? What was distracting to you during this session?)***:**

_____

_____

Proficiency Level (PL):

PL1: Does not use targeted skill appropriately.

PL2: Sometimes uses targeted skill appropriately.

PL3: Often uses targeted skill appropriately.

PL4: Regularly uses targeted skill appropriately.

PL5: Consistently and appropriately uses targeted skill.

In this exercise I feel I used *reflecting content* at PL _____.

In this exercise I feel I used *reflecting feelings* at PL _____.

In this exercise I feel I used *basic empathy* at PL _____.

In this exercise I feel I used *clarifying* at PL _____.

In this exercise I feel I used *intuitive empathy* at PL _____.

In this exercise I feel I used *metaphor* at PL _____.

Grader's Comments:

_____

_____

Student used *reflecting content* at PL _____.

Student used *reflecting feelings* at PL _____.

Student used *basic empathy* at PL _____.

Student used *clarifying* at PL _____.

Student used *intuitive empathy* at PL _____.

Student used *metaphor* at PL _____.

CHAPTER 11: CONFRONTATION (CARE-FRONTATION)

Instructions: In your small groups, conduct interviews together (a minimum of twenty-two to twenty-seven minutes, and at least six counselor responses), alternating the counselee, counselor and observer roles. Record each interview on a digital recording device with both audio and video capabilities.

In the counselor role, practice using confronting responses and other skills needed to complete the confrontation. Note: You must use confrontation appropriately, i.e., use empathic responding to give support before and after making a confrontation. Remember that confrontation involves pointing out an apparent discrepancy. Confrontation must be handled with preparation and care!

In the counselee role, be cooperative and provide sufficient information for the counselor to practice. It may be easier to role-play something from your past or the problem of a friend or family member, unless you already know there is something in your life that needs confronting! If you absolutely cannot think of something in the above categories, you can use one of the situations below (although they are likely to come across as more contrived than an actual situation).

1. An individual who has just achieved something important but continually negates that success.

2. A person whose comments indicate considerable distress about a child's leaving home but who angrily professes a lack of interest in the child's welfare.

3. A church member whose comments indicate considerable distress about the plan of the pastor to transfer. The person professes to being submissive to "God's will" but is actually very angry at God.

4. A new believer whose spouse has had a long-standing extramarital affair. The believer's comments indicate considerable distress about the matter, but the believer adamantly claims to have "learned to live with it."

5. An employee having difficulty cooperating with fellow workers who sits with arms tightly folded, avoiding eye contact and discussion in response to the personnel officer's attempts to discuss the matter.

6. A pastor having difficulty relating with the local church governing board but who avoids meetings with the district superintendent about the matter.

7. A Bible school faculty member having difficulty relating with the rest of the faculty who avoids discussion of the matter with the academic dean.

8. A worship team member who comes late to practice but who blames the team leader for the group's poor performance. The team member is talking with the pastor or pastor's spouse.

9. A young person who stays out late at night with friends and who views home as just a place he/she has to go to for food and money. The young person complains to the church youth worker about not liking to go home because "my mother nags too much."

10. A father/mother who claims to have the best interests of his/her family at heart. The parent believes that this means working three jobs so that his/her family can afford things such as seasonal ski passes, restaurant meals, a third flat-screen TV, etc., despite the fact that he/she has very little time with spouse and children.

11. An engaged person who believes that it is God's will to marry an unbeliever.

12. A young person who, when denied parental permission to attend a church activity, finds a way to sneak out and attend anyway.

In the observer role, operate the equipment and watch out for discrepancies in what the counselee says so that you can give feedback to the counselor during the post-interview discussion with regard to whether he/she confronted appropriately.

After the interview, allow the counselor to begin the discussion by talking about how it felt to be in the counselor role with this counselee. Then invite the counselee to share how it felt to be in the counselee role with this counselor: what was appreciated and what was distracting or not helpful. The observer can then give feedback based on guidelines provided in the text and anything else noticed. The discussion should be nonjudgmental and focus on effective as well as less effective responses.

CHAPTER 11: CONFRONTATION (CARE-FRONTATION)—WORKSHEET

Assignment Template

Name:

Other participants:

Written Assignment: Watch the recording of you in the counselor role. Choose a section of the recording that includes six counselor responses and complete the following form. Under "Evaluation" section, include how the counselor response rated on levels one to five of both the confrontation and empathy scales. Also rate your "better responses" on both the confrontation and empathy scales. Note: Reread the descriptions of the levels of the

confrontation scale. It is different from the empathy scales. You want to mix empathy and
confrontation, so you should not make a confrontational response each time.

Summary of what comes previous to this segment of recording:

_____

_____

Counselee response 1:

_____

Counselor response 1:

_____

Evaluation *(Why would you consider it effective or not effective; level of confrontation; level of*
empathy):

_____

_____

Better/alternate response with evaluation:

_____

_____

Counselee response 2:

_____

Counselor response 2:

_____

Evaluation:

_____

_____

Better/alternate response with evaluation:

_____

_____

Counselee response 3:

_____

Counselor response 3:

_____

Evaluation:

_____

_____

Better/alternate response with evaluation:

_____

_____

Counselee response 4:

_____

Counselor response 4:

_____

Evaluation:

_____

_____

Better/alternate response with evaluation:

_____

_____

Counselee response 5:

_____

Counselor response 5:

_____

Evaluation:

_____

_____

Better/alternate response with evaluation:

_____

_____

Counselee response 6:

_____

Counselor response 6:

_____

Evaluation:

_____

_____

Better/alternate response with evaluation:

_____

_____

Overall Skill Evaluation:

What I am doing well in this session (particularly with regard to the targeted skill)**:**

_____

_____

What do I need to continue working on?

_____

_____

Proficiency Level (PL):

PL1: Does not use targeted skill appropriately.

PL2: Sometimes uses targeted skill appropriately.

PL3: Often uses targeted skill appropriately.

PL4: Regularly uses targeted skill appropriately.

PL5: Consistently and appropriately uses targeted skill.

In this exercise I feel I used _reflecting content_ at PL _____.

In this exercise I feel I used _reflecting feelings_ at PL _____.

In this exercise I feel I used _basic empathy_ at PL _____.

In this exercise I feel I used _clarifying_ at PL _____.

In this exercise I feel I used _intuitive empathy_ at PL _____.

In this exercise I feel I used _confrontation_ at PL _____.

Grader's Comments:

_____

_____

Student used *reflecting content* at PL _____.

Student used *reflecting feelings* at PL _____.

Student used *basic empathy* at PL _____.

Student used *clarifying* at PL _____.

Student used *intuitive empathy* at PL _____.

Student used *confrontation* at PL _____.

CHAPTER 12: DEVELOPING AN INDIVIDUAL STYLE

Instructions: In your small groups, conduct interviews together (a minimum of thirty minutes and at least six counselor responses), alternating the counselee, counselor and observer roles. Record each interview on audio-recording or digital-recording device.

In the counselor role, you are free to use all of the skills that you have learned up to this point, but you are not required to use all of them. This may include practicing your attending skills (eye contact, attending posture, attention to nonverbals, etc.), in addition to any of the other skills learned throughout this process: reflecting skills, basic and advanced empathic reflection, clarifying skills, confrontation, use of metaphors, immediacy and self-disclosure. Use closed inquiry only when essential to obtain specific information. Combination responses are also appropriate, such as a paraphrase and an open inquiry. However, you will need to justify your use of specific skills at particular points in the session in the evaluation section of your write-up.

In the counselee role, be cooperative and provide sufficient information for the interviewer to practice. Using a real situation from your own life is strongly encouraged.

In the observer role, operate the equipment and note your own observations of the counselor's use of helping skills, including the use of appropriate attending behaviors.

After the interview, allow the counselor to begin the discussion by talking about how it felt to be in the counselor role with this counselee. Then invite the counselee to share how it felt to be in the counselee role with this counselor, what was appreciated and what was distracting or not helpful. The observer can then give feedback based on guidelines provided in the text and anything else noticed. The discussion should be nonjudgmental and focus on effective as well as less effective responses.

Assignment Template

Name: _____

Other participants: _____

Written Assignment: Watch the recording of you in the counselor role. Choose a section of the recording that includes six counselor responses and complete the following form. Under the "Evaluation" section, evaluate each of your counselor responses with respect to its appropriateness. For example, if you asked a question, evaluate the question itself (e.g., is it open, not multiple choice) and also discuss whether a different skill would have been better (e.g., an empathic reflection). Also, rate responses on levels one to five of the appropriate scale (e.g., empathy, confrontation). Your "better/alternate" response, therefore, may involve the same skill or a skill you think would be a better alternative. Make sure to also evaluate your "better/alternate" response. Note that you may use immediacy and self-disclosure but they are not required.

Summary of what comes previous to this segment of recording:

_____

_____

Counselee response 1:

_____

Counselor response 1:

_____

Evaluation *(Why would you consider it effective or not effective; level of confrontation; level of empathy):*

_____

_____

Better/alternate response with evaluation:

_____

_____

Counselee response 2:

_____

Counselor response 2:

_____

Evaluation:

_____

_____

Better/alternate response with evaluation:

_____

_____

Counselee response 3:

_____

Counselor response 3:

_____

Evaluation:

_____

_____

Better/alternate response with evaluation:

_____

_____

Counselee response 4:

_____

Counselor response 4:

_____

Evaluation:

_____

_____

Better/alternate response with evaluation:

_____

Counselee response 5:

Counselor response 5:

Evaluation:

Better/alternate response with evaluation:

Counselee response 6:

Counselor response 6:

Evaluation:

Better/alternate response with evaluation:

Overall Skill Evaluation:
✓ **What I am doing well in this session** (particularly with regard to the targeted skill)**?**

✓ **What do I need to continue working on?**

Proficiency Level (PL):

PL1: Does not use targeted skill appropriately.

PL2: Sometimes uses targeted skill appropriately.

PL3: Often uses targeted skill appropriately.

PL4: Regularly uses targeted skill appropriately.

PL5: Consistently and appropriately uses targeted skill.

In this exercise I feel I used *reflecting content* at PL _____.

In this exercise I feel I used *reflecting feelings* at PL _____.

In this exercise I feel I used *basic empathy* at PL _____.

In this exercise I feel I used *clarifying* at PL _____.

In this exercise I feel I used *intuitive empathy* at PL _____.

In this exercise I feel I used *confrontation* at PL _____.

In this exercise I feel I used *self-disclosure* at PL _____.

In this exercise I feel I used *immediacy* at PL _____.

Grader's Comments:

_____

_____

Student used *reflecting content* at PL _____.

Student used *reflecting feelings* at PL _____.

Student used *basic empathy* at PL _____.

Student used *clarifying* at PL _____.

Student used *intuitive empathy* at PL _____.

Student used *confrontation* at PL _____.

Student used *self-disclosure* at PL _____.

Student used *immediacy* at PL _____.

FINAL TRANSCRIPT ANALYSIS

This assignment serves as the capstone or summative project, in which students conduct a forty-five to sixty-minute helping session with a volunteer who serves in the role of counselee. Students will have all the skills needed to complete this assignment after learning "using the here and now" in chapter twelve and can conduct their session any time after that class is completed.

The volunteer counselee *cannot* be a classmate or a student within the same degree program. Additionally, it cannot be someone with whom the student/counselor already has a social or personal relationship (the volunteer *cannot* be a friend, roommate, family member, coworker, Bible study member, etc.). One option for finding a counselee is for students to "trade" friends/family/acquaintances with one another (e.g., Sarah's roommate volunteers for Kyle, and Kyle's roommate volunteers for Emily).

Instructions for submission: Please place the CD/digital recorder/flash drive into an envelope/zip-locked bag, and staple or paper-clip to your paper. Make sure your name is on the CD/digital recorder/flash drive in case it becomes separated from your paper. The video may also be uploaded to a secure shared server if one exists for your training program.

Instructions for completing the assignment: Video-record a forty-five to sixty-minute counseling session with someone outside the class as the counselee. The situation presented by the counselee should be a current, real one rather than a role-play. You will need to get signed consent from the counselee in order to use the interview for this course requirement. Following is a step-by-step guideline for how to proceed with this requirement.

The Interview Part

1. Contact the volunteer counselee and provide them with a brief explanation of what is being asked of him/her—namely, approximately one to one-and-a-half hours of their time in which they share about a current or ongoing situation in their life about which they would like to talk with someone. Inform the prospective counselee that this is for a class assignment and therefore cannot be considered an actual counseling session, although you will be utilizing counseling skills during the conversation. Inform them that this will be video recorded for the purposes of assessing the counselor's skills. Schedule a time to meet—it is recommended that you, as the counselor, plan on an hour and a half for setup, recording and packing up. You need to conduct this interview/conversation in a private and quiet location. Please talk with your instructor regarding any on-campus room options, such as library study rooms, that may be available for use.

2. Upon the counselee's arrival, have the counselee read and sign the interview consent form that has been designed by your instructor in keeping with your institution's policies. (Keep the signed form—it will be submitted with your final assignment.) Mention that confidentiality *does* apply, and verbally go over the relevant exceptions to confidentiality. This will involve using a different interactive style than you will use in the remainder of the session. Video-record your forty-five to sixty-minute session.

3. Conduct the counseling session! Remember to conclude by thanking the counselee for their time, openness and willingness to volunteer.

The Written Prep-Work Part

1. Watch your entire session, noting when you felt your skills were particularly strong or when they were particularly weak.

2. *Choose a six- to eight-minute consecutive segment* of recording you wish to critique. You need to have an absolute minimum of six counselor responses, and preferably ten or more (not including "uh huh" and "hmmm," etc.). If you need to add a couple of minutes to your transcribed section of the recording in order to make this possible, please do so. *Type out a transcript* of the recording segment you have chosen.

3. At the top of your paper, prior to the commencement of the transcript, include a statement indicating how long the total interview was, how long the transcribed section is and how many minutes into the interview the transcribed section begins. For example: "The interview was a total of 54 minutes, and the transcribed section begins 21 minutes into the interview and lasts for 7 minutes." Additionally, give a brief summary of your prior relationship to the counselee as well as what has happened up to this point in the interview. For example: "I met the counselee the day of the interview, having been connected through a mutual friend. We arranged the interview via email. Prior to where the transcript begins, she has been talking about the difficulty she is having with her mother-in-law, who is very controlling. Just before the transcript begins she has told me that her husband thinks his mother has a right to be this way because she is helping them out financially."

The Written Analysis Part

Similar to your small group exercises, you are going to go into your transcript and write assessments of each counselor response, but given that this is a *final* transcript your assessments are going to be far more involved than they were in your exercises. Each assessment needs to include the following: Why did you respond the way you did? Explain what was going on in your head at this moment and where were you hoping to go with your response. For example: "The counselee was talking on and on and I knew I had to say something in order to be graded for this assignment, but I didn't know how to stop her from talking! I was feeling panicky. I finally just jumped in, but I realize that what I said wasn't helpful. My response lacked empathy and wasn't even on topic. I should have intervened earlier on and done some empathic responding after she said . . ." Or: "I wanted to get more information about his relationship with his father, but in asking the closed question, I realize that I actually got less information! I needed to either ask an open question such as 'Can you tell me more about your relationship with your family?' or just keep reflecting content and feelings as he began to talk about family members."

Describe your attending posture at the time of the given response—pretend your instructor is unable to see your video and verbally describe for him or her what your nonverbals are communicating (remember S.O.L.E.R. as well as your facial expressions and hand/body movements).

Identify the skill you used (or attempted to use) in this particular response.

Evaluate the quality of this response using the scales and standards provided in the text. *Every* response should be rated on each dimension, even if the rating is "N/A." If you use a clarifying skill, discuss the appropriateness of its use in this response, such as was it open or closed, would an empathic reflection have been better, etc.

Provide an alternate response and *explain* your rationale for the use of the alternate response. An alternate response is required for each exchange. *Evaluate* the alternate response in the same way (on empathy, confrontation, immediacy/relational immediacy, etc.) you evaluated your actual response.

An example:

Counselor: You're angry that he didn't discuss it with you first.

Explanation: I was thinking about how annoyed and upset I would be if my friend had gone and made plans like that without talking to me first. I'm not usually comfortable using the word *angry*, but the counselee was so upset that I couldn't shake that *angry* was the right word, so I just took a risk and said it!

Attending: I was still in S.O.L.E.R. at this point, but I was sitting up straighter than usual as I was getting worked up with the counselee. My eyes are super focused on her, and I'm trying real hard to stop shaking my leg.

Skills Evaluation:

Reflecting Content: N/A

Reflecting Feeling: N/A

Empathy: Level 4—The counselee hadn't actually used such a strong word, but it was implied in the counselee's body language, therefore it is additive. The counselee confirmed the accuracy of my response by saying "I guess I do feel angry." If she had denied she felt angry, it would have been a level 1 or 2 response. I don't rate it a level 5 because the anger was quite close to the surface, just beneath the awareness of the counselee.

Clarifying: N/A

Confrontating: Level 4—Although my response was intended to be primarily empathic, and no discrepancies were pointed out, the response is actually somewhat confrontational because she hadn't actually been consciously aware that she was angry.

Immediacy: N/A

Authenticity: Level 3—I did not explicitly reveal my own emotion or opinion, but my response was not sterile or inauthentic.

Alternate Response: "On the one hand, you understand why he made the decision he made, but on the other, you feel angry that he didn't discuss it with you first."

Rationale: I chose a soft confrontation as an alternate response because the counselee kept going back and forth between trying to make sense of her friend's choice, while still needing to express how she felt about the decision.

Skills Evaluation:

Reflecting Content: N/A

Reflecting Feeling: N/A

Empathy: Level 4—Although this is a confrontation, the use of "you feel angry . . ." still communicates empathy for what was beneath the surface.

Clarifying: N/A

Confronting: Level 4—Although this is in the formula of a level 3, because she wasn't consciously aware of her anger it becomes a level 4 confrontation.

Immediacy: N/A

Authenticity: Level 3—This response neither hides nor reveals who I am or what I feel about the counselee and the situation.

1. After giving a "play-by-play," response-by-response critique, *narratively* give an *evaluation of your overall work with this counselee,* both in the segment you have transcribed and the session as a whole. Include responses to:

   - What would you do differently?

   - What would you do the same?

   - How would you evaluate your ability to develop rapport with the counselee?

   - What direction would you go if you had the opportunity to have another session or sessions with the counselee? Your response should indicate that you either understand what is happening with the counselee or have an idea of how you would attempt to find out.

   - How did the informed consent segment of the interview go? How did you feel doing this part of the interview versus the rest of the interview?

2. Attach the signed informed consent to your final document.

3. Reread the instructions above and compare it to what you have written. Did you get it all?

4. Breathe and submit your assignment (including the completed informed consent and a digital recording of your session).

5. Do a happy dance and celebrate—you made it! You are one step closer to becoming a counselor!

TRANSCRIPT ANALYSIS ASSIGNMENT—WORKSHEET

Assignment Template

Your Name: _____

Written Assignment: Watch the recording with you in the counselor role. Choose a section of the recording that includes a minimum of six counselor responses and complete the following form. Under the "Evaluation" sections, include how the counselor response rated on the levels one to five of the empathy, confrontation and authenticity scales (i.e., rate *every* response on *each* of these scales, even if the rating is N/A and include an explanation). You must also evaluate the response against the other listed skills where applicable, even if the explanation is N/A. Each of your "better/alternate responses" are to be evaluated in the same manner as your original response (again, N/A with explanation may be a sufficient rating).

Summary of prior relationship with counselee:

_____

_____

The interview was a total of _____ minutes, and the transcribed section begins _____ minutes into the interview and lasts for _____ minutes.

Summary of what comes previous to this segment of recording:

_____

_____

Counselee response 1:

_____

Counselor response 1:

_____

Evaluation:

_____

Reflecting content:

_____

Reflecting feeling:

_____

Empathy:

_____

Clarifying:

_____

Confronting:

_____

Immediacy:

_____

Authenticity:

_____

Better/alternate response with evaluation:

_____

Reflecting content:

_____

Reflecting feeling:

_____

Empathy:

_____

Clarifying:

_____

Confronting:

_____

Immediacy:

_____

Authenticity:

_____

Counselee response 2:

_____

Counselor response 2:

_____

Evaluation:

_____

Reflecting content:

_____

Reflecting feeling:

_____

Empathy:

_____

Clarifying:

_____

Confronting:

_____

Immediacy:

_____

Authenticity:

_____

Better/alternate response with evaluation:

_____

Reflecting content:

_____

Reflecting feeling:

_____

Empathy:

_____

Clarifying:

_____

Confronting:

_____

Immediacy:

_____

Authenticity:

_____

Counselee response 3:

_____

Counselor response 3:

_____

Evaluation:

_____

Reflecting Content:

_____

Reflecting Feeling:

_____

Empathy:

_____

Clarifying:

_____

Confronting:

_____

Immediacy:

_____

Authenticity:

_____

Better/alternate response with evaluation:

_____

Reflecting content:

_____

Reflecting feeling:

_____

Empathy:

_____

Clarifying:

_____

Confronting:

_____

Immediacy:

_____

Authenticity:

_____

Counselee response 4:

_____

Counselor response 4:

_____

Evaluation:

_____

Reflecting content:

_____

Reflecting feeling:

_____

Empathy:

_____

Clarifying:

_____

Confronting:

_____

Immediacy:

_____

Authenticity:

_____

Better/alternate response with evaluation:

_____

Reflecting content:

_____

Reflecting feeling:

_____

Empathy:

_____

Clarifying:

_____

Confronting:

_____

Immediacy:

_____

Authenticity:

_____

Counselee response 5:

_____

Counselor response 5:

_____

Evaluation:

_____

Reflecting content:

_____

Reflecting feeling:

_____

Empathy:

_____

Clarifying:

_____

Confronting:

_____

Immediacy:

_____

Authenticity:

_____

Better/alternate response with evaluation:

_____

Reflecting content:

_____

Reflecting feeling:

_____

Empathy:

_____

Clarifying:

_____

Confronting:

_____

Immediacy:

_____

Authenticity:

_____

Counselee response 6:

_____

Counselor response 6:

_____

Evaluation:

_____

Reflecting content:

_____

Reflecting feeling:

_____

Empathy:

_____

Clarifying:

_____

Confronting:

_____

Immediacy:

_____

Authenticity:

_____

Better/alternate response with evaluation:

_____

Reflecting content:

_____

Reflecting feeling:

_____

Empathy:

_____

Clarifying:

_____

Confronting:

_____

Immediacy:

_____

Authenticity:

_____

Repeat pattern for as many responses as you need!

Overall Skill Evaluation:

✓ **What I am doing well in this session** (particularly with regard to the targeted skill):

_____

_____

✓ *What do I need to continue working on?*

_____

_____

Proficiency Level (PL):

PL1: Does not use targeted skill appropriately.

PL2: Sometimes uses targeted skill appropriately.

PL3: Often uses targeted skill appropriately.

PL4: Regularly uses targeted skill appropriately.

PL5: Consistently and appropriately uses targeted skill.

In this exercise I feel I used *reflecting content* at PL _____.

In this exercise I feel I used *reflecting feelings* at PL _____.

In this exercise I feel I used *basic empathy* at PL _____.

In this exercise I feel I used *clarifying* at PL _____.

In this exercise I feel I used *intuitive empathy* at PL _____.

In this exercise I feel I used *confrontation* at PL _____.

Grader's Comments:

_____

_____

Student used *reflecting content* at PL _____.

Student used *reflecting feelings* at PL _____.

Student used *basic empathy* at PL _____.

Student used *clarifying* at PL _____.

Student used *intuitive empathy* at PL _____.

Student used *confrontation* at PL _____.

THE RELATIONSHIP
BETWEEN PSYCHOLOGY
AND RELIGION

AS MENTIONED IN CHAPTER FIFTEEN, this topic connects to a broader topic, well beyond the scope of this book. However, for some readers this question is at the center of what Christians interested in counseling need to understand before going further into developing the skills of effective people helping. This appendix will attempt to outline some of the issues related to this topic, admittedly from our own perspective, which may or may not mesh with yours.

PSYCHOLOGY'S INTERACTION WITH
RELIGIOUS AND SPIRITUAL EXPERIENCE

The history of psychology, and its handling of the religious dimension of human experience, includes a massive literature on the psychology of religion attesting to the significance of the topic and its relevance to counseling relationships (e.g., Leach & Sato, 2013; Walker, Gorsuch & Tan, 2004). For centuries authors have discussed human experiences that transcend the here-and-now aspects of our lives. Words like *numinous, supernatural, mystical, holy, awesome, transcendent* and *sacred* all point to something beyond our daily, embodied existence, which for many is not reducible to natural or scientific explanation. Religions can be defined as systems people have constructed to explain and often to control these experiences. The problem in modern Western culture is that we have tried to explain away these experiences and reduce them to scientific explanations. *Postmodernism* can be described as an effort to return to a worldview that values such experience in conjunction with science and other ways of knowing.

This is not only the purview of religious studies, philosophy and New Age gurus; the counseling field has also wrestled with how to respond to the tensions between a modernist, scientific worldview, based on research and empirically validated treatments and approaches, and the pre- and postmodern worldviews that see reality and the process of change as more than what can be empirically studied and understood. Psychology, in its relatively recent emergence in the history of human thought, has struggled to be seen as a science and establish its identity alongside the hard sciences like biology and physics. As such it has been suspicious of the sacred and has favored a scientific epistemology (theory of knowledge). However, in its focus of study, understanding humans and human experience, the debate still rages regarding whether everything humans are and experience is explainable scientifically. The recent emphasis on neurophysiology and psychopharmacological interventions is to a degree part of this continuing effort to explain and control human experience and behavior apart from a spiritual dimension. Our perspective, which we will lay out in the following paragraphs, is that we need both the scientific and the spiritual: it is not one or the other; it is both.

Theoretical Support

Historically counseling theories have not readily endorsed religious belief. From Freud onward, a bias has existed that essentially perceived religion and spirituality as a symptom of psychological immaturity or even pathology. Freud's *The Future of an Illusion* (1927/1978), in which he stated his belief that God and Christianity are illusions, as well as other of his writings clearly challenged the religious orientation to life and influenced generations of mental health professionals, regardless of their agreement with Freud's other theoretical hypotheses and practices.

However, not all of the major counseling theories were as negative about the role of the sacred in the helping process. Carl Jung, a disciple of Freud who broke from Freud's theoretical orientation and developed his own approach to counseling, was heavily influenced by Christianity, Eastern religions and the occult. Jung included many religious elements in his theory and openly affirmed a spiritual orientation to life. He is frequently cited as saying, "I have treated many hundreds of patients. Among those in the second half of life—that is to say, over thirty-five—there has not been one whose problem in the last resort was not that of finding a religious outlook on life" (Ulanov & Dueck, 2008).

Albert Ellis, the founder of rational emotive behavior therapy, once considered religion a source of irrational beliefs that are dysfunctional. Later on, Ellis stated, "I think I can safely say that the Judeo-Christian Bible is a self-help book that has probably enabled more people to make more extensive and intensive personality and behavioral changes than all professional therapists combined" (Ellis, 1993, p. 336).

The examples of the value of spirituality in counseling are many (cf. Frame, 2003; Gorsuch, 2002, Pargament, 2011; Richards & Bergin, 2005; Sperry, 2011), yet the predominant view, supported by a cultural backlash in the West against organized religion, continues. While spirituality in general and in the abstract is accepted, strongly held, specific religious beliefs, or the personal affirmation or allegiance to the theological doctrines of a particular religion, continue to be seen as deficient. Such adherence to particular religious doctrines is seen as restricting human freedom, interfering with the development of one's unique self, dependent on looking to others for personal affirmation and belonging, developmentally immature, or simply being out of touch with the twenty-first century.

CHRISTIANITY'S RELATIONSHIP WITH
THE SCIENCE OF PSYCHOLOGY

Christians, particularly evangelicals in the past century, have been quite suspicious of the scientific worldview because it largely rejects religion and the validity of a deistic worldview. Christians believe in a personal relationship with God, a being who is wholly Other and not simply a part of me, who both created and sustains the universe and who sent Jesus to redeem us personally. The rejection of this belief system, the associated religious systems (the church) and personal spiritual experience leave Christian counselors with a profound tension—essentially our religious beliefs and our vocation are in contradiction. A review of the decades of literature addressing this tension (cf. Stevenson, Eck & Hill, 2007 is a good overview of the literature) is not the point of this appendix, but suffice it to say that this is another example of *both/and*, not *either-or*: science, Scripture and human experience, along with other sources of knowledge, coexist with one another to form the complex human condition. Persons embedded in this complexity are drawn to understand the complexity of God, who created, sustains and heals them.

From a Christian perspective Worthington (2010), among many other writers in the field of the integration of psychology and theology (or counseling and faith) has done an admirable job of defending the scientific approach to psychology and demonstrates how psychology can benefit Christian theology, thereby helping Christians live their lives in both healthier and holier ways. At the end of this appendix is a sample list of outcomes research related to spiritual interventions. It is not only secular counseling interventions that need to be empirically validated but Christian interventions and approaches as well (see Worthington, Johnson, Hook & Aten, 2013). We need not fear applying scientific research methods to Christian interventions and approaches. Ultimately we would suggest that good science and good theology and biblical studies will not contradict each other, since human experience is both fundamentally spiritual and psychological (Benner, 1988, 1998), and, we would add, sociological.

AN APPROACH TO UNDERSTANDING
THE INTEGRATION LITERATURE

As you read various authors on integration, you will find that it is almost as if one author is talking about something completely different from another, and yet both are calling it "integration." Years ago, it became clear to us (Heather and Fred) that people were often arguing over different types or levels of integration, focusing on different components of the process. In light of this, we suggest that there are five levels of integration (Gingrich & Worthington, 2007). These are briefly described below. Specific examples of each level of integration are given in table 15.2.

1. *Presuppositional* (e.g., worldview, assumptions, beliefs, values)—what are the core beliefs?

2. *Theoretical* (e.g., models of personality, health, pathology, counseling)—what are the beliefs about the nature of personhood and how people change?

3. *Intervention* (e.g., assessment, case conceptualization, techniques, skills)—what are the beliefs about how counseling is conducted?

4. *Therapeutic relationship* (e.g., practice setting, joining, responding to resistance and growth, termination)—what are the beliefs about how the counseling relationship aids the process?

5. *Personal* (e.g., functioning as a spiritually integrated person)—in what ways are we as counselors functioning in an integrated way?

Our contention is that many of the confusions about integration occur when people are talking at different levels. For instance, are all psychological techniques of no value because the foundational presuppositions of the related counseling theory are unbiblical? Effective integration occurs at all levels, and a thoughtful model of counseling requires us to work out how psychology and spirituality are related at each level.

Table D.1. Examples of levels of integration

	Positive example	**Negative example**	**Common examples (positive or negative) related to spirituality**
Presuppositional	Persons are made in the image of God but prone to sinfulness.	Persons are intrinsically good.	Spirituality has little to do with personal problems.
Theoretical	Distortions in thinking are a common cause of emotional problems.	Emotion needs to be contained and its impact minimized.	All emotional difficulties are a result of distance from God.
Interventions	In session, asking a couple to discuss a specific topic	Using a sex surrogate to teach about sexual functioning	Practicing a biblical example of spiritual disciplines
Therapeutic Relationship	Having a final session to end well	Joking about a counselee's misunderstanding	Counselor imposing his/her spiritual beliefs onto the counselee
Personal	Being appropriately genuine with a counselee	A counselor pretending to have it all together when things are desperately falling apart	Counselor feels angry at God but attempts to help counselee work through similar issues

THE RELATIONSHIP OF FAITH-BASED
COUNSELING TO SECULAR APPROACHES

As with so many topics in the broader counseling field, there is a wide range of opinion regarding how spirituality and counseling are related. In addition, specifically within the Christian counseling field there is also a wide range regarding this topic. Johnson

(2010) edited the "Five Views" book, which describes the range of predominantly evangelical Protestant views on integration. A brief and probably overly simplistic summary of the models is the *biblical* counseling view (the Bible is the manual for counseling, providing all we need to discern truth through the power of the Spirit); the *Christian psychology* view (constructing an explicitly Christian "psychology" entirely from Christian principles with Christian methods founded on Scripture, theology and the history of the church, while not denying some value to modern psychology and empirical research); the *perspectival* view (each academic discipline, psychology, theology, linguistics, etc., has a unique perspective to offer; they may disagree at times but one does not negate the other); the *transformational* view (the doing of psychology is grounded in the person of the counselor and the processes of doing counseling are fundamentally Christian in spirit); and the *integration* view (special revelation, given to us by God in the Bible, is ultimately consistent with general revelation, discovered in science). These five approaches are illustrated using the same case study in Greggo and Sisemore's edited book (2012).

Guiding Principles for Addressing Spiritual Issues
(Richards & Bergin, 2005)

✓ respect for the counselee's autonomy and freedom
✓ sensitivity to and empathy for the counselee's R/S beliefs
✓ flexibility and responsiveness to counselee's R/S beliefs

In the broader counseling field the Association for the Spiritual, Ethical and Religious Values in Counseling (ASERVIC, 2009), whose standards have since been endorsed by the American Counseling Association (ACA), is a voice that advocates for the inclusion of spiritual issues in counseling. These standards serve to affirm the essentially spiritual nature of counseling and people, going beyond any one religion's specific values and emphasizing the innately spiritual elements that make someone human. The ASERVIC competencies (see below) present a compelling case that not only are there specific ways in which counselors need to function, but there are skills and training that counselors should have. The history of the development of the competencies is detailed in Robertson and Young (2011). The competencies cover such topics as culture and worldview, counselor self-awareness, human and spiritual development, communication about spiritual issues, assessment, and diagnosis and treatment (see also Brownell, 2015). Whether or not your counseling conversations are in contexts that are explicitly faith based, and whether or not your counselee is willing to have conversations regarding spirituality, these competencies help the counselor make decisions regarding why, how and when to address spiritual issues. The guiding values in this regard are relatively simple: respect, sensitivity, empathy, flexibility and responsiveness are essential (Richards & Bergin, 2005).

Whether counseling is occurring in an explicitly faith-based context or not, the autonomy of the counselee is considered paramount. We have no right to impose our beliefs on others; however, we can share our beliefs if the counselee gives consent (as with so many issues in counseling, the counselee's *informed* consent is the key). Empathy can also be applied to a counselee's religious beliefs. Our focus should be on seeking to understand the counselee's unique spiritual journey rather than subtly or explicitly judging the veracity and orthodoxy of his or her theology. Even for Christians, there can be a wide range of beliefs on many spiritual topics. Being flexible in our consideration of how counselees interpret and apply their beliefs, and how we respond to their beliefs, is central to an effective helping process. Remember that empathy does not mean agreement or endorsement.

On the following pages are three related documents. The first is the ASERVIC competencies, introduced in the paragraphs above. It is very encouraging that the American Counseling Association, the major professional counseling association in the United States, has endorsed these competencies. It allows Christians, and people from all R/S orientations, to address R/S issues in counseling—of course with appropriate cautions and ethical awareness.

Related to the need to carefully discern the use of R/S interventions in counseling, the second document extends Chapelle's (2000) model of decision making, discussed in chapter fifteen, with descriptions of the steps and case examples. The application of R/S interventions needs to be carefully considered.

The third document is a brief list of research studies on R/S interventions. Reading the article titles provides a sense of the kind of research being done to show that at least some R/S interventions are effective. This empirical validation supports the integrative belief that accurate biblical interpretation, sound theology, healthy spirituality and robust scientific evidence are ultimately compatible. This confirms our belief that God's revelation of himself in nature and in Scripture is ultimately unified.

ASERVIC Competencies for Addressing Spiritual and Religious Issues in Counseling (2009)

Preamble

The Competencies for Addressing Spiritual and Religious Issues in Counseling are guidelines that complement, not supersede, the values and standards espoused in the ACA Code of Ethics.

Consistent with the ACA Code of Ethics (2005), the purpose of the ASERVIC Competencies is to "recognize diversity and embrace a cross-cultural approach in support of the worth, dignity, potential, and uniqueness of people within their social and cultural contexts" (p. 3). These Competencies are intended to be used in conjunction with counseling approaches that are evidence-based and that align with best practices in counseling.

This Preamble must accompany any publication or dissemination, in whole or in part, of the ASERVIC Competencies.

Culture and Worldview

1. The professional counselor can describe the similarities and differences between spirituality and religion, including the basic beliefs of various spiritual systems, major world religions, agnosticism, and atheism.

2. The professional counselor recognizes that the counselee's beliefs (or absence of beliefs) about spirituality and/or religion are central to his or her worldview and can influence psychosocial functioning.

Counselor Self-Awareness

3. The professional counselor actively explores his or her own attitudes, beliefs, and values about spirituality and/or religion.

4. The professional counselor continuously evaluates the influence of his or her own spiritual and/or religious beliefs and values on the counselee and the counseling process.

5. The professional counselor can identify the limits of his or her understanding of the counselee's spiritual and/or religious perspective and is acquainted with religious and spiritual resources, including leaders, who can be avenues for consultation and to whom the counselor can refer.

Human and Spiritual Development

6. The professional counselor can describe and apply various models of spiritual and/or religious development and their relationship to human development.

Communication

7. The professional counselor responds to counselee communications about spirituality and/or religion with acceptance and sensitivity.

8. The professional counselor uses spiritual and/or religious concepts that are consistent with the counselee's spiritual and/or religious perspectives and that are acceptable to the counselee.

9. The professional counselor can recognize spiritual and/or religious themes in counselee communication and is able to address these with the counselee when they are therapeutically relevant.

Assessment

10. During the intake and assessment processes, the professional counselor strives to understand a counselee's spiritual and/or religious perspective by gathering information from the counselee and/or other sources.

Diagnosis and Treatment

11. When making a diagnosis, the professional counselor recognizes that the counselee's spiritual and/or religious perspectives can (a) enhance well-being; (b) contribute to counselee problems; and/or (c) exacerbate symptoms.

12. The professional counselor sets goals with the counselee that are consistent with the counselee's spiritual and/or religious perspectives.

13. The professional counselor is able to (a) modify therapeutic techniques to include a counselee's spiritual and/or religious perspectives, and (b) utilize spiritual and/or religious practices as techniques when appropriate and acceptable to a counselee's viewpoint.

14. The professional counselor can therapeutically apply theory and current research supporting the inclusion of a counselee's spiritual and/or religious perspectives and practices.

Table D.2. A process for applying spiritual interventions in counseling

Step	Description	Reflections	Examples
1	Why is the counselee seeking help, and are R/S issues relevant?	Is the use of spiritual interventions relevant to the counselee's presenting problem? We have no right to use an intervention because we like it when it does not directly relate to why the counselee came to see you.	If the counselee wants financial advice, career guidance or time-management tips, introducing meditation may not feel very respectful to the counselee.
2	Check the appropriateness of using R/S interventions in this context/setting.	Is it appropriate to use spiritual interventions given the public or private setting in which the counseling is occurring? Is it appropriate to use spiritual interventions given the boundaries and responsibilities of one's helping role?	Practicing inner healing prayer in a fast food restaurant is probably not appropriate. Even if the setting is private, is the R/S intervention open to alternate interpretations if observed by someone else (e.g., laying on of hands)? If your role is a professional counselor in a secular agency, be careful about using spiritual interventions.
3	Assess the compatibility of your faith perspective with the counselee's faith perspective.	The counselor role is very influential; the counselor is seen as an expert in many regards. Add to that any role (e.g., ordination, church leader) or training (e.g., seminary) you might have and your influence increases.	Even within the same faith tradition (e.g., evangelical or Roman Catholic), there is a wide range regarding theological and worship perspectives. Of course, our Christian R/S interventions may not be appropriate with counselees representing different world religions.
4	Assess your competency in using a relevant R/S intervention.	Do your own homework to obtain the necessary education and training. Many R/S interventions have specific applications depending on specific church or denominational contexts and traditions. Empirical research has been conducted on many interventions (e.g., inner healing). Respect these sources and expertise.	Solitude can produce unintended internal distress for a counselee. Do you know how to handle such a situation? Have you engaged the literature on the use and misuse of prayer and meditation, for example? Religious rites and sacraments (e.g., the Lord's Supper) have significant meanings and procedures, and may require specific qualifications in some traditions.
5	Obtain informed consent from the counselee (ask their permission!).	Describe and discuss the interventions you want to use and seek permission from the counselee before using spiritual interventions.	It only takes a moment to explain the value of Scripture, and many people are not against Scripture; rather, they just do not know how it applies.

Step	Description	Reflections	Examples
6	In the midst of using an R/S intervention continue to use what you know about helpful counseling.	Using an R/S intervention does not mean that other counseling skills are not relevant.	Empathy is important during the use of R/S interventions as well.
7	Prioritize respect for the counselee's beliefs and practices and their right to choose.	Do not proselytize or use counseling as a "pulpit" for imposing your own religious values on the counselee. The counselee's right to freely choose, without any feeling of coercion, is essential for safety.	The goal is to help the counselee experience God in a different way that will open up new possibilities. The counselee's agreement with your beliefs and values is not the goal.
8	Depending on the context and your role, document the use of spiritual interventions carefully.	As appropriate to the context, maintain a record that clearly describes the rationale, use and effectiveness of each spiritual intervention employed in the process of counseling.	Even in informal counseling contexts, keeping notes of the length and locations of meetings, the topics of discussion and the interventions suggested can indicate a level of concern and attention, as well as remind you the next time you meet of what happened last time.
9	Connect the R/S intervention to the reason the counselee is seeking help and promote the overall well-being of the counselee.	R/S interventions that are not relevant to the counselee's presenting problem are more easily mistaken as coercive. Always consider the safety and well-being of the counselee with any intervention that is employed in the process of counseling.	This is particularly important with more dramatic and powerful interventions (e.g., deliverance/exorcism). However, even for more common interventions it is possible, for instance, for prayer to be misunderstood, misapplied and mismanaged.

Source: Modified from Chapelle, 2000.

A Sample of Outcomes Research Related to Spiritual Interventions

The following titles of research articles are only a small sampling of the many intriguing studies on spiritual interventions. The first six are focused on prayer as an intervention; the last three provide examples of spiritual interventions in general.

✓ Functions of Christian prayer in the coping process (Bade & Cook, 2008)
✓ A new look at children's understanding of mind and emotion: The case of prayer (Bamford & Lagattuta, 2010)
✓ Praying in a secularized society: An empirical study of praying practices and varieties (Bänziger, Janssen & Scheepers, 2008)
✓ Christian counselees' preferences regarding prayer as a counseling intervention (Weld & Eriksen, 2007)
✓ A qualitative exploration into how the use of prayer in counselling and psychotherapy might be ethically problematic (Gubi, 2009)
✓ Theophostic prayer ministry in clinical practice: Issues and concerns (Hunter & Yarhouse, 2009b)
✓ Clinical use of explicit religious approaches: Christian role integration issues (Hathaway, 2009)

✓ Counseling students' perceptions of religious/spiritual counseling training: A qualitative study (Henriksen, Polonyi, Bornsheuer-Boswell, Greger & Watts, 2015)

✓ Considerations and recommendations for the use of religiously-based interventions in a licensed setting (Hunter & Yarhouse, 2009a)

✓ Prayer and subjective well-being: An examination of six different types of prayer (Whittington & Scher, 2010)

REFERENCES

Adams, J. E. (1970). *Competent to counsel.* Phillipsburg, NJ: Presbyterian and Reformed.

———. (1981). *Ready to restore: A layman's guide to Christian counseling.* Phillipsburg, NJ: Presbyterian and Reformed.

Alcoholics Anonymous World Services (2002). *Twelve steps and twelve traditions.* New York, NY: Author.

Allen, V. B., Folger, W. A., & Pehrsson, D. (2007). Reflective process in play therapy: A practical model for supervising counseling students. *Education, 127*(4), 472-79.

American Counseling Association (2014). *ACA Code of Ethics.* Alexandria, VA: Author.

American Psychiatric Association (2013). *Diagnostic and statistics manual of mental disorders* (5th ed.; DSM-5). Washington, DC: Author.

Anderson, L. W., & Krathwohl, D. R. (2001). *A taxonomy for learning, teaching and assessing: A revision of Bloom's Taxonomy.* New York, NY: Longman.

Anderson, N. T. (1990). *The bondage breaker.* Eugene, OR: Harvest House.

Anderson, N. T., Zuehlke, T. E., & Zuehlke, J. S. (2000). *Christ centered therapy: The practical integration of theology and psychology.* Grand Rapids, MI: Zondervan.

Anderson, R., & Ross, V. (1998). *Questions of communication: A practical introduction to theory* (2nd ed.). Boston, MA: Bedford/St. Martin's.

Antony, M. M. (2014). Behavior therapy. In D. Wedding & R. J. Corsini (Eds.), *Current psychotherapies* (10th ed.) (193-230). Belmont, CA: Brooks/Cole.

Appleby, D. W., & Ohlschlager, G. (Eds.). (2013). *Transformative encounters: The intervention of God in Christian counseling and pastoral care.* Downers Grove, IL: InterVarsity Press.

Arterburn, S., & Felton, J. (1991). *Toxic faith: Understanding and overcoming religious addiction.* Nashville, TN: Thomas Nelson.

Association for the Spiritual, Ethical, and Religious Values in Counseling (ASERVIC). (2009). *Competencies for addressing spiritual and religious issues in counseling.* Retrieved from www.aservic.org/resources/spiritual-competencies/.

Aten, J. D., & Leach, M. M. (Eds.). (2008). *Spirituality and the therapeutic process: A comprehensive resource from intake to termination.* Washington, DC: American Psychological Association.

Augsburger, D. W. (1986). *Pastoral counseling across cultures.* Philadelphia, PA: Westminster.

Averbeck, R. E. (2008). Spirit, community, and mission: A biblical theology for spiritual formation. *Journal of Spiritual Formation & Soul Care, 1,* 27-53.

Backus, W. (2006). *Telling each other the truth.* Minneapolis, MN: Bethany House.

Backus, W., & Chapian, M. (2014). *Telling yourself the truth*. Minneapolis, MN: Bethany House.

Bade, M. K., & Cook, S. W. (2008). Functions of Christian prayer in the coping process. *Journal for the Scientific Study of Religion, 47*(1), 123-33.

Baker, H. (1998). *Soul keeping: Ancient paths of spiritual direction*. Colorado Springs, CO: NavPress.

Baker, S. B., Daniels, T. G., & Greeley, A. T. (1990). Systematic training of graduate level counselors: Narrative and meta-analytic reviews of three major programs. *The Counseling Psychologist, 18*, 355-421.

Ball, R. A., & Goodyear, R. K. (1991). Self-reported professional practices of Christian psychotherapists. *Journal of Psychology and Christianity, 10*(2), 144-53.

Bamford, C., & Lagattuta, K. H. (2010). A new look at children's understanding of mind and emotion: The case of prayer. *Developmental Psychology, 46*(1), 78-92.

Bänziger, S., Janssen, J., & Scheepers, P. (2008). Praying in a secularized society: An empirical study of praying practices and varieties. *International Journal for the Psychology of Religion, 18*(3), 256-65.

Barker, P. (1985). *Using metaphors in psychotherapy*. New York, NY: Brunner/Mazel.

Barnett, J. E. (1998). Should psychotherapists self-disclose? Clinical and ethical considerations. In J. L. Thomas, S. Knapp & L. VandeCreek (Eds.), *Innovations in clinical practice: A sourcebook: Vol. 16* (419-28). Sarasota, FL: Professional Resource Press.

Bartholomew, K., & Horowitz, L. M. (1991). Attachment styles among young adults: A test of a four-category model. *Journal of Personality and Social Psychology, 61*, 226-44.

Barton, R. H. (2009). *Sacred rhythms: Arranging our lives for spiritual transformation*. Downers Grove, IL: InterVarsity Press.

Bayne, R., & Thompson, K L. (2000). Counsellor response to clients' metaphors: An evaluation and refinement of Strong's model. *Counselling Psychology Quarterly, 13*, 37-49.

Beck, J. R. (1999). *Jesus and personality theory*. Downers Grove, IL: InterVarsity Press.

Beck, J. R., & Demarest, B. (2005). *The human person in theological and psychological perspective: A biblical anthropology for the twenty-first century*. Grand Rapids, MI: Kregel.

Beck, T. D. (2009). The divine dis-comforter: The Holy Spirit's role in transformative suffering. *Journal of Spiritual Formation & Soul Care, 2*, 199-218.

Benn, A. E., Jones, G. W., & Rosenfield, S. (2008). Analysis of instructional consultants' questions and alternatives to questions during the problem identification interview. *Journal of Educational & Psychological Consultation, 18*(1), 54-80. doi:10.1080/10474410701864115

Benner, D. G. (1983). The incarnation as a metaphor for psychotherapy. *Journal of Psychology and Theology, 11*, 287-94.

———. (1988). *Psychotherapy and the spiritual quest*. Grand Rapids, MI: Baker.

———. (1998). *Care of souls: Revisioning Christian nurture and counsel*. Grand Rapids, MI: Baker Books.

———. (2002). *Sacred companions: The gift of spiritual friendship & direction*. Downers Grove, IL: InterVarsity Press.

———. (2003). *Surrender to love: Discovering the heart of Christian spirituality*. Downers Grove, IL: InterVarsity Press.

———. (2004). *The gift of being yourself: The sacred call to self-discovery*. Downers Grove, IL: InterVarsity Press.

————. (2005). *Desiring God's will: Aligning our hearts with the heart of God.* Downers Grove, IL: InterVarsity Press.

————. (2010). *Opening to God: Lectio divina and life as prayer.* Downers Grove, IL: InterVarsity Press.

————. (2015). Then and now: Response from David G. Benner. *The EMCAPP Journal: Christian Psychology Around the World, 7 Canada.* Retrieved from http://emcapp.ignis.de/7.

Bernard, J. M., Clingerman, T. L., & Gilbride, D. D. (2011). Personality type and clinical supervision interventions. *Counselor Education & Supervision, 50*(3), 154-70.

Bernard, J. M., & Goodyear, R. K. (2013). *Fundamentals of clinical supervision* (5th ed.). Upper Saddle River, NJ: Pearson.

Blomberg, C. L. (2012). *Interpreting the parables* (2nd ed.). Downers Grove, IL: IVP Academic.

Bloom, B. S., Engelhart, M. D., Furst, E. J., Hill, W. H., & Krathwohl, D. R. (1956). *Taxonomy of educational objectives: The classification of educational goals. Book I: Cognitive domain.* New York, NY: David McKay.

Bonhoeffer, D. (1937/1995). *The cost of discipleship.* New York, NY: Touchstone.

Bowen, M. (1978). *Family therapy in clinical practice.* New York, NY: Jason Aronson.

Bowlby, J. (1988). *A secure base: Clinical applications of attachment theory.* New York, NY: Basic Books.

Boyatzis, C. J., & Varghese, R. (1994). Children's emotional associations with colors. *The Journal of Genetic Psychology, 155*(1), 77-85.

Brodsky, S. L., & Lichtenstein, B. (1999). Don't ask questions: A psychotherapeutic strategy for treatment of involuntary clients. *American Journal of Psychotherapy, 53*(2), 215-20.

Bronfenbrenner, U. (1999). Environments in developmental perspective: Theoretical and operational models. In S. L. Friedman & T. D. Wachs (Eds.), *Measuring environment across the life span: Emerging methods and concepts* (3-28). Washington, DC: American Psychological Association Press.

Brown, B. (2012). *Daring greatly: How the courage to be vulnerable transforms the way we live, love, parent, and lead.* New York, NY: Gotham Books.

Brown, J. E. (1997). The Question Cube: A model for developing question repertoire in training couple and family therapist. *Journal of Marital and Family Therapist, 23*(1).

Brownell, P. (2015). *Spiritual competency in psychotherapy.* New York, NY: Springer.

Buckland, S. (2006). *Netherlands—culture smart! The essential guide to customs & culture.* New York, NY: Random House.

Buechler, S. (2002). Fromm's spirited values and analytic neutrality. *International Forum of Psychoanalysis, 11,* 275-78.

Cade, B., & O'Hanlon, W. H. (1993). *A brief guide to brief therapy.* New York, NY: Norton.

Calhoun, A. A. (2015). *Spiritual disciplines handbook: Practices that transform us.* Downers Grove, IL: InterVarsity Press.

Carlson, D. (1976). Jesus' style of relating: The search for a biblical view of counseling. *Journal of Psychology and Theology, 4,* 181-92.

Carter, J. D., & Narramore, B. (1979). *The integration of psychology and theology: An introduction.* Grand Rapids, MI: Zondervan.

Casey, J. A. (1999). Computer assisted simulation for counselor training of basic skills. *Journal of Technology in Counseling 1*(1).

Cashwell, C. S., Young, J. S., Fulton, C. L., Willis, B. T., Giordano, A., Daniel, L. W., Crockett, J., Tate, B. N., & Welch, M. L. (2013). Clinical behaviors for addressing religious/spiritual issues: Do we practice what we preach? *Counseling and Values, 58,* 45-58. doi: 10.1002/j.2161-007X.2013.00024.x

Chan, S., & Lee, E. (2004). Families with Asian roots. In E. W. Lynch & M. J. Hanson (Eds.), *Developing cross-cultural competence: A guide for working with children and their families* (3rd ed.) (219-98). Baltimore, MD: Brookes.

Chang, V., Scott, S., & Decker, C. (2013). *Developing helping skills: A step-by-step approach to competency* (2nd ed.). Belmont, CA: Brooks/Cole.

Chao, R. C.-L. (2011). Managing stress and maintaining well-being: Social support, problem-focused coping, and avoidant coping. *Journal of Counseling & Development, 89,* 338-48.

Chapelle, W. (2000). A series of progressive legal and ethical decision making steps for using Christian spiritual interventions in psychotherapy. *Journal of Psychology and Theology, 28*(1), 43-53.

Chudler, E. H. (2014). *Autonomic nervous system.* Retrieved from https://faculty.washington.edu/chudler/auto.html

Clinton, T., & Sibcy, G. (2002). *Attachments: Why you love, feel and act the way you do.* Brentwood, TN: Integrity.

Cloud, H., & Townsend, J. (1994). *False assumptions.* Grand Rapids, MI: Zondervan.

———. (2001). *How people grow: What the Bible reveals about personal growth.* Grand Rapids, MI: Zondervan.

Coe, J. H. (2000). Musings on the Dark Night of the Soul: Insights from St. John of the Cross on a developmental spirituality. *Journal of Psychology and Theology, 28,* 293-307.

Collins, B. (2012). Metaphorical communication in working with couples. *Psychodynamic Practice, 18,* 339-44.

Cook, M. (2011). *Graduate counseling students' use of Facebook privacy settings: Implications for self-disclosure* (Unpublished MA thesis). Denver Seminary, Denver, CO.

Cooper, M. L., Albino, A. W., Orcutt, H. K., & Williams, N. (2004). Attachment styles and intrapersonal adjustment: A longitudinal study from adolescence into young adulthood. In W. S. Rholes & J. A. Simpson (Eds.), *Adult attachment: Theory, research, and clinical implications* (438-66). New York, NY: Guilford.

Corey, G. (2013). *Theory and practice of counseling and psychotherapy* (9th ed.). Belmont, CA: Brooks/Cole.

Corey, G., & Corey, M. S. (2011). *Becoming a helper* (6th ed.). Stamford, CT: Cengage Learning.

Crabb, L. (1988). *Inside out: Real change is possible if you are willing to start from the inside out.* Colorado Springs, CO: NavPress.

———. (1997). *Connecting: Healing for ourselves and our relationships.* Nashville, TN: Nelson.

———. (1999). *The safest place on earth: Where people connect and are forever changed.* Nashville, TN: Nelson.

Dael, N., Mortillaro, M., & Scherer, K. R. (2012). Emotion expression in body action and posture. *Emotion, 12*(5), 1085-1101. doi:10.1037/a0025737

Damasio, A. R. (2012). *Self comes to mind: Constructing the conscious brain.* New York, NY: Vintage Books.

Day-Vines, N. L., Wood, S. M., Grothaus, T., Graigen, L., Holman, A., Dotson-Blake, K., & Douglass, M. J. (2007). Broaching the subjects of race, ethnicity, and culture during the counseling process. *Journal of Counseling and Development, 85,* 401-9.

De Stefano, J., Mann-Feder, V., & Gazzola, N. (2010). A qualitative study of client experiences of working with novice counsellors. *Counselling & Psychotherapy Research, 10*(2), 139-46. doi:10.1080/14733141003770713

Decenteceo, E. T. (1997). *Rehab: Psychosocial rehabilitation for social transformation—some programs and concepts.* Manila, Philippines: Bukal Publications.

Decker, E. E., Jr.,(2002). The Holy Spirit in counseling: A review of Christian counseling journal articles (1985–1999). *Journal of Psychology and Christianity, 21,* 21-28.

Demarest, B. (1999). *Satisfy your soul: Restoring the heart of Christian spirituality.* Colorado Springs, CO: NavPress.

———. (2009). *Seasons of the soul: Stages of spiritual development.* Downers Grove, IL: Inter-Varsity Press.

Denney, R. M., Aten, J. D., & Gingrich, F. (2008). Using spiritual self-disclosure in counseling and psychotherapy. *Journal of Psychology & Theology, 36*(4), 294-302.

Diel, P. (1975/1986). *Symbolism in the Bible: Its psychological significance.* San Francisco, CA: Harper & Row.

Doherty, W. J. (1999). Morality and spirituality in therapy. In F. Walsh (Ed.), *Spiritual resources in family therapy* (189-91). New York, NY: Guilford.

Dougherty, R. M. (1995). *Group spiritual direction: Community for discernment.* Mahwah, NJ: Paulist.

Dueck, A., & Reimer, K. (2009). *A peaceable psychology: Christian therapy in a world of many cultures.* Grand Rapids, MI: Brazos.

Duru, E. (2008). The predictive analysis of adjustment difficulties from loneliness, social support, and social connectedness. *Educational Sciences, Theory & Practice, 8*(3), 849-56.

Eckert, K. G., & Kimball, C. N. (2003). God as a secure base and haven of safety: Attachment theory as a framework for understanding relationship to God. In T. W. Hall & M. R. McMinn (Eds.), *Spiritual formation, counseling, and psychotherapy* (105-23). New York, NY: Nova Science Publishers.

Egan, A. (2010). Conscience, spirit, discernment: The Holy Spirit, the spiritual exercises and the formation of moral conscience. *Journal of Theology for Southern Africa, 138,* 57-70.

Egan, G. (2014). *The skilled helper: A problem-management and opportunity-development approach to helping* (10th ed.). Belmont, CA: Brooks/Cole.

Elliot, A. J., & Maier, M. A. (2007). Color and psychological functioning. *Current Direction in Psychological Science, 16*(5), 250-54. doi: 10.111/j.1467-8721.2007.00514.x

Elliott, M. (2006). *Faithful feelings: Rethinking emotion in the New Testament.* Grand Rapids, MI: Kregel.

————. (2014). *Feel: The power of listening to your heart.* Grand Rapids, MI: Kregel.

Ellis, A. (1993). The advantages and disadvantages of self-help therapy materials. *Professional Psychology: Research and Practice, 24*(3), 335-39.

Enroth, R. M. (1992). *Churches that abuse.* Grand Rapids, MI: Zondervan.

————. (1994). *Recovering from churches that abuse.* Grand Rapids, MI: Zondervan.

Entwistle, D. N. (2010). *Integrative approaches to psychology and Christianity: An introduction to worldview issues, philosophical foundations, and models of integration* (2nd ed.). Eugene, OR: Cascade Books.

Evans, D. R., Hearn, M. T., Uhlemann, M. R., & Ivey, A. E. (2011). *Essential interviewing: A programmed approach to effective communication* (8th ed.). Belmont, CA: Brooks/Cole.

Faranda, F. (2014). Working with images in psychotherapy: An embodied experience of play and metaphor. *Journal of Psychotherapy Integration, 24,* 65-77.

Foley, V. D. (1979). Family therapy. In R. J. Corsini (Ed.), *Current psychotherapies* (2nd ed.) (460-99). Itasca, IL: F. E. Peacock.

Foster, R. J. (1998). *Streams of living water: Celebrating the great traditions of the faith.* San Francisco, CA: HarperCollins.

————. (2002). *Celebration of discipline: The path to spiritual growth.* San Francisco, CA: Harper.

Fowler, J. W. (1984). *Becoming adult, becoming Christian: Adult development and Christian faith.* San Francisco, CA: Harper & Row.

Frame, M. W. (2003). *Integrating religion and spirituality into counseling.* Pacific Grove, CA: Brooks/Cole.

Freud, S. (1927/1978). *The future of an illusion.* London, England: Hogarth.

Friedman, E. (1985). *Generation to generation: Family process in church and synagogue.* New York, NY: Guilford.

Fryling, A. (2008). *Seeking God together: An introduction to group spiritual direction.* Downers Grove, IL: InterVarsity Press.

Garland, D. R. (1999). *Family ministry: A comprehensive guide.* Downers Grove, IL: InterVarsity Press.

Garrett, M. T., & Portman, T. A. A. (2011). *Counseling Native Americans.* Belmont, CA: Cengage.

Garwick, A. (2000). What do providers need to know about American Indian culture? Recommendations from urban Indian family caregivers. *Families, Systems & Health: The Journal of Collaborative Family Healthcare, 18*(2), 177-89.

Gazda, G. M., Balzer, F. J., Childers, W. C., Nealy, A. U., Phelps, R. E., & Walters, R. P. (2005). *Human relations development: A manual for educators* (7th ed.). Boston, MA: Pearson.

Gelo, O. C. G., & Mergenthaler, E. (2012). Unconventional metaphors and emotional-cognitive regulation in a metacognitive interpersonal therapy. *Psychotherapy Research, 22,* 159-75.

Gingrich, F., & Smith, B. M. (Eds.). (2014). Special Issue: Psychology in the global context. *Journal of Psychology and Christianity, 33*(2).

Gingrich, F., & Smith, B. M. (in press). *Global mental health: Expanding the church's transforming mission.* Downers Grove, IL: InterVarsity Press.

Gingrich, F., & Worthington, E. L., Jr. (2007). Supervision and the integration of faith into clinical practice: Research considerations. *Journal of Psychology and Christianity, 26*, 342-55.

Gingrich, H. D. (2013). *Restoring the shattered self: A Christian counselor's guide to complex trauma.* Downers Grove, IL: IVP Academic.

Goleman, D. (2006). Social intelligence: The new science of human relationships. New York, NY: Bantam.

Goldstein, G., & Suzuki, J. (2015). The analyst's authenticity: "If you see something, say something." *Journal of Clinical Psychology: In Session, 71*(5), 451-56.

Gorsuch, R. L. (2002). *Integrating psychology and spirituality?* Westport, CN: Praeger.

Gottman, J. M., & Gottman, J. S. (2007). *And baby makes three: The six-step plan for preserving marital intimacy and rekindling romance after baby arrives.* New York, NY: Crown.

Gottman, J. M., & Silver, N. (2000). *The seven principles for making marriage work: A practical guide from the country's foremost relationship expert.* New York, NY: Three Rivers.

Green, H. (1964/2004). *I never promised you a rose garden: A novel.* New York, NY: St. Martin's Press.

Greggo, S. P. (2007). Biblical metaphors for corrective emotional relationships in group work. *Journal of Psychology and Theology, 35*, 153-62.

―――. (2016, in press). *Assessment in Christian counseling.* Downers Grove, IL: IVP Academic.

Greggo, S. P., & Lawrence, K. (2012). Clinical appraisal of spirituality: In search of Rapid Assessment Instruments (RAIs) for Christian counseling. *Journal of Psychology and Christianity, 31*(3), 253-66.

Greggo, S. P., & Sisemore, T. (Eds.). (2012). *Counseling and Christianity: Five approaches.* Downers Grove, IL: InterVarsity Press.

Gross, J. J. (2014). Emotional regulation: Conceptual and empirical foundations. In J. J. Gross (Ed.), *Handbook of Emotion Regulation* (2nd ed.). New York, NY: Guilford.

Gubi, P. M. (2009). A qualitative exploration into how the use of prayer in counselling and psychotherapy might be ethically problematic. *Counselling and Psychotherapy Research, 9*(2), 115-21.

Guernsey, D., & Guernsey, L (1991). *Birthmarks: Breaking free from the destructive imprints of your family history.* Dallas, TX: Word.

Hall, T. W., & McMinn, M. R. (Eds.). (2003). *Spiritual formation, counseling and psychotherapy.* New York, NY: Nova Science.

Hammond, D. C., Hepworth, D. H., & Smith, V. G. (1977). *Improving therapeutic communication.* San Francisco, CA: Jossey-Bass.

―――. (2002). *Improving therapeutic communication: A guide for developing effective techniques.* San Francisco, CA: Jossey-Bass.

Hampson, P. (2012). "By knowledge and by love": The integrative role of *habitus* in Christian psychology. *Edification, 6*(1), 5-18. (See also the commentaries on this article, pp. 19-42).

Hankle, D. D. (2010). The therapeutic implications of the imprecatory psalms in the Christian counseling setting. *Journal of Psychology & Theology, 38*(4), 275-80.

Hansen, G. W. (1997, Feb. 3). The emotions of Jesus and why we need to experience them. *Christianity Today, 43.*

Hathaway, W. L. (2009). Clinical use of explicit religious approaches: Christian role integration issues. *Journal of Psychology and Christianity, 28*(2), 105-22.

Hayes, B. G. (2008). Counselor education: Integration of teaching strategies. *Journal of Technology in Counseling, 5*(1).

Hearn, M. (1976). *Three models of training counselors: A comparative study.* Ontario, Canada: University of Western Ontario Press.

Henriksen, R. C., Polonyi, M. A., Bornsheuer-Boswell, J. N., Greger, R. G., & Watts, R. E. (2015). Counseling students' perceptions of religious/spiritual counseling training: A qualitative study. *Journal of Counseling and Development, 93*, 59-69.

Hill, C., & O'Brien, K. (1999). *Helping skills.* Washington, DC: American Psychological Association.

Hollon, S. D., & Ponniah, K. (2010). A review of empirically supported psychological therapies for mood disorders in adults. *Depression & Anxiety (1091-4269), 27*(10), 891-932.

Hunter, L. A., & Yarhouse, M. A. (2009a). Considerations and recommendations for the use of religiously-based interventions in a licensed setting. *Journal of Psychology and Christianity, 28*(2), 159-66.

———. (2009b). Theophostic prayer ministry in clinical practice: Issues and concerns. *Journal of Psychology and Christianity, 28*(2), 149-58.

Hutchison, A. N., & Gerstein, L. H. (2012). What's in a face? Counseling trainees' ability to read emotions. *Training and Education in Professional Psychology, 6*(2), 100-112. doi:10.1037/a0028807

Ivey, A. E., Ivey, M. B., & Zalaquett, C. P. (2014). *Intentional interviewing and counseling: Facilitating client development in a multicultural society* (8th ed.). Boston, MA: Brooks/Cole.

Jack, R. E. (2013). Culture and facial expressions of emotion. *Visual Cognition, 21*(9/10), 1248-86. doi:10.1080/13506285.2013.835367

Jensen, J. V. (1985). *Perspective on nonverbal intercultural communication.* In L. A. Samovar & R. E. Porter (Eds.), *Intercultural communication: A reader* (256-72). Belmont, CA: Wadsworth.

Jocano, F. L. (1997). *Filipino value system: A cultural definition.* Quezon City, Philippines: PUNLAD Research House.

Johnson, E. L. (Ed.). (2010). *Psychology and Christianity: Five views.* Downers Grove, IL: InterVarsity Press.

Johnson, S. M. (2004a). Attachment theory: A guide for healing couple relationships. In W. S. Rholes & J. A. Simpson (Eds.), *Adult attachment: Theory, research, and clinical implications* (367-87). New York, NY: Guilford.

———. (2004b). *The practice of emotionally focused couple therapy: Creating connection* (2nd ed.). New York, NY: Brunner-Routledge.

Jones, S. L., & Butman, R. E. (2011). *Modern psychotherapies: A comprehensive Christian appraisal* (2nd ed.). Downers Grove, IL: InterVarsity Press.

Kaya, N., & Epps, H. H. (2004). Relationship between color and emotion: A study of college students. *College Student Journal, 38*(3), 396-405.

Kearney, R. (2007). Narrating pain: The power of catharsis. *Paragraph, 30*(1), 51-66.

Killen, M., & Coplan, R. J. (Eds.). (2011). *Social development in childhood and adolescence: A contemporary reader.* Hoboken, NJ: Wiley-Blackwell.

Kim-van Daalen, L. (2012). The Holy Spirit, common grace, and secular psychotherapy. *Journal of Psychology & Theology, 40*, 229-39.

King, J., trans. (1847–1850). *Calvin's commentaries, 33, Matthew, Mark and Luke, Part III.* Retrieved from www.sacred-texts.com

Kinnaman, D., & Lyons, G. (2012). *unChristian: What a new generation really thinks about Christianity . . . and why it matters.* Grand Rapids, MI: Baker.

Kleinman, A., Eisenberg, L., & Good, B. (1978). Culture, illness, and care: Clinical lessons from anthropologic and cross-cultural research. *Annals of Internal Medicine, 88*, 83-93.

Klofstad, C. A., Anderson, R. C., & Peters, S. (2012). Sounds like a winner: Voice pitch influences perception of leadership capacity in both men and women. *Proceedings of the Royal Society B.* doi:10.1098/rspb.2012.0311

Koenig, H. G. (2011). *Spirituality and health research: Methodology, measurement, analyses, and resources.* West Conshohocken, PA: Templeton.

———. (2012). Religion, spirituality, and health: The research and clinical implications. *International Scholarly Research Network (ISRN) Psychiatry.* Article ID 278730. doi:10.5402/2012/278730

Koenig, H. G., King, D., & Carson, V. B. (2012). *Handbook of religion and health* (2nd ed.). New York, NY: Oxford University Press.

Kopp, R. R., & Craw, M. J. (1998). Metaphoric language, metaphoric cognition, and cognitive therapy. *Psychotherapy, 35*, 306-11.

Kudler, H. S., Krupnick, J. L., Blank, A. S., Jr., Herman, J. L., & Horowitz, M. J. (2010). Psychodynamic therapy for adults. In E. B. Foa, T. M. Keane, M. J. Friedman & J. A. Cohen (Eds.), *Effective treatments for PTSD* (2nd ed.) (346-69). New York, NY: Guildford Press.

Kuntze, J., van der Molen, H. T., & Born, M. P. (2009). Increase in counselling communication skills after basic and advanced microskills training. *British Journal of Educational Psychology, 79*, 175-88.

LaBarre, W. (1985). Paralinguistics, kinesics and cultural anthropology. In L. A. Samovar & R. E. Porter (Eds.), *Intercultural communication: A reader* (272-79). Belmont, CA: Wadsworth.

L'Abate, L. (Ed). (1998). *Family psychopathology: The relational roots of dysfunctional behavior.* New York, NY: Guilford.

Lambert, M. J., & Barley, D. E. (2002). Research summary on the therapeutic relationship and psychotherapy outcome. In J. C. Norcross (Ed.), *Psychotherapy relationships that work: Therapist contributions and responsiveness to patients.* New York, NY: Oxford University Press.

Lanier, S. (2006). *Foreign to familiar: A guide to understanding hot and cold climate cultures.* Hagerstown, MD: McDougal.

Larkin, E. E. (1967). The three spiritual ways. In *The published articles of Ernest E. Larkin.* Retrieved from http://carmelnet.org/larkin/larkin092.pdf

Leach, M. M., & Sato, T. (2013). A content analysis of the *Psychology of Religion and Spirituality* journal: The initial four years. *Psychology of Religion and Spirituality, 5*(2), 61-68. doi:10.1037/a0032602

Lee, R. W, & Jordan, J. L. (2008). Counseling laboratories and clinics: Making the most of technology. *Journal of Technology in Counseling, 5*(1). Retrieved from http://techcounseling.net/Archive/Vol5_1/Lee.htm

Leibert, T. W., Smith, J. B., & Agaskar, V. R. (2011). Relationship between the working alliance and social support on counseling outcome. *Journal of Clinical Psychology, 67*(7), 709-19. doi: 10.1002/jclp.2080

Levine, A., & Heller, R. (2010). *Attached: The new science of adult attachment and how it can help you find—and keep—love.* New York, NY: Tarcher.

Lewis, C. S. (1950/1977). *The lion, the witch, and the wardrobe.* Middlesex, UK: Puffin.

Linehan, M. (1993). Cognitive-behavioral treatment of borderline personality disorder. New York, NY: Guilford.

Little, C., Packman, J., Smaby, M. H., & Maddux, C. D. (2005). The Skilled Counselor Training Model: Skills acquisition, self-assessment, and cognitive complexity. *Counselor Education & Supervision, 44,* 189-200.

Lyddon, W. J., Clay, A. L., & Sparks, C. L. (2001). Metaphor and change in counseling. *Journal of Counseling & Development, 79,* 269-74.

Manning, B. (2002). *Abba's child: The cry of the heart for intimate belonging.* Colorado Springs, CO: NavPress.

———. (2004). *The wisdom of tenderness: What happens when God's fierce mercy transforms our lives.* New York, NY: HarperOne.

———. (2005). *The ragamuffin gospel: Good news for the bedraggled, beat-up, and burnt out.* Colorado Springs, CO: Multnomah.

———. (2009). *Ruthless trust: The ragamuffin's path to God.* New York, NY: HarperCollins.

———. (2009). *The furious longing of God.* Colorado Springs, CO: David C. Cook.

Mason, M. (1985). *The mystery of marriage: Meditations on the miracle.* Sisters, OR: Multnomah.

McCarthy, A. K. (2014). Relationship between rehabilitation counselor efficacy for counseling skills and client outcomes. *Journal of Rehabilitation, 80*(2), 3-11.

McGee, R. (2003). *The search for significance: Seeing your true worth through God's eyes.* Nashville, TN: Thomas Nelson.

McHenry, B., & McHenry, J. (2015). *What therapists say and why they say it: Effective therapeutic responses and techniques.* New York, NY: Routledge.

McMinn, M. R. (1996). *Psychology, theology, and spirituality in Christian counseling.* Wheaton, IL: Tyndale.

McMinn, M. R., & Campbell, C. D. (2007). *Integrative psychotherapy: Toward a comprehensive Christian approach.* Downers Grove, IL: IVP Academic.

McRay, B. W., Yarhouse, M. A., & Butman, R. E. (2016). *Modern psychopathologies: A comprehensive Christian appraisal.* (2nd ed.). Downers Grove, IL: InterVarsity Press.

McWilliams, N. (2011). *Psychoanalytic diagnosis: Understanding personality structure in the clinical process* (2nd ed.). New York, NY: Guilford.

Mehrabian, A. (1971). *Silent messages.* Belmont, CA: Wadsworth.

Meyer, E. (2014). *The culture map: Breaking through the invisible boundaries of global business.* New York, NY: Public Affairs.

Miles, A. (2011). *Domestic violence: What every pastor needs to know* (2nd ed.). Minneapolis, MN: Augsburg Fortress.

Monroe, P. (2005, Oct.). *Connecting people to God: Guidelines for using Scripture in counseling.* Seminar presented at AACC Conference, Nashville, TN.

Moon, G. W. (1997). *Homesick for Eden: A soul's journey to joy.* Ann Arbor, MI: Vine.

Moon, G. W., Bailey, J. W., Kwasny, J. C., & Willis, D. E. (1991). Training in the use of Christian disciplines as counseling techniques within religiously oriented graduate training programs. *Journal of Psychology and Christianity, 10*(2), 154-65.

Moon, G. W., & Benner, D. G. (Eds.). (2004). *Spiritual direction & the care of souls: A guide to Christian approaches and practice.* Downers Grove, IL: InterVarsity Press.

Morrison, J. (2014). *Diagnosis made easier: Principles and techniques for mental health clinicians.* New York, NY: Guilford.

Mulholland, M. R., Jr. (1993). *Invitation to a journey: A roadmap for spiritual formation.* Downers Grove, IL: InterVarsity Press.

Murphy, B. C., & Dillon, C. (2008). *Interviewing in action in a multicultural world* (3rd ed.). Belmont, CA: Thompson Brooks/Cole.

Mwiti, G. K., & Dueck, A. (2006). *Christian counseling: An African indigenous perspective.* Pasadena, CA: Fuller Seminary Press.

Newell, J. P. (2000). *Celtic benediction: Morning and night prayer.* Grand Rapids, MI: Eerdmans.

Nisbett, R. E. (2003). *The geography of thought: How Asians and Westerners think differently . . . and why.* New York, NY: Free Press.

Norcross, J. C. (2010). The therapeutic relationship. In B. L. Duncan, S. D. Miller, B. E. Wampold, & M. A. Hubble (Eds.), *The heart and soul of change* (2nd ed., pp. 113-41). Washington, DC: American Psychological Association.

———. (2011). *Psychotherapy relationships that work* (2nd ed.). New York, NY: Oxford University Press.

Nouwen, H. J. M. (1972). *The wounded healer: Ministry in contemporary society.* New York, NY: Doubleday.

———. (1994). *Here and now: Living in the Spirit.* New York, NY: Crossroad.

Nydell, M. K. (1996). *Understanding Arabs: A guide for Westerners.* Yarmouth, ME: Intercultural Press.

Oden, T. C. (1987). *Classical pastoral care, Vol. 3, Pastoral counsel.* Grand Rapids, MI: Baker.

Okun, B. F., & Kantrowitz, R. E. (2015). *Effective helping: Interviewing and counseling techniques* (8th ed.). Boston, MA: Cengage Learning.

Orlowski, B. (2010). *Spiritual abuse recovery: Dynamic research on finding a place of wholeness.* Eugene, OR: Wipf and Stock.

Ortberg, J. (2015). *The life you've always wanted: Spiritual disciplines for ordinary people.* Grand Rapids, MI: Zondervan.

Palmer, P. (1999). *The active life: A spirituality of work, creativity, and caring.* New York, NY: Jossey-Bass.

Pargament, K. I. (2011). *Spiritually integrated psychotherapy: Understanding and addressing the sacred.* New York, NY: Guilford.

PDM Task Force. (2006). *Psychodynamic Diagnostic Manual.* Silver Spring, MD: Alliance of Psychoanalytic Organizations.

Pedersen, P. B., & Ivey, A. (1993). *Culture-centered counseling and interviewing skills: A practical guide.* Westport, CT: Praeger.

Pedersen, P. B., Lonner, W. J., Draguns, J. G., Trimble, J. E., & Scharrón-del Rio, M. R. (2016). *Counseling across cultures.* Thousand Oaks, CA: Sage.

Peterman, G. W. (2013). *Joy and tears: The emotional life of the Christian.* Chicago, IL: Moody.

Plante, T. G. (2009). *Spiritual practices in psychotherapy.* Washington, DC: APA.

———. (2014). Four steps to improve religious/spiritual cultural competence in professional psychology. *Spirituality in Clinical Practice, 1*(4), 288-92. doi:10.1037/scp0000047

Polcin, D. L., Mulia, N., & Jones, L. (2012). Substance users' perspectives on helpful and unhelpful confrontation: Implications for recovery. *Journal of Psychoactive Drugs, 44*(2), 144-52. doi:10.1080/02791072.2012.684626

Powlison, D. (2010). *The biblical counseling movement: History and context.* Greensboro, NC: New Growth.

Prechtel, D. L. (2012). *Where two or three are gathered: Spiritual direction for small groups.* New York, NY: Morehouse.

Press, B. (2011). *I am because we are: African wisdom in image and proverb.* St. Paul, MN: Books for Africa.

Prochaska, J. O., & DiClemente, C. C. (1983). Stages and processes of self-change of smoking: Towards an integrative model of change. *Journal of Consulting and Clinical Psychology, 51,* 390-95.

Prochaska, J. O., & Norcross, J. C. (2013). *Systems of psychotherapy: A transtheoretical analysis* (8th ed.). Stamford, CT: Cengage Learning.

Rautalinko, E. (2013). Reflective listening and open-ended questions in counselling: Preferences moderated by social skills and cognitive ability. *Counselling & Psychotherapy Research, 13*(1), 24-31. doi:10.1080/14733145.2012.687387

Ray, D. (2004). Supervision of basic and advanced skills in play therapy. *Journal of Professional Counseling: Practice, Theory & Research, 32*(2), 28-41.

Reinert, D. F., Edwards, C. E., & Hendrix, R. R. (2009). Attachment theory and religiosity: A summary of empirical research with implications for counseling Christian clients. *Counseling and Values, 53,* 112-25.

Richards, P. S., & Bergin, A. E. (2005). *A spiritual strategy for counseling and psychotherapy* (2nd ed.). Washington, DC: American Psychological Association.

Robert, T. E., & Kelly, V. A. (2010). Metaphor as an instrument for orchestrating change in counselor training and the counseling process. *Journal of Counseling & Development, 88,* 182-88.

———. (Eds.). (2014). *Critical incidents in integrating spirituality into counseling.* Alexandria, VA: American Counseling Association.

Robertson, L. A., & Young, M. E. (2011). The revised ASERVIC spiritual competencies. In C. S. Cashwell & J. S. Young (Eds.), *Integrating spirituality and religion into counseling: A guide to competent practice* (2nd ed.) (25-42). Alexandria, VA: American Counseling Association.

Robinson, T. L., & Howard-Hamilton, M. F. (2000). *The convergence of race, ethnicity, and gender.* Columbus, OH: Merrill.

Rogers, C. R. (1957/1992). The necessary and sufficient conditions of therapeutic personality change. *Journal of Consulting Psychology, 21*(2), 95-103. doi:10.1037/h0045357; *Journal of Consulting and Clinical Psychology, 60*, 827-32. doi:10.1037/0022-006X.60.6.827

——. (1961/1992). *On becoming a person: A therapist's view of psychotherapy.* New York, NY: Houghton Mifflin.

Rollnick, S., & Miller, W. R. (1995). What is motivational interviewing? *Behavioural and Cognitive Psychotherapy, 23*, 325-34.

Rothbaum, F., Morelli, G., Pott, M., & Liu-Constant, Y. (2000). Immigrant-Chinese and Euro-American parents' physical closeness with young children: Themes of family relatedness. *Journal of Family Psychology, 14*, 334-38.

Sanders, R. K. (Ed.). (2013). *Christian counseling ethics: A handbook for psychologists, therapists and pastors* (2nd ed.). Downers Grove, IL: IVP Academic.

Scazzero, P. (2006). *Emotionally healthy spirituality: It's impossible to be spiritually mature while remaining emotionally immature.* Grand Rapids, MI: Zondervan.

Schaub, B. G., & Schaub, R. (1990). The use of mental imagery techniques in psychodynamic psychotherapy. *Journal of Mental Health Counseling, 12*, 405-14.

Seligman, L., & Reichenberg, L. W. (2014). *Selecting effective treatments: A comprehensive systematic guide to treating mental disorders* (4th ed.). San Francisco, CA: John Wiley.

Shallcross, S. L., Frazier, P. A., & Anders, S. L. (2014). Social resources mediate the relations between attachment dimensions and distress following potentially traumatic events. *Journal of Counseling Psychology, 61*(3), 352-62. doi:10.1037/a0036583

Sharpley, C. F., Jeffrey, A. M., & McMah, T. (2006). Counsellor facial expression and client-perceived rapport. *Counselling Psychology Quarterly, 19*(4), 343-56. doi:10.1080/09515 070601058706

Sherer, M., & Rogers, R. W. (1980). Effects of therapist's nonverbal communication on rated skill and effectiveness. *Journal of Clinical Psychology, 36*(3), 696-700.

Siegel, D. (2007). *The mindful brain.* New York, NY: Norton.

Sims, P. A. (2003). Working with metaphor. *American Journal of Psychotherapy, 57*, 528-36.

Sims, P. A., & Whynot, C. A. (1997). Hearing metaphor: An approach to working with family-generated metaphor. *Family Process, 36*, 341-55. doi:10.1111/j.1545-5300.1997.00341.x

Smith, E. M. (2005). *Healing life's hurts through Theophostic Prayer.* Campbellsville, KY: New Creation.

Smith, J. B. (2009). *The good and beautiful God: Falling in love with the God Jesus knows.* Downers Grove, IL: InterVarsity Press.

Solomon, A. (2008, Oct. 29). Notes on an exorcism. *The Moth* [podcast]. Retrieved from http://themoth.org/posts/stories/notes-on-an-exorcism

Sommers-Flanagan, J., & Sommers-Flanagan, R. (2014). *Clinical interviewing* (5th ed.). New York, NY: Wiley.

Sperry, L. (2003). Integrating spiritual direction functions in the practice of psychotherapy. *Journal of Psychology and Theology, 31*, 3-13.

Sperry, L. (2011). *Spirituality in clinical practice: Theory and practice of spiritually oriented psychotherapy* (2nd ed.). New York, NY: Routledge.

Stark, M. (1999). *Modes of therapeutic action: Enhancement of knowledge, provision of experience, and engagement in relationship*. Northvale, NJ: Jason Aronson.

Stevenson, D. H., Eck, B. E., & Hill, P. C. (Eds.). (2007). *Psychology and Christianity integration: Seminal works that shaped the movement*. Batavia, IL: Christian Association of Psychological Studies.

Strong, T. (1989). Metaphors and client change in counselling. *International Journal for the Advancement of Counseling, 12*, 203-13.

Sue, D. W., & Sue, D. (2016). *Counseling the culturally diverse: Theory and practice* (7th ed). New York, NY: John Wiley & Sons.

Tallman, B. (2005). *Archetypes for spiritual direction: Discovering the heroes within*. Mahwah, NJ: Paulist.

Tamase, K., & Katu, M. (1990). Effect of questions about factual and affective aspects of life events on an introspective interview. *Bulletin of Institute for Educational Research* (Nara University of Education), *39*, 151-63.

Tan, S-Y. (1994). Ethical considerations in religious psychotherapy: Potential pitfalls and unique resources. *Journal of Psychology and Theology, 22*(4), 389-94.

———. (1996). Practicing the presence of God: The work of Richard J. Foster and its applications to psychotherapeutic practice. *Journal of Psychology and Christianity, 15*(1), 17-28.

———. (2011a). *Counseling and psychotherapy: A Christian perspective*. Grand Rapids, MI: Baker.

———. (2011b). Mindfulness and Acceptance-Based Cognitive Behavioral Therapies: Empirical evidence and clinical applications from a Christian perspective. *Journal of Psychology and Christianity, 30*(3), 243-49.

Tan, S-Y., & Castillo, M. (2014). Self-care and beyond: A brief literature review from a Christian perspective. *Journal of Psychology & Christianity, 33*(1), 90-95.

Tan, S-Y., & Gregg, D. (1997). *Disciplines of the Holy Spirit: How to connect to the Spirit's power and presence*. Grand Rapids, MI: Zondervan.

Tay, D. (2012). Applying the notion of metaphor types to enhance counseling protocols. *Journal of Counseling & Development, 90*, 142-49.

Taylor, A. (1980). The systematic skill-building approach to counselor training for clergy. *The Journal of Pastoral Care, 34*(3), 159-67.

Thompson, C. (2010). *Anatomy of the soul: Surprising connections between neuroscience and spiritual practices that can transform your life and relationships*. Carol Stream, IL: Tyndale House.

Tisdale, T. C., Doehring, C. E., & Lorraine-Poirier, V. (2004). Three voices, one song: Perspectives on the care of persons from a psychologist, spiritual director and pastoral counselor. In G. W. Moon & D. G. Benner (Eds.), *Spiritual direction and the care of souls: A guide to Christian approaches and practices* (219-42). Downers Grove, IL: InterVarsity Press.

Toporek, R. L., Lewis, J. A., & Ratts, M. J. (2010). The ACA advocacy competencies: An overview. In M. J. Ratts, R. L. Toporek & J. A. Lewis, *ACA advocacy competencies: A social justice framework for counselors* (11-20). Alexandria, VA: American Counseling Association.

Tozer, A. W. (1959). *The value of a sanctified imagination.* Retrieved from http://lovestthoume. com/FeedMySheep/SanctifiedImagination.html

Treat, S., & Hof, L. (1987). *Pastoral marital therapy: A practical primer for ministry to couples.* Mahwah, NJ: Paulist.

Turnell, A., & Lipchik, E. (1999). The role of empathy in brief therapy: The overlooked but vital context. *Australian and New Zealand Journal of Family Therapy, 20*(4), 177-82.

Turock, A. (1978). Effective challenging through additive empathy. *Personnel & Guidance Journal, 57*(3), 144-49.

Ulanov, A. B., & Dueck, A. (2008). *The living God and our living psyche: What Christians can learn from Carl Jung.* Grand Rapids, MI: Eerdmans.

University College, London Institute of Cognitive Neuroscience. (2011). *Autonomic bodily responses.* Retrieved from www.icn.ucl.ac.uk/Experimental-Techniques/Autonomic-bodily-responses/Autonomic-bodily-responses.htm

van Velsor, P. (2004). Revisiting basic counseling skills with children. *Journal of Counseling & Development, 82,* 313-18.

Von Glahn, J. (2012). Nondirectivity and the facilitation of a therapeutic cathartic release. *Person-Centered & Experiential Psychotherapies, 11*(4), 277-88.

Walker, D. F., Gorsuch, R. L., & Tan, S. (2004). Therapists' integration of religion and spirituality in counseling: A meta-analysis. *Counseling & Values, 49*(1), 69-80.

Ward, D. E. (1984). Termination of individual counseling: Concepts and strategies. *Journal of Counseling and Development, 63*(1), 21-25.

Webb, H. P., & Peterson, E. H. (2009). *Small group leadership as spiritual direction.* Grand Rapids, MI: Zondervan.

Weld, C., & Eriksen, K. (2007). Christian clients' preferences regarding prayer as a counseling intervention. *Journal of Psychology and Theology, 35,* 328-41.

Whittington, B. L., & Scher, S. J. (2010). Prayer and subjective well-being: An examination of six different types of prayer. *International Journal for the Psychology of Religion, 20*(1), 59-68.

Wilson, G. T. (2005). Behavior therapy. In R. J. Corsini & D. Wedding (Eds.), *Current Psychotherapies* (7th ed.) (202-68). Belmont, CA: Brooks/Cole.

Witteman, C. L. M., Spaanjaars, N. L., & Aarts, A. A. (2012). Clinical intuition in mental health care: A discussion and focus groups. *Counseling Psychology Quarterly, 25*(1), 19-29.

Wong, Y. J., & Rochlen, A. B. (2005). Demystifying men's emotional behavior: New directions and implications for counseling and research. *Psychology of Men & Masculinity, 6,* 62-72. doi:10.1037/1524-9220.6.1.62

Wood, J. T. (1995). Gendered interaction: Masculine and feminine styles of verbal communication. In K. S. Verderber (Ed.), *VOICES: A selection of multicultural readings* (18-29). Belmont, CA: Wadsworth.

Worthington, E. L., Jr. (2001). *Five steps to forgiveness: The art and science of forgiving.* New York, NY: Crown.

———. (2010). *Coming to peace with psychology: What Christians can learn from psychological science.* Downers Grove, IL: InterVarsity Press.

Worthington, E. L., Jr., Johnson, E. L., Hook, J. N., & Aten, J. D. (Eds.). (2013). *Evidence-based practices for Christian counseling and psychotherapy.* Downers Grove, IL: InterVarsity Press.

Wright, H. N. (1984). *Training Christians to counsel.* Eugene, OR: Harvest House.

———. (1986*). Self-talk, imagery, and prayer in counseling.* Dallas, TX: Word.

Young, M. E. (1992). *Counseling methods and techniques: An eclectic approach.* New York, NY: Macmillan.

———. (2009). *Learning the art of helping: Building blocks and techniques* (4th ed.). Upper Saddle River, NJ: Pearson.

AUTHOR AND SUBJECT INDEX

SCRIPTURE INDEX

An Association for Christian Psychologists,
Therapists, Counselors and Academicians

CAPS is a vibrant Christian organization with a rich tradition. Founded in 1956 by a small group of Christian mental health professionals, chaplains and pastors, CAPS has grown to more than 2,100 members in the U.S., Canada and more than 25 other countries.

CAPS encourages in-depth consideration of therapeutic, research, theoretical and theological issues. The association is a forum for creative new ideas. In fact, their publications and conferences are the birthplace for many of the formative concepts in our field today.

CAPS members represent a variety of denominations, professional groups and theoretical orientations; yet all are united in their commitment to Christ and to professional excellence.

CAPS is a non-profit, member-supported organization. It is led by a fully functioning board of directors, and the membership has a voice in the direction of CAPS.

CAPS is more than a professional association. It is a fellowship, and in addition to national and international activities, the organization strongly encourages regional, local and area activities which provide networking and fellowship opportunities as well as professional enrichment.

To learn more about CAPS, visit www.caps.net.

The joint publishing venture between IVP Academic and CAPS aims to promote the understanding of the relationship between Christianity and the behavioral sciences at both the clinical/counseling and the theoretical/research levels. These books will be of particular value for students and practitioners, teachers and researchers.

For more information about CAPS Books, visit InterVarsity Press's website at www.ivpress.com/cgi-ivpress/book.pl/code=2801.

Finding the Textbook You Need

The IVP Academic Textbook Selector
is an online tool for instantly finding the IVP books
suitable for over 250 courses across 24 disciplines.

---

www.ivpress.com/academic/

Anyone in a helping profession—including professional counselors, spiritual directors, pastoral counselors, chaplains and others—needs to develop effective counseling skills. Suitable for both beginning students and seasoned practitioners, *Skills for Effective Counseling* provides a biblically integrated approach that trains the reader to use specific microskills such as perceiving, attending, validating emotion and empathic connection.

This textbook and the accompanying IVP Instructor Resources include all of the activities and assignments needed to execute a graduate, undergraduate or lay course in foundational counseling skills. Professors teaching within CACREP-accredited professional counseling programs will be able to connect specific material in the textbook to the latest CACREP Standards.

"This is a comprehensive, readable text that is a fully integrated Christian and psychological model for being an effective helper. Regardless of your discipline or theoretical approach, you'll love it."

EVERETT L. WORTHINGTON JR.
coauthor of *Couple Therapy*

"Wow. What a delightful surprise. . . . If you want to upgrade your therapeutic toolkit and increase both your confidence and effectiveness, read this book. It's that good."

GARY J. OLIVER
executive director, The Center for Healthy Relationships, John Brown University

"This is a much-needed book for the effective training of Christian professional counselors as well as lay counselors. Highly recommended!"

SIANG-YANG TAN
Fuller Theological Seminary, author of *Counseling and Psychotherapy*

"This book combines clarity and reader-friendliness with an academically solid, up-to-date approach to counseling skills."

BRADFORD M. SMITH
Belhaven University

"Whether you are a beginning student, seasoned clinician or pastor, *Skills for Effective Counseling* is a must-add to your library."

TIM CLINTON
president, American Association of Christian Counselors

"This book unfolds a helping process that is realistic, hopeful and, most importantly, biblically faithful. Finally, a faith-sensitive microskills text for the next generation of people helpers."

STEPHEN P. GREGGO
Trinity Evangelical Divinity School

"*Skills for Effective Counseling* is a comprehensive yet accessible textbook written from decades of professional practice by the authors."

GARY W. MOON
executive director, Martin Institute and Dallas Willard Center, Westmont College

"Finally! We have been given a competent textbook that tackles the need for training graduate students in skills for effective counseling that also addresses faith-based integration."

C. GARY BARNES
Dallas Theological Seminary

ELISABETH A. NESBIT SBANOTTO is a consultant, speaker, writer, counselor and educator. She is assistant professor of counseling at Denver Seminary and the coauthor with Craig Blomberg of *Effective Generational Ministry*. A licensed professional counselor, she maintains a private practice in Littleton, Colorado.

HEATHER DAVEDIUK GINGRICH is a counselor, scholar, teacher and former missionary. She is professor of counseling at Denver Seminary and maintains a small private practice working with complex trauma survivors. She is the author of *Restoring the Shattered Self*.

FRED C. GINGRICH is professor of counseling at Denver Seminary and served as division chair from 2007 to 2015. He practiced and taught in Ontario for fourteen years prior to directing MA and EdD degrees in counseling at seminaries in the Philippines.

ISBN 978-0-8308-2860-9

RELIGION / Christian Ministry / Counseling & Recovery

CAPS BOOKS
from IVP Academic

www.ivpacademic.com

INSTRUCTOR
RESOURCES
from IVP ACADEMIC

9 780830 828609